The Holocaust and
the West German Historians

George L. Mosse Series in Modern European Cultural and Intellectual History

The Holocaust and the West German Historians

Historical Interpretation and Autobiographical Memory

Nicolas Berg

Translated and edited by
Joel Golb

The University of Wisconsin Press

Publication of this volume has been made possible, in part,
through support from the George L. Mosse Program
at the University of Wisconsin–Madison.

The University of Wisconsin Press
1930 Monroe Street, 3rd Floor
Madison, Wisconsin 53711-2059
uwpress.wisc.edu

3 Henrietta Street, Covent Garden
London WC2E 8LU, United Kingdom
eurospanbookstore.com

Originally published as *Der Holocaust und die westdeutschen Historiker: Erforschung und Erinnerung*,
© 2003 by Wallstein Verlag, Göttingen

Printed in the United States of America

Library of Congress Cataloging-in-Publication Data

Berg, Nicolas, author.
[Holocaust und die westdeutschen Historiker. English]
The Holocaust and the West German historians: historical interpretation and
autobiographical memory / Nicolas Berg; translated and edited by Joel Golb.
pages   cm — (George L. Mosse series in modern European cultural and intellectual history)
Includes bibliographical references and index.
ISBN 978-0-299-30084-5 (pbk.: alk. paper)
ISBN 978-0-299-30083-8 (e-book)
1. Historiography—Germany (West).   2. Holocaust, Jewish (1939–1945)—Historiography.
3. Historians—Germany (West).   4. Germany—History—1933–1945—Historiography.
I. Title.   II. Series: George L. Mosse series in modern European cultural and intellectual history.
DD86.B4713   2015
940.53'18072043—dc23
2014007449

Contents

Preface

I would like to express my warmest thanks to all those who helped make the present translation possible. For the support he gave to the idea of having this book published in English, and for both the good will and extreme patience it took to see through these plans, John Tortorice of the University of Wisconsin Press's George L. Mosse Series merits special thanks. Such gratitude is likewise extended to his kind colleagues at the press, who maintained extraordinary trust over an exceptionally long working period. I still think back with pleasure to my visit to Madison on the occasion of a conference held at the University of Wisconsin in the spring of 2005, when the idea for this American edition took on its first contours. I likewise warmly thank Steven Aschheim (Mosse Program and Jerusalem) for recognizing the project's merits and initiating the translation through his friendly intercession. I feel deep gratitude as well to a great many other friends and colleagues who conveyed strong interest in the research that culminated in my German-language book and who also expressed corresponding encouragement, among them Dan Diner (Leipzig and Jerusalem), Jan Eike Dunkhase (Berlin), Jörg Ganzenmüller (Jena), Ulrich Herbert (Freiburg), and Bernd Martin (Freiburg). I am especially grateful to my wife, Karoline Mueller-Stahl (Leipzig), for the help and support she offered in that period and beyond. Finally, I would like to express my heartfelt thanks to Joel Golb for an extraordinary period of cooperative work on what was at once a translating and editing project, for the sharp advice and insight he offered in both interconnected domains, and for the friendship that has emerged between Berlin and Leipzig.

Nicolas Berg

Summer 2014

Editorial Note

This book is an edited and shortened version of a study by Nicolas Berg first published in Germany in 2003. A second edition followed that same year and a third, corrected edition in 2004; the book quickly became the focal point of intense controversy among German historians and journalists, a controversy the author addresses in his introduction to the present volume. The editing undertaken for this English-language text was aimed at making it accessible to a general American readership interested in the basic historical questions it raises. At the same time, all the material on the great—and in his time ostracized— Polish Jewish historian Joseph Wulf, located in various chapters of the original edition, has now been brought together in a single chapter forming a unified narrative. This American edition of Nicolas Berg's important study thus serves as a memorial to both Joseph Wulf and his distinguished collaborator and fellow Holocaust survivor, the Russian-French Jewish historian Léon Poliakov.

From 1945 to the present, the way historians have approached the Holocaust has posed far-reaching problems regarding choice of language. In the postwar context this book addresses, such problems have involved the particular discursive arsenal German historians had at their disposal—an ideological legacy they sometimes struggled to come to terms with, to one or another degree. The book is consequently as much about language as it is about facts, and a wide range of idiosyncratic German terms are thus a crucial element of its narrative. For this reason, I ask readers to bear with the presence throughout these chapters of many such terms in the original German, for the most part placed in brackets following their approximate English equivalents.

The new introduction by Nicolas Berg for this edition offers a summary of the most important recent scholarly literature on the book's central topic. By contrast, references in the main body of the book have only occasionally been brought up to date.

JOEL GOLB

Berlin, August 2014

The Holocaust and
the West German Historians

Introduction
to the American Edition

This book owes much to an approach most precisely formulated by the French philosopher Paul Ricœur. In his work examining basic questions of historical theory and method, *Memory, History, Forgetting*,[1] Ricœur treats history and memory as distinct forces with diametrically differing logics that are nonetheless intimately interwoven. Historical writing, he argues, is not only a record of events and the end result of professionalized research or a dialogue between history professors; rather, it is "the very operation in which historical knowing is grasped at work."[2] Consequently, for Ricœur a special epistemological procedure is grounded in the "historiographical act"—a general method of historical understanding. He is less concerned, then, with an internal specialist discourse, more with a "hermeneutics of the historical condition" and the "autonomous status" of that hermeneutics as a humanistic enterprise.[3] This does not mean, however, taking the historian's representation of the past at face value; rather, crucially, the problems emerging from that procedure need to be explored. To explain what he means in more detail, Ricœur distinguishes between "intending the truth of history" and "the intention of being faithful to memory."[4] Through this distinction, with the cultural-historical work of Michel de Certeau, Pierre Nora, and Jacques Le Goff as his starting point, he draws attention to three basic historiographical phases: a "documentary phase" taking in the canon and archives; a phase of "explanation/understanding" tied to both hermeneutics and interpretation; and a "representative phase," the only one to cover the act of writing itself.[5] Importantly, the historiographical operations within this triadic conceptual figure are not categorically separated; rather, each one feels the impact of the others, for Ricœur here is speaking directly of "methodological moments" that are "interwoven with one another."[6] In his view each of these

3

"moments" forms part of the epistemological act and is thus the foundation for the two others, all three in this way correcting and influencing one another. This historiographical model offers a schema based on a movement from the *archive* (in which documents are meant to be discovered or from which they are simply drawn) to both *understanding* and *explanation* (of said documents) to *representation* (i.e., through the freshly written text). And Ricœur avoids any hierarchization among the three phases or moments of history-writing: he sees memory at work in all the phases of the historiographical act; in turn he has tried to historically understand this memory, as present in the archive, in explanation, and in the representation of history.

This synthetic theory of memory and historiography is the starting point for my study of Holocaust historiography in West Germany's early postwar decades; the theory also functions as a methodological principle running through all the study's chapters.[7] The chapters lay no claim to being a contribution to the philosophy of history or to the understanding of historical methodology. Nevertheless, synthesizing two forms of history, one centered on German memory, the other on German historiography itself, is crucial to my argumentation. This is because doing so makes it possible to reflect on both: on the contributions of individual historians and their particular memories *and* on the generational, collectively defining forces characterizing the zeitgeist.[8] These forces generated a conceptual framework for the historiography stamping Germany's postwar decades.[9] The intertwining of historical interpretation and autobiographical memory constitutes the central motif running through the five chapters of this book's English version. It is a motif that emerges in the full-length studies and shorter essays, lectures, and minutes, memoirs, letters, and many other autobiographical documents by Friedrich Meinecke (chap. 1), Gerhard Ritter and Hans Rothfels (chap. 2), Hermann Heimpel, Reinhard Wittram, and Fritz Ernst (chap. 3), and onward to historians from a younger generation, Hermann Mau and later Martin Broszat at the newly founded Institute for Contemporary History (Institut für Zeitgeschichte; IfZ) in Munich (chap. 4). And it emerges in the work of the Polish Jewish survivor of the Holocaust, Joseph Wulf (chap. 5), working as an academic outsider and freelance scholar in West Berlin starting in the 1950s and dedicating his life to publishing facts about the Holocaust's planners, collaborators, perpetrators, and victims. He did so in books, radio essays, and above all a series of documentary volumes, initially written together with the great Russian-French Jewish historian Léon Poliakov: a life work, for a long time neglected, that was extensively evaluated for the first time in this book's first German edition. (Since then an excellent biography of Joseph Wulf by Klaus Kempter as well as several full-length studies focused on Jewish Holocaust historiography and documentation in

early postwar Europe in general have appeared.[10]) The subject addressed in
the following chapters is thus the history of how historians perceived, and failed
to perceive, the Holocaust, how they interpreted and misinterpreted that historical fact, using an arsenal of terms and concepts, arguments and explanations
in the first three decades of the West German state.

Since the German defeat, a broad range of facts tied to the Third Reich
and the events transpiring in Germany's domain between 1933 and 1945 have
been described and interpreted in many different ways. Historical writing allows
no "definitive version" but only a body of approximations that change in the
course of time—something all the more the case with historiography of the Holocaust. Saul Friedländer—arguably the greatest living Holocaust historian—
has observed that a putatively objective description of the events can at best
only be "pure chronicle," and that even as such the objectivity remains a theoretically unreachable goal; explicitly or implicitly, every description of the past
has to be based on a value system and is thus "not only an image of this past but
also a mirror of the society from which the description emerged."[11] Change in
the historiographical confrontation with the Third Reich's defining crime as a
reflection of postwar West German society stands at the center of this study.

It is clear that when it came to the relationship between the event itself and
the slowly beginning process rendering it into historical knowledge, the situation
in Germany was marked by special difficulties. These had a great deal to do
with strategies of denial and intentionally false statements, with the influence
exerted by participants in the events (by observers, fellow travelers, bureau-
cratic planners, and even, albeit rarely, those who directly supervised and participated in the murder process, in personal accounts, memoirs, interviews, and
so forth) on the German historians' image of the past. In retrospect it is striking
that precisely historians who before 1945—to follow a classic definition offered
by George Mosse—had participated in defining *Volk* as the "union of a group
of people with a transcendental 'essence,'"[12] now, after 1945, were infuriated by
one thing more than anything else: the assumption of a German community of
perpetrators; and that their response to the question of collective German responsibility for what had happened was to lay sole and urgent emphasis on
each single, "individual case."[13] But together with the fact that here the successor society to the former "people's community," the *Volksgemeinschaft*,[14] was
meant to explicate its own crimes, the difficulties in Germany were also due, as
was also the case elsewhere in the world, to individual and collective overload,
resulting from the need for repeatedly new efforts to assimilate the shockwaves
generated by the mass crimes' significance.[15] This was particularly the case in
the immediate postwar period.[16] Hence in these pages we will see in detail how
German historians, for instance, Gerhard Ritter, engaged in nothing less than

a struggle "to avoid teaching . . . German history with an appalled gaze focused on Hitler's horrific deeds alone" (chap. 2). But for a long time, such a burden would make it difficult for Jewish intellectuals, and historians in particular, to participate in German academic research on the horrific events or indeed receive acknowledgment by the community of German researchers. With the great exception of Hans Rothfels, who shared that community's basic premises (chap. 2), when German Jewish historians returned to Germany, they were offered no stable academic foundation from which to speak. They also lacked institutional backing because in their particular case—as opposed to that of Geman historians who had been in the Hitler Youth, the Nazi Party, the SS—witness status and personal proximity to the events were perceived as tantamount to epistemological disqualification.[17]

All specific differences notwithstanding, German historians such as Gerhard Ritter, the Eastern Europe specialist Hermann Aubin, and Siegfried A. Kaehler, who specialized in nineteenth- and early twentieth-century Prussian and German history, mistrusted all criticism of Germany and its history. Quite often, the old ways that historians thought and wrote were clearly evident in their postwar writing. In private letters from May 1945, Kaehler referred in Nazi jargon to "already ongoing defamation through democratic-Jewish propaganda," an Allied "campaign of revenge," "Anglo-Saxon self-righteousness,"[18] and he drew a parallel between Germany's suffering in 1945 and that of German Jewry in the Kristallnacht period.[19] As late as 1956, Aubin published an essay on Eastern Europe in which we read that Hitler "introduced an unmixing of *Volk*-entities [*Entmischung der Volkstümer*]—not without violence against non-Germans [*Undeutsche*]."[20] These were, as indicated, still entirely intact formulas from a period that was now, however, meant to be analyzed, its consequences confronted. The mix of bias and irritation toward both German Jewish emigrants to America[21] and "foreign countries"—*das Ausland*—in general itself hardened a reflexive rebuff of any "anti-German" observations or references to German culpability. Such an inability to accept intellectual responsibility for what had taken place was the stamp placed on many commentaries from the period around 1950. All efforts to shape a "German picture of history" were aimed at preserving the "German character"[22] and thus part of what Kaehler understood as a "battle [*Kampf*]" against the "outside," against "the victors"—and against interpretations of one's own history that did not come from Germany. "Even if the actual criminals within the SS amounted to 100,000 men," insisted Kaehler, "in a population of more than 60 million people this does not carry so much weight that we need to recognize and accept that this *Volk* represents a new type of human being; rather, eradicable manifestations of degeneration [*ausmerzbare Entartungserscheinungen*] are at work here."[23] The talk was of a "demonic threat to our existence," itself containing a "threat to the German human being in particular."[24] For a long time the social historian Werner Conze, in whose work the Holocaust remained a blatant "void" (as Jan Eike Dunkhase has shown in his first-rate biography),[25] cast scorn on any consideration of continuities for the explanation of recent German history. Even in the mid-1960s, Conze held the conviction that most Germans had been subject to a form of "double terror" in the Nazi period, that of the party and that of the Allied bombs; National Socialism itself had "not penetrated deeply" in Germany.[26] Conze was here very consciously pursuing a goal he saw as *geschichtspolitisch*, "political-historical."[27] He tied the "catastrophes of 1945" to the "severity of the victors' decisions" and the "occupiers' rule,"[28] in the process reinterpreting the concept of "catastrophe" away from the question of the Nazi Party's rise to that of the consequences of World War II for the Germans. In a 1963 overview of German national history, he points to the Versailles Treaty as responsible for Hitler's rise and describes Germany in the 1930s as "the first European country occupied by the National Socialists."[29] Hajo Holborn, a former student of Meinecke who had emigrated to the United States, bluntly refers to such avowals as "completely unbearable," then reminds German readers, perhaps with some sarcasm, of "wounds for which there are no amends, inflicted not only on one's own *Volk* but on other *Völker*."[30] Another former Meinecke student, the German Jewish medievalist Helene Wieruszowski, who would survive the Holocaust and retain a sense of personal gratitude to her teacher despite being driven out of Germany, wrote him in 1946 from New York as follows: "Too much has happened, the dimensions are too enormous, the collective deeds go beyond the episodic and individual. . . . Germany, your great Germany, Herr Geheimrat, as I first grasped it in your book *Weltbürgertum*, disappeared in the Germany of the Third Reich; at least I cannot retrieve it."[31]

The students of the older generation of historians, above all Hermann Heimpel and Reinhard Wittram in Göttingen, took such gestures of departure from *Weltbürgertum*, from a worldly bourgeois Germany, more seriously than their teachers did. They declined to carry forward a pathos, meant to defend German national history, that in the end conceived of Hitler as alien to that history, a pathos that avoided confronting Nazism's origins by evoking a "malignant disease" and "raging epidemic" that had fallen upon "not only Germany but the peoples of the world [*die Völker der Welt*]."[32] In contrast to Rothfels, who had been driven out of Germany on racist grounds, to Ritter, who had been close to the resistance, and to Meinecke, who was already over seventy when Hitler came to power, this generation felt rightly guilty for what had happened on very concrete, personal grounds. Hermann Heimpel, a medievalist at the University of Göttingen born in 1901, is a good example of a distinguished West German academic who had incurred guilt during the Third Reich; at the same time, like no other German historian he personifies a process of shame-ridden public meditation on guilt in the framework of his professional and personal self-understanding (chap. 3). In 1933 Heimpel had supported, with wholehearted conviction, Heidegger's call for a new role for German universities under Nazism. In the 1940s he taught at what had been renamed the "Reich University" in what was now officially called Straßburg, delivering lectures about the German Reich as a guardian of order against a "barbarian world" without culture or history. Also, in Leipzig he was appointed to the chair of his distinguished Jewish teacher Siegmund Hellmann, who had been deported in 1942 and murdered in Theresienstadt.

After 1945, even before any historiographical renewal on his part, Heimpel began to reflect on his guilt in a quasi-confessional autobiographical text; he announced, then abandoned, a planned second volume focused on his career as a historian. The mix of confession and despair at the simple facticity of events led him to take up the concept of *Vergangenheitsbewältigung*, a term meaning literally "overcoming the past" but that is essentially untranslatable in its encapsulation of German self-reflection in the face of guilt for war and extermination;[33] Heimpel began to use the term more frequently and in an increasingly existential way. Phenomenologically, the term represented a Protestant gesture of atonement that Heimpel conveyed from personal memory into the public sphere. This marked a clear-cut change vis-à-vis his teachers. But in the 1950s and 1960s, he did not succeed in rendering his new approach, his avowal of guilt, into a basis for a fresh way of presenting his *Deutsche Geschichte*—a project on which he had labored for years. His conception and arrangement of the project clearly emerge in the lecture-course manuscript that we have: Heimpel divided all of German history into a series of important loci of memory, with Aachen and Wittenberg, Frankfurt and Potsdam, Weimar and Berlin each symbolizing and representing an entire age. But unmistakably, the closer he approached the present, the more obvious it became that the series of place-names moved, in the end, toward Dachau and Auschwitz, as—from his unavoidable perspective—the de facto culmination of modern German history. He could make this clear to his students in lectures, but he failed to express it in writing and evidently did not want it to see print.

For its part, the new academic discipline of modern history emerging in West Germany, both at the IfZ in Munich starting in the 1950s and later in the universities, sincerely pursued research on the "German catastrophe." But the discipline had an exaggerated sense of its own objectivity, tending to equate, as did Meinecke's biographer Walther Hofer directly, "objective" analysis with a presentation of documents (chaps. 4 and 5). The almost untempered optimism at work here was sometimes informed by honorable arguments but often displayed a marked one-sidedness. Already in the late 1950s, the Third Reich was thus being declared—with an emphatic insistence that now seems astonishing— the best-researched epoch of German history: a topos elevating the status of budding research to nothing less than a fetish. We thus find Hans Mommsen stating in the early 1960s that the external course of the persecution of the Jews was basically firmly understood; Karl Dietrich Bracher beginning his book on "the German dictatorship" (*Die deutsche Diktatur*, 1969) with the statement that Nazism had been "largely researched" and a "nearly complete view of the rule of the Hitler regime in Germany and Europe" had successfully emerged; Martin Broszat stating that "individual questions may still need answering, but doing so will not change the overall assessment"; and both Karl Dietrich Erdmann and Helmut Krausnick making claims of the same sort (chap. 4). But the work of Jewish historian Joseph Wulf, who in his own way wished to see facts emerge from documents, and who—in contrast to the IfZ historians—did not develop any interpretive model based on "totalitarianism" or "structuralism" to come to terms with these facts, was not granted a stamp of "objectivity." On the German side, his great documentary volumes were not understood as a contribution to historical scholarship but rather were denounced as an "accusation," an extension of the "Nuremberg Trials." In this way his oeuvre was expelled, a priori, from the realm of German scholarly discourse (chap. 5).

Present-day research on National Socialism owes much to basic work on the Nazi period by the postwar generation of West German historians. The historians refused only one thing categorically: to openly contemplate their own, complex intellectual-ideological origins and perspective—to problematize their own memory—thus relativizing the range of their own explanations. Instead, they presented that perspective as "objective," "scientific," and "sober," thus allowing that memory to expand into their scholarship. At the same time, as Joseph Wulf's travail most dramatically shows, they maintained an aggressive lack of interest when it came to the experience of others, with the disinterest's main focus being the work of Jewish scholars. We see this in the exaggerated polemic aimed at Gerald Reitlinger; the decades-long neglect of Raul Hilberg's monumental research; the resentment-laden feud with Wulf; the collapse of the cooperative arrangement between the IfZ and H. G. Adler. But in the end, Jews were absent from postwar West German discourse on Nazism and the Holocaust not because they articulated other memories, but because they had, tied to this, another historiographical perspective. The scholarly exclusion of Jewish witnessing with simultaneous exaggeration by these historians of their own viewpoint regarding the past they had experienced is thus the central, underlying problem I address in this book.

In the late 1980s, German historians were still seeking ideas and methods to adequately describe and conceptualize the extermination of European Jewry. The famous—and in West Germany heavily publicized—"historians' controversy" that unfolded between 1986 and 1989 was focused on concepts such as the Russian Revolution's status as a "factual prius" and "causal nexus" when it came to the rise of Hitler (the terms were Ernst Nolte's), "comparability" between the Stalinist mass murders and the Nazi genocide, and the range and limits of the term "singularity." The memoirs and other published witness accounts by survivors were still being classified within the profession, with a certain helplessness, as *Literatur*. For myself as a student in this period, this was hard to understand. Initially, my reservations about a pseudo-dichotomy between "hard" history and "soft" *Literatur* were intuitive; later the division increasingly interested me as a problem calling for exploration. The discursive aporias at work in Holocaust historiography thus constituted one of my basic experiences when I began my graduate studies in the early 1990s. The second such experience was reading new studies of the Holocaust by Götz Aly, Ulrich Herbert, Christian Gerlach, and Dieter Pohl, among others that were coming out in the 1990s and that together were making one thing clear: in many respects empirical research on the Holocaust, understood in the sense of Raul Hilberg, had only just begun in Germany.[34] The panel on "German historiography after 1945" at the German Historians' Conference in Frankfurt am Main in September 1998 marked an important moment in this development (see Figure 1). This was naturally not the first occasion for self-critique on the part of German historians after the war. But here for the first time, the careers of three central figures—former chairmen of the German Historians' Association Theodor Schieder, Werner Conze, and Hermann Heimpel—were publicly and officially subjected to critical scrutiny. The present book offers the long prehistory leading up to that conference.

One text in particular offered me a key to understanding the aporias of a Holocaust historiography caught between the requirements of historical research and the problem of memory: the published exchange of letters between Saul Friedländer and Martin Broszat concerning the historical, methodological, and communicative difficulties evident in the very discourse used to discuss the Holocaust.[35] This volume addressed everything being left unsaid at the time by historians about two interrelated problems: the problem of the difficulties involved in finding a language adequate for the event; and the problem of the individual perspectives that historians, with their specific life experiences, inevitably brought to its study. All told, by the mid-1990s, the situation was changing rapidly, as a result of both new studies and new theoretical approaches for considering the diverse tendencies they reflected. Consideration of Auschwitz as a "rupture in civilization" (the term is Dan Diner's),[36] the relationship between witnessing and documentation and between theory and empiricism, the ways in which the perspectives of perpetrators, fellow travelers, and victims inform historical writing: all of this was in the process of becoming its own research subject and thus had a very strong influence on my own approach to the emerging issues.

In 1988 Herbert A. Strauss gave a lecture whose title is roughly translatable as "Reflections on the Possibilities for a Scientific and Human Approach [lit.: *Annäherung*, "approximation" or "drawing near"] to the Holocaust."[37] The title's formulation doubtless contains an allusion to what Charles S. Maier has referred to as "the inflamed German debate" known as the "historians' controversy";[38] from our perspective the lecture's contents have their own historical resonance. With the distance we now enjoy, it is also clear that the text actually does not undertake the process of "drawing near" referred to in its title. Large portions are a thoroughly professional introduction to Holocaust research. Strauss does point to limits he sees facing historical scholarship because the Holocaust had "no rationally graspable meaning."[39] Survivors, he observes, reported on "an unprecedented event."[40] But he is here not speaking of himself. Rather, what he himself experienced is only present for readers in a few light, parenthetical, sometimes skeptical remarks, such as when he mentions that an impression dominates in victims' and survivors' accounts "that here there is no interlocutor and perhaps none is possible," the authors thus often being "condemned to the loneliness of their judgments."[41] At the time, Strauss did not wish to grant readers more autobiographical closeness. Only the appearance of his autobiography *In the Eye of the Storm* some years later would make clear that the historian Strauss had chosen to speak in separate capacities as a scholar and as a witness.[42] For survivors such as himself or Otto Dov Kulka, born in Prague in 1933 and whose Auschwitz memoir *Landscapes of the Metropolis of Death* was published recently,[43] the guiding rule was thus: if they wished to contribute as historians to discourse about the recent past, they would have to remain private as witnesses.

Strauss, born in 1918, had experienced the November 1938 pogroms (Kristallnacht) in his home town of Würzburg, during which his father was arrested by the Gestapo[44] and then subsequently murdered in Treblinka; Strauss himself managed to escape to Switzerland in 1943. After the war, he emigrated to the United States, then returned many years later to become the founding director of the Center for Research on Antisemitism at the Technical University in Berlin. In his autobiography, he expresses great anger regarding the German crimes, at one point acknowledging that "from the distance of half a century that has burned the murder of a people into the world's consciousness, the emotions still revolt against what my memory has retained."[45] But at the same time, he often addresses the difficulties of transforming memory into history. The difficulties are present, for example, in the following passages:

> Few of the men and women whose lives had touched mine ever returned. The images I can recall are fixed like photographs frozen in time.[46]

> It was just too unbelievable and fantastic that innocent people would be "exterminated" by those they passed on the streets every day and experienced as "average" or "normal" in their behavior. I do not recall when the ambiguities of "knowing" gave way, piece by piece, to panic and defeat in "accepting" what would be forever unacceptable, the final loss of the people to whom our dead belonged, and to find a way of mourning adequate to their unlived lives.[47]

The problem was that for the witnesses' generation it was becoming increasingly difficult "to recognize the history they themselves experienced in the sober and abstract language of science," as Christhard Hoffmann has put it in a book edited by Strauss.[48] Similarly, more than fifteen years ago Raul Hilberg—who was a professional Holocaust historian par excellence—expressed concern that the emergence of many new professional research terms and concepts was affecting the approach taken in Holocaust historiography to events of the 1940s.[49] Saul Friedländer has repeatedly expressed similar feelings,[50] but without abandoning the claim to scientific rationality in the face of his skepticism. The simultaneous presence of strong skepticism and a firm adherence to the premises informing scholarly discourse makes clear that however tense their relationship, past experience and its present analysis are not to be pitted against each other, neither scientifically nor autobiographically. Strauss was speaking not only as a survivor, and as a man who had returned to Germany, but also as a professional historian when he expressed a strong sense of being surrounded there by people "who did not share the memory of ten years of growing up in a multitiered culture of persecution."[51]

In the period during which the German edition of this book was conceived and written, the hiatus between research and memory had emerged as a problem for historiography itself, research on the Holocaust thus having entered a new phase. For this reason, from the book's inception its basic arguments and approach were intended not to maintain this epistemological gap but to make it into a fundamental theme. The way these intentions were realized received a great deal of attention in Germany: first in national newspapers and weekly magazines;[52] then in local papers;[53] then, with the normal delay, in professional publications and specialized Internet forums.[54] Parallel to this was an international response as well, taking in Switzerland,[55] the United States,[56] Israel,[57] England,[58] France,[59] Holland,[60] Sweden,[61] and Poland.[62] What merits special emphasis is an extended debate in February 2004 taking up the "Forum" section of the professional Internet journal *H-Soz-u-Kult*, initiated and edited by Astrid Eckert and Vera Ziegeldorf. This was the framework for critical and affirmative voices and additional insight from America (Claudia Koonz, Gerhard Weinberg, Alan E. Steinweis, Robert P. Erickson), England (Ian Kershaw, Stefan Berger), and Germany (Peter Longerich, Habbo Knoch, Hanno Loewy), followed by my own extended response to these contributions.[63] A number of programs on German radio also focused on the book.[64] It was eventually taken up as a theme by a few "high-end" cultural magazines as well, was chosen as a "book of the month" by several leading German publications,[65] and had three print runs in the first year.

So many different positions were staked out within the unusually intense response to the book that any attempt to pin down a basic pattern runs into contradictory material. At first it seemed that critical voices mainly stemmed from an older generation, but later it became clear that this was not the case with an entire group of important reviews—that there were both colleagues of my generation who wished to maintain distance from my approach and conclusions and those from my teachers' generation (which is to say, old enough to be students of some of those I was writing about) who wholeheartedly embraced the book's arguments. And while after the first edition's appearance German reviews seemed to be generally critical, those from other countries generally positive, a number of evaluations stemming from particularly well-known voices defied that pattern: there was, for example, the positive review in the influential weekly German newspaper *Die Zeit* by Volker Ulrich, who ended his thoughtful discussion with the comment that the approach taken to the Holocaust—"here we must endorse the author"—did "not constitute a glorious chapter of German research in modern history"; and writing in *The Times Literary Supplement*, the British scholar of the "Third Reich" Ian Kershaw indicated that "something ahistorical" clung to my chapter treating the early years of the IfZ.[66] Others among the large body of reviews expressly praised my dispensing with "accusations and unmasking" in favor of explaining "the different ways of approaching and viewing the apparently incomprehensible event of the Holocaust in terms of their period and scholarly context,"[67] while some were annoyed by what they considered not the only but still an especially outspoken effort at a "fundamental critique" of older historical research, one reflecting a "tendency" to "arbitrarily" inflict a particular "verdict" on the historians concerned: that they "delayed a reckoning with the criminal policies of the National Socialist regime and above all omitted the Holocaust from their historical memory."[68]

On a substantive level, the various critics and commentators were grouped around three debates or controversies, each of them reported on in the media. The first of these centered on the early IfZ—on the general approach taken there to historians who were Jewish survivors, together with the particular question of the young Martin Broszat's possible membership in the Nazi Party.[69] In both respects, I also presented my arguments in an essay in the *Süddeutsche Zeitung*.[70] The second debate also involved the IfZ, but here focused on the question of Hans Rothfels' influence on the institution's foundational phase, and also took on the broader question of the ideological-conceptual currents informing German postwar historiography.[71] In the context of this debate, I laid out my interpretation in a detailed English-language essay that appeared in 2004 in the Leo Baeck Institute's *Year Book*.[72] Each of these thematic constellations generated entire conferences—both my work and that of other historians were decisive in this respect.[73] The two constellations are of essential importance for the basic issues raised in the German-language book, and the discussion of them there has been largely retained, partly in revised form, in this English version. In respect to the IfZ, Hans Woller and Jürgen Zarusky, both members of the editorial board of the institute's prominent historical journal, the *Vierteljahrshefte für Zeitgeschichte*, recently stated that "a major research project" on the history of the institute's personnel, program, and historical practice was overdue.[74]

For American nonspecialist readers, most aspects of the third debate are of secondary importance, as here the focus was on a methodological question discussed in the German book but not taken up in the English version, as I will explain later. One of the book's most vociferous critics was the historian Hans Mommsen, who had taught at the University of Bochum over a long career after beginning his work in the late 1950s at the IfZ. The veteran historian emphatically rejected the book's methodology, warning against its lack of a "genetic approach to the problem [*genetische Fragestellung*]"[75] and its "political-moral approach to the history of National Socialism." My judgments, Mommsen opined, reflected "a preconceived decisionistic-moralizing position"; I had, he insisted, displayed no interest "in explaining a historiographical process."[76] The historian offered these views emphatically in various forums,[77] in this way attempting vigorously (if arguably highly inaccurately) to come to terms with my critical scrutiny of the IfZ's early history. Now the context of that scrutiny was my discussion of the development between the late 1960s and the 1980s of "structuralism" or "functionalism" in Holocaust research (briefly: the presumption of an *absence* of any concrete master plan to murder the Jews prior to 1941, with stress placed instead on the role played by competition and cumulative radicalization inside the Nazi Party apparatus) as an approach opposed to "intentionalism" (briefly: the presumption that antisemitic ideology, as already laid out in Hitler's *Mein Kampf* in the 1920s, was a central catalyst for the Holocaust). Mommsen had contributed significantly to that development, which, as indicated, is not addressed in this American edition of the book but which of course continues to invite consideration by specialists and others in the German edition. I there examine Mommsen's work at the time of his influential study of Nazi German officialdom, together with preceding essays and expert evaluations, most importantly, his—eventually published—evaluation of the "area of duties and responsibility" of Wilhelm Kritzinger, one of the leading officials in Nazi Germany, the second in command in the Reich Chancellery behind Hans Lammers and a participant in the Wannsee Conference (and thus self-evidently in the plans for mass murder laid out at the conference in January 1942).[78]

Despite Hans Mommsen's objections to this book, the relationship between methodology and empiricism I strive for in it was, happily, received far more sympathetically by many other reviewers. It is, to be sure, not false that, as one reviewer remarked, the book's basic approach and contents leave the question open of the reasons for the "avoidance discourse" of my own generation, born around 1968: I do not address, so to speak, my own blind spots.[79] That actually seems too much to expect from any book. In contrast to such criticism, which seemed to suggest that I failed to address the theme by not thematizing myself, other commentators in any event insisted, to the exact contrary, that the methodology I used and the treatment of the material in general were what made the insights I laid out possible in the first place.[80]

These many responses and points of criticism made clear how intense the interest was in Germany in 2003 in the debates, controversies, and concepts tied to historians' discourse about the Holocaust in the—now reunited—country's early postwar period. In my view, the decisive thing here is not merely a lack of previous research on the topic, but rather that my book also represented the first attempt at a detailed overview and interpretation. Meanwhile, entire lexicons have been published on the phenomenon of *Vergangenheitsbewältigung*, attempting to systematize the debates and arguments and referring to the German book in the process.[81] Also, over the past several years a number of new editions have appeared of correspondence by historians whom I discuss in these pages: Eduard Mühle's edition of Aubin's letters; the already-cited correspondence collection edited by Gerhard A. Ritter offering important documentation on Meinecke's relationship with his emigrated students and containing a detailed discussion of my book; and another volume of Meinecke's letters and documents, again edited by Ritter together with Gisela Bock as the tenth volume of the historian's collected works.[82] Finally, we now have an impressive group of new biographies of West German historians. I have already referred to the books on Conze by Dunkhase and Wulf by Kempter. Also noteworthy are the following biographies: Jan Eckel's of Rothfels, Eduard Mühle's of Hermann Aubin, David Thimme's of Percy Ernst Schramm, and Franz Hocheneder's of H. G. Adler.[83] Most recently, however, Christoph Nonn's study of Theodor Schieder has, unfortunately, palliated that historian's failure to address the Holocaust.[84] This direct "historicizing of the historians," an expression used several times in reviews and in commentaries on the debate about the book,[85] has had its complement in studies that had not appeared when the German book was in preparation and that illuminate the context of German's postwar period in great detail. Two outstanding examples here are Astrid Eckert's book— now available in English translation—on the early efforts of German historians to have files confiscated by the Western Allies after World War II returned to Germany and Ruth Nattermann's account of the founding of the Leo Baeck Institutes in London, New York, and Jerusalem. Another example is offered by the two volumes of collected articles that Hartmut Lehmann and Otto Gerhard Oexle have edited on Nazism within German cultural studies before and after 1945.[86]

A conviction this study shares with a number of the previously mentioned works is that the history of how history has been written can to some extent close the gap between past events and narrated memories. A historiography wishing to understand itself as more than the opposite of these memories, one that indeed sees belonging to them as a basic premise, gains another quality. Its discourse is no longer shared only by specialists seeking to correct incomplete, distorting, or false memories; rather, it tries to incorporate the logic of memory into its own struggle to understand the past. History and memory are here intertwined and comment on each other. Without the work of historians there is no social-political memory, but no historian works free of his or her own memories.

I

Tragedy, Fate, and Breach

Friedrich Meinecke's The German Catastrophe (1946) and the Paradoxes of "National-Historical" Interpretation

Knowledge, not Memory

"Before 1945 . . . I knew nothing about the mass murders." This often-cited statement was also made by the forty-six-year-old contemporary historian Hans-Günter Zmarzlik in the "retrospective concerning his own person" he presented as a lecture in 1968 and then had published two years later. But in these memories of his own path before and after 1945, not the remembered events but the memories themselves confronted him with "ever-more question marks," as Zmarzlik put it, now unsure of himself and self-probing:

> Perhaps I did not wish to know. Afterward it is hard to say whether one had not sometimes decided not to hear [*nicht weggehört hat*] when something of it seeped through in the anonymity of a furlough train heading back from the front. For many knew about it. In a trip through Upper Silesia in 1944, my sister, who could only tell me this after the war, heard a woman whisper to her neighbor: "You see the smoke over there? People are being cremated there." But for me in the summer of 1945 . . . Auschwitz still did not exist.[1]

From the war's end onward, the elemental constellation of accusation and defense, questions and answers, was predetermined. Who "knew" and who didn't? What could have been "known" and what not? How much had been "known" and how precisely? However the question was formulated and to whomever it was posed, which is to say to oneself or others, at the beginning stood the question of knowledge, not memory. What now is discussed as "history" was then the present, not the past. The discourse on Auschwitz began quantitatively, and it received its first criteria for judgment from the question of the relation between "knowing" and "not having known." In the postwar period, contemporary observers quite often confirmed this approach with a certain unease, with even the most understanding commentators remarking that the "not knowing . . . [was] not complete."[2] Some years ago, researchers with an interest in the history of mentalities turned around this discursive paradigm, confirming that the real question was not "how—and how much—the Germans knew of the genocide." The question was rather: "how did the Germans deal with their knowledge?"[3] The question of "knowing" versus "not knowing" is evidently inadequate, since there was a consistent absence of what might be termed "knowledge of knowledge": immediately after the end of the war, Auschwitz was not the symbol of an epoch or indeed a century. Fritz Klein's observation that "the qualitative difference between Auschwitz and Buchenwald was only realized slowly" can stand in for many similar statements.[4] Even Raul Hilberg made various statements to the effect that initially he was "unaware of the extermination's full extent. . . . Only later, in 1946 . . . did I grasp that every third Jew in the world was dead. And no one knew how to deal with this fact. For there was no so-called memory; it was a shock. Everyone went on as if nothing had happened."[5]

When it came to the German situation, although the problem was the same, the circumstances were entirely different. Here what loomed was not incredulity in the face of the dimension—succinctly described by Hilberg—of a mass-killing process that had just seen its end. In Germany not only was information lacking but also—crucially—recognition of the German nation's own perpetrating role: "Whoever designates the Germans as accessories in the murder of millions must count on simply no longer being listened to" is the way the Freiburg University medievalist Gerd Tellenbach puts it in his book, already published in 1945, on "the German plight as guilt and fate" (*Die deutsche Not als Schuld und Schicksal*).[6] Beyond the issue of individual credibility, the quotation shows that discursive borders revealed themselves very quickly by way of the question of "knowing": after 1945 whoever assumed complicity or merely cognizance was obliged to prove it—not those who denied one or the other. In

1947 merely a nonspecific secret knowledge was conceded, a whispering "mouth to ear . . . of dark lore from the concentration camps."[7] Tellenbach accordingly did not so much inquire into the precarious status of such half-knowledge as polemicize against the occupying Americans with a reflex representative of the time. His concern was the emergence of a "Germany as a no man's land" and a "fateful break with tradition," where no "cultured people"— *Kulturvolk*—could live "without historical consciousness."[8] The question of how the German image of history, that "of one of the great Western spiritual peoples" (*eines der großen abendländischen Geistesvölker*) was to become "composed" (*einkomponiert*) within the "entire European-American cultural circle" was pressing.[9] But half-knowledge and bad conscience correspond. In his book on Germany's "plight," Tellenbach, using the key terms "guilt" and "honor," began an implicit reflection on the destruction of European Jewry, but at that time this could only unfold as a conglomeration of disbelief and reluctance, depression and a defensive stance: the catch phrases "guilt of National Socialism" and "responsibility of the German *Volk*" make clear what was understood as the "anathema [*Bann*] and burden of the past," a burden responded to with vehement resistance, at times by those actually searching for explanations.

In the postwar period every thought that seemed capable of modifying facts and self-image was seized on, for these thoughts thus offered grounds not so much for explanation as for the display of something like endless elucidation. According to Tellenbach's conviction, for example, the persecution of the Jews originated in "unhealthy phenomena" (*krankhafte Erscheinungen*) "that (among other things) require medical research," which is to say phenomena such as sexual perversion and sadism. The idea of the responsibility of modern administrative apparatuses, however, also fitted into the explanatory framework, since, as the Freiburg historian struggled to put it, not all the perpetrators were "lacking all human feeling."[10] And then again, he compared the "mania about Jews"—*Judenwahn*—with the "entirely related phenomenon" of mania about witches, that is, with a power ruling totally over the masses, before characterizing the extermination as "disgracefully rational" and as "coldly conscious," without noting the contradiction between the two etiologies.

But importantly, there were exceptions. At the beginning of June 1945, in a private communication to his University of Göttingen colleague Siegfried Kaehler, the Cologne University historian Peter Rassow indicated that he had just read Hitler's *Mein Kampf* for the first time. His summary of the reading centered on the event in question not in terms of something mystifying or mysterious but rather as a precisely laid out and announced plan that was then carried out while everyone watched:

The most important conclusion seems to me that no followers of his may assert they bear no guilt for the camp atrocities because they knew nothing of them. For everything essential to making the horror possible can be clearly read in the book. And approval of the basic principles encompasses approval of the horror. Also whoever experienced the deportation of the Jews in throes intensified to the end would have to have told himself that in the treatment of these unfortunates any beastliness was possible and thus certain.[11]

The historian Annelise Thimme herself recalled gnawing questions of guilt. But she was twenty years younger than Tellenbach and at the time still a student; the questions led not to sweeping explanations and theories but to reading that was downright compulsive:

Although we did not even know the entire extent of what happened, what we knew was horrible enough, so that everything possible that the Allies would perhaps do with the Germans could be pictured. It is the case that later on I took in necessary details of the Nazi crimes by necessity, but in the end I could not gain any worse and more terrible an idea of them than I already had in 1945, although I certainly did not know the details of Auschwitz and the other concentration camps. When I spoke once full of disgust and horror about the Nazis with my uncle, who was employed in the Potsdam military archives, he said: "If you knew what I know . . ." Since I have retained a memory of the remark, but at least presently no longer recall whether I knew anything even approximate about Auschwitz, I assume he did not tell me what he knew. Later I could figure it out. It was the systematic murder of the Jews. After 1945 people learned everything relatively fast. When in the spring of 1947 I was in Switzerland for seven weeks, friends lent me the latest German literature about that period, and I remember that I read for entire nights long.[12]

In Tellenbach's case we have an invocation of Western cultural values; in Rassow's a concern with Hitler's weltanschauung and memory of the deportation of Jews from the midst of society; in Thimme's nightly readings. On the one hand, we are offered wide-ranging explanations and apologies for the Germans; on the other hand, reflections on the responsibility incurred by one's own witnessing of the events or else a hunger for information. And again, on the one hand, an effort to preserve national continuities; on the other hand, a renewed recollection of the event or appropriation of its details. Diametric differences in reactions to knowledge of the genocide had already emerged in the 1940s. The events posed a "question of will to knowledge"[13] both before and after 1945.

Twenty years later, Erich Kosthorst came up with the formula *dies also war deutschen-möglich*, which although untranslatable can be roughly rendered as "so this was German-possible":[14] the encapsulation of an insight remaining private in the immediate postwar years. Like Zmarzlik and Kosthorst, Fritz Klein, later one of the best-known East German contemporary historians, waited until his memoirs to report on conversations between Wehrmacht soldiers in 1943, in the dark of packed train cars, that dealt with the systematic killing of Jews: "Whoever wanted to understand . . . understood: a people was being murdered by Germans."[15]

Rhetoric of Universalization

Under pressure to acknowledge the "German" contents of the theme and render the relation between knowledge and event definable, German historians initially discovered their nation's own victimization or took the defensive path of what Zmarzlik termed "trumpeters of morality and cellists of culture."[16] The basic structure informing both national narratives is revealed not in one or another term or argument but in a deeply anchored conviction that more than anyone else, it was the German *Volk* who had been delivered to fate by Hitler, a "tempter and seducer"—and an "Austrian" as well: "No other *Volk* had to endure such a hard trial," Tellenbach thus declared.[17] Discovering one's own suffering was one response to recent events; its counterpart was the nurturing of straightforward political escapism. Referring to his university days, Zmarzlik recalled, "People ensconced themselves in a kind of cultural world bourgeoisie. Behind the rubble of national state power politics and *Realpolitik*, we discovered the arcades of poets and thinkers. From the fatherland that had perished, we crossed directly over to the Occident, which promised imperishable values."[18]

As described by Nicolaus Sombart, son of the economic theorist Werner Sombart, in the postwar years, students at Heidelberg could celebrate a "rendezvous with the world spirit" with their teachers, but the need to interpret Nazism's advent placed the "German question" on the agenda—and did so in a way leading to the central role of the murder of the Jews remaining unacknowledged.[19] To be sure, the "horrific documentary films" were duly viewed, sparking indignation and a desire to see the criminals punished. But the event's interpretation remained something like Germany's domestic political riddle, mediated to students in the following form: "The atrocities were the work of a band of criminals that had organized itself as a state within the state—a secret criminal organization, a sort of political mafia, that had carried through its sinister plans for rule with brutal means and in a certain way had held the German *Volk* hostage, the majority of 'decent Germans.'"[20]

Retrospective assessments like Sombart's make clear that this cultural escapism was by no means unpolitical. Behind the demonization of the Nazi period was an arsenal of interpretive interests and struggles over memory; we thus find the historian Ludwig Dehio, in an essay collection that appeared in 1955, asserting, "In attributing supreme significance to the leading concept [of the demonic], I am already moving a little away from interpretations that do without it."[21] Such distancing was aimed above all at any explanations "that in isolating consideration simply see the German events of [the] epoch as having grown from German roots";[22] the strong emphasis placed on differentiated interpretations was thus not seldom an argumentative step taken for the sake of, for example, being "forced to perceive" what Dehio termed "volkish irredenta" as "a glowing stream of *Volk*-grounded passions [*volkstümlicher Leidenschaften*]" from "beyond the borders."[23]

The apologetics of the first discussions by German historians of the genocide of the Jews—apologetics that can almost be termed structural in nature— were nourished by a mixture of horror and mental overload. This mixture, leading to a sweepingly universalizing rhetoric, corresponded to the relation between the facticity of the event and an inherited self-image as intellectual representatives of everything national and historical. But bringing event and image together could not work. There was either a belief that rendering the destruction of the Jews into a theme was the same as denouncing national values; or, in the reverse case, a dead end immediately loomed when it came to maintaining one's own model of historical explication, grounded in positive concepts of power, state, and *Reich*, in other words, a form of intellectual suicide. (In asides in the texts in question, we find statements such as Friedrich Meinecke's that the situation paralyzed a will "to continue living.")[24] Put somewhat differently: traditionally accustomed to viewing world events through a national-historical lens, the historians suddenly faced the task of confronting a universal-historical caesura of the most destructive sort imaginable—a caesura both identifying the German nation with a war of conquest and genocide and demanding explanation.

But the efforts at understanding rarely extended beyond a "sentimental interiorizing of the German debacle" or an "adventistic 'zero-hour' awareness."[25] Such "explanations," which from our own perspective say nothing about the event but a great deal about the speechless embarrassment of those who advanced them, are the sources of a discourse in which that shock-centered existentialism could maintain itself. From the "high mountain" composed of "fragments of one's own experience,"[26] the older generation of historians tried to find concepts for interpretation. In the diaries of the historian Ulrich Kahrstedt, who chose to delve deeply into Nazi ideology, we find inserted newspaper clippings with banner headlines like "New Atrocities Discovered" and "Maidanek and Auschwitz," alongside printed photos of the "German torture camp Belsen" and an illustration of a "Polish shrunken head."[27] Where such lurid news items could be easily shrugged off as propaganda—and with them the theme itself—the general stream of photos, reports of criminal accusations, and newspaper articles on what had transpired were taken to demonstrate that precisely not the Germans but rather general anthropological phenomena such as modernity and mass society were what required research and study. German national history was what needed defending; it was thus the structural determinant of the first postwar historiography: melancholy and deterministic as the history of a tragic failure ("false path," "riddle," "hazard"); apologetic as verification of the nationally nonspecific within National Socialism; revisionistic as a search for a rescuing counternarrative of the good and other Germany.[28] We thus find the theme of "Auschwitz" present not as a narrative but rather as its avoidance—and nonetheless the presence is nearly continuous, albeit in a negative form not adequately definable in simplifying categories of "repression" and "coming to terms" with the event. It is conceptually there but not articulated, or else articulated and in the same breath contrasted, counterpointed, subject to revision.[29] In this respect, one unmistakable marker of the national historiographical self-understanding was a demonstrative shift away from the national state and toward an invocation of values like "culture" and "Christianity"[30] or suprastate and global concepts such as "Europe," "Central Europe," and *Abendland*, "the Occident." "Germany was beaten and dismembered," Eva Reichmann succinctly observed, "but 'Europe' was on every German's lips."[31] At the same time, a "renaissance of national topoi" took place "beneath the surface of discourse"; the *nation* "subtext" was the catalyst for the large questions of continuity at work in the debate about what *Germany* actually meant.[32] In this manner the national was redefined universally, and what was morally unsettling was grasped in terms of a Christian sin and atonement metaphorics, with concrete events bound into a metaphysical philosophy.

Recoiling from the facticity of the event could also occur when it was addressed directly. For example, in a remarkable passage of his at the time widely read and often cited book *Hitler in uns selbst*, published in 1946, the conservative Swiss Christian cultural philosopher Max Picard offers a metaphysical reflection on the relation between "gassing and forgetting" in the section titled "The Human Being without Memory" (*Der Mensch ohne Erinnerung*) and a thesis regarding modern "disconnection":

> The Nazi forgets everything because he has no continuity. He is always
> only the thing within him that the moment has thrown at him. . . . On the
> inside of such a human being, nothing from the past is ever there. This is
> the reason why at present everything can happen, the human being dares
> everything. . . . He undertakes the wickedest actions; they are all tossed
> into the abyss of amnesia. . . . This, then, characterizes the Nazi: not only
> that he murders but above all this: that he forgets that he murders.[33]

This observation about the "abyss of amnesia" clearly reveals recognition of
the social construction of "forgetting." But at the same time it locates the Nazi
crimes outside history, hence removes them from critical questions regarding
tradition. An argumentation linking a crime and memory in which that which
is "sinful" is defined as "everything that happened in the past" being "in the
German case interrupted by the present"[34] encapsulates the dilemma of the
German historians' interpretive efforts in the late 1940s, caught between particularity and universalization. In the effort to understand the events of the past
decade and a half through recourse to Germany's national character, but doing
so with a vocabulary of forgetting centered on momentariness, disconnection,
and discontinuity, Nazism very quickly turned into a "wound" or "illness" from
which the whole world suffered. "Thus is the Nazi," Picard declares, "we have
already said it: without memory, without inner continuity, disconnected. But
thus is the German today in general, only not as markedly as the Nazi, and thus
are nearly all Europeans and Americans today."[35] Within such a framework,
the German has been given the task to represent the world in the battle against
such discontinuity and disconnection:

> For a short time evil, the disconnected [*das Zusammenhangslose*], was summed
> up [*zusammengefaßt*] as a German phenomenon, in the Hitler phenomenon.
> Otherwise it would have established itself in all countries of the earth. . . .
> It would have destroyed all countries of the earth. But in this way, by
> forming and clearly standing there as the world of the Nazis, it set itself off
> from everything else; it remained bunched together here in Germany; it
> concentrated itself *here*. It is as if a body has disease-producing materials
> in it that are scattered everywhere until they finally gather into a distinct
> illness and make themselves visible in a single organ. . . . In the same way,
> what had been present within the German *Volk*, and not only in the German
> *Volk* but in almost all countries of the earth, was also expressed in National
> Socialism as a distinct phenomenon.

And Picard continues: "Much of the evil done in Germany took place
representing others; here in Germany what in other countries unfolded only

here and there and less violently and distinctly became a distinctly formed phenomenon."[36]

Within such a stance, universalization of Christian conservative provenance is recognizable as a reaction to the specifically German contents of the "final solution":

> In the face of the atrocities of the concentration camps, we cannot speak of individual guilt and collective guilt. . . . The concentration camp atrocities were . . . so horrible that this distinction is insufficient. Neither the guilt of the individual person nor that of the collective corresponds to these atrocities. Not the individual and not the collective of a *Volk* [*sic*], but only all humanity, the evil that is within all men [*das in den ganzen Menschen darin ist*] and has accumulated within these atrocities, only the guilt of all humanity corresponds to these atrocities. Not the juridical, not the moral, but only the metaphysical here offers a satisfactory explanation.[37]

Picard here is transparently alluding to Karl Jaspers's distinction, likewise referring to the recent Nazi past, between four kinds of guilt: criminal, political, moral, and metaphysical.[38] In this period, the sort of ahistorical deconcretization manifest in Picard's text was aimed not at enlightenment but at exculpation.[39] Starting with the Picardian thesis of a "Hitlerian world of discontinuity," the distance was not great to interpreting Nazism as a "matter playing itself out outside history, alongside it, in its effluents." At the center of Picard's approach was a belief that "National Socialism is not a part of history, not an episode in it; National Socialism is an intrusion into history, it is without history. . . . History is interrupted by Nazism."[40] In this context, the idea that history is "destiny," *Verhängnis*, that it is not made but befalls us "in inescapable decisions,"[41] contains an aggressive core. Even as late as 1957, Hermann Aubin was referring to the "episode of National Socialism,"[42] whereby the German crimes become marginalized within this perspective as "exaggerations." The formula that sometimes things did not transpire "without violence against non-Germans," *Undeutsche*,[43] reveals less a bad conscience than a conviction of a historical necessity of suffering and death in the execution of a historical mission. This is manifest not least of all in the concept of "the Occident," *das Abendland*, which accomplished the two main tasks: helping salvage earlier values and camouflaging an idea of superiority that was virulent, now as previously.

The Self-Image of the German Historians

The historians, however, were not only able to paradoxically maintain a nationalist tenor in their reflections; in the process, they could also preserve their self-image as *praeceptor germaniae*, mystified, as suggested, into a sense of being administrators of the national heritage and "guardians of the holy fire on the altars of the past."[44] In 1949 the sixty-two-year-old Heidelberg professor Johannes Kühn, who a few years earlier had published a text, strongly reflecting his Nazi commitment, on the "meaning of the present war,"[45] could speak with unbroken pathos, in a quasi-defiant gesture, of the *Abendland* as the "highest stage" until that point—which is to say until immediately after the war—in the movement of historical "truth": "The truth of history has never been more exactly, sharply, and richly determined . . . than in the Occidental cultural circle. . . . It has never [emerged] into light with such revelatory wealth. . . . But this is only the highest stage reached until now, under special circumstances, behind which those elsewhere remained far behind."[46]

But after 1945, the "revelatory wealth" of the historical truth of the "Occidental cultural circle" included the crimes of the Germans throughout Europe. It is to a high degree symptomatic that reflection about this led—often in a manner seeming to reflect a quasi-Heideggerian polarity between authentic *Geschichte* and vulgar *Historie*—to a cognitive theory capable of polemicizing against, in Kühn's words, *Richtigkeitswissen*, "knowing what is correct." In turn, it led to constructing a reality in which "Auschwitz" had no need to appear, since it represented an event on the "surface" whose cause still needed to be plumbed to the "depths." The guiding scholarly discipline here was theology: for aged Walter Goetz, World War II was the greatest event since the days of Saint Augustine, and never "since the *Civitas Dei* was it so emphatically clear that really great historical events demand theological interpretation."[47] The historian, Kühn stipulated, was not an antiquarian "but a sage." What was at stake here was not "being able to pile up facts" but "struggling for the shape of true history."[48]

For his part, in his *Weltgeschichte Europas*, Hans Freyer, a Leipzig sociologist and universal historian who himself had been a sometimes enthusiastic follower of Nazism, distinguishes the "historically illuminated realms of the past" from the "dark well-chambers of present decisions."[49] Presenting his book's "essence" and "self-consciousness" as "five thousand years of the past," Freyer defines his method, following Hegel, as a "decision to philosophize in facts" and as "thinking contemplation," hence philosophy—albeit a "philosophy of history with dates."[50] And although in the good tradition of historicism Freyer repeatedly inserts reflections about "actuality" and "individuality" into his history, he is less concerned with "demonstrating a cause and effect relationship" than with both "an effort at interpreting an entire epoch" and the "unity of world history," just as "within the variety of nature the careful researcher is concerned with the unity of creation."[51] Within these lofty parameters, Freyer can achieve his two main goals: continuing his work as a philosophical commentator while disparaging all those "falling" upon the "monstrous events" as moralists: "No wonder that shaken humankind, possessing the will to learn, to experience, to judge, falls [*stürzt*] upon the monstrous events. . . . Nevertheless for now the judgments are more moral and political than historical."[52]

The models for this approach were the Greek historians and tragedians. Freyer admired Thucydides and the virtue he displayed in maintaining the principles of historical critique in the face of crisis. But even when it came to this great model from antiquity, he admired not the critique in itself but rather the renunciation of "attribution of share of guilt"—that Thucydides was not so much interested in "research on causes" as in furthering "insight into the involvement of disaster-bringing forces [*unheilbringende Kräfte*]."[53] In the same vein, Paul Egon Hübinger compared life at the time in Germany to the "situation of Greece in the second century BC"—a situation historiographically mastered by Polybius, and he added that an effort was needed to reach the point where "a gifted historian accomplishes the same thing for us."[54] Likewise, Gisbert Beyerhaus discovered an achievement in the ranks of world literature in the published version of interviews that British military historian Basil Liddell Hart conducted with former Wehrmacht generals, which in Beyerhaus's view "demonstrated" the "maintenance [*Aufrechterhaltung*] of a 'code of decency' [English in original] by the Germans": "If we search for parallels, then only an antique parallel can be named for this book—the 'Persians' of Aeschylus."[55] And Golo Mann as well concedes in the preliminary remarks to his book on the Third Reich that "observations of the sort Roman historians cultivated" meant more to him than "all modern academic history."[56]

In this way, a professional self-understanding prevailed within which the central task of one's own historical labor was to identify "the angels of world history."[57] The events themselves paled in the process: what counted was thinking them through, not describing them. The contemporary metaphorics of "unsealing" the events make clear how great the emphasis was on the events' mysteriousness, hermetic qualities, inaccessibility, within the postwar German historians' cognitive-theoretical framework. In a variation on the great counter-Enlightenment German author Johann Georg Hamann, Johannes Kühn could thus write: "We live in the feeling of the future, and only thus do we unseal the past. For this reason, a capacity to read the past as the future must be demanded of historians."[58]

The basic problem at work here can be illuminated by considering certain argumentative structures in the postwar historical writing of the doyen of German historians, eighty-four-year-old Friedrich Meinecke, and in the work of Gerhard

Ritter and Hans Rothfels as well (for Ritter and Rothfels, see chap. 2), writing
that arguably is stamped by a paradox, inherent in a certain kind of apologetics,
endowing its analysis with a dialectic content. "Auschwitz" is not a theme for
any of these postwar German historiographers; because they avoided coherent
discussion of the extermination of the Jews, asking them how they approached
the topic professionally and as contemporaries of that crime would not have
been possible. But since not only what is remembered is of interest to the history
of memory but also what has been forgotten or remains unarticulated, the
question emerging in this context is how each of the three historians inserted
the Third Reich into the sequence of German history without rendering the
extermination an object of reflection and research. It would appear that in the
late 1940s their intellectual labor involved a displacement of the immediate
reality of the Holocaust's civilizational break into a complex of meta-themes,
and that only a historical unpacking of this displacement makes clear what they
wished to avoid. Despite this situation, all three unquestionably speak to us
with the authority of contemporary witnesses. Likewise, through their choice
of actual themes, the form of their historical narrative, and their theoretical
premises, all three offer a mirror of a deep professional and personal upheaval,[59]
but one only manifest as apologetic reaction. For Meinecke—whose reception
will be discussed in juxtaposition to a famous postwar work by Eugen Kogon—
the apologetics unfolded in a field defined by a group of key concepts including
"catastrophe," "fate," and "chance" (*Katastrophe, Schicksal, Zufall*) and as the fixing
of basic historical premises culminating in the conception of a "vertical" historiography. For Ritter it was manifested as a remarkably elaborate and highly
influential effort to deny that the "catastrophe" was German, accompanied by
a failure to confront the extermination of Europe's Jews. And for Rothfels, it
was expressed as a sustained attempt at building "bridges" between Germans
and Germans—bridges that once again entirely bypassed the Jews.

Friedrich Meinecke's *The German Catastrophe*

Annelise Thimme has offered us an illuminating report on the University of
Göttingen of the early postwar period. In the following passage, she recalls a
visit fifty years in the past with the aged Friedrich Meinecke (see Figure 2), then
living in the apartment of his former student Siegfried August Kaehler:

> Whereas during the war he was ailing to the point that everything was too
> much for him, especially longer, demanding conversations, now we sat
> together for up to three hours, and if someone expressed some sort of Nazi
> nonsense, which in the end sometimes happened, although not often, then

he went into a rage and pounded the table with his fist, becoming so furious
that the other person stopped his nonsense. . . . This was in the months of
1945–46, when he wrote his little book on "*The German Catastrophe*," thus
being the first historian to grapple in writing with the past of German history [*die Vergangenheit der deutschen Geschichte*]. Perhaps the title was not such
a happy one, for which catastrophe might he have in mind: that of 1933 or
that of 1945 or even the earlier one? He also "puzzled" [*rätselte*] about German "fate," whereas fate for me always signifies the intercession of alien
powers or of arbitrary chance effecting non-participating and innocent
people.[60]

In her evaluation, Thimme emphasizes two points closely tied together in
Meinecke's case: his rage at "Nazi nonsense" and the ambivalence conveyed in
a title that became proverbial, *Die deutsche Katastrophe* (although this work was
translated into English in 1950, we use our own translation). The undefined
relationship between the title's two main terms is expressed both incisively and
suggestively, in a way that allows opposing readings: the catastrophic as something caused by Germany or as something descending upon it.[61] In reality, the
non-determinability of the reference is a constitutive moment not only in
Meinecke's text but in almost all comparable personal accounts. "Five and a
half, no, twelve years, always the same question: when is the end coming?" is
the way, for instance, that Wilhelm Hoffmann, director of the Württemberg
State Library, corrects himself in the first sentence of his *Nach der Katastrophe*
(After the Catastrophe). The text appeared in the summer of 1945 with a first
print run of ten thousand and was out of print in a year; given the rubble
fields in all the destroyed German cities, most retrospective contemplation
could locate the war and Nazism under a single conceptual roof.[62] Repeatedly,
Meinecke and others actualized the natural implications of the term "catastrophe," its proximity to the passive, the state of being conveyed, the sphere of
storms, deluges, and earthquakes. Meinecke spoke of the "headwaters [*Quellge-
wässer*] of National Socialism," of the "heavy gales" (*Sturmwinden*) of the Hitler
movement and "waves of the epoch" (*Wellen des Zeitalters*);[63] *Wellen* is an omni-
present basic metaphor of the book, and a chapter heading. Hans Freyer likewise
evoked "wave crests" (*Wellenberge*) together with a "spark-bolt" (*Funkenschlag*)
and—not inaptly—"firestorm" (*Feuersbrunst*). After 1945 Johannes Haller—who
in the various prewar editions of his *Die Epochen der deutschen Geschichte* had
longingly invoked the day when the nation's "deepest debasement" would be
overcome and then proclaimed in 1939, "What was belief and hope has become
reality. The day has come!"—directly compared history to natural catastrophe,
thus merely spelling out what was already implied by the term or what could

be derived from citations of Goethe.[64] Like nature, history was "a great dissi-
pater, not even familiar with pity. Without mercy, through catastrophe, storm,
and flood, earthquakes and volcanic eruptions, it destroys the existence of innumerable animals and plants and lets thousands of human beings perish. No
guilt or punishment exists in its eyes, only relentless necessity—it really seems
to have no heart."[65]

But even in the absence of such analogies with nature, in the historical
writing of the postwar years the form of expression was diffuse, thus requiring
interpretation. In his *Vor den Ruinen Deutschlands* (Before the ruins of Germany),
F. A. Kramer identifies the "actual catastrophe of German history" as the subjugation of the western and southern German lands to Prussia long before the
Third Reich;[66] in Fritz Helling's Communist perspective on the "path of catastrophe of German history," the entire history of the German people was a
"failure" (*mißraten*);[67] and in contrast as late as 1953 Werner Conze could speak,
in the plural, of the "catastrophes of 1945," explicitly referring to the "severity
of the victors' decisions" and "occupational rule" (*Besatzungsherrschaft*).[68] Years
later, Theodor Schieder, for example, could distinguish the "events of 1933"
from the "catastrophe of 1945,"[69] und Percy E. Schramm used the same term,
long since a fixed formula, at the beginning of the 1960s.[70] If the term's meaning
was not directly changed, as here, to fit a politics for the past, it could simply
experience an extension into non-specificity through historical analogization.
Hence when in one of his many apologies for Prussia, Siegfried A. Kaehler
spoke to students of the "catastrophe of 1945," he tied it to the idea that what
was here at stake was, once again as in 1918, an "interpretive struggle over the
German conception of history that was imposed" on the Germans.[71] For his
part, Hans Freyer spoke, like many others, of the "permanent catastrophe that
began with the shots at Sarajevo";[72] and even Ludwig Dehio, in his reflective
revision of his own historical approach, uses the term "catastrophe of peace"
alongside "catastrophe of 1918" to designate the period that followed, confirming that in those interwar years, "the soul of every" German was ruled by a
"longing to extinguish a catastrophe."[73]

Perhaps unsurprisingly, what was here being repeatedly expressed contrasted sharply with the reading of German history by various German Jewish
historians. While Eva Reichmann, for instance, uses the term "catastrophe"
quite often in her writing, she also spells out at one point that it was to be seen
"not in the lost war but in the reversion to a barbarity disguised as National Socialism."[74] And looking back in the 1960s, the Prague-born historian of nationalism Hans Kohn, who had lived in the Soviet Union, London, and Palestine
before moving to America, describes 1933 as a "catastrophe for the Germans,

the Jews, and the entire world."[75] In the context of his efforts to understand the collapse of the modern state, Kohn favors a comparative approach to German history between the French Revolution and Nazism, understood as a cohesive epoch: a model oriented explicitly toward a specifically German political, institutional, social, and intellectual developmental path—a *Sonderweg*—deviating from that of the West in general.[76] "In reality the 'German catastrophe,'" he observes, began in 1871, when Berlin became the German capital for the first time and Germany an enlarged Prussia."[77]

After 1945 the idea of basic continuity between Prussia and the Third Reich was perceived as extraordinarily provocative and vehemently opposed by the bulk of German historians—not, however, by Friedrich Meinecke. For precisely his little book deviates from the historians' consensus; all in all his argument hardly differs from Kohn's. For despite the expansion of the catastrophe metaphor into the generality of Western history and the apologetic self-referentiality of the argumentation (the focus on German suffering through war and expulsion and loss of the national state), Meinecke's own ideas of "catastrophe" were themselves closely tied to the thesis of an erroneous German development that had not suddenly begun in 1933. Without a doubt, these ideas had reference to the defeat of 1918 and the end of Wilhelminian Germany; and he frequently spoke of a "century of catastrophes"[78] whose causes lay in the nineteenth century and whose "final catastrophe" would continue to preoccupy the coming centuries.[79] He here also meant the catastrophe *for* Germany, speaking to an emigrated student of a "world turn"—a *Weltenwende*—and of the "fearful catastrophes for those of us who have remained here."[80] But the man Fritz Stern has called the best-known twentieth-century German historian[81] was not only one of the first to speak out about what had happened but also—and this should not be overlooked—one of the most self-critical: he clearly criticized Prussian militarism, attacked the imperialism of Germany before both Weimar and Nazism, as well as the hyperbolic nationalism of German history in general; even the bourgeoisie of the Wilhelminian period and the early twentieth century— hence his own class—was not spared Meinecke's critique. These were all topics that the established historians' guild was very reluctant to critically examine. Hence Meinecke's "master narrative" of a German catastrophe is more complex than might first appear. One of the main sources of the repeated interest it sparks is its highly specific mixture of pronounced critique, analytic approach, and flight into something approaching demonizing irrationalism, together rendering the book hard to interpret.[82] On the one hand, the text was often downright mocked; on the other hand, even in the 1990s it was described as an "unexcelled" and "outstanding" historical essay. It was read as an apology

for the Nazi period, but in 1996 Meinecke was also praised by a prominent
feuilletonist for the "impressive honesty" of his inquiry into the grounds of the
German catastrophe.[83]

Autobiographical Authenticity

In what rhetorical-thematic form did Meinecke present his historical understanding and approach in *The German Catastrophe*—his articulation of concern
for Germany after Nazism? His text represents both an emotional-religious
confessional text and develops an explanatory model for the "Hitlerism" of
individual Germans. It has documentary, reportorial, and explanatory passages, with apology and critique often alternating directly. Meinecke's little book
thus amalgamates very different substantive and formal areas. But the decisive
factor, at least for its successful reception, was the historian's reflection on the
"West," the "German character," and "chance" in history—but also the tone
of unassailable autobiographical authenticity conveyed by passages on the
origins of Nazism, its "idea," and its violent realization. ("German spirit, Christianity, the Occident: we must live, believe, and hope within this triad."[84])
Interestingly, despite the subtitle "Reflections and Memories" (*Betrachtungen und
Erinnerungen*), Meinecke's introductory remarks in that spirit, the many self-
references in the main text, and the nature of the book's reception by contemporary readers, *The German Catastrophe* has seldom been closely considered as an
autobiography. (The book was, however, placed in the autobiographical volume
of Meinecke's selected works.[85]) Meinecke himself scarcely reflected on autobiography as a genre. At one point in his book, he speaks, entirely in passing, of
the effort manifest in autobiographical texts "to fuse one's own harmless life
with serious scientific and intellectual experiences."[86] And in a letter, he refers,
likewise in passing, to the boom in memoirs as a "natural and justified reaction
of the tormented soul to everything experienced."[87] For Meinecke, "memory"—
Gedächtnis—was itself not a category that increased perception. It surfaces in the
book's forward in entirely traditional form, as an explanation that circumstances allowed him nothing more than an appeal to himself, with his report
lacking objective material as a result of weak vision and an absence of sources,
thus emerging from memory alone.[88] In his memoirs, he observes—writing in
World War II and referring to Germany's revolutionary November days of
1918—that with "memories [*Erinnerungen*] emerging out of such deeply exciting
days as those we are now experiencing . . . recollection [*das Gedächtnis*] is only
firmly maintained by brightly illuminated individual moments—like lightning
interrupting night's darkness." Despite the marginality of such passages, we

can speak in Meinecke's case of an "autobiographization" of history, marking a shift in his basic ideas about history itself, the general interest in it, and its effects on human beings. In a letter to his student Kaehler in January 1945, in which his slow turn to Jacob Burckhardt over the war's course becomes clear, he equated this insight with a regular program: "Instead of continuing to inquire into deeds and effects, we now ask—how the deeds and works effect the human soul itself! Hence—history of humanity as the future's great historical task—as long as any form of historical research is still possible."[89] (Meinecke's short re-mark on a postcard fifteen months later itself points to the length and intensity of his shift of paradigm: "At the moment the Ranke-Burckhardt opposition completely preoccupies me."[90])

It thus becomes clear that the special quality of Meinecke's little autobiog-raphy in relation to the time of the "German catastrophe" consists neither in the "fate" and "riddle" centered metaphorics alone nor in the focus on his own person—both were a constitutive element of many texts of the period. Decisive for the book's impact was the "autobiographization" process—the question, posed with Burckhardt, of how "deeds and works affect the human soul itself," which is to say the effort at an analysis of historical effect. Tied to this was a systematically executed notion of personal and national catharsis articulated in the following terms: "May my notations, as limited as their value can be at present, contribute to beginning a new, bowed down [*gebeugt*] but nonetheless spiritually more pure existence, and to strengthening the decision to invest the remainder of our own strength for the sake of rescuing the little that remains of German national and cultural substance [*deutscher Volk- und Kultursubstanz*]."[91] "Under the impression of our experiences," Meinecke explained, he had "found some new perspectives that surprised even myself. The dictum *Historia vitae magistra* [history is life's teacher] must be inversed!: *Historiae vita magistra*. That this involves encountering cliffs is clear; but with vigilant self-critique, they can perhaps be circumvented."[92]

In a letter to Ludwig Dehio from the same period, Meinecke articulated his historical leaning more concisely and clearly: "The main thing is that in the midst of all the burgeoning pseudo-history and radicalinsky-history, German scientific history finally again announces itself and gives confused souls hope that at least within this very small realm of life, the old culture is still at hand."[93] But regardless of whether modest ("bowed down") longing for a "more pure existence" or an unbroken faith in "German scientific history" was in play, in both these seemingly countervailing citations, Meinecke expressed the same idea that he had already expounded on theoretically in a work written during the war:[94] rescue through the old culture.

An Anti-Catastrophic Interpretive Model

The cultural concept on which Meinecke based his interpretation of the nineteenth century, and which he rendered credible as his own work's autobiographical struggle, culminated in the formulation of a theory of "vertical historiography" containing both idiosyncratic-personal elements and those that might be considered historistic and typical of the time. A "horizontal contemplation [*Betrachtung*] of history," the historian argued, needed to be connected to a "vertical contemplation," as the only foundation for demonstrating, "in the middle of the tragedy, traces of authentic culture intermingling everywhere in the preponderant mass of human insufficiency, infirmity, and sin."[95] The "vertical" alignment here was of the contemporary experiential poles of good and evil, now appearing not as two possibilities of human existence but as a dichotomy between the human and the divine worlds. The world's wickedness was conceptualized as Antichrist: Hitler's work, for Meinecke, had to be "counted as one of the breakthroughs of a satanic principle in world history."[96] Correspondingly, Nazism was an expression of defiance at the Christian order: "Without knowing as much, Niemöller represented far more than only his church's faith. The entire Christian-Occidental past of two millennia arose within him and called to the usurper of this past: My empire [*Reich*], says God, is not of this world; but your empire, which you wish to found, is that of Satan."[97] In *The German Catastrophe*—and this is especially important—Christianity has become almost everything, including liberalism and democracy, "1789," and the humanist Freemasons.[98]

The philosopher Benedetto Croce sharply criticized Meinecke for falling into a "dualistic trap: such dualism amounted to "the ruin of all thinking and at the same time the source of everything religious and supersensible." Meinecke, he argued, admitted no dialectic thinking: "Without the protective weapon of this conceptual form, philosophy has to succumb to the temptation of grasping oppositions as something extrahuman, diabolical, with which he then really delivers himself to the devil, who for him is no longer a servant of God but rather represents a power opposed to God."[99] Be this as it may, Meinecke's "vertical contemplation of history" itself meant much more than the faith of his church. In the previously cited four-page essay titled "Irrwege in unserer Geschichte?" (Wrong tracks in our history?), he once again took up his theme of Germany's decadent historical course as laid out three years earlier in *The German Catastrophe*—albeit with a significant historiographical change. He now addressed the question of how the "treasure of historical memories" was to be rescued from each historical epoch. For this collection of "historical values," which Meinecke defined—in explicit distancing from the "horizontal contemplation, meant to be initially practiced, that follows the temporal course of things"—as "immune to crisis" and "inviolable," was, he indicated, the task of a history not only deepening knowledge "but also offering an ethical and religious foothold." Hence Meinecke's critical effort to revise the path taken in recent (Prussian-) German history was not substantive in nature, but rather involved a repetition of his idea that "contemplated horizontally," that history would never cease "to be tragedy."[100] As so often is the case, the basic tenor of this brief text is manifest in its key terms: "mistaken path" and "path of misfor-tune" (*Irrweg/ Unglücksweg*) appear fourteen times; "tragedy"/"tragic" and "fate"/"fateful/fate-determined" (*Schicksal/ schicksalsmäßig/ schicksalsbestimmt*) six times each; "abyss," "demonism"/"demonic," and "ghost light" (*Irrlicht*) twice each. "Demonism" was, in the end, Meinecke's term for how unintended evil could emerge from good. "In Prussian-German history," he explained, "salva-tion and perdition" (*Heil und Unheil*) were often "inseparably grown into each other."[101] As his biographer Walther Hofer accurately if uncritically observes, for the historian "all history [is] simultaneously tragedy."[102] The indelible char-acter of German cultural values, evoked in purely religious terms in the last chapter of *The German Catastrophe*, was now reformulated in a terminology of historical method—hence not as national ethical reflection in general but as an invocation of Germany's most famous historian, as the embodiment of a scholarly-ethical program, in particular:

> It is the contemplation, taught to us by Ranke, of historical epochs and formations *sub specie aeterni*, in their direct relationship to God. Or as this can also be expressed: it is the vertical contemplation of history. . . . [It] as it were holds the individual fleeing entities, i.e., the epochs and formations of history, firmly in its hands, allows them to linger, and tries to look at them face to face, and if possible into their heart, to convey their special achievement and special value for the highest human concerns and tasks.[103]

The postwar German historians' fusion, through religious introspection and aesthetic solace, of historical memory and ahistorical antimemory was rarely expressed with more conviction and economy than in Meinecke's detemporal-izing plea for a "vertical contemplation of history." The grasping of fleeting time, as a prototypical moment of historical inquiry, here was transformed into temporally removed confession and into art: "In what individual form—this the question posed by the vertical contemplation of the formation requiring scrutiny—have you produced cultural values of the true, the beautiful, and the sacred?" Meinecke himself formulated the corollary: "Now we no longer inquire into false paths taken by the individual person or the individual nation."[104]

(Elsewhere he spoke of the "quiet and healing values of memory and the past that are among the soul's vitamins.")[105] Hence the important thing for this sort of history was not "the question of success and failure, of effects and the further course of history in general," since now and previously that was the task of German history's "horizontal contemplation." What was decisive was seeking, finding, and rescuing "authentic culture," a culture located, as we have seen, "in the middle" of tragedy, "intermingling everywhere in the preponderant mass of human insufficiency, infirmity, and sin." And further: "Vertical in this manner, considered as an individual formation, this so deeply split epoch can even lift its eye directly to God and await a mild judgment."[106]

One letter from a reader expressed thanks for this "mild judgment": "Whoever wished to maintain that all, simply all phenomena tied to the Third Reich had been reprehensible and inherently bad? Despite all the pressure and terror?" A second saw the essay as itself representing "the hopeless confusion of political obfuscation—if not to say a falsification of the German historical picture" and a "license that . . . would tidily suit Hitler."[107] In actuality, within this plea for a "mild judgment," we can discover a revision of Meinecke's revision. The plea seems to form the conceptual center of his mixture of hope and apology, representative speaking for Germany and conservative self-interpretations. Karl Dietrich Erdmann, in rejecting the charge leveled at Meinecke that "a lack of readiness for genuine research on causes could be hidden" in a "false sense of fate," described the "verticality" notion as reflecting a "deeply grounded will to subject the world of the real, history, to the strictest standards available."[108] Erdmann saw absolutely no "side-step into the irrational" whatsoever at work in Meinecke, but defended him with the words of Hyperion to Diotima in Hölderlin's *Hyperion*: "Everywhere a joy still remains with us. True pain causes delight. Whoever treads on his misery stands higher. And it is splendid that we only truly find our soul's freedom in suffering." In the same period, Hans Schlange-Schöningen articulated a similar heroics of suffering in the pathos-laden final sentence of his apologia for Nazism: in view of the "horror and devastation," a glimmer of hope lay in the thought that "deepest misfortune . . . also has its dignity when the unfortunate one understands how to maintain it."[109] As absurd as such sentences—however benign or malevolent their discursive form—may sound when juxtaposed with the suffering caused *by* Germany, they were simply meant to bring the cathartic function of German history's tragedy to a logical head.

On the General Reception of *The German Catastrophe*

There was also criticism of Meinecke's text, for instance by Gerhard Ritter, who explicitly argued against the "vertical aspect" of Meinecke's history, seeing it as "an intentional abandonment of historical thinking" and very much recognizing the presence of "Goethe's beliefs" in the historian's theory.[110] Hans Rothfels also privately expressed a negative opinion, speaking of "world-distant cloudiness," "an old man's style," and "jargon"; he was of the opinion that Meinecke had never "been more deeply touched . . . by the really massive things in historical life."[111] For its part, Erdmann's reading of Meinecke's text in itself makes one thing clear: the reception of *The German Catastrophe* was one of its constitutive elements. For in the context of what Jaspers termed "the question of guilt" after 1945, the text's authorization through the life of its author took on a special function revealed through its various readings. This is manifest, for a start, in two longer comments, the first of which was offered by Eduard Spranger in late September 1946 in a letter to Meinecke:

> In writing, I will presumably not deviate strongly from your own feelings when I say that with the title *The German Catastrophe*, every reader initially fears receiving new wounds in an already wounded state, or at least being irritated because, for instance, the gloomy fog has not yet dissipated enough for things to be seen properly. I assure you that I have found no passage where I could have experienced this. Everything is full of a mild wisdom. You have in my view developed the highest degree of judiciousness [*Gerechtigkeit*] achievable at present, in the process not sparing your own people [*Volk*], but also have said what was necessary to the other side, where it was more dangerous. . . . This is the direction one has to take: from whence came these disturbances of balance, this subjugation of an entire high-standing people?. . . The inserted personal memories are exhilarating. You emerge as having been an antagonist over the entire twelve years. The receptive reader will understand it as a nice coincidence [*Fügung*] — alongside all the blindly arbitrary (chap. VIII) — that you, the old master of the history of ideas [*Geistesgeschichte*], still wield the cause of "spirit" [*Geist*] against the world's crime and wickedness [*Ungeist*] and thus could crown your oeuvre. . . . Many will be as grateful to you as I am.[112]

And in a long letter to his teacher in late October 1946, Siegfried A. Kaehler described the book, which he also reviewed,[113] in the following terms:

> I would like to now focus on one aspect of your "Reflections and Memories" revealing its special significance to me: the book appears as a memoir, apparently without claims to higher value [*höherer Geltungsanspruch*], and then proves from the first to last page to be a fully valid [*vollgiltig (sic)*] work of history, although written without "sources" and staking its claim without "evidence." And this has been possible by the "naive" form of the personal

account making use of the analytic method—applied to personal experience and refined over long decades—to integrate the personally perceived
into an outline of the elemental forces of the age. In this manner, from the
personal report an outline of modern history emerges whose questions and
assessments will influence all further problems posed—whether in agreement or disagreement. . . . Such a tie between simple report and refined
analysis, [emerging] from the wealth of the life experience of decades-
long intellectual labor, is the highest point a work of modern history can
reach—what enviable fortune that you could win this supreme accomplishment not only from your advanced years but also from the oppressive
circumstances under which you lived! You thus not only stand chronologi-
cally at the head of the generation of historians that presently has to move
along the dark path of the German people into the future, but you have
also assumed leadership in the process of clearing the thicket of misunderstandings and errors through which this path has to be opened.[114]

In his review Kaehler referred to Meinecke's book as a "breakwater."[115] It is
the case that in a private letter he cautiously articulated a criticism that is only
vaguely intimated in the review. But the critique was of a particular nature: he
found the book essentially *too* critical, too "exaggerated," above all because
Meinecke granted no justice to "the mass of 'idealistic fellow travelers'" from
1930–33. Meinecke responded simply: he maintained, he indicated, his critique of the German bourgeoisie.[116] All told, it is clear that both Spranger
and Kaehler—the colleague and the former student, the philosopher and the
historian—ennobled Meinecke's book as a guidepost and crowning moment,
standing, in Kaehler's view, against the "rising flood of daily journalism" and,
as he observed farsightedly, setting the direction for the "coming confrontation
about our fateful questions."[117] At the same time, neither failed to notice the
special form of the book as a mix of a personal account, a historical source, and a
historical study. And both argued dialectically: the book's extreme importance,
each insisted in his own way, was due to its being supplied with personality—
the "outline of modern history" developing from the "personal report."[118]
Such observations point to the actual explosiveness of the book's reception, as
understood from our present perspective: to an extraordinarily high degree,
Meinecke's *German Catastrophe* could generate *consensus*, despite its clear critique
of German traditions. The type and form of Meinecke's self-criticism was perceived as acceptable by Germans of all political orientations and social strata,
by readers at home and abroad, opponents of the Nazi state and former party
members, fellow travelers and victims. Albert Brackmann spoke of a "deep
emotion" and a "feeling of hallowed atmosphere" (*Gefühl der Weihestimmung*) that

came over him on reading the book's conclusion.[119] Gerhard Brück, who was, as he indicated, a German nationalist of Austrian Jewish origin who had converted to Christianity, and who had been deported to Dachau in 1938 before escaping to Sweden the following year, thanked Meinecke in a "Good Friday mood" for the "nearly uprooting force" evoked by his "own confessional text," by "royal thoughts from this spring of wise perception." He especially praised Meinecke for the chapter on the "positive contents of Hitlerism."[120] A younger reader wrote that he had read the book "avidly": "Yes, that is how it is. . . . So much resonates in me just as with you. . . . I see things perhaps a little less tragically than you do, somewhat less conscious of guilt, since as someone younger I perhaps even more strongly feel the guilt of others, of the other side. It is a tragedy of the times that crimes on one side sparked crimes on the other."[121]

There was also much praise for the book's historiographical form. Karl Dietrich Erdmann even singled out the method as more important than Meinecke's findings: "In a first outline, the categories of understanding adequate to our fate have here become visible."[122] The liberal historian Franz Schnabel praised the book's "moral consideration of history," neglected in modern historical scholarship; the Berlin medievalist Friedrich Baethgen wished to have Meinecke as a "leader and advisor" (*Führer und Berater*) in the search for "revision of some older viewpoints"; the Institute for Contemporary History (IfZ) in Munich observed that the historian had "also offered research in modern history orientating insight"; and in a message written by Hermann Heimpel, the German Historian's Association sent the following ninetieth-birthday congratulations in 1958: "To the spiritualizer [*Vergeistiger*] of the national idea . . . / to the explorer of causality / And guardian of values in the radiance of the fatherland and in two defeats / Who did his share for . . . new reflection at a biblical age in the midst of the catastrophe."[123] Together, West Germany's minister of the interior and minister for all-German affairs sent their own congratulations: "Thank you for your meritorious achievements as interpreter of our history."[124] That such thanks was centered on more than the mood of sacral self-reflection is made clear in a letter characterizing *The German Catastrophe* as *homeopathic*—as "world medicine" that both hurt and did good: "For me the satanic element of the recent past lies above all else in that all of Germany's justified historical claims appear buried by the devilish things that occurred; they can simply no longer come up for discussion."[125] Even Michael Müller-Claudius could begin his unspeakable pamphlet with the title *Deutsche und jüdische Tragik* (German and Jewish tragedy), treating the "senseless annihilation of millions of Jews and Christians at once," with a bow to the "pure wisdom of the historian at the evening of his life."[126] And under the title

"Farewell to Prussia," Munich's most prominent newspaper, the *Süddeutsche Zeitung*, offered thanks for Meinecke's "fragments toward a history of degeneration [*Entartungsgeschichte*]."[127]

The aged author was widely praised for rejecting "ressentiment and factional passion [*Parteileidenschaft*],"[128] and gratitude was expressed for the fact that he had declined to "speak of guilt,"[129] that he had contributed to "healing" "the German *Volk*" and relieving it "from the inner burden of the recent past."[130] There was also considerable focus—both affirmative and critical—on Meinecke's establishment of "coincidence" (*Zufall*) as a historical category.[131] A Nuremberg newspaper described the historian as one of the first such figures to return from exile, emphasizing his function as a "mediator . . . between his disoriented *Volk* and those who defeated it."[132] In a letter to Meinecke, the Leibniz publishing house praised his book's "decisive overview of the events," its "objective, crystalline clarity" emerging from the "highest, most all-encompassing watchtower." The historian, the letter continued, had the capacity, "in the moment itself," to "decisively assess" history in a "truly *sub specie aeternitatis*" manner.[133] And Berlin's newspaper *Der Tagesspiegel* summarized Meinecke's scholarly achievement as the demonstration of a specific tragedy, "that for the sake of human beings politics must be more than merely violence [*Gewalt*] but can never manage without violence."[134]

The book was essentially beyond criticism for some commentators outside Germany as well. "The slender volume is by far the best book written by a German" concerning "the disasters of the Hitler era," exclaimed Felix E. Hirsch in the *New York Herald Tribune* in 1952, while the Harvard and Yale historian Sidney B. Fay simply spoke in a letter to Meinecke of "the best short analysis of the reasons for, and the significance of, Hitler's rise to power." The Danish historian Aage Friis was more fulsome: Meinecke had been a "victim of National Socialism" and a "resistance fighter," "one of the greatest German historians of our century," who had described, "with deep human and political understanding . . . and remarkable mastery," how Germany fell "into the hands of a band of criminals hostile to culture."[135] And the above-cited Swiss historian Walther Hofer suggested that "German fate" (*deutsches Schicksal*) itself was speaking in *The German Catastrophe*: Meinecke's "life and work," he argued, was "intertwined in the narrowest possible way with the general fate of the German spirit," his "thinking and creating" nothing less than the "condensation of a supra-individual substance of a *Volk* and a time":

> Speaking to us here is a person who has shared the experience and suffering of the entire frightful vortex [*Wirbel*] of recent German history. . . . And what a fate this is! . . . What must it mean for Meinecke, the thinking and

feeling man, for above all the German historian Meinecke, to have experienced 1871 as a child [the reference here was of course to Germany's unifi-
cation] and 1945 as an aged man! . . . As if with threads of life, Meinecke
encompasses the entire fateful development of German humanity [*deutsches
Menschentum*] from Bismarck on to Hitler. . . . His historiography can never
be understood through purely scientific categories, since it is always more
than science: a conscious avowal of weltanschauung and expression of
active experiencing. *Historical fate*—that is the last and highest stage of
thinking about the meaning and essence of history that the aged historian
would attain—is tragic fate; the sense of history is experience of the tragic;
history fulfillment of a tragedy.[136]

Hofer added that only those who knew the sociology of totalitarianism through
their own experience could completely understand the path traveled by the
Germans: "Meinecke's work is an ideal-typical confirmation of the insight that
all contents of a worldview and view of history in the end rest on a life context."
For that reason, the dean of German history had a "profound right to speak
about German fate" and "gradually let us grasp this horrendous development."
Meinecke had been forced, Hofer continued, "to fight through within himself
everything now inclined to appear as crimes of the German human being [*Verbrechen des deutschen Menschen*]."[137]

A Countertext to Eugen Kogon's *SS State*?

In his review of *The German Catastrophe*, Hofer thus rendered homage to both the
book and its author. As suggested, Hofer placed strong emphasis on the long
duration of Friedrich Meinecke's mnemonic capacity, underscoring the fact
that as a child the old master of historicism could still feel wonder in the presence of veterans of the early nineteenth century's Napoleonic Wars, marching
through the Brandenburg Gate in Germany's unificatory celebrations of 1871.
But Hofer here was not only revealing a student's reverence for his most important teacher; the *longue durée* of biographical memory was also being cited as an
argument in the struggle for relevance unfolding between different forms of
memory. A context for this struggle is here suggested that may point to the first
and in its time most important book on Nazism by a German historian as being
an indirect counterbook to a range of depictions of concentration camp imprisonment. Alongside Eugen Kogon's report on and study of the SS state, which
was published at the same time as Meinecke's book,[138] many texts appeared
directly after 1949 that together established a new genre of memoir, using concepts such as fate, hell, and tragedy in a very different way than did Meinecke.

But these memoirs and descriptions placed German readers in the role of in-criminated parties, demanded answers and explanations, and, each in its own way, represented a kind of monument to a collective suffering of which there was no desire to be reminded. Against this backdrop, Hofer's expression of thanks that Meinecke "placed the role of admonisher so thoroughly in the background" sounds rather like an appeal to forgetting. In this period, many readers desired to read books that authentically conveyed the way they had themselves been overwhelmed by the Nazis, not those provoking a bad con-science regarding their own indifference. Accordingly, in a private letter to the author of *The German Catastrophe*, the archaeologist Erich Boehringer made the following observations concerning the Nazi crimes:

> We [have to] see things from the perspective of heaven, from very far away, and then it seems to me concerning this historical development, which as you say began with the Enlightenment and the French Revolu-tion, that Nazism . . . is only a small sub-segment, although—perhaps— the most horrible and naked. We have probably moved past the culmina-tion of this trajectory. The course of things will now go more quickly. I could imagine that in sixty to seventy years these things will be at peace.[139]

In writing his book, Eugen Kogon was keenly aware of such ressentiment and thus felt himself obliged to polemicize against "the flood of personal reports" in order to defend his own stance. He consequently called his account a *Sachbe-richt*, an "objective report" meant as a plea to acknowledge truth and reality.[140] He wanted to describe "the system," precisely not merely individual events, as he explained, and hence to expose "the organizational structure" and what was typical within it. To that end, he broadly laid out the circumstances of the text's origins, underscoring the fact that out of a four-hundred-page work written together with other prisoners in the summer of 1945, containing both a main report and 150 memoirs, he had now fashioned an entirely "new manuscript"; it was meant to be read as an analysis, not as an expression of an individual's ressentiment, thus not describing the "singular case" of Buchenwald (the camp he himself had survived) but rather the entire camp system. At the same time, he apologetically explained how carbon copies of separate portions of the text could be published in the Russian Zone of Occupation under the title *KL Bu* (=*Konzentrationslager Buchenwald*).

Structured in a markedly systematic manner,[141] *Der SS-Staat* (hereafter re-ferred to as *The SS State*), alongside basic chapters and subchapters on "the goal of the National Socialist state," the "psychology of camp prisoners," the step-by-step radicalization of the camp system, and the inner organization of the camps, also contained detailed descriptions of exemplary daily prisoners' routines, forced labor and the penal system, the situation regarding nourishment, and hygiene and sanitary circumstances. In chapter 14, Kogon turned to "special facilities such as crematoria, gas chambers, and medical-experiment stations"; and the following chapter discussed "group fates and special actions," taking in the mass murder of the Jews, the liquidation of Russian war prisoners, and the destruction of "life unworthy of living." Kogon described the system of external camps, the corruption of the SS, and the prisoners' economic exploitation. One chapter was devoted to the "anti-fascist forces" inside the camps and their fight against the SS, another to the liberation of the camps; the last chapter, titled "The German *Volk* and the Concentration Camps," was a critical confrontation with the "thesis of German collective guilt."

Through such a critique, Kogon in fact meant the chapter to serve as a defense against what he anticipated as the reproach of engaging in propaganda on behalf of Germany's enemies. And actually from our present perspective, the precision of Kogon's differentiated descriptions and sharpness of vision is not half as remarkable as his frequent expression of misgiving regarding his report even being published. In his foreword, he voices concern about "the dark burden . . . that I have brought to light,"[142] warning his readers about individual chapters that would be hard for many men and women "with pure hearts" to read. The foreword's first sentence in fact virtually implores readers to accept the legitimacy of the reasons he offers for deciding to publish: it is meant as an "ecce homo mirror," not an accusation against "Germanness," *Deutschtum*.[143] Likewise in the foreword, he recommends that the final chapter be read twice, once at the start and once at the end. In the final chapter, he puts aside his objective diction, naming the Third Reich the "twelve rough years" and confessing to himself and his readers that in the Nazi period something "metaphysical" occurred with the Germans—something scarcely graspable through reason alone. Here again, he grapples with the credibility of his analysis, with the arguments against a focus on the reality of the camps, and with the function of his book in general: a function he identifies above all as contributing to Germany's renewal. But the chapter's core remains the adamant rejection of the thesis of German collective guilt. The horrific facts, Kogon indicates, could not have an impact in connection with that unjustified accusation; they would have led to more insight if they had been "directly" entrusted to the German conscience:

> Before it could touch the sphere of deepest feeling for law and humanity,
> indeed of the religious, where the German would have still offered enough
> resistance to the twelve years of Hitler rule and its spiritual influence, the

concentration camp propaganda was already rejected, because he realized
that he was meant to be pushed even more inescapably into greater guilt.
Every one of them sensed that a higher judge would not have placed them
in one and the same dock with criminals and activists of the Nazi Party.[144]

As a subtext and in a structurally defensive manner, Kogon went so far on his
foreword's first page as to point demonstratively to putative American crimes
in Japan—the atom bomb, he insisted, had reduced the Americans to the level
of the SS.[145] He criticized German obduracy and the pharisaic non-German
world on equal terms, shielding himself with urgency, as suggested, against imputations of ressentiment, sensational reporting, the intention of producing an
"atrocity report." In this way Kogon anticipated nearly every conceivable ob-
jection against the publication of his *SS State*; already in 1945, he was concerned
with parrying the criticism that too much had already been said and written
about the camps. In that respect, he referred in highly generalizing sentences to
his mistrust of "human nature," emphasized the character of "uncanny complicity" in a guilt extending far beyond Germany, and offered the reassurance
that the camp inmates had to survive in the face not only of the SS but also of
the "terror and arrogance" of fellow prisoners.[146] He anxiously considered his
book's impact, assuming it might actually not simply preserve a memory of evil
in documentary form but actually keep the evil alive. For that reason, he stated,
"I sometimes . . . was tempted to burn the manuscript during its writing."[147]

Eugen Kogon was by no means against descriptions of the "German catastrophe" in the tone and style of Meinecke's work. In the cited chapter on
the approach of postwar Germans to the fact of the camps, he himself recommended that, after their stifling of humanity, they now descend "into their own
submerged depths" where "the gold of high German qualities, indeed: the gold!"
lay buried; through such "gold," "the historical and national-psychological
roots of guilt" were meant to be uncovered, in order to be transformed after
"generations of patience," reemerging with a "purified essence" for the sake of
"fulfilling Germany's true task in Europe and the world." This was precisely
Meinecke's own desire, and for that reason it is not surprising that Kogon made
clear his deep respect in his review of Meinecke's book, seeing it as "the start of
a revision of German historiography" possessing "splendid" passages.[148] At the
same time, Kogon strictly dismissed any speculation over the "positive contents
of Hitlerism" and "chance in history" as a "*deus ex machine*" and "emergency
exit" for German nationalist ressentiment. All told, he aptly assessed the book
as an effort "to save as much as possible from the past."[149]

Germany's guild of professional historians responded to this moderate
criticism with a major essay by Gisbert Beyerhaus in their chief organ, the

Historische Zeitschrift, in which that author began by declaring—with a discernibly threatening undertone—that Meinecke represents "the voice of the spiritual and political countercamp to Hitler."[150] The goal of his own essay, Beyerhaus explained, was to "further develop" Meinecke's great achievement "and offer a spur to further research." To this end, he placed his main focus on the eighth chapter of the historian's book—the chapter criticized by Kogon—in order to expound on a passively understood "catastrophe of the German *Volk*": the shift from democracy into "caesarism," Beyerhaus observed, was no merely "German problem" but rather a general "sign of decaying culture"; "the battle of Hitlerism against Christianity" had been a consequential campaign of extermination by the totalitarian state against "the last bulwark of the constitutional state and freedom of conscience." Hitler, he continued, was "the singular, unexpected incursion of an alien [*fremdartig*] factor into Western history." And further: with his dictum, referring to Hitler, that "this person actually doesn't really belong to our race," Otto Hintze had properly posed the question of "whether this essential foreignness [*Wesensfremdheit*]" of Hitler "was not in fact of purely biological origin," for after all, his ancestors were "from the Balkans," his despotism "Asian," his success a "breakthrough of the satanic."[151]

In direct correspondence with Meinecke, Beyerhaus indicated that he had identified the chapter on "Chance and Generality in History" as the core of his book, and the point where he anchored his effort "to convert Herr Eugen Kogon through *positive* analysis and show him . . . the foolishness of his assumptions." Kogon's thesis, he wrote,

> that through recourse to chance you intended to create an emergency exit for German nationalism [*für Deutschnationale*] condemns itself. Educators coming from all directions need to promptly inform him of the baleful [*unheilvoll*] effects on youthful souls of his book *The SS State*. . . . My friend the philosopher Joachim Ritter considers *The SS State* so pernicious [*verderblich*], that he would approve its being locked away [*für Sekretierung*]![152]

When Meinecke had not yet answered in the fall of 1949, Beyerhaus wrote again, stating, "You will understand that my sense of how successful I have been in using the right weapons to defend your book against Kogon's attack in the *Frankfurter Hefte* depend on your judgment in particular."[153] Beyerhaus was here trying to instrumentalize Meinecke's *German Catastrophe*. In defining the historian as representing a conception of German victimization and by emphasizing a Nazi anti-Christian exterminatory campaign, he initiated a process of overwriting the experience of camp imprisonment that Kogon had conveyed in his own book; in doing so he endowed the reception of Meinecke's book with an orientation that became firmly attached to it.

At the same time, the metaphor of the "SS state" would become very popular in the period after Kogon's book appeared—it too could be applied in highly flexible fashion. In his 1954 text on the officers' revolt of 20 July 1944 against Hitler, Siegfried A. Kaehler would thus speak of a "revolt against the SS state" and a "deeply rooted counterrevolution against National Socialist rule over the European world" that tried to erect a constitutional state in place of the "SS state."[154] Leaving aside the question of whether the history of the military resistance to Hitler can be reasonably formulated in such terms: during this period the frequent, hence urgent recourse to the metaphor had a connotation extending well past Kogon's effort to define the camp system to encompass Germany's general circumstances under Nazism.[155] Within the framework of such a reading of German domestic politics between 1933 and 1945, the Greifenverlag chose to ask Meinecke in August 1948 whether he wished to contribute to, as the publisher's letter put it, "a culturally and politically significant *Bekenntnis-Buch*"—the untranslatable German term suggested a volume presenting professions of creed—in which "the fates of prominent personalities of German intellectual life [*deutsches Geistesleben*] forced over the past twelve years into so-called 'inner emigration' or abroad" would be brought together in "self-portrayals." The collection was meant, the letter explained, "to offer the most complete possible description of the history of an oppressed, persecuted, and suffering spiritual Germany in the 1933–1945 period, before the eyes of the international public and for the benefit of the German *Volk*."[156] In the context of reception history, the implicit ties between Meinecke's personal account and his book carried a specific, highly important resonance, with the book itself functioning as a kind of counterbook to the accounts of surviving camp inmates. A linkage of autobiographical experience with historical instruction in a message deemed acceptable by the Germans was crucial for the work of postwar German historians of the recent past.

Meinecke, the culturally conservative historian, was forthright in respect to the nationalist tenor of his oeuvre. In a remark on the occasion of a highly reserved English review of *The German Catastrophe*, a review by G. B. Gooch that Meinecke described as "amusing . . . , not unfriendly, but malicious,"[157] he responded to those observing that his concept of freedom simply meant the freedom to write books that although the critique contained "a grain of truth," "it is not entirely accurate."[158] He also conceded, however, that the "framework of an authoritarian state" the reviewer discerned in his book "unfortunately" could "not so easily" be shaken off.[159]

2

"A Large Dark Stain on the German Shield of Honor"

Gerhard Ritter, Hans Rothfels, and the Denationalization of National Socialism

Considered retrospectively, it is difficult to grasp the critical potency of Meinecke's ambivalent reflections on the "false path" of German history. This difficulty is above all grounded in his blurring of historical realities into the equation of Germany's historical path with that of a tragic hero, a great man gone astray. Gerhard Ritter spoke up persistently against what he termed an "obscuring"—*Verdunkelung*—of German history, vehemently protesting against its description as a "catastrophe"; this marked his distance from Meinecke's melancholy cultural nationalism. But if he did not, like Meinecke, embrace German culture of the Goethe period as the measure for evaluating the recent events, how did he defend the nation's traditions? What themes did he choose, and what positions did he draw on in the process? What was his terminology, and in what way did he speak of Nazism and the extermination of the Jews?

Ritter's full commitment to an understanding of both politics and history in terms of the nation-state is known and has often been criticized.[1] His interpretation of Nazism was less escapist than Meinecke's, but in essence narrower and more reductionist—albeit consistent to an almost breathtaking degree. Even following 1945, the Freiburg historian viewed the nation as a connotative historiographical center—what endowed history with a sense that was the opposite of a quintessentially "senseless" Nazism. For Ritter, misfortune, coincidence, and hard political circumstances basically explained the Nazi Party's rise to power, which could have happened in any other nation facing similar burdens. "Is it not senseless that an individual man can cause this horrendous intrusion of barbarism onto the Occident that we have experienced—that through his mere will he could literally set the entire world aflame? . . . Indeed, one would like to believe that with the abrupt end of our national state, the general sense of our mysterious history has become conclusively obscure. For where the future is no longer visible, interpreting the past also remains denied."[2] But Ritter added as consolation for such rhetorical skepticism: Nazism had nothing at all to do with one's own national tradition. To the contrary, it had caused severe damage to that tradition, which freed from "barbarism," needed to be mobilized in strengthened form. In Ritter's idea of the "individual man," that is, Hitler, bringing misfortune over Germany, the West, and the entire world, the view of the Third Reich as a *Betriebsunfall* of German history, an "industrial accident," was not merely implicit but indeed clearly enunciated.[3] Similarly to Meinecke, who had speculated on "historical coincidence" for a long time, with Ritter the other leading postwar German historian had embraced an approach meant to diminish German guilt in general. Germany was here characterized as completely surprised by and unprepared for Nazism, the "Hitler movement" evaluated not as an event emerging from German history but as "a result of the surging up [*Aufwallen*] of confused times."[4] Ritter thus underscored the contingency and discontinuity of the event. The repeated articulated credo of his scholarly efforts after 1945 reflected, accordingly, a search not for the Nazi period's roots within German history but rather for proof that Nazism was alien to Germany's own true traditions. What is here astonishing is the consistently denied contradiction at work between an ideal of scientific objectivity, on the one hand, and the proclamation of a prescriptive political history, on the other hand; clearly, his essential concern was not defining the nation's incriminated traditions but purifying the national self-consciousness.[5] Regularly Ritter would arrive at a point where in order to maintain an axiom of continuity central to his basic historical convictions and scholarly method,[6] he had to proclaim an equally central axiom of discontinuity in Germany historical development: the Third Reich had to be marginalized, both in its prehistory and in assessing its consequences.

Scandalization of the Continuity Question

Ritter did not stand alone in such convictions. For example, Siegfried A. Kaehler, his colleague at the University of Göttingen, likewise polemicized against the idea of a German "false path," referring to it with the disparaging term "historical optative," by which he meant an a posteriori view of past events.[7] The idea, he indicated in a letter to Meinecke from October 1949, was excessively in debt to universalism;[8] perhaps, he suggested in another letter to Meinecke written a year later, "the tortuous wrestling about the sense and meaning of 'path' and 'false path" is itself a great false path of our genus [*Geschlecht*]."[9] And adhering to a dialectic then inherent in the theme of "research problems" of National Socialism, Heinrich Heffter (first head of the research group, founded in 1949, on the "History of the City of Hamburg between 1933 and 1945"), alluding to Ritter, remarked that "however much of the German, all too German spiritual heritage flowed into National Socialism, the strict fuehrer-principle must be named un-German and un-Germanic [*undeutsch und ungermanisch*], particularly when the desire is to preserve a purely national line and banish [*verfehmen*] all foreign influences."[10]

Already in the earlier cited reflections of Max Picard from 1946, published under the easily misunderstood title *Hitler in uns selbst* (Hitler in Ourselves), Hitler was interpreted as the strong expression of a disease—one that in any event characterized the entire epoch. Picard molded this argument into a concept illuminating the relationship between crime and nation in a paradigmatic way: the concept of a "disconnection" or "discontinuity" between the events of 1933–45 and the totality of German history. At times, this concept took on obsessive qualities, operating as the guilt fantasy of an obverse, and frequently denounced, *failed* national tradition starting with Bismarck or Frederick the Great, even Luther or the Middle Ages. In actuality, lurking within Ritter's scientifically couched postulate of objectivity is the Picardian fantasy of "disconnected man"—a fantasy representing a vulgarized version of a Weberian modernization thesis. Picard had developed the notion that Nazism had no place in history whatsoever—not even as "an episode"; Nazism was, he argued, an "intrusion into history, something "without history," and inversely history was "broken through" by Nazism.[11] Ritter oriented himself around this notion of a "situation of discontinuity" stamping modern civilization; it represented the subtext of a mission of national rescue that he made his chief personal, scholarly, and national-pedagogic task into the 1960s. For Ritter, engaging in "revision" in postwar Germany was not so much offering a corrective to Nazi ideology as correcting its critique. The first of these alternatives in his view took care of itself, since the Third Reich was simply the "senseless rupture of a magnificent ascent,"[12] something that needed to be borne with dignity but not explained. What he believed needed explaining—indeed considered unbearable—were the explanations themselves, above all ones focused on German history's false, and inescapable, path.

The question of the relationship between continuity and break then formed the template for the decisive caesura in postwar German historiography, the so-called Fischer controversy of the early 1960s.[13] This debate over the causes of World War I and Germany's military policies, the last of Ritter's major interpretive battles, owed its intensity to the fact that the "discontinuity thesis" still lay over the question of World War II's causes like a tranquilizing blanket. It is now very clear that the controversy was, as Gerd Krumeich observed in 1999 in the *Frankfurter Allgemeine Zeitung*, a kind of proxy discussion, its generation-determined absolutism reflecting, not least of all, the start of a confrontation with "Auschwitz." In Krumeich's view, none of the participants could have used a terminology of "continuity" and "discontinuity" without thinking, at least tacitly, of the Nazi crimes. His observations are worth citing at greater length:

> If we search for those who were the "moderns" in this *querelle des anciens et des modernes*, then we will come across the hundreds of young students attending Fischer's lectures in Hamburg. Within this anonymous mass of students, no one, whether in Hamburg or elsewhere, had ever reflected on Germany's war aims in the First World War or the July crisis of 1914. But everyone understood that someone had shown the courage to turn against the establishment and pose the "continuity" question as the students wanted it posed. We followed Fischer above all because he brought the staid older gentlemen holding seminars over the "demonism of power," German spirit and German fate, Bismarck's historical greatness, and the like into a white heat. In truth, the controversy over the war's outbreak had the role of a proxy war. For actually we had an entirely different question that, to be sure, only very few of us dared ask. It was the question of Auschwitz and how that could have happened.[14]

In this context, Krumeich cited the trial held against former *Einsatz* group (special killing unit) members in Ulm in 1958, the founding of the "C Commission" (the Central Office of the State Justice Administration for the Investigation of National Socialist Crimes) in Ludwigsburg that same year, the appearance of Gerhard Schoenberner's pathbreaking *Der gelbe Stern* in 1960, and the Auschwitz trials themselves. He then continued:

> In the Fischer controversy, there was no direct talk of all of that, but everyone who spoke of "continuity" or claimed discontinuity in German history from Bismarck by way of Hitler to Adenauer, knew or suspected they were actually speaking of Auschwitz. . . . In view of the shock of the gold star

and Auschwitz, the young were then demanding an accounting from the old. . . . What was above all at stake was destroying the understanding "we" of the older historians who had grown up in the Wilhelminian period or, like Gerhard Ritter, had been soldiers in the First World War, for the sake of historical critique.[15]

Gerhard Ritter had no understanding for such "accounting by the old." For him, that was synonymous with something he specifically named "self-doubt"—no answer to pressing questions but part of the problem against which he was campaigning. Ritter saw *precisely here* an echo of the national "hubris" practiced by the Nazi and meant to be opposed by "sobriety";[16] that was his message to German participants in the controversy. This notwithstanding, he offered effusive thanks abroad to colleagues showing "genuine, empathic understanding for the situation of the average German": having "hate for the German *Volk*," he argued, was "unworthy of a *historicus*"—his message to a Dutch colleague whom he thanked "as a German" for being "so bravely and openly against a revival of old feelings of hate among your countrymen."[17] In general, Ritter's work from this period symbolized recourse to a stock of knowledge and values stemming from the pre-Nazi period and thus capable of being stylized into blamelessness. They were, so to speak, topical and obsolete at once, in that they followed a zeitgeist generally trying to establish an intellectual anchoring in paradigms from the Wilhelminian epoch.

Post-1945 Self-Stylizations

In the German academic context, exercising *Vergangenheitspolitik* (the untranslatable term designates either a politics or a policy meant to deal with the past)[18] refers to a culture of knowledge in which the "selection, transmission, and circulation of stories is organized by way of past events in the discipline."[19] That after 1945 this process unfolded in a palliative manner is well known. What now seems far more interesting is the question of the semantic strategies used in the process. In the postwar years, a "rhetoric of elision" took in a wide range of procedures relatively recently encapsulated under the term *Vergangenheitsmanagement* (management of the past). What is in any case correct is that the definition of divergent opinions as taboo and scandalous, the staging of a "new beginning," the systematic elisions combined with demands for "objectivity," marked out a field that determined the way the theme was to be discussed from the start. This included all the argumentative figures devaluing criticism of institutions by invoking decency, on the part of either the individual or the discipline. For a long time such myths were diligently transferred into historiography—

very much as if academics, and historians in particular, stood beyond critical usage of sources.

Now if Ritter offered an "accounting" of his own role in the Hitler years, then he did so defiantly, like someone who had already known everything in advance and had to merely correct himself in details but otherwise could remain true to his view of the world: "I was a passionate opponent of National Socialism long before 1933," he declared in a letter written in 1961, "and was one completely starting with the so-called seizure of power. . . . The only thing I greeted in National Socialism was—aside from the defeat of unemployment— the fact that in 1938 the unfortunate 'Greater German-Lesser German' problem appeared to be overcome by Austria's incorporation into the Reich." Ritter continued: "I was never National-Socialistic, and also not imperialist, but rather patriotic."[20] And this was not in fact inaccurate, in that there are no indications of any Nazi rhetoric on his part in the 1933–45 period, and his few antisemitic remarks had been well within the framework of standard academic opinion at the time. Also, in the 1930s Ritter had suffered personally from moderate harassment, had been arrested a few months before the war's end as a member of the "Freiburg circle" of anti-Nazi professors, and then survived a period of mortal danger in a Gestapo prison and the Ravensbrück concentration camp.[21] Against this backdrop of personal integrity and in light of the various possibilities for "managing the past," he had to engage in far less "constructing" or altering when it came to his role and function in the Nazi years than did many colleagues. And just this had great importance for his conceptualizing of both the Hitler phenomenon and Nazism in general, since he was the bearer of the proper credentials for consistently defining the Third Reich as nothing other than a calamity that befell Germany, hence as the opposite of genuinely German political and cultural traditions. But this interpretation could only succeed to the extent that he understood Nazism, in a conservative-elitist manner, as an "uprising of the masses," and with this, as an abuse of precisely those values that he and his generation championed. When he expressed himself about the mass crimes and especially the Final Solution, the results were catastrophic—his biographer Cornelißen speaks of constitutive "perceptive pitfalls."[22] Either he dealt with these topics through the usual stylizations, or he avoided them because of his own denunciation of their circulating in Germany and abroad as an effort to politically delegitimize the German nation.

In a long interview with Helmut Heiber at the start of the 1960s for Heiber's great study of academic history in the Nazi period,[23] we thus find Ritter presenting himself as a veritable seer—one who peremptorily placed the placating German formulas of the period in Jewish mouths:

"From the first moment it was clear to me," explained Ritter, "when this persecution of Jews began in April, that this would develop into an unprecedented catastrophe. I remember standing in the Kaiserstrasse with my half-Jewish colleague Brie, the scholar of English literature, and taking in the dreadful impression with bitterness; then I said: Dear Brie, that will be a cultural catastrophe of the sort we've never experienced. He remarked guilelessly [harmlos]: Oh, those are initial revolutionary phenomena; they'll eventually blow over. I said: Dear friend, in two years you'll be sitting in a camp; you'll experience that. Which then happened, to be sure, only for a few days."[24]

In the same interview, Ritter also recalled his young doctoral student, "who on 1 April stood in uniform before a wreaked Jewish shop that he had helped destroy. . . . Naturally I very clearly expressed my displeasure to the man across from me, and he was himself ashamed." The contrast between these recollections and many other passages in the interview where Ritter offers self-exculpating arguments—a paradigmatic mix of belated insight and gaps in memory—seems peculiar: Heiber: "Book burning?" Ritter: "Yes, that did not take place here." Heiber: "This operation of 10 May 1933 wasn't carried out here in Freiburg?" Ritter: "I know nothing about that."[25] Likewise: the elimination of the "Jewish or half-Jewish professors was carried out entirely silently [ganz in der Stille]";[26] the Nazi Students' Association, in Ritter's words, "often got on his nerves," but "as said, all that was outside the more narrow circle of my own following.—National Socialist infiltration? I don't know what's meant by that."[27] Again: the "basic tone" at the University of Freiburg was "not exactly Nazi-friendly." "Here in Baden-country" everything was different, for "the natural good-heartedness of the population and also the Catholic tradition" made it possible to "somewhat dampen" Nazism;[28] "by and large most people really were unpolitical, in fact the case now as well." "I would think," Ritter went on, "that . . . contamination by the brown flood was not so bad among the professors as elsewhere. . . . But naturally we as well were not spared being forced to appoint all sorts of National Socialist elements, of whose scholarly achievements we thought very little."[29]

In general, Ritter recalled, the students who came to his lectures—"in the hope of hearing something to strength their hearts against the Nazi tyranny"—were very "gratifying." In this context, he used the term "resistance" without great hesitation, then retracted it somewhat later in the following, rhetorically skillful manner: "Ach, in the case of most [professors], we shouldn't speak of opposition or resistance; it was perhaps only the professors' inability to suddenly change their ways. . . . Scholars basically have an unpolitical nature and can't be suddenly made into preachers. In the 'quiet resistance,' I see no achievement but simply a fact."[30] And after 1945, "[we] succeeded in our faculty . . . being extensively again cured [*sic*]."[31]

With this choice of words, Ritter was alluding to his key role, as held in his memory, in the "self-purging" (the French authorities referred to it in even more medical terms as *Auto-Epuration*) of Freiburg University after the war.[32] In actuality, it was above all the sugarcoated evaluations Ritter handed out to his colleagues that made a positive image of the University of Freiburg in the Third Reich possible. Heidegger, he indicated, had lived in an unpolitical world before 1933 and took that with him after joining the party; he had prevented "crass Jew-baiting . . . in the university's halls" and in the end held out "in an attitude of sharpest inner opposition" to the regime. The committee under Ritter wrote an attestation for the professor of ancient history Joseph Vogt, who had adapted to the Nazi state with essays informed by biological racism, indicating that he had joined the SA in 1933 and the party in 1937 in order to help in the "overcoming of class differences" and save "Germany and the Occident from communism." And even the eugenicist and "racial researcher" Hans F. Günther, who could not receive certification that his work and teaching had remained free of Nazi influences, and who was excluded from the university, his chair terminated, received an attestation of his "humanly decent attitude." Consistently, the argumentation in these cases and many others reveal one of two patterns: either "sharp oppositional views" were belatedly underscored—this for instance the phrasing in the certificate for the art historian Kurt Bauch, who had spoken up for Nazism in the first years after 1933— or else party membership and Nazi ideology were explained by the fact that younger candidates had to advance through a party detour. As Cornelißen summarizes, in respect to this crucial process in fixing the university's postwar self-image, hardly any expression was resorted to as often as "determined opponent of National Socialism."[33] Hence in the Heiber interview, the referential center of Ritter's retrospect on the Nazi era was his own interpretation of history, not that history itself.

The palliative rhetoric to the effect that in Freiburg things had not really been so bad was supplemented by a melodramatic narrative regarding the Jewish deportation from the area. In private correspondence rather than published form, Ritter here outlined a personalized scenario whose key terms—"pangs of conscience," "despair," "pistols," "choked with tears," "martyrdom"—recall literature more than political reality:

> Allow me a few words about my own answer to the question of whether
> the German people are responsible for the crimes [*Untaten*] of Hitler and

his accomplices. Naturally you are completely right in saying that it is non-sense to demand a confession of guilt [*Schuldbekenntnis*] from every single German for things that largely happened without them knowing and at the same time remained outside their sphere of influence, meaning that they could in no way prevent them. Nevertheless, I admit that it always cause me pangs of conscience to so often have to observe something horrible happening. I will never forget what I felt like when one morning I heard that a Jewish married couple with whom I was friends was just taken away to a transport to southern France . . . to be killed there. I still owned a pistol and struggled with myself over whether I should gun down the policeman who was taking them away. In the end I did not do so because it was sense-less, and I later learned that the police officer was a former regiment comrade of our Jewish friend and had demanded that the married couple leave their apartment with despair in his heart, indeed choked with tears. There were thousands of cases of this sort, and even martyrdom of some-one wishing to resist evil would have been practically fruitless, for it would have been kept secret from the public.[34]

The discursive significance of this story lies in its melodrama taking place within Ritter, the central theme thus being removed from the political-public sphere; Ritter now attached moral-theological reflections that he normally strictly rejected:

But somehow there was a feeling of some moral responsibility when one simply remained silent in such cases. Beyond this, I would like to also express the view that a people living in a democratic state [*ein demokratisches Staatsvolk*] is in some way responsible before history (not before the judge and not before the neutral foreigner) for whom it applauds and thus brings to power. . . . Nevertheless, for me it remained a saddening and as a German repeatedly shaming fact that so many Germans—extending into the ranks of my "colleagues"—were never hindered by moral reluctance [*Widerwillen*], by indignation at such hypocritical, brutal, and mendacious discourse by the rabble-rouser [*Rattenfänger*], from ever giving him and his partners their vote. It isn't the political error, but definitely what I'd like to term the "moral horse's nose" [*moralische Pferdenase*], which is to say a com-pletely blunt nose, that I perceive as the guilt or perhaps the ethical failure [*sittliches Versagen*] of a large, very large part of the German *Volk*, with fateful consequences. That afterward, once he had come to power, a revolting pack of conscienceless position hunters, sycophants, cowards, and also sadists, i.e., scoundrels ended up on top and spread out was nothing other than what was to be expected and depressed me less than that "horse's nose." For in every nation . . . under the veneer of civilization—a very thin veneer—there always lives a type of person resembling a beast of prey and only waiting for his moment to become active.[35]

In Ritter's letters and publications after 1945, these are the most critical words he expressed regarding German responsibility. The use of feeble words such as "somehow" and "in some way" and the pileup of invective, the simultaneous antipathy toward judges and foreigners, the immediate rendering abstract of concrete guilt, which simply stands "before history," a picture of the perpetrators ("beasts of prey") that through a strict separation of sadists or scoundrels from the *Volk*, in the end manages, after all, to externalize Nazism, and the lament over the generally very thin veneer of civilization—all this indicates that Ritter was offering a portrait of Nazism in which the events at the end of the 1930s were kept from view of the majority of German people. Furthermore, Ritter's limited critical assessments, as manifest in both the longer passages quoted here, remained without consequences. In the same letter, he presented the basic "past-political" conviction he consistently followed as a historian: the German *Volk*, "in all its layers," was presently so deeply convinced of the depravity of Hitler's regime and "so deeply affected by the misfortune" he had caused

> that the Hitler period is felt to be a large dark stain on the German shield of honor. There's no need in that respect for instruction in the schools, as is taking place daily. And the same for instruction from abroad. . . . For my part, I believe that the time is past where such confessions of guilt were useful. I feel that it is nothing less than a danger that the former excess of patriotic self-glorification has perhaps now been often followed in schools and universities by a super-revisionism that no longer concedes a shred of good to the German past.[36]

The last sentence was already aimed explicitly at "the latest product of this fashionable current": Fritz Fischer's *Griff nach der Weltmacht* (Grasp for World Power, 1961),[37] which Ritter condemned as a renewal of the "Versailles guilt accusation" and as a prime example of "super-revisionism." All told, his argumentation was aimed not only at avowals of guilt perceived as superfluous and "instruction" from abroad but also already against a presentation of the facts themselves—against a historical concern with the entire theme and an analysis of a body of sources that he found disagreeable.

If we read it as an initial text in post-1945 modern German historiography, Meinecke's *The German Catastrophe* was basically a document inverting the inherited definition of such historiography. In view of the disastrous results of twelve years of Nazi rule, he wrote no "history of the fathers" but rather, as a father, a "history of the sons," to whom, he argued, one's own nineteenth-century cultural values had failed to be transmitted. Ritter saw things differently. He wrote not about the sons as historical actors within Nazism, but wholeheartedly out of the context of his own generation, in a defensive tenor and without the melancholia that so strongly stamped Meinecke's approach. The image Ritter drew of the Third Reich has such a distorted effect because he completely elided the role of the intellectuals and universities in the Nazi system; but the image was compatible with his own views, including those that had been expressed earlier, and, importantly, with his own behavior in the Nazi period.[38] But his insistence on maintaining such a perspective meant keeping some absolutely central themes out of the complex of problems he meant to scrutinize, with disastrous consequences for his interpretation of the period. Since Ritter did not say anything cohesive about the Nazi genocide and related mass crimes and thus also failed to assess their consequence for German historical self-understanding, in his case, as well, we can only argue in terms of an absence.

Against the death camps' backdrop, Ritter's explication of what Nazism was simply has no graspable sense, or formulated inversely: he could only maintain the sense of his own historical interpretation by approaching the camp system, plunder and dispossession, deportation, extermination, as outgrowths of Nazism to be sure, but emphatically not as essential to defining what took place in the twelve years of the Nazi regime. What Ritter wished to understand by "National Socialism" was so narrowly conceived that he could present his arguments with a particular sort of biographical authenticity and historiographical authority, a sort that even found its own zealous confirmation in refutation and critique. But the fact that so many themes, questions, and problems posed by the international public after 1945 were absent from his view of the Third Reich renders it doubtful that his work should even have been evaluated in respect to an altered context—one whose caesura was defined by World War II and the Holocaust. Rather, its special quality seems to lie in its needing to be read within the constellation of the *Great War*, that war's own question of guilt and consequences.

Resistance as a Historical Lesson

What Ritter did consider worthy of research was German resistance, which was closely tied to his self-image and represented the only theme that could be positively tied to the Nazi years.[39] Allowing a fusion of historical research and biographical labor of memory, the theme has undeniable advantages for personal and professional authority. In November 1949, Ritter could thus still express astonishment, writing to members of the board of the German Historians' Association, that overcoming objections to cooperation with the International Historians' Association had likely been facilitated by Ritter himself being perceived as a resistance fighter ("more so than I would have believed") and hence as guarantor of an anti-Nazi attitude within the new German history.[40] (This perception, let us note, was also at work in the early East German state. We thus find the Communist historian Leo (Jonas Leib) Stern, while sharply criticizing Ritter's postwar publications, adding the following remark in the same talk: "Allow me . . . some words on Gerhard Ritter, doubtless one of the great German bourgeois historians. . . . Ritter belonged to the group of conspirators against Hitler called to account by the Gestapo after 20 July 1944."[41]) But already in March 1946, Ritter had spoken self-confidently of the "moral fundament for my continued influence," possessed, he indicated, by no other German historian and, as he put it, "at present priceless [*unschätzbar*], when we have moved from one set of coercive circumstances [*Zwangsverhältnis*] to a new one, provisionally even more oppressive in many respects."[42] And even earlier, he had asserted that he had "neither a restricted nor a total sense of guilt," but rather believed that he had all grounds for a good conscience, both being the only German historian who "had dared to touch the hot iron of this delicate [*heikel*] problem" and also counting among those who had "demonstrated their fulfillment of duty through Gestapo dungeons and mortal danger."[43]

In this manner, Ritter's research on resistance, in particular his 1956 book on the conservative opponent of Nazism Carl Goerdeler and the German resistance movement,[44] itself lived off of his sense of affiliation, thus gaining entry into his general picture of the Third Reich. Here, where he saw himself as a "spiritual ally," he wrote with his "heart's blood"; in one private letter he unhesitatingly acknowledged that "passionate participation" and a "large portion of my own experience" informed the book.[45] In a letter to his publisher Stolz, he similarly wrote that as a biographer he had "directly shared" his hero's life, his description thus being destined to have the effect of "an original source."[46] But crucially, with Carl Goerdeler Ritter had chosen, as a central historiographical theme, a resistance organizer who, he suggested, "not only was inwardly averse beforehand" to the plans for assassination and overthrow of 20 July but had "afterward radically renounced them." In his cell, Goerdeler, Ritter argued, became a "model of an upright confessor"; "possessed by the idea of peace and justice," he had ascended into the fantasy of mediating between the Nazis and Allies for the sake of protecting Germany: "whoever wishes to understand him must conceptually enter very deeply into his way of seeing the world."[47] Written from this perspective, Ritter's "labor of interpretation and thinking"[48] had to present the "basic stance" of the German resistance through Goerdeler's personal "obsession"; it had to demonstrate that despite ultimate failure, it had been comprehensive and principled, broadly supported by a German elite: no officers' putsch, but the "effort at revolt of an entire *Volk*," "the voice of a hard-pressed conscience," and expression of true patriotism. Its underlying gesture, Ritter passionately insisted, "was not for the sake of one's own person and its historical legacy but for the sake of Germany."[49]

Even in those cases where speaking as a witness was empirically impossible, the interpretations of the resistance by Ritter, his colleagues, and their followers were authenticating self-stylizations or "texts of passage" in the sense of Arnold van Gennep, with a strikingly high share of biographical content. Through mutual citation, the "authority of the insider's view" could here be transmitted, with a "strategy of exclusion" thus becoming an argument. With such texts, the authors could negotiate Nazi-period careers, described for readers in exemplary form.[50] In this way everything could be achieved at once: the apologetic historical-political exoneration of Nazi-era Germany and the spiriting away of disagreeable historiographical themes; the manifestation of an imaginary self-image in which none would be forced to abruptly abandon his own traditional values. At the same time, a "view of these men," which is to say the resisters, also offered a possibility of "again discovering a bridge to the good German past," as Ritter unambiguously described his book's function.[51]

Jan Eckel has explored these discursive connections, consistently offering a balanced view of the political and mental functions of such "autobiographical strategies for authentication." His argument that a type of self-generated intellectual transformation could establish itself in precisely those texts opening a path to the community of values embraced in the early West German state renders plausible the constitutive proximity of research and memory in respect to the key "period of historical reconstitution and new definition";[52] this is especially the case when we take into account the reception history of such books—a history strikingly neglected even in the case of Ritter's book on Goerdeler. We thus find Ritter's arrest by the Gestapo and flight from Berlin "almost" reminding his colleague Kaehler "of the legendary liberation reports of the apostles' history."[53] Of all of Ritter's books, this one received the broadest response, with the commentaries by the press and colleagues mainly positive and sometimes euphoric, with those from abroad tending toward skepticism or rejection. (There were also positive reactions from outside Germany, but these were distinctly "more dissonant"; the Hitler biographer Alan Bullock thus rightly indicated that the book marginalized the resistance groups that were not National-Conservative.[54]) The *Stuttgarter Zeitung* expressed the hope that the Goerdeler biography would become "a political book for the German *Volk* and house"; the medievalist Heinrich Bornkamm praised the study's pedagogic value, thanking Ritter for having furnished readers with a "basis for a new spiritual order" through the men of the resistance movement; and Göttingen colleague Percy E. Schramm likewise thanked Ritter for his "service," through which something "decisive" had been achieved "freeing us from the nightmare of our recent past."

In October 1939, Ritter stylized himself into an "emigrant among my own *Volk*."[55] However much we take this statement at face value, in the context of the leading role of both Meinecke and Ritter in the German historians' profession after 1945, the significance of the above-described response can hardly be overestimated. The costs of autobiographical dominance were immense, since inversely, the closeness of emigrants, surviving victims of Nazism, and those outside the German historians' guild to the events they experienced was unanimously seen as grounds for rejection—in the name of objective science. (We will return to this later in the present chapter, and then later in the book in respect to Joseph Wulf, where the situation was manifest in its full tragic effect.)

Controversies and a Struggle for German Honor

The debates Ritter had been engaged in—some were regular battles; others either involuntarily sparked or ones that he tried to bring to an end in an authoritarian way—were both strategic and polemic on all levels and in all their forms: in scholarly publications and newspapers, private correspondence, and above all the work for boards guiding academic politics. The picture that emerges is of a historian engaged in a constant struggle for one thing: the restoration of Germany's honor and the rescue of the nation's political traditions; the struggle was sometimes carried out through scholarship with empirical claims, and sometimes in the "form of politics engaged in by historical means."[56] The latter activity passed as the "eros" of Ritter in his role as the "political educator of his age": a figure destined, for example, to be praised at his funeral by Heinrich Bornkamm for his "decisive nature," leading him "to also endure and maintain enmities for the sake of what was at issue."[57] The "enmities" surrounding Ritter in the prehistory and early period of the West German state make two things clear: that his "defensive mentality" encapsulated the country's stance in those years; and why there was no place for acknowledging the *Jewish* catastrophe alongside that of the Germans.

As the first chairman of the German Historians' Association and opening speaker at the first German Historians' Conference after the war, Ritter was, as suggested, the dominant figure in the freshly forming academic discipline (see Figure 3).[58] In this respect, in a letter to Ritter, Fritz Hartung observed that, "Precisely the connection between undisputedly serious scholarship and an absolutely blameless political stance in the years '33–'45 makes you the association's most suitable chairman. That you are known as a good and national German seems to me a thoroughly positive thing; if it were otherwise, it would be difficult for you to count on the trust of the majority of German historians."[59] Ritter repeatedly stressed the association's "purely scholarly" orientation; he nevertheless formulated decidedly political claims, without ever perceiving this as a contradiction.[60] The historians' conference was itself meant to follow the principle of normalcy and solid scholarship, as fixed by Ritter; we thus find the decision taken, in an early stage of planning when Frankfurt was still the conference's intended venue, not to gather at St. Paul's Church because of the event's "scholarly character." At the same time, "only such themata" were to be dealt with "that also [had] special meaning for the political thinking of modern man."[61] The program Ritter desired thus united scholarship with efficacy. In a letter to a W. Philipp written in March 1949, he thus explained that, "In this first conference of German historians since the catastrophe, we do not wish the topics covered to depend on the preferences of those invited, but rather to implement a program suited in its entirety to convey a sense to the outside world of the sustaining power [*Lebenstüchtigkeit*] of authentic historical research, i.e., to demonstrate that genuine stocktaking and a healthy new orientation by the German *Volk* is impossible without historical studies."[62] In a letter to Rudolf Stadelmann from December 1946, Ritter had already addressed his own work's function even more clearly. His main focus, he indicated, was "documenting before the public how we conceive of the renewal of German history [*Historie*]: no total revision in the sense of alien impositions [*fremde Zumutungen*], but also not simply the old routine"—to which he added that in his view "precisely medieval history with its highly one-sided cultivation of learned-antiquarian research" needed "some revising."[63] In its particular historical context, Ritter's opening speech thus necessarily involved a balancing act between, on the one hand, his deeply held premises—his mistrust of opposition, perceived as an "alien imposition," to a narrowly "national historical" perspective—and, on the other hand, a widely expected defining statement on the restoration of national self-assurance.

It was characteristic of Ritter that in the Munich speech the most pressing problem was apparently whether, as enunciated at the start, following the "cultural catastrophe" historians could still reach "the nation's ear."[64] Although maintaining critical distance from the hypostatization of the state in the German historiographical tradition, the chaired Freiburg professor was nonetheless convinced that "German history" could not abandon its heritage "without betraying itself, i.e., the final, highest sense of its work."[65] Accordingly, after presenting scattered examples of bias and exaggeration, at a central point Ritter announced his credo, to the effect that he did not believe his own scholarship presently had any reason to "essentially alter" its fundament.[66] All in all, he indicated, he was of the pragmatic view that what was needed was not great words but rather modesty, earnest self-reflection and "illusion-free sobriety," unreserved critical scrutiny of traditions, and an execution of existing tasks, again without illusion.[67] At the same time, he rejected "laborious and practically useless belated self-accusation or self-justification by our discipline."[68] The important thing was not criticizing but understanding, a "clarification and cleansing of the national self-consciousness" beyond opportunism and nationalism.[69] Here Ritter could not deny himself a jab at the only critical biography of Bismarck then available, a much-discussed study by the German Jewish jurist and emigrant Erich Eyck, disqualified by the historian for a "mistaken" and "schoolmasterish basic approach."[70]

In the course of the speech, Nazism emerged as a problem concerning the Germans alone, the main element in "the history of our misfortune," to be described, as seen, alone, without help from the "outside":[71] "The German *Volk*, which for twelve long years only heard the droning loudspeakers of Hitler's propaganda, has for a long time fervently desired to finally hear the peaceful, pure voice of the historical truth, objective historical scholarship."[72] The picture of Nazism Ritter here drew presented a Germany forced to endure the regime as a yoke and an everyday life marked by no shelter from its claims; he thus defined the Third Reich in terms of bellowing SA masses. With that perceived reality as his backdrop, Ritter could comment that there was "certainly much to do to protect . . . German history from unjust vilification [*Verunglimpfung*]."[73] In this manner, all the historical events making their way into the speech were meant to demonstrate German suffering: the separation from "the so-called Eastern Zone, which in truth includes the center, the heart of Germany"; the loss of Prussia; and the war losses.[74] There was no mention of the German crimes in general, and the Final Solution in particular; instead, there was an abstract and laconic reference to Nazism as something non-German. In a summarizing gesture that here seemed intended, nevertheless, to succinctly outdo Meinecke, Ritter referred to the Nazi years as the result of "demonic forces of the deep."

Emphatically, he initiated no turn from old positions through this apologia and the concession of a few past mistakes.[75] Rather the reverse: we here find a restoration of traditional positions, with a key function being accorded to a rhetorical demarcation from nationalism and National Socialism, and to the rhetorical figures of the "peaceful, pure voice of the historical truth" and "objective historical scholarship," beyond the "atmosphere of attack and defense."[76] It is important to note that Ritter's hovering middle position composed of measured critique of tradition and programmatic scholarly orientation toward the future indeed had an expected "politically very favorable" impact: "The headlines that the *Neue Zeitung* [a newspaper published by the American Information Control Division in Berlin's American Zone between 1945 and 1956] gave its two reports: 'German Historians against Nationalism' and 'History Writing without Blinkers' [*Deutsche Historiker gegen Nationalismus / Geschichtsschreibung ohne Scheuklappen*] speak for the outward effect."[77] Shortly after the Munich conferences, Ritter had his impression confirmed by Hans Nabholz, interim president of the Comité Internationale des Sciences Historiques, who conveyed his "excellent impression" of the conference.[78]

Denationalization of National Socialism as a Program

Ritter tried to show that Nazism was something non-German in many of his postwar works—and this not only through metaphorical rhetoric but also in concrete historical interpretations. On the one hand, he maintained a strict, and for his time nearly ritual, distinction "between the German *Volk* and its National Socialist leadership."[79] But in its elaborateness, the substantive nature of the distinction takes on interest. For a start, he argued that Nazism was itself a product of non-German developments, picked up by Hitler, "the born Austrian,"[80] from Mussolini's Italian fascism. In any event, he viewed the actual historical source of the Nazi movement in the French Revolution; the Third Reich's racism and antisemitism stemmed, he pointed out, from the "French Gobineau," the book of the "German-English" Chamberlain, and the "fermenting national chaos [*gärendes Völkerchaos*] of the Donau area" that Hitler had "imported [*eingeschleppt*] to Germany." Finally, as the highpoint of this historical theory, he assigned responsibility for antisemitism to the Jews themselves: "a political antisemitism on a grand scale only emerged after the world war [i.e., World War I], in connection with the mass influx of the Jewish population from the east."[81] And as the political ideology and theory of *Lebensraum* was, according to Ritter, the core of any imperialist doctrine, "not merely a German but an international phenomenon" was manifest here as well.[82] In a downright sententious manner, Ritter, for instance, attributed to the German resistance the idea that Nazism was "a satanic falsification of authentic German tradition."[83] It was "utterly wrong," he insisted, to derive it from the premises of German history. ("In the core of its essence, National Socialism is not any sort of original German growth [*Gewächs*]."[84])

Ritter's *Europa und die deutsche Frage* (Europe and the German Question) was his book that most clearly argued for a denationalizing of National Socialism, moving in sharply dialectic form against the idea of the Third Reich as a German catastrophe. The French Revolution was defined as the movement's source not only "analogically" but explicitly "genealogically" as well,[85] this because Ritter conceived of the Hitler regime as a "revolt of the masses," the radical realization of a "total democracy." Ritter was here defending the tradition of the German theory of state as on the same level as Western (i.e., British, French, and American) constitutional theory. The reactions to this stance were a mirror of the book itself, its reception thus confirming what it described, and also what it wanted to be: a thoroughly German book. For abroad, mystification and rejection predominated; Ritter thus complained, for example, to Hans Rothfels: "The fearfulness of American publishers when it comes to having my book translated" seems nothing short of "grotesque": "Here one book after another is translated from English, large and small. The German publishers have no fear of this, although they are all in dire financial straits, and these gentlemen in the land of the dollar have now been considering ¾ of a year and can't bring themselves to decide." He could not, Ritter confessed, shake off "the bitter feeling that distaste at even hearing the voice of a German is actually in play here."[86] In contrast, the German reception was highly enthusiastic. Even Ludwig Dehio, who later distanced himself from Ritter, wrote him to confirm that the Third Reich resembled a "curved mirror" that, although reflecting back German features, nevertheless "distorts through circumstance that should not only be derived from German developments but also from European and indeed global ones as well." *Europa und die deutsche Frage*, Dehio asserted, had helped restore the self-consciousness of German youth, in that here Ritter had refuted the principle of "after this, hence because of this" (*post hoc ergo propter hoc*). In doing so, he had been able to "do [the German] *Volk* a service" as no one else could.[87]

Even years later, Dehio tried to work through his own approach in this respect with the help of Ritter's concepts. At the 1951 historians' conference in Marburg—the first such postwar conference to incorporate a section on modern history—he himself formulated a firm rejection of any "overemphasis on the German special way," an "isolated consideration" simply seeing "the German events of our epoch as growing from German roots," "without steadily keeping in mind the intertwining of these events with the environment." At the same time, he cited Ritter's term "demonism of power" as having "paramount [*überragend*] importance," while resorting to a corresponding metaphorical arsenal: Germany as having been subject to "demonic temptation"; Hitler as a "corporeal demon in the extreme hegemonic struggle"; and Hitler as a "satanic genius" who lifted Germany upward on a "dark wave of crisis [stemming] from the rising forces of civilization," "constantly also spurred onward by the admired rival, Bolshevism."[88] That only a short time later Dehio and Ritter entered into a sharp controversy over principles, centered on the tradition of German militarism, makes one thing very clear: On the one hand, Ritter dominated the postwar German historical profession with his basic concepts, early books, and voluminous theorizing, in the process forcing those objecting to some of the concepts onto his own terrain. But on the other hand, he remained so unmoving in his unbroken Wilhelminian canon of values that even those lightly criticizing German political continuities quickly found themselves taking a diametrically opposing direction. In light of Ritter's rigid defense of Prussia and Bismarck, the reproach of immobility he leveled at others takes on significance. For Ritter, Dehio's general description of Prussia, which included a sometimes critical discussion of the continuity problem, was thus proof that even before 1961 the author had been caught in the "mood of catastrophe" of 1945.[89]

Objections by Outsiders and Polemics against Foreigners

As an example of the constant polemics and critiques in which Ritter was caught up, his relationship with East German historiography is especially revealing, since the opposing attacks were here formulated in particularly sharp fashion. Importantly, this enduring quarrel is not reducible to an ever-"colder" conflict between systems. For example, Ritter's reference in *Geschichte als Bildungsmacht* (History as an Educational Force) to the "power of evil and blind chance" in the struggle between "God and Satan"[90] provoked indignant criticism from Leo Stern that remains solid despite its Communist theory of agency. For Stern, understanding modern German history required no "learned-profound Baroque language" but simply "showing what is"; there was nothing mysterious in that history if it were not interpretively mystified from the start. (Unfortunately, Stern had his sober and solid critique culminate in the reproach that Ritter's conception of history "objectively exonerated the powers of German monopoly capitalism that pushed Hitler into power, because he was the most compliant and unscrupulous tool for realizing their imperialist plans of plunder." In this way even Stern became a spokesman for the general East German critique of West German historiography, with its own, glaringly ideological blind spots.[91]) In any case, Ritter rarely reacted with annoyance to criticism from the East—he in fact hardly ever reacted at all.

In West Germany and abroad, no publication of the Freiburg historian failed to spark a polarized response. Already his first postwar article, an apologetic piece on the "German professor" in the Third Reich, evoked astonishment on the part of readers who had been chased out of the German universities: Hannah Arendt confronted Ritter's theory of institutional resistance by the academic elite with the assertion that in 1933 those universities had "lost their honor." In a letter to Karl Jaspers she agreed with him that restoring their reputation seemed virtually impossible:

> For they have made themselves ridiculous. Denazification, certainly very important, is still only a word there; for the institution itself, and worse the position of the scholars, have become ridiculous. What is decisive here is not that professors did not turn into heroes but rather their humorlessness, assiduousness [*Beflissenheit*], anxiety at missing the connection. . . . Now I know that many, perhaps even a majority, were never seriously Nazis. Only this as well becomes questionable when for instance we see what, e.g., Gerhard Ritter . . . chooses to say about this. He had an article in the *Gegenwart* that unfortunately also appeared here.[92]

Ritter's rhetorical distinction between politics and history, meant to endow dignity to his own works as interpreter of the past, was already rejected by his contemporaries; its claims remained without influence. Ritter scorned the outsiders who criticized him for the distinction, such as Johann von Rantzau, as "unsatisfied private lecturers." (In mid-March 1951, Rantzau had written: "Herr Ritter fails to observe one fact of basic importance: namely, that historical work can be draw into politics at any time, indeed that, for example, his text on the German question is *essentially politics*."[93])

The hardball at work in the clash of different historical conceptions is also apparent in the early struggle for influence in the IfZ. This struggle will be discussed in detail later; at this point, what must be noted is that Ritter's main resistance was directed at the person of Gerhard Kroll (1910–63), a jurist and economist from Breslau who had begun his postwar career as a Christian Social Party delegate in the state parliament and, starting in 1949, was the institute's founding director (it was still known then as the Deutsches Institut für Geschichte der nationalsozialistischen Zeit). Kroll advocated a revised Catholic-Occidental history with a basic critical perspective on Prussia that he wished to establish at the institute. As a result, he fell into direct conflict with Ritter, the Protestant by conviction, who had a dominant influence at the institute for a short time. Ritter arranged Kroll's dismissal by threatening to otherwise resign from its board.[94] Parallel to this, in a controversy centered on the Catholic publicist Otto B. Roegele's critique of reigning Catholic traditionalism, Ritter battled against the reproach that his own stance regarding national politics was inadequate: the reproach, in fact, simply strengthened him in defining any critique—whether centered on the German past, Germany's historical profession, or his own person—as precisely the treacherous disturbance that needed to be fought against. In an article with the title *"Nationalismus und Vaterlandsliebe"* (Nationalism and Love for the Fatherland), he lamented that the critique leveled at him had "again destroyed the arduously built bridges of personal trust to the German historians' profession."[95] As argued, if such trust existed in Ritter's case it was based mainly on his reputation as a resistance fighter.

Ritter's missionary self-understanding as an embodiment of the "great national-political task of the contemporary historian," responsible for securing the "continuity of historical thinking" (or the "future fate of German history"),[96] apparently was perceived by him as sufficient legitimation for polemics against foreigners and emigrants—and this in a way going far beyond the usual apodictic assessments. He accused critics of Bismarck such as Erich Eyck and Golo Mann of wishing to practice a historiography evoking the extremely hard, and anti-Prussian, line taken by British chief diplomatic advisor Robert Vansittart toward Germany both during the war and afterward; their "clichéd image," he claimed, merely confirmed the usual foreign prejudices regarding German history. In the end, he wrote Golo Mann, "the forty-three Bismarck years were the only epoch of great political fortune in the long centuries of ever-renewed catastrophes and hardships. Should it be presented so darkly to the Germans? Shouldn't they also be able to retain some sort of joy in their history?"[97] The reproach of *Verdunkelung*—darkening, obscuring, or obfuscation—was directed not only at commentators on German history from abroad; Ritter was rather convinced, as a matter of principle, that "penitential sermons of the unbidden" (*die Bußpredigten der Unberufenen*) were carrying on hostile wartime propaganda, and that "Germans being instructed about their own history by foreigners" was a unique scandal.[98]

De facto, Ritter not only denounced foreign voices but also, as itself innately foreign, any critical perspective on his work. German emigrants were likewise foreign, and those who had then returned remained so. This marked, once more, a basic difference from Meinecke, whose Jewish students exchanged frequent letters with him after 1945, and whose position as honorary president of Berlin's Free University (FU) (founded in 1948) offered him an entirely different view of the fate of Jewish survivors and emigrants. Hence in 1951 Meinecke initiated and signed the invitation extended by the university's philosophy department, on the advice of the historian Hans Rosenberg, to Adolf Leschnitzer (1899–1980), a German Jewish historian and specialist in German literature who had emigrated in 1939 to the United States via England. In its invitation, the new university explicitly asked Leschnitzer to lecture "on the history and problematics of German-Jewish relations," and this "in the framework of the Department of Philosophy and also for auditors in all the divisions." We read further: "It is our heartfelt desire to do everything to objectively treat these grave problems and make our contribution to paving the way for a reconciliation that helps us move past the horrifying events of the past years."[99] Leschnitzer accepted the invitation and then taught between 1952 and 1972 at the FU's Historical Institute in Berlin-Dahlem, later named after Friedrich Meinecke.

The sharp difference in Ritter's approach to critical views by Jewish emigrants regarding modern German history emerges in a controversy that had unfolded shortly before (1949–50) between him and Hans Rosenberg. The controversy makes one thing very clear: Ritter not only introduced topics for discussion but kept others out. Rosenberg's guest professorship in this period at Berlin's Free University—participants in his seminar included Gerhard A. Ritter, Helga Grebing, Wolfgang Sauer, and Gerhard Schulz—had an undeniably enduring impact: his call for a "new critical interpretation of Prussian-German history as a moral duty"[100] sparked, in Gerhard A. Ritter's words, a "process of fermentative rethinking" among the students.[101] But Rosenberg's effort to replace an "aristocratic" with a "democratic" perspective within German historiography needed a generational change—the emergence into positions of academic authority of a range of social historians sharing that perspective—to show results.[102] During his Berlin stay, while working on his book *Bureaucracy, Aristocracy and Autocracy: The Prussian Experience, 1660–1815* (begun in the 1940s, it would finally appear in 1958), Rosenberg developed the now well-known idea of a German *Sonderweg*, a historical "special path," without ever using the term itself; although he had not invented the idea, he certainly decisively prepared its advent as a subject of intense debate.[103] His effort to render the preconditions for the German susceptibility to Nazism into a theme naturally stood diametrically opposed to the conservative German historiography of the time. At stake here was defining the reasons why long-term traditions, while "not necessarily leading to Hitler and thus to Auschwitz," nevertheless constituted a political-conceptual framework that made the development possible.[104] Above all his postscript attacked the "naive and superficial interpretation" of the Third Reich as simply a tragic accident or fatal aberration.[105]

As we might suspect, Gerhard Ritter intervened and prevented publication of a German edition of the book through a brusquely negative evaluation for the press considering it;[106] the intervention, however, would not succeed in blocking Rosenberg's influence on the revision of postwar German ideas concerning German history between the nineteenth century and 1945.[107] Ritter executed his intense historiographical politics as a conscious defensive gesture, since he perceived himself as regularly "persecuted" by criticism from emigrant circles in the postwar period. He made a basic distinction between "two sorts" of emigrants: those damaging Germany and those benefiting it.[108] For this reason, the individual reasons for controversies with "foreign countries," *das Ausland*, were almost of peripheral concern to him. As Christoph Cornelißen has put it, "he experienced opposition between the European nations as self-evident"; beyond this, within academic history, he identified what he referred to as "the portion of national self-reflection" that made it impossible for him to interact with foreign members of his profession in any way other than conflictually.[109] (Involved here were convictions grounded in the Great War and its interpretation after it ended; they belonged, as suggested, to the basic stock of Ritter's historical awareness.[110]) Geoffrey Barraclough and A. J. P. Taylor, two British colleagues of Ritter who, each in his own way, had cast critical light on German historical traditions and the widespread German conception of history, were consequently referred to with epithets such as "well-bred Communist" (*Edelkommunist*), "weird codger" (*wunderlicher Kauz*), "impudent half-journalist with, finally, an anti-German attitude" (*schnoddriger Halbjournalist von letztlich deutschfeindlicher Einstellung*). A constitutive element of trips abroad was, correspondingly, an astonishment at the "natural distance from German things"; Ritter thus traveled to a conference in Monaco on "the origins of National Socialism" with an awareness he was meant to represent "the cause of Germany [*die Sache Deutschlands*]," and to do so "as the only German expert among nothing but emigrants and foreigners damaged by the Nazis or hostile to Germany [*lauter Emigranten und Nazigeschädigten oder deutschfeindlichen Ausländern*]."[111]

Despite numerous assertions to the contrary documented both in private sources and in his publications, for Ritter emigrants were responsible for the negative view of Germany held abroad. In actuality, the older emigrants tended to be far milder and more understanding in their judgment of German traditions than Ritter was able to perceive. Thus in the preliminary remarks to his *Geschichte der Deutschen*, even Veit Valentin, who already well before the Nazi ascent to power had suffered greatly at the hands of German rightists, asserted that everything he had written reflected "love for the best Germany from the past," that there was "something immortal in Germanness [*Deutschtum*]," and that he had always remained a "German patriot."[112] As such deep and enduring sentiments make clear, Karina Urbach is correct in suggesting that Ritter's antinomian polemics against emigrants involved a fundamental failure to acknowledge one fact in particular: that following their flight or expulsion from Germany, these individuals did not become "foreigners" in Ritter's sense but rather remained representatives of the Weimar Republic and its culture; his disparagement of them was thus aimed, not least of all, at a German tradition *other* than the one he chose as his own.[113]

A Historiography of "German Consciousness"

The ostentatious effort of Gerhard Ritter to avoid acknowledging the extermination of European Jewry as a theme worthy of history was made—to apply his own words—"for the sake of Germany." His warning of the danger of young people becoming alienated from German history if it were depicted "only in the blackest colors" culminated in disparaging remarks about the "daily fashion" of modern history—which he nevertheless zealously engaged in.[114] He in any event understood it in a contrapuntal sense to the gradually increasing significance that "Auschwitz" had begun to take on in the public consciousness. His demonstrative disdain for "actualized history," which he juxtaposed with "non-actualized, i.e., authentic, history,"[115] reveals little of the sovereignty with which he surrounded himself: "Much too much is already being said at present about weariness with history and a 'farewell to history.' This fails to impress me. By far most such talk is merely rhetoric by literati. Naturally it is difficult to again find, beyond the immense breach of 1933–45, a connection to the past and emerge once again from the mood of catastrophe. But this must and will finally take place."[116] Even in 1962, he declared unambiguously that his concern was for values such as "fatherland" and "patriotism"; "we must be careful," he insisted, "to avoid teaching general and German history with an appalled gaze focused on Hitler's horrific deeds alone."[117] Although the theory of Nazism as an especially unfortunate "industrial accident" was no invention of Ritter, as an undisputed specialist and in the course of many controversies, he energetically endowed the idea's emergence and transmission with conviction, wide circulation, and endurance: after all, as we have seen, as a conservative nationalist member of the Confessing Church, he had himself resisted and been persecuted by the Nazi regime (albeit following initial enthusiasm for it). Having defended and praised the German professorial guild in his first important postwar essay (the "most influential" such defense, as Steven P. Remy has indicated[118]) a few months before his death in 1966 he lashed out against "the political tendency" and "daily fashion" "presently wishing to see the entire German past in light of the Hitler period"—a tendency, he indicated that rendered the study of history an object of "disgust" for young people.[119]

Notwithstanding Ritter's constitutive invocation of scientific objectivity, his position as a victim of the Nazi regime, and his anxiety at "actualized history," what he viewed as "critical revision" was itself merely a mildly purged form of nationalism. By defining the Nazi system as having been, as it were, present beforehand in non-German origins, the "authentically" national could continue to be understood in opposition to the Hitler period, on interacting biographical, historiographical, and political levels. Ritter's search for non-German causes reflected the general difficulties involved in "national historical" interpretations, which had their apotheosis in the Third Reich's denationalization and "extraterritorialization." Even in Hajo Holborn's careful critique of Meinecke's approach to Nazism "as the result of tragic coincidences of an individual and general sort," we find him arguing that although Hitler was not to be "considered an 'extra-German' event," he did "to a certain degree represent an intrusion of the alien into German history. In a higher sense, he was more a stranger [*Fremdling*] than the Corsican Napoleon inside France. Hitler's original political ideas, above all his racial theory, grew out of the swampy soil of the decaying Habsburg Empire."[120]

Ritter raised such arguments to a regular program, summarized as follows: "A *Volk* . . . that has doubts about its past no longer has any real hope in the future. To prevent this seems to me the most immediately pressing and finest task of political education."[121] That the traditional realm of nationalist values and the inescapable critique of recent historical facts never met, or at most at an infinite future point as with parallel lines, reflected Ritter's research axiom rather than the result of his historiographical labor. The "break that the year 1945 brought into our historical development" was hypostasized, with a subsequent effort to overcome it. Ritter's key questions centered on backward ties, which he did not wish to see called into question, even when what was at issue was state-organized industrial murder. Already in the early 1930s, in a letter to Hans Rothfels he expressed the conviction that the "proper historian . . . simply has to be naive," with the empirical substance of his scholarship forcing a certain "simplicity" on him—by which he meant a complexly weighed mix of pure empiricism and "secondary political intentions";[122] at the same time he assumed that every historian had to have "something like a philosophical head."[123] True history writing," he argued, allowed, as it were, "the things . . . themselves to speak," taking place beyond "eternal judging."[124] It was aimed at a "clear idea of the inner course of historical events," at the "meaning of the inner *state* in history and the relationship between state and church," and finally at "the characteristic element" defining German being or the German essence, *deutsches Wesen*.[125] As a result of the defensive position vis-à-vis Nazism through which he expressed his hypostatization of the national, he was able to champion the same thing after 1945 that he had before 1933: a "deepening of the unbearably flattened concept of the 'national idea,' hence German-consciousness [*Deutschbewußtsein*]."[126]

Ritter's idea of a "German form of spirit," "*deutsche Geistesart*," was a fixed element in his "program of national history writing."[127] And he tried to defend the program against Nazism both before and after its defeat. Within the Third Reich, the defense was against demands leveled by Nazi history itself; it was expressed in exemplary form in his renunciation of further collaboration with the *Historische Zeitschrift*, reflecting awareness of a "shared responsibility for the fate of German history [*deutsche Historie*]," after the so-called Oncken affair (the forced retirement of historian Hermann Oncken from his chair at the University of Heidelberg in 1935 following personal attacks on him by his student Walter Frank in the Nazi *Völkische Beobachter*).[128] At the beginning of February 1933, he had already confirmed, without appearing to sense the congruence of his rhetoric with the new age, "a very clearly recognizable national mission," an "educational mission" for the historian. As long as "everyone is chasing after those who are bellowing," he commented, no one wanted to hear voices such as his own; instead of going along with the *nationale Phrasengedröhn* (literally the "national droning of phrases"), he preferred to "prepare the auxiliary positions."[129]

After the Nazi collapse, Ritter's defense was against interpretations of the Nazi years from what he considered an anti-German perspective. He now made clear that he would not refrain from "serving my *Volk* as a publicist," noting in passing that he would "now consciously shelve pure scholarship for a time in order to offer something like historical-political emergency help."[130] His authority in this respect was based on fidelity to his own views, not to their modification or revision. Ritter gladly polemicized against the notion that a historian had to "simply photograph a past somehow standing ready before him"; in contrast, his own historiographical self-image developed into a volatile mixture equally composed of capacity, art, and struggle: a mixture to which he nonetheless attributed historical objectivity and authenticity. He thus laid claim at one point to a "higher locus" and "clear perspective";[131] at another point he claimed that "the few people who (like the author) already knew then" that Germany had fallen into the hands of an "unconscionable adventurer" "now still clearly recall the deep despair that overcame them in light of this blindness: in tormented foresight into an inexorably arriving cultural catastrophe."[132] But such claims could not be plausibly grounded. At yet another point, in the foreword to his book on Goerdeler, Ritter insisted that the historian must not wait until legend solidified but rather had to "himself put his hand to the forms of the historical image of our age." Here, in contrast to the two other cited passages, Ritter—who had labored with his entire person and authority to prevent increased acknowledgment and knowledge of the German catastrophe inflicted on the Jews—succeeded in accurately describing his own historical work.

Hans Rothfels
and the Problem of Split Epistemology

On 13 March 1950, Elliot Cohen, a "Jew, American citizenship" as he described himself, and founder-editor of *Commentary* magazine, gave a remarkable speech in Berlin at the invitation of the Society for Christian-Jewish Cooperation.[133] This was his first visit to Germany, and very likely his last, and his talk focused on the "abyss" of experience separating Germans and Jews, the impossibility of "bridging this chasm . . . through a few friendly words and good intentions." "Between us," he stated, "lies an abyss as wide as the ocean, and no trace can be seen of a bridge above its depths." "Abyss," "chasm," and "bridge" were regularly repeated terms in the speech, and Cohen left no doubt how they were meant to be understood. He was attacking the silence reigning in Germany, voicing an expectation of the start of a dialogue from the German side, with the hope of a "first arch in that bridge over the abyss" to begin there. Cohen ended his speech with the "feeling of having said much more" than he had originally intended, "and at the same time to not have really begun." He attributed this contradiction to his feeling "so intensively . . . that the start cannot be made by a Jew but has to come from the other side."

The published version of Cohen's speech was commented on by Germans; these responses are interesting mainly because for the most part they were efforts to explain the "silence" he had criticized. The silence, one reader's letter suggested, was the expression of a "speechless contempt for the crime," for when "facing the fact of the racial murders" the Germans were "as stunned as the Jews." But now precisely this silence drew the "suspicion" of itself being "suspect," something rendering it impossible for decent people, "in view of the many guilty people who in no way feel guilty," to speak up for their own guiltlessness.[134] This logic was no less dialectic than the problem itself. It distinguished between two sorts of silence, a decent sort maintained by the guiltless and a "false" sort maintained by the guilty—an in principle correct phenomenology but nonetheless solipsistic in that from the outside the two sorts could not be distinguished from each other. In requesting, as an American Jewish outsider visiting a defeated Germany, that the silence be broken, Cohen was consciously addressing writers, scholars, and among these, explicitly, historians;[135] he was thus not calling for private confessions but appealing to those responsible for preserving cultural memory. His request for a "word" was aimed neither at individual admissions of guilt nor at hairsplitting explanations of why these were lacking, but rather at assuming responsibility though memory.

At this time Hans Rothfels was still in American exile from Germany, teaching at the University of Chicago (see Figure 4). The contrast between his stance, that of a Prussian conservative of Jewish origin, and that of Cohen could not be greater. He would neither formulate a similar request nor sympathize with something of that sort. Following 1945, his expulsion from Nazi Germany furnished him de facto with a bridging function—but in a directly opposite sense than that presented by Cohen. In contrast to Cohen, Rothfels, like most post-"catastrophe" German historians, was convinced that silence was a place of potential transformation—a place opening up the possibility of something like testing or probation. "Without silence," Max Picard proclaimed, "there is no forgetting and no forgiving. Just as time itself enters silence, what takes place in time enters it as well, and thus through silence . . . human beings are led to forgetting and forgiving."[136] In view of the "shadow cast on German honor," Gerd Tellenbach had likewise proposed a "command of shamefaced silence" as a serious option.[137] It was approached as a positive sign and a sublime substance. The Picard citation here is from an entire book he wrote devoted to "the world of silence"—to silence's holy function as a "primal phenomenon," the human being's "anthropological center." Within this neo-pietist weltanschauung, with all forms of "analysis" being in the end destructive, suffering and silence belonged together: "The spirit is certainly the cause of transformation, but without silence the transformation cannot be realized, for in the transformation process, human beings are able to leave all that transpired in the past behind only when silence can be placed between the past and the new."[138]

Rothfels confirmed this position de facto. We would even say that none of the essential figures in postwar German academic history chose "speaking silence"[139] (Hermann Lübbe's approving term was "communicative silence"[140]) as consciously as he did, and with as much intensity. Stigmatized as a Jew in the Third Reich and forced into exile despite his declarations of loyalty, he represented the greatest possible potential danger to the German historical profession after 1945: he was now a highly respected historian in the Anglo-American world, possessing nothing less than an ideal-typical position because of the scandalous and shabby expulsion. But he offered no reproaches—or even raised questions—either publicly or privately; and what he had to say about Nazism amounted to forms of dehistorization, a passing over of historical problems in silence, or else their replacement by moral pathos. His post-1945 bridging efforts had nothing to do with the German-Jewish chasm and everything to do with Germany's historical chronology. They were real acts of keeping something silent that approached the 1933–45 period as a task to be bridged, passing over the empirical-moral reality of historical experiences emerging from it.

Certainly partly as a result of awareness of Rothfels' American years, hardly any other figure is mentioned as frequently in relation to a key problem presently occupying the borderland between contemporary history and the culture of memory: the problem of split or schizoid epistemology, challenging historians to analyze specific processes at work within scholarship, as well as the individual's location within these processes. In the context of early postwar Germany—both an extreme example of the challenges faced in developing a post-totalitarian academic self-understanding and as it were a laboratory for such analytic efforts—over the past years Mitchell G. Ash, Otto G. Oexle, and Bernd Weisbrod have all pointed to the problem's dual aspect: the need to guarantee the individual both a capacity for change *and* personal authenticity. In other words, in relevant situations both individual scholarly careers and broad perspectives must first be disentangled from complicity or collaboration with the old system, past achievements transposed to new temporal and spatial loci within the framework of a new status quo. And this must be done with distinct stress placed on supposed continuities. An individual had to be willing and able to learn—while remaining the same familiar person.[141]

Within the various scholarly disciplines, the history of historiography is challenged in a special way by the figure of Rothfels, though principally through intimation, in reference to the broader context.[142] Conversely, as a basic dimension of his attempts at "bridging," hardly any figure in the field of contemporary history better illustrates the intertwining of the new and the old, of positions before 1933 and after 1945, of transformations in the rhetorical cloak of the old and continuities appearing as seeming innovations. The dominance he established within his discipline is becoming ever clearer. Even in the retrospective interviews contained in Konrad Jarausch and Rüdiger Hohls' *Versäumte Fragen*, it sometimes appears impossible for those historians being interviewed to render fair judgment of Rothfels' students Theodor Schieder and Werner Conze, as well as of contemporary German history in postwar Germany in general, without first turning to the life and ideas of their teacher.

In controversies centered on such history, observations by Rothfels had foundational importance. In this light, his presence on the postwar West German historiographical scene relativizes the thesis, proposed on occasion, that the influence of emigrant historians on that scene was basically minor.[143] At the same time, the basic points emerging from both personal recollections of Rothfels and assessments of his place in scholarship are highly disparate. For example, Wolfram Fischer's emphasis on his role as an educator in the period after his remigration is not without a certain undertone of discontent. Many of his students from Tübingen in the 1950s themselves describe a generally "distanced" demeanor and the "dry," "wooden," and "old-fashioned" tenor of his lectures (the terms are Hartmut Lehmann's).[144] But within the smaller circle composed of his doctoral candidates and assistants in Königsberg before the Second

World War, Rothfels' word was authoritative. In that circle, he was revered, in Wolfgang Mommsen's words, as a kind of "deity," his books as "scripture."[145] Over the span of several recent decades, testimonials from these different periods—from his pupils in the 1930s and again in the 1950s and 1960s—shaped Rothfels' image. For a long time there was, in fact, no genuinely historical (or even historiographical) interest in his writings or person, aside from work by Peter Thomas Walther: a doctoral thesis on Rothfels that appeared in the United States in 1989; two short essays published in the mid-1980s, dealing in part with Rothfels, but then precisely and knowledgeably, hence with lasting value.[146] In any case, for a number of years after Rothfels' death in 1976, articles by Werner Conze and Hans Mommsen had the strongest influence on the general understanding of his work.[147] These articles were based in part on unpublished material but were still written in the basically adulatory spirit of the collection of open letters presented to him on the occasion of his seventieth birthday.[148] Examinations of Rothfels' historiography had to wait until the 1990s, when a handful of studies on specialized questions appeared,[149] along with initial efforts at a synthesis; such efforts have taken an increasingly critical perspective.[150]

This shift, an acknowledgment of the "all too positive image of Rothfels in the postwar generation,"[151] was first manifested mainly in efforts to explore the milieu of the so-called Rothfels group, the most outstanding example being Ingo Haar's study of historians under Nazism, which deals extensively although not exclusively with Rothfels and several of his Königsberg pupils, along with their networks.[152] Attention has also been paid to the power of his personality to forge a community of like-minded individuals after his return to the University of Tübingen. Thus in his study of German postwar historiography published in 2001, Thomas Etzemüller repeatedly refers to Rothfels as a "father figure," characterizing his role, in the Foucaultian sense, as that of group "spokesperson," or "mentor" or "patriarch."[153] Gerhard Ritter, coining the term "Rothfelsians," had already expressed his surprise at the group's coherence around their guiding light in 1962.[154]

Nevertheless, despite such scholarly evolution, no comparably intensive research has yet been undertaken on Rothfels' function as a scholar and historian in the postwar era. There have been recent signs that a "Rothfels debate" is emerging.[155] But now as previously, the discussion is dominated by the question of Rothfels' presumed proclivities toward Nazi ideology and the politics he articulated before his forced emigration in 1938.[156] Karl Heinz Roth, in several articles appearing over recent years, has been the only scholar to examine Rothfels as a "politician of history"; he has advanced the thesis that Rothfels worked to rehabilitate two separate discredited phases of past German history, and did so in two separate periods: after World War I, and after 1945. In this manner, Roth argues, Rothfels' influence helped "delay by decades" the formulation of decisive questions about Nazi society and rule.[157] Such an approach sharpens the critique that Winfried Schulze leveled in a far more cautious manner in an essay published in 1995 in a festschrift for Hans Mommsen. Already here significant stress was placed on Rothfels as a "strategic personality" for the postwar period. In his analysis Schulze moved significantly forward from his earlier position and elaborated a wide-ranging study of postwar German historiography.[158] Schulze has criticized the approach manifest in even the most recent debates, arguing that Rothfels and his "key function" were being sorely neglected; he has emphasized the need for a "critical biography of Rothfels."[159]

A Fractured Unity:
Life and Scholarship in Rothfels' Career

We can assume that such a biography would pay due attention to the "unusual development of a conservative-revolutionary Prussian who had had scant scholarly impact in the United States into a magnanimous *grandseigneur* of professional historians in West Germany."[160] Indeed, writing in 1986 Peter Thomas Walther sensed that Rothfels' career trajectory was marked by a "certain irony," since as an "emigrant and Jew," he had become a veritable "figure of legitimation" for postwar German historiography.[161] At the time, Walther did not pursue this line of inquiry, but he did call attention to the fundamentally contrary nature of Rothfels' influence: after his remigration and his "encouragement of research on contemporary history," he in effect paved a road for the—as Walther termed it—"antiquated guild" (*verkrustete Zunft*) to begin critically examining the political and academic views of those to whom he had been closely allied before 1933, making them the object of its sharpest critique. Shortly after Rothfels' death in 1976, Konrad Kwiet termed it a "rewarding research task" to probe his attitude toward Judaism. Kwiet was correctly assuming that the fact of Rothfels' "Jewish origins" was "little known." Yet his assimilation, Kwiet stressed even then, was apparently "so total that it did not allow for any ties whatsoever to Judaism. At best it allowed some memories to be aired, in an intimate circle, of the earlier discrimination he had experienced as a student and historian."[162] However, Kwiet's suggestion did not bear fruit at the time: no detailed methodological-epistemological study followed—one that would have taken appropriate account of memory, perspective, and emotion.[163]

In this context, from a present-day viewpoint an apparent contradiction seems provocative: namely, that in previous discussions of Rothfels, the dominant opinion has been that he succeeded, in an especially reflective manner, in fusing the key biographical questions of the century with his chosen agenda of research, producing a striking harmony of the personal and the professional. Hence Hans Mommsen refers to his "ability . . . to overcome the dissonances between his own world of experience and his intellectual character, achieving a unity of private life and scholarly work, and this despite a chain of interlinking personal and general perils."[164] Mommsen, in any case, does not further analyze this "ability" or relate it to his mentor's forced emigration and exile. Likewise, in his eulogy for Rothfels, and drawing on Rothfels' own autobiographical writings, Theodor Schieder has placed special emphasis on his "unobtrusively preshaped unity of scholarship and way of living" (*unaufdringlich vorgeprägte Einheit von Wissenschaft und Lebenshaltung*). In Schieder's view, Rothfels "repeatedly sought to reconstitute" this unity "whenever he confronted new situations."[165] Such an assessment may be accurate in regard to Rothfels' image of Bismarck, or his ideas regarding nationhood and nationalities in Eastern Europe—a theme that his Königsberg professorship had helped make highly topical—but not in regard to Nazism and antisemitism. Although he felt "a sense of bitterness over the forced separation" and gratitude for the "enrichment that the American environment had meant for him," in his relationship to Germany and the Germans, "he had nonetheless never drawn that inner line of separation," as another famous pupil of his, Conze, put it in an eulogy for his teacher.[166]

The failure to draw that "internal line of separation" had a significant impact on the development of postwar German historiography. Hans Rothfels repeatedly referred to his reacquisition of a "community of experience" with the Germans. And he tried to achieve this not only in the private realm but also in that of academic history, in the form of a return to the old "community of interpretation." However, since Rothfels' view of himself and his pupils' view of their teacher have prevailed in both general evaluations in newspapers and professional journals and specialized studies in postwar German historiography, we need to look more carefully at the problem of revoking the "inner line"—or the refusal to draw it in the first place. For this problem lies, after all, at the uncommented heart of all previous interpretations of Rothfels. Can his historiography be read as part of a *Jewish* narrative, beyond any political provenance, through which the Nazis' victims helped shape the postwar scholarly and public image of the terrible recent events and their meaning? Is a cognitive vector inscribed in his historical works—a vector addressing his personal historical experiences, or at least preserving and protecting them?

A central premise of this discussion is that in Rothfels' case, a unity of life and work was anything but uniform. Rothfels had a decisive impact on the emerging field of contemporary history in the German Federal Republic. In exerting such impact, he excluded a significant portion of his "bitter personal experience" from the problems meriting inquiry: namely, the portion encompassing topics such as antisemitism, Aryanization, expulsion, exile, and the mass murder of the European Jews. These were, to be sure, topics that contemporary history in West Germany dealt with only hesitatingly, generally favoring the topic of German resistance to Nazism, foregrounding the many and diverse apologies formulated on behalf of the German nation-state and its traditions, and favorably emphasizing the role of the bourgeois elites. This tendency was bolstered by Rothfels' opinion-shaping historical studies. In this manner his "function as a bridge" in the politics of the past—his role in generating a restitution of "German questions" in the realm of scholarship—was an option whose personal legitimacy and biographical consequences require more probing scrutiny than is possible here. But as its significance was not only private and personal, in coming to terms with the meaning of Rothfels' career one needs to take into account the impact of both an unarticulated process of remembering and an unstated experience of history.

In exploring such factors, we must avoid hasty prejudgments regarding specific life decisions that Rothfels made in the course of his career, since we still know far too little about them. Rather, our interest here will focus on the returned emigrant as founder of a German postwar historiographical discourse—on his enduring importance for both the history of his profession and the image its members articulated, in Germany for Germans, over a span of nearly three decades. One argument that will be made here is that through his important role in constructing this image, Rothfels served, despite his own recent exile, to marginalize the experiences of those who had fled Germany or been persecuted by the Nazi regime.

It is now possible to confirm Hans Mommsen's 1982 assessment of an "elemental relation to history" in Rothfels' writing in a different way than was originally intended: such a relation is indeed present in Rothfels' generation as a whole; their work before 1933 and after 1945 was indeed significantly shaped by their ability to "ultimately harmonize historical knowledge and individual self-discovery."[167] But "historical knowledge" and "individual self-discovery" were possible in Rothfels' case—and in that of German contemporary historiography as a whole—because neither Rothfels nor his discipline were prepared to transpose specifically Jewish experiences of history onto an epistemological plane in an effort to grasp historical meaning and forge forms of individual self-knowledge.

Born in the 1891 in Kassel, Rothfels was a student of Friedrich Meinecke in Freiburg before the First World War. While fighting on the front, he sustained a serious wound that would leave him handicapped for the rest of his life. After the war, he studied with Max Lenz, Hans Delbrück, and Otto Hintze in Berlin and Heidelberg, where he wrote a doctoral dissertation under Hermann Oncken on Clausewitz. In the crisis years of the Weimar Republic, he wrote his habilitation thesis for Meinecke in Berlin on the social policies of Theodor Lohmann.[168] In 1926 he received a professorship at the University of Königsberg, where he devoted his research to nationality problems in Eastern Europe. He filtered his views on the history of the state through the prism of the new *Volksgeschichte*, now espousing a program of "total folk history"—*ganzheitliche Volksgeschichte*—to supplant the concept of the state as a power-political entity, a *Machtstaat*.[169] In respect to this conceptual focus, Rothfels would later write his colleague Reinhard Wittram that he felt he basically shared some responsibility for the rise of Nazism: "Didn't the Nazis have a certain diabolical skill for slithering inside everything that was 'genuine'? . . . In part, we assisted them in that, and I don't exclude myself from this blame."[170]

Although Rothfels converted to Protestantism in 1910 at the age of nineteen, as the son of Jewish parents he would become a victim of Nazi racial policy. The fact that he was not immediately subject in 1933 to the "Law on the Restoration of the Professional Civil Service" was due to his war injury. In the eyes of the Nazi Party, Rothfels was a "Jewish professor." It was "totally unacceptable that a person of alien blood should teach the coming generation of young Germans about German history."[171] In an open letter, his students defended "all of Prof. Rothfels' work in teaching and research," and his "attacks against the destructive tendencies mentioned and against ruinous individualism." They considered him one of the "very best now paving the way for a new spirit in scholarship."[172] Likewise, a letter from the students to Rothfels himself, also from early July 1934, contained the following sentences: "In recent weeks we have experienced with you the beginning of a new Germany, and have welcomed the long-hoped-for change. . . . Under your guidance, the insight into national and social questions has broadened our perspective on the development and essence of the new Reich."[173] Moreover, the university's *Kurator*, who had no reservations about seeing Rothfels as "one of those now preparing the path for the new Germany," wrote to the Ministry of Science, Art, and National Education in Berlin to praise Rothfels for the "always genuine German courage of his convictions." He suggested creating exceptions to the pending "de-Judaization" of the German university system, noting that in Königsberg, Rothfels had "constructed a world of ideas basically identical with the one that has created the new Germany." The *Kurator* remarked in closing, "Our new state is so strong that it can easily place itself behind a man like Rothfels."[174] Yet despite such testimonials on his behalf, the Protestant and Prussian conservative was dismissed from his post and stripped of his title and honors. He always regarded this as an "error," and in taking leave from his students he articulated something like an oath of allegiance or alliance: "Allow us to be in essence something resembling a community of the intellect [*eine intelligible Gemeinschaft*]."[175]

What followed Rothfels' academic expulsion was the then-familiar chain of events: initially, the *Historische Zeitschrift* spurned his reviews. Later, during the November 1938 nationwide pogrom, he was arrested. But in his case luck played its part, and he was released.[176] That same year he left Germany and headed for England, where after the outbreak of the war he was detained as a German and sent to an internment camp on the Isle of Man. Eventually he was offered a professorship at Brown University in Providence, Rhode Island, and after the war he was awarded one of the most respected chairs at the University of Chicago. Still in the United States, he wrote what is probably his most famous book, *The German Opposition to Hitler* (Hindsdale, Illinois, 1948), which would pave the way for his return to Germany, initially as a guest lecturer in Tübingen and Göttingen, and then from 1951 onward as a full professor in Tübingen.

In debates about Rothfels, it has at times been possible to gain an impression that the various phases of his life could be separated into five different blocks representing five layers of memory and time within German history, each individually negotiable: *Kaiserreich*, Weimar Republic, National Socialism, emigration, and Federal Republic. But the different character of Rothfels' life within these phases of evolving experience is not what has made him a key personality in German postwar and scholarly history. Rather, this has emerged from his labor to bridge biographical breaks and gullies, to distill something that endures in the midst of change. To begin to grasp the meaning of Rothfels' career, one must consider the way in which his work of historical interpretation was counterposed to these ruptures in historical flow—especially his influential reading of the Third Reich, which resonated powerfully within the self-understanding of the early Federal Republic, indeed helping it to formulate its sense of identity. By contrast, defining Rothfels as a representative of a "unique patriotism of German-Jewish symbiosis" (*einzigartiger Patriotismus deutsch-jüdischer Symbiose*)[177] merely serves to distort the nature of the discursive-communicative historical path that Rothfels traveled. Put briefly, such a definition disregards the fact that his function in the years after 1945 lay in an interplay of perspectives. It is true that as a foreigner, émigré, and expelled Jew, he was ascribed special importance—but not because of any new perspective he championed. Rather, its source was his re-importation of old views, his formulations of the positions of a German patriot that his colleagues could no longer afford to profess.

The Other Remigrant—Rothfels as an Exception

Hans Rothfels was "the other" remigrant. Contemporaries very consciously perceived and used this unique function of Rothfels for the postwar discipline of contemporary German history. Siegfried A. Kaehler, before the remigration of his friend—a move he constantly tried to dissuade him from taking—spoke quite bluntly about Rothfels' situation: his "current position between two spheres of Western scholarship is so unique and special that it is presumably more in the German interest if he remains in his new place of influence [*Wirkungsstätte*], perceiving our intellectual concerns [*geistige Belange*] from that vantage point."[178] After the war, Friedrich Meinecke officially referred to Rothfels as a "bridge builder." In his introduction to the Rothfels festschrift, he explicitly praises his "masterfully balanced 1949 Munich lecture on Bismarck," extolling Rothfels' "striving" for "unification" as the "leitmotif of your life and work as a teacher and scholar."[179] Meinecke here makes no explicit reference to the events in Rothfels' life linked to Nazi "de-Judaization." Instead, he praises his former student for his ability "to combine, with a strong sense of character, loyalty towards everything good in your German past with an inner obligation to your new environment." "Germany," Meinecke declares, "will never forget that you were able to write the book *The German Opposition to Hitler*. . . . You were in a position to dare to venture forth as a defender of German values—because now you were observing things from a higher vantage point than that offered by a merely national-historical perspective."[180]

What becomes clear here is the entire paradox of a national exculpation for which one was meant to be emphatically grateful—because, although it was "defense," it seemed to spring from a "higher vantage point" than that of the mere "national-historical perspective" historians who had remained in Germany might have been expected to share. In view of the interpretative model of German national history prevailing in the Nazi period, Meinecke explicitly acknowledged the exculpatory utility inherent in Rothfels' "inner universalism," which he glossed as follows: "Today, in this shattering time of transition for the world and its peoples [*in der heutigen erschütternden Zeit einer Völker- und Weltenwende*], how bitterly we need such an inner universalism. A universalism that, rooted in respect for the positive values of one's own people, turns into respect for the positive values and common ground of all peoples, building bridges to everything that is truly and universally human in them. You have become such a bridge builder."[181] Of course Meinecke also wrote similar lines to other star students of his who had emigrated, such as Hajo Holborn and Gerhard Masur. But he did not thank anyone else as emphatically for his work as he thanked Rothfels. For example, in reference to Rothfels' English essay treating the mass flight of Germans from the east Meinecke commented: "The fact that you, precisely, have written this is a deed for which I warmly shake your hand. Let our motto be *Treue um Treue* [faithfulness everlasting]."[182] The history of a specific discourse unfolds in such private letters. The "handshake" Meinecke offered Rothfels accurately looked forward to the program of return that was successfully implemented later. From the emphatic expression of gratitude for the essay at the start, to Meinecke's suggestive invocation of "closeness," "consoling elements," and "our deeper shared common ground," conciliation was not so much pleaded for or negotiated but rather proclaimed. What remained implicit was the highly consequential tacit agreement to remain silent about differences, conflicts, contrary perceptions.

As perhaps suggested already by the case of Ritter, feelings of resentment against returning emigrants were widespread in postwar Germany;[183] from the start their judgments were regarded as skewed. In indicating that "whoever wishes to speak about Germany and pass judgment has to have remained here," the poet—and for a time admirer of Nazism—Gottfried Benn offered an accurate formulation of this view.[184] Following the defeat of Germany, the Munich social and economic historian Friedrich Lütge published a long memorandum on the relation between "party members" and "non-party members" addressed to the American occupiers.[185] At the memorandum's beginning, he explicitly excluded information on Germany offered by emigrants before and during the Nazi period as, a priori, devoid of value—an extreme hypostasizing of the Third Reich's "internal development" typical of the text as a whole. In order to reinstall the "goddess of justice" to her throne, Lütge argued, the only acceptable basis for assessment was "insight into the internal situation," the "internal events," "internal development," "inner attitude," and a most "deep and personal conviction." The only adequate yardstick for evaluation was "the honest will" (*ehrliche Wille*), the "feeling of social responsibility," the "pangs of conscience" of individuals during the war, as well as their constant efforts to "mitigate and improve" the situation—not any "superficial" formal party membership or modes of social action demanded under compulsion by "terrorists in the party."

In a letter to Carl Schmitt in 1950, the sociologist Helmut Schelsky expressed a sweeping and pejorative rejection of "remigratory scholarship" (*remigratorische Wissenschaft*)."[186] Even such a liberally minded historian as Franz Schnabel was capable, at the end of the 1950s, of commenting as follows on Eric Voegelin's appointment to a newly created chair in political science at the University of Munich: "Well, now they've hauled the flotsam and jetsam of emigration [*das letzte Strandgut der Emigration*] back onto dry land."[187]

Emigrants defended themselves at times against such "selective perception"—against a dictum that Germany could be understood only by Germans who had stayed in the country under the Nazis, itself equivalent to a form of epistemological marginalization. But that notwithstanding, returnees frequently either found themselves confronted with ever-stronger feelings of resentment or were praised with such strategic exuberance that their role in the system was narrowly circumscribed and their position rigidly fixed right from the start. Of course, some returnees gladly withheld any critical observations, thus fulfilling the special hopes invested in them by colleagues who had remained in Germany. This was the case, for example, with Arnold Bergsträsser, a colleague of Rothfels at the University of Chicago, whose anthology *Deutsche Beiträge zur geistigen Überlieferung* (German Contributions to Intellectual Transmission), published by the University of Chicago Press in 1947—unusual for an American academic press, the various contributions by emigrants from Germany were in German—was enthusiastically welcomed by Ludwig Dehio in a review in the *Historische Zeitschrift*, where it was referred to as "tidings from the old Germany" and a "monument of German intellectual life overseas."[188] This particular sort of "coming home" characterized Rothfels' career to a far greater degree (his contribution to Bergsträsser's *Beiträge* recommended the "timelessness" of the Prussian reformers to those calling for a political "reawakening").[189] Heinrich Ritter von Srbik clearly sensed this would be so, that should Rothfels return to Germany, it would be "a ray of sunlight in the darkness of the hour."[190]

Thus Rothfels was, and not only in Meinecke's eyes, an exception to the prejudicial rule established by German historians against their newly returned Jewish colleagues. Nor was Meinecke the only one to note Rothfels' strategic position as someone spared from the prejudice otherwise directed against émigrés. When plans were afoot at the IfZ to establish a new periodical (the *Vierteljahrshefte für Zeitgeschichte*), Rothfels was also regarded as "*the* right man" to direct it, as Hellmuth Becker, a member of the journal's new advisory board, put it. Similarly, in a testimonial for Rothfels submitted to the board, Otto Vossler noted: "There is someone else who is downright predestined for this job, Mr. Rothfels in Tübingen. He is *the* obvious and absolutely ideal solution. What more could one possibly want?"[191]

Restoration of the "Community of Experience": The German Opposition (1948)

So how did Rothfels provoke such German expectations? And, in particular, how did he fulfill them? To answer these questions, let us note for a start his remark, made while commenting on the American public, that "only a few foreigners were prepared to realize that Germany after 1933 was an 'occupied country.'"[192] Rothfels' description of Nazi Germany as "occupied" in fact both defined and sanctioned an entire style of thought. This style is also apparent in his studies of the German resistance to Nazism, where he wished to demonstrate, in his forthright words, "the fiction of any identity between what is German and what is National Socialist."[193] The German resistance had shown itself to be a "moral rebellion against evil as such." Foregrounding a concept of "man" and his "humanity" that was universalistic in a specific way, Rothfels established a concept of resistance that, viewed politically, was pronouncedly opportunistic: resistance as the "legacy of humanness in extremis" (*Vermächtnis des Menschentums in extremis*) and as a "breakthrough into freedom" (*Durchbruch ins Freie*) opposed to the "arrogance of totalitarianism in all its colors, brown or red."[194]

The English version of *German Opposition*, its plea for a better Germany explicitly directed at the American public, turned out on closer scrutiny to have two sets of addressees. In fact, the book implicitly targeted a German audience, and Rothfels had more success with it in Germany than in America. A book by Allen Welsh Dulles had already been published in 1947 with the suggestive title *Germany's Underground*, and Rothfels' review of the book is revealing. He praised both the author's "insight into the conditions and problems faced by an opposition under the totalitarian form of rule" and his "spirit of uninhibited analysis and evaluation." But Rothfels' complaints are more instructive. He particularly criticized Dulles's concept of "opposition" for being too narrow, adding that "anonymous forces and the problems of a silent or potential opposition are hardly touched on." As a whole, what he found lacking in the study was insight into the overall character of the resistance movement, which in his view had crossed all boundaries between classes, professions, and parties. And he viewed the book as lacking, not least of all, clear criticism of the United States. In short, Rothfels here offered a blueprint for his own upcoming book; its appearance was announced in the last sentence of the review, concluding with an exclamation mark.[195]

Germany had been discussing its resistance to Hitler without waiting for Rothfels to give the go-ahead. Even before the book's original version began to make the rounds in Germany, the *Historische Zeitschrift* had published a long review essay on the topic;[196] Rothfels' book was given a separate review in the journal, by none other than Gerhard Ritter, in addition to its mention in this essay.[197] The force of his voice from "outside" was thus immediately acknowledged, and Ritter now set to work arranging a translation of the book into German. With this volume, Rothfels not only opened up the field of "contemporary history" for himself personally but also prepared the way for his return to Germany. As a preliminary step, he mailed no fewer than a hundred copies to colleagues.[198] In the radio interview with Rothfels by Viktor von Oertzen and Hubert Locher, cited earlier, he emphasized his good fortune in finding a topic "that went beyond being merely a welter of flagellation and self-accusations, although these were naturally unavoidable."

But this mode of inquiry did not constitute historical research. Rather, it involved the construction of an "invented autobiography," to use a phrase aptly coined by Ulrich Raulff.[199] Through such a project, Rothfels transformed the general apologetic reflexes of the Germans after 1945 into an academic discipline. The "justified" resistance of would-be assassins of Hitler was now expanded to cover Germany and the German people as a whole. As early as 1947, Rothfels noted in a letter to Siegfried A. Kaehler that "it was necessary to make substantial modifications regarding the so-called failure of the German intelligentsia," and that he hoped to "do something along those lines in a pamphlet on the resistance movement."[200] "Justice for a nation collectively discriminated against" was important for him.[201] Rothfels' use of the ciphers Buchenwald, Oranienburg, and Dachau was reductionist to an extreme degree, since these ciphers were being used to refer explicitly to *German* victims. He talked about the sense of outrage in the postwar years, the "indescribable atrocities" in the camps in Russia and Poland, continuing with the following breathtaking statement: "When these proofs of 'German bestiality' appeared, little was said about the great number of *Germans* among the victims."[202] And alongside some biting remarks about the French "camps" in southern Germany and the American war against the Native American Indians, Rothfels could not resist offering his own explanation of the facts: "All available evidence and the results of sober and unbiased examination will demonstrate that modern mass civilization produces from its own depths a reservoir of dark forces whose release spells pure and naked barbarism, while by the same token it should also be clear that potential material for both torturers and martyrs is present in every nation, should a politics of hatred and revenge choose to overlook this."[203] The conclusion was left unstated but crystal clear: to talk about the camps meant to perpetuate a "politics of hatred and revenge." The overwhelming pathos in Rothfels' book, his constant invocation of the human element "in the borderline situation [*Grenzsituation*] as such,"[204] is in significant measure a result of the fact that he had to depart from the concrete plane where such "humanity" had actually been negated in order to legitimize his self-chosen theme of "resistance" in the first place. At the same time, he suggestively juxtaposed scholarship with politics, spoke up for conciliation, took distance from revenge—indeed co-opted the gesture of enlightenment in opposition to repression, speaking in the name of "truth" against "ideology."[205] In this way, a model of German resistance was established in German historiography and German memory.

As its yardstick, the model had concepts such as "resistance," "courage," "the power of suffering," "steadfastness," "composure," "martyrdom," "moral self-assertion," and "Christianity as an anchor" in chaos. These concepts appear within three pages of *German Opposition*. In concord with the historians who had remained in Germany, Rothfels made no attempt whatsoever to ask any questions about the expulsion, expropriation, despoiling, destruction, and murder of the Jews. Emigrants who wished to be properly recognized in Germany had to toe the line: they could only speak about the German past within the accepted German forms of discourse. In Rothfels' words, remigration to Germany was a "return to the nature-given locus" (*Rückkehr an den naturgegebenen Standort*).[206] Rothfels was convinced that any true pedagogical effectiveness had to be grounded on a "community of experience"—an *Erlebnisgemeinschaft*; the loss and restoration of this *Erlebnisgemeinschaft* through a "filling in of the gaps in experience" was a recurrent metaphor clearly and unequivocally foregrounding the question of one's own identity and sense of belonging. In June 1947, he explained his doubts about a possible return to Germany by the fact that he had not been inside the "positive and negative community of experience of the past eight years" and that it was difficult to bridge over these "gaps in experience."[207] It is striking that Hans Mommsen does not cite the concept of "gap in experience [in the *Erlebnisgemeinschaft*]" in his 1976 portrait of Rothfels but rather cites (probably mistakenly) another expression, "gap in knowledge [in the *Wissensgemeinschaft*]."[208] But for Rothfels—as for other returned emigrants—the problem was not to gain insight and knowledge as rapidly as possible (one could do that on one's own); rather, it was centered on the task of restoring community—and for this, one of course needed an alliance with the other side. Rothfels responded to this gap, solving the task of returning to Germany and constructing through scholarship an image of it he could sustain, with his book on the German resistance. And a short time later, having ascertaining through guest professorships at several German universities that "a ten-year absence is no problem in my relationship to the present generation of students,"[209] the gap had apparently closed; it seemed that reestablishing the *Erlebnisgemeinschaft* was not much of a problem. But the process drew on and tapped memories that were "German," not "Jewish." If it indeed succeeded, this was in the general way we have noted between Meinecke and Rothfels: as a strange offer of alliance held out by Germans to Jewish emigrants, an offer that emphasized acceptance of the thematic canon of German traditions. Valorizing the "other Germany" had become a prerequisite for speaking at all about German history.

"Counter-Images":
The Reception and Meaning of Hans Rothfels' Work

Against this backdrop, the enthusiastic reception of *German Opposition* serves as a typical element in the reception of his work in general, since it was itself one of the programmatic documents of the restoration in progress at the time. The reviews of the book by Gerhard Ritter and Karl Dietrich Erdmann in, respectively, the first volume of the *Historische Zeitschrift* and the first issue of *Geschichte in Wissenschaft und Unterricht* put forward the official reading.[210] Ritter did not skimp on honesty and effort, sketching in his first sentence the framework within which he saw the book's importance: "The literature by German emigrants in America and England on the German problem has given rise to more confusion than enlightenment. A feeling of resentment, where it reigns unchecked, is not favorable soil for sober and objective historiography, and estrangement over many years from German soil easily leads to a distorted view of reality."[211]

This precisely identified the consensus of German historiography of the time: emigrants did not write "sober and objectively" but rather in a fashion distorted by "resentment." The exception represented by Rothfels' book was all the more "heartening," noted Ritter. In his view, the book combined "noble humanism" and a "masterful control" of the subject. Although the author had been "tested by suffering," he was completely free of "blind passion and bitterness." And although Rothfels had himself suffered heavily from being persecuted as a Jew, "he is able to render his judgments with admirable objectivity, far removed from making the entire German *Volk* responsible for the atrocities." According to Ritter, Rothfels' exacting approach, precision, caution, and intellectual mastery of the material led to his book's persuasive basic premise, which with "great clarity illuminates the political and moral emphasis of this opposition movement, while proving the working notion that all Germans obeyed the Hitler tyranny [*die Hitlertyrannei*] and offered no resistance to be a legend."

In Ritter's eyes, a "just assessment" meant focusing on the breadth of the movement, the depth of its motives, the truth of its basic religious convictions, and the "fateful and mysterious nature" of the failed assassination attempts, while looking at both church and military "with a deep sense of understanding" for their position. In the course of his review, he formulated what amounted to an official welcoming speech for Rothfels on behalf of the German historians' profession, lauding, his words, the ethos and ability "of our old colleague and friend, whose voice we are pleased to hear once again, after such a long period of silence, coming now from across the sea." Ritter continued by asserting that there can "hardly be better proof of the fact that the scholarly maturity of the genuine historian leads to a reflective high ground where the bickering of daily politics fades into silence."

Friedrich Meinecke, Karl Dietrich Erdmann, Werner Conze, Theodor Schieder, and Siegfried Kaehler all stressed that Rothfels could not possibly be partisan—that he looked at recent history from a healthy distance, able to demonstrate objectively, in Kaehler's words, the "exculpation," *Rechtfertigung*, of "substantial sections of the German *Volk*."[212] In this connection, Kaehler spoke of 20 July 1944 as a genuine "German freedom movement." Meinecke, "deeply moved," called the book an "air bridge" (*Luftbrücke*) linking the United States with Germany.[213] The "bridge" metaphor, symbolically so important for Rothfels' historiographical architecture, here naturally involved a word-play, referring as it did to a concrete contemporary event—the Berlin blockade and General Lucius D. Clay's airlift to the city, with up to a thousand daily flights between late June 1948 and May 1949, representing the first great confrontation of the Cold War. Meinecke went on to note that when reading Rothfels' description of events linked to the German resistance, "all my conversations with Kaiser and Beck came vividly back to me. Yes, it was exactly like that; it seemed to us a simple human obligation of conscience to eliminate the monster [i.e., Hitler] and then rebuild an ethically purer Germany [*ein ethisch reineres Deutschland*]."[214]

This citation makes clear how Rothfels regularly imparted to both his colleagues who had stayed in Germany and his readership what they had—or wished they had—experienced. But it was not only his fellow professional historians who praised the book, its topic and premises, and the ethos of its author. Eventually, the German Foreign Office itself would voice sincere gratitude for a work that had served, for so many, as a form of "liberation," a work that had understood the tasks of politics.[215] The similar reception of Rothfels' book by professional historians and the public, running across the political spectrum, illuminates a German longing for a narrative of resistance: a longing whose expression must be termed an "invention of tradition," because the narrative was not shaped for the sake of genuine history but was meant to serve as a great counter-narrative to Nazism. Rothfels' "little book," as he put it, "had many peculiar effects," provoking a response by readers that amounted to a "barely endurable burden of letters."[216] He answered the deep longing generated by his ideas as best he could: through manifold encounters with his former colleagues, industrious correspondence with friends, and numerous scholarly publications. In a letter to Kaehler, he once termed this continuous activity "laying emergency footbridges over the old pillars."[217]

Rothfels' exchange with Kaehler makes it clear that he maintained correspondences with others for one main purpose: to promote "matters of importance within the framework of internal German discussion."[218] At one point Kaehler confirmed to Rothfels, innocently but accurately, that in reading his letters he had the feeling that "the past years had not really taken place and today was directly attached to the day before yesterday."[219] It is evident that such bridges spanning the Nazi period—presented paradigmatically in this private correspondence—were a basic part of the politics of scholarship and science of their time. Rothfels had no doubt that the emphasis on equating

Nazis and Germans was created to legitimate "Potsdam"—that is, that treaty's ceding to Poland of the formerly German soil on the other side of the Oder-Neisse Line—and that the concentration camps were a "piece of propaganda" designed to legitimate the division of Germany.[220] As in his book, Rothfels here implied that the camps were largely a means of compulsion used by the state against Germans; and the fact that after the Allied victory they had been instrumentalized a second time against Germany now called for "counterimages" (*Gegenbilder*).[221]

Rothfels was dedicated to the task of formulating such "counterimages." In the private sphere, he had repeatedly sought new beginnings, "built bridges," strung out "emergency footbridges," and proclaimed the need for conciliation. In 1949, commenting on Ernst Jünger's diary *Strahlungen*, Peter de Mendelssohn had diagnosed Jünger's "total blindness" and "complete inability to see the other side."[222] From our present perspective, the same diagnosis would seem to apply to Rothfels, helping to illuminate his role as something like a postwar German-academic discursive center, indeed magnetic field—someone around whom the hopes, interests, and intentions of the historians who had stayed in Germany were concentrated. In turn, exploring this role supplies some answers to the question of why in the immediate postwar period German historians were unable to perceive the Jewish catastrophe.

A "Sense for History" and the "Task of Memory"

As an example of interaction between former academic exiles and colleagues who had stayed in Germany, it is clear that Rothfels' experience marks a significant exception, for his own return was nothing less than a great success. But looked at soberly, it is clear that the success came at a very great cost, that of something like a discursive erasure. In contrast with other emigrated colleagues, Rothfels did not hesitate to pay this form of tribute; his contribution to historiography can be understood as confirming an intellectual alliance with the German elites in which their offer was mixed with his reaction to it. The foundation underpinning this alliance was a concept of Nazism as the "absolute other" within German history. The true Germany, Rothfels suggested, in the process acting somewhat like a stage prompter whispering lines to his grateful German colleagues, had been the Germany that resisted and opposed Hitler.

Against this backdrop, one can cogently argue that none of the key figures in postwar German historiography chose "communicative silence" as consciously as did Hans Rothfels. Put otherwise, his "bridge building" was in fact a concrete act of suppression, based on a view of the years between 1933 and

1945 as years that needed to be "bridged over," and on a refusal to juxtapose the historical experiences emerging from their murderous matrix.

In his recent autobiography, the historian Georg Iggers reminisces about his studies in Chicago, where he himself attended two seminars taught by Rothfels, one in the winter of 1948–49 on the Prussian reforms of Freiherr von Stein and another the following summer on the Frankfurt-based German national parliament of 1848–49. Iggers expresses surprise that Rothfels was so "conservative and German-national" in his thinking. And he comments that as a young man, he had never understood why Rothfels had in fact emigrated. "Only later did I learn that he had been raised in a Jewish home."[223] The Chicago encounter between Iggers and Rothfels was marked by decided feelings of antipathy. Iggers recalls that Rothfels told him "straight to his face" that it would be wise to give up his studies since "I had no sense for history."[224]

This meeting between two emigrants from Germany shortly after the end of World War II has been preserved only in the mode of a personal memory. Whatever the reason for their mutual antipathy during the late 1940s, and whatever led Rothfels to make the assessment he did about Iggers as a student, from today's perspective the space between them takes on more than anecdotal interest. It might, in fact, serve as an emblem for the present discussion.

Georg G. Iggers was born in 1926 in Hamburg as Georg Igertsheimer; his parents changed their name when they emigrated in 1938. Iggers, who would live in America for many years, dates the "transition . . . from a patriotic German who identified completely with the other kids at school and the teacher to a nationally minded and religious Jew" to the years preceding his flight from Germany.[225] Expelled from Königsberg in 1938 without telling his children at the time why,[226] and returning to Germany shortly after the end of the war, Rothfels experienced no comparable confrontation with his Jewish origins. His devotion, as a conservative German nationalist, to the putative gap between "National Socialism" and the German nation forms a stark contrast to Iggers' attempt to fathom the overburdened traditions of German history over the *longue durée*.[227] Rothfels became the dean of German contemporary history, head of the German Historians' Association, board member of the IfZ, editor of its *Vierteljahrshefte für Zeitgeschichte*, author of programmatic studies reflective of the era of restoration in the Federal Republic. Iggers, on the other hand, devoted himself to fundamental studies in the history of historiography, historicizing his own doubts about the dignity and integrity of the historical profession in Germany. Put briefly: Rothfels represented the dominant line in the foundational discourse of postwar German historical studies, and Iggers embodied the skeptical resistance to that line.

Indeed, the contrast between Rothfels, born in Wilhelminian Germany, and Iggers, thirty-five years his junior, could not be more pronounced. Rothfels was a full professor, holding one of the most respected chairs in American academe, while Iggers was partly supporting himself at the time by working as a lift operator in the University of Chicago's library.[228] The fundamental difference of generation and status helps account for the two men's divergent paths—their views on history express entirely different times, values, interests, perspectives. In this light, it is not surprising that Rothfels misread Iggers' criticism of the traditions of the nation-state—traditions that he himself still represented as a veteran of World War I—as a basic inability "to think historically," nor perhaps is it surprising that one of the earliest criticisms of Rothfels' function and role in postwar West German historiography would be formulated by Iggers two decades later. Initially, this criticism was conveyed in a broader context of Iggers' questioning of nationalist traditions within German historiography as a whole.[229] It was then articulated more clearly and directly in later writings.[230]

Nevertheless, the differences between the two historians cannot be sufficiently explained by a gap in chronology and career. This was not a private conflict, the reflection of a purely generational difference discharging itself in personal animosity. Rather, a real clash was at work here between very different views of the Nazi period, indeed of that period's prehistory. In understanding the latter in the framework of a crisis-charged continuum of German history itself, Iggers gave theoretical expression to Jewish historical experience, thus locating the expulsion of Germany's Jewish minority in an epistemological space.[231] In Rothfels' case, just the opposite is true. Starting with his participation as an enlisted soldier in the Great War, his dominant historical experiences remained "national German," subsequently attached to the imperial German model of German history—a model that by no means became antiquated or invalid in the Weimar period.[232] Consequently, when it came to Rothfels' self-identity, he always remained, before, during, and after his emigration from Germany, a Prussian conservative in the Protestant tradition and that of Bismarck's nation-state. He may well have considered his "Jewish extraction," as defined by Nazi racist ideology, as a type of misunderstanding; in any event, as indicated he rarely expressed himself in public on the matter, thus leaving it in the realm of "implicit memory" or "unarticulated history." Because his perception as a "Jew" came in the form of an externally imposed and denigrating stigmatization through Nazi ideology, the continuity of his own self-perception is not something incomprehensible or counterintuitive. Seen in these terms, Rothfels perceived the de facto experiences he endured of "Aryanization"—dismissal, expulsion, antisemitic and racist rejection—as elements incompatible with his own self-understanding, an alien ascription.

This experience was, then, basically incongruous with Rothfels' own being, with his political views, education, and impressive career as a historian in Germany. Thus, on the level of individual formation of memory, his ideological choices were no more or less than those West German postwar society had made in general—and that contemporary German historiography had opted for in particular.

Figure 1. Panel discussion at the Conference of German Historians, Frankfurt am Main, 8–11 September 1998. The debate about the role of German historians in the Third Reich unfolded in an overfilled auditorium at the University of Frankfurt, before many professional historians and their students (including the author). The debate left an enduring echo in both the public and professional realms. At the podium is Peter Schöttler, who had organized this section together with Winfried Schulze, Otto G. Oexle (*both on the left*), and Jürgen Kocka (*far right*). The Strasbourg historian Pierre Racine (*far left*) spoke on Hermann Heimpel. In addition there were lectures by Götz Aly, Michael Fahlbusch, and Mathias Beer (*right side, from left to right*) on, respectively, Theodor Schieder and Werner Conze, the so-called *Volksdeutsche Forschungsgemeinschaften* (Nazi research associations for studying the ethnic German regions) established in the 1930s, and the major research project on "Expulsions of the Germans from Eastern Central Europe" undertaken in the 1950s. (Wonge Bergmann)

Figure 2 (*at right*). Friedrich Meinecke (1862–1954) at his desk at home in Berlin-Dahlem, where he lived the last four decades of his life. The photograph by Fritz Eschen shows the elderly scholar — for many years one of the main representatives of German historiography — in 1950. With his book *Die deutsche Katastrophe* (published in 1946; begun toward the war's end) Meinecke initiated a still ongoing public debate about Germany's efforts to come to terms with the historical reality of the Third Reich. Not least because of that book, at the time the photo was taken Meinecke was serving as the first rector of Berlin's Free University. Starting already in the Kaiserreich with his *Weltbürgertum und Nationalstaat* (1908, published in English as *Cosmopolitanism and the National State*) and especially during the Weimar Republic period, the historian's work attracted many Jewish students, including Gerhard Masur, Hajo Holborn, Hans Baron, Felix Gilbert, and Gustav Mayer. Some of them retained a strong sense of gratitude toward their teacher, resuming contact with him after 1945. (bpk Berlin)

Figure 3. Gerhard Ritter (1888–1967) in September 1949 at the first German Historians' Conference, held in Munich, following World War II. Ritter (*foreground, far right*) was at the time chairman of the German Historians' Association. A Lutheran of nationalist-conservative leanings, Ritter had maintained his distance from Nazi ideology; as a result of his detention by the Gestapo shortly before the war's end, he possessed undisputed authority abroad. He was thus an ideal personality for the reestablishment of the historians' association. His central guiding principle was regaining recognition for the importance of German national historiography; he thus considered its criticism misguided and counterproductive. Also seated in the first row is Walter Goetz (*fourth from the right*); while teaching at the University of Leipzig he had left his stamp on the beginnings of contemporary historiography in Germany following the Great War. We also see Hermann Heimpel (*fifth from the right*) and Hans Rothfels (*eleventh from the right*), both of whom are discussed extensively in chapters 2 and 3. In the second row behind Ritter is the University of Munich historian Franz Schnabel (*with mustache*). (Nicolas Berg)

Figure 4. Hans Rothfels (1891–1976) was one of the most influential German historians in Germany's postwar period. A nationalist conservative of Jewish ancestry, Rothfels (*seated, with cane*) had to flee Germany in 1938, returning from American exile—and a professorship at the University of Chicago—in 1951 to teach at the University of Tübingen. Intellectually and institutionally, Rothfels was one of the handful of German historians to define the concept of *Zeitgeschichte*, "contemporary history," its methods and the choice of questions deemed relevant for study in the years after Germany's defeat. He was chairman of the German Historians' Association between 1958 and 1962; coeditor of the Institute for Contemporary History's influential quarterly, *Vierteljahrshefte für Zeitgeschichte*; and a member of various influential academic boards, including the Commission for Documentation of the Expulsion of Germans from the East. Already before his return to Germany, he had great success there through his manner of presenting Nazism and German resistance to Nazism as two sides of a page. This photo was taken at the German Historians' Conference held in Berlin in October 1964. It shows Rothfels in conversation with Karl Dietrich Erdmann (*standing*), his successor as conference chairman. (picture-alliance/dpa)

Figure 5. Fritz Ernst (1905–63) was a student of Johannes Haller. He received his habilitation (qualification to teach in German universities) in 1932 in the area of medieval studies and then taught at the University of Heidelberg, where he served as rector from 1961 to 1963. At the beginning of his rectorship, Ernst gave an influential lecture course; soon after, the lectures were published in Germany as *Die Deutschen und ihre jüngste Vergangenheit* (1963, published in English as *The Germans and Their Modern History*), a book that would represent one of the most well-known reflections by a German historian on coming to terms with the Nazi past. In this book, *Zeitgeschichte* and autobiography were nearly indistinguishable: a feature of all retrospective discussions by West German historians of the period. For whether or not they acknowledged it, in the picture they presented of the Nazi period, the historians were always also offering an assessment of their own behavior between 1933 and 1945. (Heidelberg University Archives, photo by H. Speck)

Figure 6. Hermann Heimpel (1901–88) was an important medieval historian and director of the Max Planck Institute for History in Göttingen after the war. His significance with respect to the ways in which the crimes of the Third Reich were spoken about in West Germany during the late 1950s can hardly be overestimated—precisely because, in contrast to many of his colleagues, he openly expressed shame and remorse over his own behavior in the Nazi period. Heimpel's public authority was thus not so much grounded in scholarly criteria as in lectures and speeches on German history and a range of autobiographic texts projecting a reflective, warning voice. In this way he can be seen as one of the founders and main representatives of a special form of Protestant self-criticism aimed not at what the Germans refer to as a *Schlußstrich*—a line drawn with the recent past—but rather at what is termed *Vergangenheitsbewältigung*—overcoming or coming to terms with that past. That term would become ubiquitous in postwar West Germany. Although Heimpel did not invent it, he saw to its promulgation and its abiding relevance. (picture-alliance/dpa)

Figure 7. The Institute for Contemporary History in Munich in its founding year. The institute, today internationally renowned, was established a few years after the end of World War II as the German Institute for the History of the National Socialist Period with a pair of researchers in tight quarters. This is a photo from 1950 with an unknown visitor at the entranceway to Reitmoorstraße 29. At that time the institute, which in 2013 incorporated a Center for Holocaust Studies, initiated empirical research in Germany on political developments during the Nazi period, first under the directorship of Hermann Mau (1951–52), then Helmut Krausnick (1959–72), and Martin Broszat (1972–89). This work was begun long before history departments at German universities even contemplated taking up the subject. From our present perspective, we can thus understand the Munich institute's history as encapsulating two dimensions: on the one hand, resistance to its work and related difficulties tied to the onset of historical processing of the Nazi years in the early German Federal Republic; on the other hand, a rather quickly established new emphasis on what was perceived as scholarly sobriety and a form of research strictly centered on facts (see chapter 4). In its early period, the ideas of "objectivity" at work in the institute led to Jewish colleagues voicing reservations about the research being conducted there and to a frequent assessment by institute researchers that other (non-German) perspectives and themes were insufficiently objective or were biased (see especially chapter 5). (bpk/Bavarian State Library, Munich)

Figure 8. Martin Broszat (1926–89) was one of the most prominent West German researchers on contemporary history. In the early 1950s he wrote his dissertation on the antisemitic movement in the Kaiserreich at the University of Cologne under Theodor Schieder. He then moved to the newly founded Institute of Contemporary History, where he remained throughout the rest of his lifetime, for a long time as a researcher and, starting in the early 1970s, as the institute's director. In the 1960s, Broszat was involved in a long epistolary controversy with the historian Joseph Wulf (see Figure 9) concerning methods as well as the proper factual questions to be focused on in research on the Holocaust; the correspondence attests to sharp differences of perspective. In the photograph Broszat is standing between the historians Czesław Madajczyk (based in Warsaw) and Sybil Milton (based in New York) during a conference held on 9 November 1987 in Berlin. The conference had been arranged to discuss future planning for the villa in Berlin-Wannsee where, as is now notorious, on 20 January 1942 Reinhard Heydrich convened a conference to discuss the murder of all of European Jewry. In 1992, on the fiftieth anniversary of that conference, the villa was opened as a memorial and education center; this would mark belated fulfillment of an idea that Joseph Wulf had developed and passionately argued for in the 1960s. The idea had been very concrete but failed at the time because of insufficient social and political backing in West Germany. (picture-alliance/dpa)

Figure 9. Joseph Wulf (1912–74) at his desk at home in Berlin-Charlottenburg. We know from reports of colleagues and intimate friends that, from the 1950s onward, the Jewish historian, documentarian, and Auschwitz survivor worked here eighteen hours daily on his pioneering source-collections and other historical publications. From this workplace he corresponded with colleagues throughout the world, with figures from politics, society, and the church, with various authors, former Nazis, resistance fighters, and Jewish survivors. And on 10 October 1974 he took his life in this apartment. In the background above the file tray we see a sign with the imperative "Zachor!" in Hebrew, beneath which (partly covered in the photo) was placed the figure "6000 000." Wulf's documentary books—*The Third Reich and the Jews, The Third Reich and Its Thinkers, The Third Reich and Its Servants*, and *The Third Reich and Its Executioners*—were developed and written together with Léon Poliakov, a distinguished Paris-based historian of antisemitism of Russian Jewish descent; this work offered the first comprehensive depiction of the Holocaust and its perpetrators, masterminds and ideologues, diplomats and soldiers, bureaucrats, jurists, medical doctors, profiteers, and countless fellow travelers: a horrifying panorama. In another series of books Wulf focused in the 1960s on art, music, literature, film, and journalism in the Third Reich. (Ursula Böhme, from Klaus Kempter, *Joseph Wulf: Ein Historikerschicksal in Deutschland*, Göttingen, 2012, page 171)

3

Hermann Heimpel,
Reinhard Wittram, and
Fritz Ernst

A "Demonstration of Protestant
Penitence" in 1950s Germany

"Schlußstrich" versus "Professors of Guilt and Repentance"

In a radio conversation with the University of Vienna historian Forst de Battalia on 22 January 1958 in the studios of Westdeutscher Rundfunk under the title "Is Prussia Actually Responsible for Everything?"[1] Peter Rassow declared in annoyance, and formulated in pronouncedly general terms, that "the historian as such," which was to say the academic specialist, had no necessary knowledge of the word "guilt." Guilt was, he observed, a moral and religious concept, but not one meant to inform historical research. It was an "unpleasant use" of everyday language when guilt and the causes of something were confounded. "Now allow me to tell you as a historian," he continued irritably, "that I won't go along with this confusion of guilt and cause."[2] From a commentary on the conversation by Siegfried A. Kaehler, Rassow's colleague at the University of Göttingen, who opined that de Battalia swept together, "with refinement," "rather all kinds of historical garbage [Unrat]" that eluded "any form of rebuttal,"[3] the reason for Rassow's annoyance becomes clear: in one remark de Battalia had simply referred to the concentration camps.

103

With polemic intent, Rassow posed the question of how a historian would need to be "constituted," *beschaffen*, if "the events of history" were evaluated "before him and by him" according to criteria of guilt. But through this polemic, he was evading a basic aporia of the time. For alongside the moral and religious implications, in this period speaking of guilt meant, first and foremost, critically assessing individual attitudes and collective action. Rassow's conceptual retreat into what he postulated as strict scholarship involved playing off "cause" against such assessment—in the process giving expression to a widespread opinion while at the same time hypostasizing disciplinary obstinacy. Elsewhere, in a clear look back at Jaspers, he put it thus: "The question of guilt is no historian's question."[4] In the typically defensive stance they reflected, such words were superimposed on the problem that the separation Rassow championed of guilt from cause was artificial. At the historians' convention in Ulm in 1956, Hermann Heimpel thus placed emphasis not on the concepts' separation but on their connection, speaking of a "change in the significance of the facts" and an "almost legal triad" in historical research moving from "the question of guilt" to "the question of causes" and onward to "the question of structure."[5]

We need to look more closely at both Rassow's and Heimpel's sententious definitions. It is clear that in the context of their time, they emerged from a widespread space of resonance in which a specific chain of terms was extraordinarily popular in German theology, philosophy, and academic history. These terms included "atonement" (*Sühne*), "healing" or "cleansing" (*Heilung*), and "purification" (*Läuterung, Reinigung*), but also "conciliation," with a valence that took in both "propitiation" and, again, "atonement" (*Versöhnung*) and "responsibility" (*Verantwortung*). This is the backdrop to an observation Reinhard Wittram offered in 1958 in *Das Interesse an der Geschichte* (The Interest in History): "History is always concerned with guilt. It is the secret motor that keeps the gears moving, mostly hidden, always active, the actual *perpetuum mobile* of world history."[6]

In any case, if we measure such excursions into the moral-pedagogic sphere against their contribution to concrete education about the Nazi period or indeed against the standard of what the authors involved had themselves done and written in that period, the results are lamentable. At the time historiographical apologies were being articulated not only as opportunistic declarations by what Erwin Klinger has termed "clean break" ethicists, *Schlussstrichethiker*, but also in declamations by "professors of guilt and repentance."[7] Concerning the latter, in his study of "master thinkers in a stateless period," Klinger offers citations by Karl Jaspers, Carl Schmitt, Hans-Georg Gadamer, Joachim Ritter, and others that make clear the extent to which eternal verities were now clung to with a mixture of engagement and callousness. In respect to direct approaches to the recent past, in official circles the atonement theme was underscored to such an extent that its connection with guilt was no longer apparent. Historians who were deeply implicated in National Socialism in one way or another were now certified as having *personal* integrity. Following the death of Heinrich Ritter von Srbik—Austrian historian, specialist on Metternich, champion of pan-Germanism, honored Nazi Party member, between 1938 and 1945 a party delegate in the pan-German Reichstag—in 1952, we thus find Werner Näf writing in the *Historische Zeitschrift*, with esteem, that Srbik had lived "in Ehrwald in asylum" in the Nazi period, for him a "time of silence and mourning he himself referred to as a time of purification." The historian's doctrine, Näf conceded, was subject to "ideological abuse." But once "idea and reality met in 1938" (in other words, once the pan-German unification of Germany and Austria, evoked by Srbik over many years, could be realized), then "the idea was not fulfilled"; rather, its "pure substance was soiled," and "its dignity had to shield what was unworthy" (*ihre Würde mußte Unwürdiges decken*). The apologia's conclusion was simple: "But an idea can remain correct even if denatured by ideology. Srbik's work and its creator with it had been usurped by a political will." The work "in itself," Näf continued, had not been created for political purposes but had emerged in a purely scholarly framework "from deeply felt attachment to fatherland and history"; there could be no doubts concerning Srbik's "constantly alert human conscientiousness."[8]

However strained and extreme Näf's apologetic diction, his obituary, appearing in Germany's leading professional journal of history, both reflected and promoted a broad view that individuals of continued prominence who had been active in the Nazi Party (thus, by any normal standards of present judgment, who had endorsed, passively and actively, the party's program and horrific exercise of hate) had been "abused" or had simply become "entangled," *verstrickt* (another extremely popular term of the time), without ever having actually done anything wrong. Against the backdrop of the semantic refurbishing of biographies and scholarship required in the 1950s, palimpsests of the old and the new emerged, steeped in evocations of purification, silence, and mourning— whatever that referred to in individual cases. Another, less lurid example is that of the legal historian Heinrich Mitteis, who examined the Third Reich in a number of texts that his biographer Georg Brun termed "brooding" (*grüblerisch*).[9] As chairman of the Rostock branch of the Cultural Association for the Renewal of Germany, Mitteis held several "anti-fascist addresses," for instance at the dedication of Rostock's Monument for the Victims of Fascism as early as the end of November 1945. In his writing and activities, he was "fully intent on reconciliation" (*ganz auf Versöhnung eingestellt*), as he put it in a letter written about a month earlier.[10] This is hardly surprising since Mitteis was now criticizing precisely the same "renewal of law" he had himself promoted in the 1930s, complained about what he saw as the period's positivist legislation as the "worst abuse of legal thinking . . . that the German's have had to suffer through," und reflected generally on what he rather oddly termed the "knife-sharp sheath [*messerscharfe Scheide*] between guilt and fate."[11] After having promulgated a legal-historical justification of Hitler's war policy in his pre-1945 writing (for example, in his article "Staatliche Konzentrationsbewegungen im großgermanischen Raum" [State Movements of Concentration in the Pan-Germanic Area], written in 1941 for a Nazified series on legal and economic history),[12] Mitteis thus now saw science and scholarship as the principle victim, degraded "into an instrument of propaganda for the power politics of the total state." Following the collapse of the Third Reich, he saw his main task in the end as helping restore German culture, not contemplating the recent past—"in any event I am happy," he asserted, "when I need to speak of those things as little as possible."[13]

Experience and Confession:
Fritz Ernst

The situation was different with the next generation of historians, who spoke a great deal about "those things," indeed couching a great portion of their work in a "confessional" diction. One of the less-known examples of such literature is *Die Deutschen und ihre jüngste Vergangenheit: Beobachtungen und Bemerkungen zum deutschen Schicksal der letzten fünfzig Jahre, 1911–1961* (The Germans and Their Recent Past: Observations and Comments on German Fate over the Past Fifty Years, 1911–1961; translated as *The Germans and Their Modern History*, New York, 1966), a "confessional book" by the University of Heidelberg historian Fritz Ernst (1905–63), based on lectures held in 1961–62 and published in Stuttgart in 1963 (see Figure 5). The book—whose title, while now seeming bombastic, would have drawn attention at the time—constituted something like a legacy, since Ernst died that year. In its nine short chapters, it unified two normally separate ways of communicating preoccupation with the Third Reich and German extermination of the Jews; it can be read as a documentation of the transition from pure national apologia to a new mode stamped by guilty sadness and consternation. As a student of the national-conservative medieval historian—and Nazi sympathizer—Johannes Haller, Ernst was interested in aligning his focus on atmosphere and experience, and his interest in the general conduct of the Germans over the ages, with what later became known as the "history of mentality."[14] The starting point for his reflections was a conviction that "for all Germans born in this century, whether or not they were for Hitler, National Socialism has been the central event."[15] Ernst was convinced that since

1918–19 the Germans had been "forced" to consider their present circumstances historically.[16] In June 1940, following the victory over France, he himself gave a speech in what the Germans and both Alsatian and scattered Lorraine separatists termed "Nanzig" (Nancy); it closed with the words: "After centuries filled with French pillaging raids [*welsche Raubzüge*], the force of the newly unified German *Volk* is in the process of shaping the future of this border area."[17] In their time such commentaries were so ubiquitous that looking back we can take them more or less for granted. But for those confronting their own ideological grandiloquence, a need to explain was present—although very few were willing to do so publicly. Ernst's book thus tested a middle path between "exaggerated German confessions of guilt" and "self-examination," a compromise structure that, while making its task recognition of "horrendous things"[18] and trying to restore credibility before oneself, colleagues, and students, often oscillated without mediation between harsh justificatory ideologems and self-incrimination. This notwithstanding, the students' generation was impressed by the result; Wolfgang Mommsen, for example, saw the text as containing an "account" written "more by the contemporary who shared the experience of all of this . . . than the critical historian."[19] Ernst's cautious plea for understanding, Mommsen insisted, generally deserved "attention and highest respect." The younger colleague was sure that if there were more such lectures at German universities "the present deep trench of non-understanding" between the generations would be smaller.

In his "history of the experience of the German *Volk*," Ernst presents apologia and confession in a methodic manner: "Both the need for historical truth and the attempt to educate the younger generation demand that history be presented as it was experienced." The turn from Ranke's famous dictum of history "as it actually was" was being made by other historians as well, albeit without expressing it openly. It was so ambivalent because basically it represented a consistently controlled but nonetheless subject-centered justification: a narrative concerning the theme of what one had believed, hoped, or desired and the places where one was gripped by fear. Ernst thus offered less information about the events than about himself: "For those who do not try to present the entire atmosphere of the time, this will be flat and colorless, merely a period of crime. The human element has removed itself from history. In the process, the period becomes incomprehensible and implausible, and those who shared the experience, whatever their personal position, turn away from such descriptions with bitterness."[20] This effort to retain the "human element" in a narrative about the Third Reich and Nazism constitutes the subtext of much of the historiographical production of the late 1950s. In Ernst's text, it surfaced as a near 140-page account based on the axiom that only those who experienced a

period could understand it. There were enough good descriptions in compen-
dia of modern German history, Ernst insisted; he in any case strongly advised
against "learning about the event whose witnesses were from books alone."[21]
For it was hardly possible any more to explain the "emergence and functioning"
of the dictatorship to younger people in that way: "When one spoke to students
in recent years about certain phenomena of the Hitler Reich, one could often
hear laughter—the superiority of those who say: 'That sort of thing couldn't
happen to us.'"[22] For that reason, he doggedly abstained from any talk of guilt,
the danger existing "that people would simply 'wallow in their own mistakes'
and apply standards to what took place that cannot be applied." But this formula in Ernst's foreword was basically a concession to the "old patriotism,"
since in his text he essentially spoke of nothing other than becoming guilty—
unmistakably in a defensive and exculpatory sense, but still publicly. Ernst put
it thus: "If we ask how the horrendous things that happened were possible, if
we try to explain—we cannot after all, abstain from judging. Many Germans
have presently forgotten what they themselves said in 1946," but the silence
and sugarcoating now being frequently practiced was "just as one-sided and
much more dangerous"—it would "exact terrible vengeance if it prevailed."[23]

Apology and Obsession as a Confessional Locus

In actuality, the apologias at work in this text were both unrestrained and
countless. Ernst polemicized against the Germans who groveled in the badness
of their own *Volk* after 1945; warned against cheap pharisaism; conflated the
dictatorship of everyday life, which he termed the "essence of dictatorship";[24]
whitewashed both the German army (the "spirituality" of its general staff, he
indicated, was to be contrasted with Hitler's brutality)[25] and the universities;[26]
and scattered easy anti-Communist phrases[27] while drawing a blunt parallel
between the fate of the German churches and that of the Jews (for example, in
his reference to *Juden- und Kirchenverfolgung*, "persecution of the Jews and the
church").[28] But even more unbearable are certain contradictions in the text, for
example, Ernst's never neglecting an opportunity to underscore ignorance in
the homeland about the annihilation of the Jews, then suddenly focusing on the
role of political jokes indicating the opposite, offering one of the most uncanny
as an example: "In the extermination of the Jews [*Judenvernichtung*] in Poland a
drunk SS *Sturmführer* tells a Jew, 'I have a glass eye. I'll grant you your life if you
can guess which eye's my glass eye.' The Jew inspects him: 'The left one!'
'Good, but how did you see that my left eye's the glass eye?' 'It looks so kind,
Herr Sturmführer!'"[29]

In the winter of 1961–62, Fritz Ernst had offered this joke to his student listeners without any commentary, and the drastic tactlessness is revealing on various levels: for the historian, the extermination was not only that which had been meant to be hidden, what could only be "suspected"; at the same time— and the point seems to have been obsessive—it was *the* argument for a German turn way from Nazism:

> Outside Germany [*im Ausland*] the Germans are reproached for having only turned away from Hitler when it became clear he had lost the war. . . . Our students were already indignant when they suspected the increasing persecution of Jews during the war, to be sure in the relatively mild forms in which it could be suspected in Germany, at least initially mild in comparison with the mass killings already being carried out at that time in Poland and soon after Russia, of which the masses in Germany could know nothing until the collapse.[30]

If we judge Ernst's confessional book according to its accuracy alone, we overlook its novelty: not just the apologia but also the obsession was one of the confession's cornerstones; together they thus functioned, unmistakably, not as its contrary but as its medium. But looking back from our perspective, the text's excitatory quality, the *how* of Ernst's helpless efforts at mastering recent history and shameless assertions, together with the fact that here the extermination was discovered as a historical argument concerning memory and not history itself, is more interesting than a relativization that was typical for the time. Ernst was in fact publicizing neither research nor memory but rather attempting to use the latter as a vehicle for exploring the "power that national myths have over human beings."[31] Ernst spoke explicitly of the "structure and significance of national emotions."[32] Not only history in itself but its relationship to the present, hence measuring a difference within it, had now become a focus of attention: we all stand in the shadow of Hitler's rule, Ernst observed, and referred to the year 1911, which is to say fifty years previously, to "be able to understand, for the present, the problem that concerns us."[33] Like Heimpel and Wittram, West German president Theodor Heuss, and others, Ernst himself had "discovered" memory and the present at once, perceived both how new experience "alters memory of what has occurred"[34] and the pitfalls to which memory in general is tied: "In ten years we will know more and less at one and the same time; we will have learned and forgotten. But on every step of the learning and forgetting it is possible to contribute to a judgment of the past events."[35]

For Ernst's generation, Nazism was three things at once: first, a temptation at a crucial juncture in their own careers to which they succumbed in their thirties without resistance; second, "the greatest disgrace in German history"[36] following the Third Reich's collapse (and this as a failure understood as thoroughly personal); and thus, third, a constant reference point for biographical reflection in view of the future—one's own and that of younger people, in the years of a new beginning: "Only ruins and mass graves remained," the "sense and essence of the twelve years" quickly acquiring "something askew," since "the balance is negative"—hundreds of thousands of "German soldiers" and "at the same time millions of Jews" had been "killed in mass extermination camps and mass shootings."[37] Even if the generation of Nazi actors consistently referred to its own suffering in the same breath as its mention of Jewish suffering, post-1945 self-scrutiny had led to an acknowledgment of responsibility:[38] "The mass extermination camps of the SS wiped out millions, and in 1945 this contempt for humanity [*Menschenverachtung*] . . . fell back upon us."[39] Against voices already arguing at the end of the 1940s that "what later was called 'overcoming the past'" had already been completed, Ernst insisted that what the Germans already called *Vergangenheitsbewältigung* had to be made fruitful. He addresses his audience directly:

> As long as you are German, no one can either grant you this Germany or challenge you for it, but at the same time no one can free you from it. You have grown into it—you have taken over a legacy you cannot escape, and while you did not create the legacy you are responsible for it in the sense that you can shape it. We only "come to terms" with the past by working for the future; in the end the past only gains its sense through what is in the future.[40]

Despite the process having been repetitively updated since the 1950s, this remains the consensus regarding *Vergangenheitsbewältigung*: its specific nomenclature, reflecting a shift of the vocabulary of "responsibility" to the discursive center, has been maintained by every generation, and by each in the same way.

"What Was Known about Treatment of the Jews . . ."

Ernst left an eighteen-page communication, not meant for publication, that was probably written between 1956 and 1959 but was discovered much later by chance in London's Institute of Contemporary History and Wiener Library.[41] It can be used to more closely scrutinize his political credo in respect to the recent past. It is in a way an autobiographical outline of the 1963 "confessional" book;

it serves a representative function both in respect to the 1950s and the lectures
Ernst delivered a few years later, with their underlying didactic tone, their in-
sistent use of a "watchman's vocabulary" (e.g., "warning too much against this
would be impossible"),[42] and their incessantly repeated appeals to understanding (e.g., laments at the "lack of understanding of the Western opponents"; the
reflexive, formulaic use of "one must understand").[43] Written at a time running
parallel to Ernst's key essay "Current Events and Historiography,"[44] the short
text is generally even more direct and subjective than the book of 1963—at one
point Ernst speaks of a "personal reckoning."[45] In this "reckoning," the basic
confrontation with the persecution and extermination of the Jews, although
only touched on, is manifested on a more personal level than in the book—the
author here, as it were, testing "consideration of his own past from the outside."[46] The short text's editor, Diethard Aschoff, emphasizes the solid memory
and simultaneous critical distance of the "historically schooled witness" it reveals;
the author, he observes, shows no hesitation in taking clear positions and naming
names.[47] But in actuality the high value as a source that Aschoff ascribes to the
text largely reflects his own interest in the history of the University of Heidelberg:
with the exception of the correspondence between Karl Jaspers and Karl Heinrich Bauer (an exchange itself not initiated until 1945),[48] no other relatively
concentrated report on the university's situation in the Nazi period exists. The
text's broader relevance and importance clearly lies not in mnemonic sharpness
or critical distance but in its status as an act of private denazification.

The years at Heidelberg that Fritz Ernst here looks back on are 1937 to
1946. The parallel to the chapters of *The Germans and Their Modern History* titled
"Hitler's Rule" and "The Second World War" are evident, as is the historian's
conviction of his role as a superior witness. Why Ernst chose to "as it were hide
away" the reminiscence "in a foreign, Jewish archive"[49] is unclear. As indicated, the theme of "extermination of the Jews" is here intermittently addressed
with a very unusual openness:

> Since I myself had no friends among the first victims of National Social-
> ism, my own situation carried far more weight than say the general fate of
> the Jews, whose details I myself only learned of for the first time when at
> the war's start a [former] pupil—she was an enthusiastic Nazi supporter—
> sent me a few pages from the *Times* of 1 November 1939 from the [Ger-
> man] Foreign Office, presenting excerpts from the English white paper on
> the initial survey of persecuted Jews. . . . In 1935 I accidentally ran into my
> only Jewish schoolmate, with whom I had lost contact in 1927. We spoke
> for a long time in his apartment. At the time we were relatively optimistic
> since the regime was showing signs of internal weakness. Later I heard he

had succeeded in emigrating to the United States. We came into contact
again after '45. What was otherwise known . . . about treatment of the Jews
was of course bad enough, and no German can say he did not know. But it
belonged to what was generally humiliating on the side of the regime, as
long as it did not affect someone you were close to. During the war I then
heard much more through the BBC, always more horrible. I knew much
more than the small-time party comrade, but this knowledge burdened
me and my wife alone. I could not communicate it further.[50]

In his private text, Ernst thus indicates that he basically had known everything
but was not especially interested in the fate of the Jews—at most, as one aspect
of general burdens. He had observed the fate of the church more closely, "since
I had many theological friends and there were also ties with Catholic theology." When at the end of November 1938 the Nazi Party representative on the
Heidelberg faculty had requested for a second time that he join the party, he
had explained, we read, that none of his Swabian relatives would shake his
hand "if after the swinish episode [*Schweinerei*] of '*Kristallnacht*' I now joined the
party." But, Ernst adds, this did not take much courage: "I knew he was also
ashamed"; it was the case that at that point not a single Jewish apartment had
been entered, but "south of the Neckar not only the synagogues were destroyed
but also apartments demolished."[51] Ernst himself saw efforts to interpret moments of dissatisfaction or halfhearted compromise as resistance as inadequate:
"It is natural to have a better view, in retrospect, of the cases of resistance. and
nevertheless classifying all of us within the collective-guilt formula was something hard to swallow, as justified as it may have been."[52] (A similar self-
corrective is evident in his recollection, elsewhere, of the "half-Jewess" student
Cornely, who was able to finish her PhD dissertation at Heidelberg in 1944 and
would then survive by "disappearing" into a bookshop in Kaiserslautern. Ernst
seems to consider the protection she received through the university as a kind
of bonus on his account, but then notes how precarious the half-heartedness of
this enterprise was; later, he indicates, he became "worried" about her—he
only learned where she had been after 1945.)

Against this backdrop, Ernst's general assessment was vaguely hopeful in
respect to "jaded" youth and the two "present powers, large-scale capitalism
and Catholicism," but exact in respect to behavior (in particular his own)
within the Third Reich. Where in his lectures he expressed a presumption that
in a dictatorship the individual could "keep himself free,"[53] in the earlier, private
text we read the following: "A dictatorship also changes people who inwardly
resist it. It determines their conversational themes. In a dictatorship, one
can become familiar with the greatness of a human being but also with his

dependence. And the belief: '*Ach*, they will survive the dictatorship inwardly safe' is an illusion. That people fall under a dictatorship must be prevented. Furthermore, no modern dictatorship is overthrown from within. This is not said to excuse the Germans, but it is an insight."[54]

Reinhard Wittram's Christian Conception of History

Reinhard Wittram likewise theorized about his relationship with tradition following the war, starting with a perception that a "turn"—*Wende*—had taken place that could only be compared "with the largest known historical upheavals."[55] As a historian of Eastern Europe and, like Fritz Ernst, a student of Johannes Haller, between 1928 and 1939 he served as lecturer at the Herder University in Riga and (following the resettlement of the Baltic Germans) at the Reich University in Posen, where he was also dean of the philosophy department. Wittram strongly contributed to the volkish ideologization of German academic history; he became a Nazi Party member in 1941, delivering talks for the führer and against a Bolshevism that was *artfremd*—"alien to one's kind." After 1945, Wittram became one of the main figures in the rebuilding of research into Baltic history at Göttingen, where he adapted a critical stance, warning against the "style of mythologization." Alongside Heimpel, Wittram is generally considered one of the few historians who did not evade a critical evaluation of his own role in the Nazi period, although he himself was especially incriminated.[56] In a letter to Peter Rassow written in May 1945, Siegfried Kaehler referred to Wittram as a "romantic fallen from the clouds of Baltic dreams of Germanness [*baltische Deutschtumsträume*]."[57] He began teaching in Göttingen in February 1946 and in the history department in the winter of 1947; in 1955 he was appointed to a professorship in medieval, modern, and Eastern European history. He inaugurated this chair in the winter semester of 1955–56 with a series of twelve lectures that would become famous as the above-mentioned *Interesse an der Geschichte*, recalled by one former student, Herbert Obenaus, as a momentous event marking nothing less than a "breakthrough of conscience into scholarly reflection"[58] and by another, Gerhard Sauter, as possessing individual phrases that remained unforgettable years later.[59] The great theme of the series was historical progress and its opposite: the "rediscovery of evil in history and in the human being." The diction of the published lectures was itself highly suggestive, alternating as it did between melancholy, a "search for warmth," and a "pastoral propensity": "one" turned into "I"; "conscience," Wittram declared, "has representative force."[60]

But Wittram's "Demonstration of Protestant Penitence"[61] actually began earlier. In a generally neglected lecture he gave at Göttingen University's

Evangelical Students' Association at the beginning of July 1952 with the title
"Public Evil and the Eighth Commandment,"[62] Wittram used concepts from
the Hebrew and Christian Bibles to pose the question of the conditions for
historiography in a dictatorship. In the context of both that question and the
Mosaic injunction "Thou shalt not bear false witness against thy neighbor" (the
eighth commandment in Luther's translation of the Hebrew Bible), the basic
terms presented at the beginning of the lecture were to the point: court, witness,
commandment, sin, honor, disgrace. Wittram referred to Luther, the German
hymn writer Paul Gerhardt, theological literature, and sermons. What does it
presently mean, he asked, to have become "publicly" wicked? Does it mean a
"loss of reputation and honor"?[63] The manner in which Wittram worked to
challenge theology for the problems he broached by historicizing them is here
highly striking. In a tour de force extending from the medieval heretics and
early modern religious wars to the French Revolution and Napoleon, and onward to the "spiritual struggles of the present,"[64] he presented his listeners and
readers with an anthropologized Christian perspective that against the backdrop of the mass murders of the Nazi period and its huge numbers of victims
and perpetrators has a quality nothing short of eerie:

> The question is under what circumstances we atone when we try to under-
> stand everything, since our office is indeed to repeatedly set about anew
> trying to understand the alien and repulsive. The defining feature of the
> Christian approach to history is not the general rule of undifferentiated
> acceptance but something else: knowledge of human beings. If we do not
> inquire into human beings, the past will be a city of the dead for us. The
> dead are up high with God. But we demand a meeting with them; we have
> them appear before us in the garments and disposition of their time and
> concern ourselves with their honor and reputation. We cannot do other-
> wise, for a spell is cast by legend that we cannot surrender ourselves to
> without examination. However defenseless the dead may be, they are
> simultaneously powerful. We have to resist suggestions, offer testimony
> doing justice to the perpetrators and thinkers in their own terms, and
> simultaneously take a stand—as if they were still quarreling with us. When
> they have been unjustifiably vilified, we should defend and protect them.
> In other cases we have to understand and nevertheless judge. This is only
> possible when we are sure of solidarity with the bones of the dead in our
> humanity before God, who is timeless.[65]

In view of this vague and generalizing reasoning, is the feeling justified that
Wittram is here grappling intellectually with Auschwitz? Are the expressions

"city of the dead" and "perpetrators" and the reference to a simultaneous defenselessness and power of the dead sufficient to align this passage with the German prose of the 1950s aimed at "coming to terms with the past"? The answer here is, in fact, affirmative, since at his lecture's end Wittram directly articulates what previously could only be suspected:

> Here I have reached the last point I wished to consider. Our shared guilt is always present. There is an objective form of guilt that is nearly independent of our good will. Those who remained silent about the mass outlawing [*Massenverfemung*; Wittram is here referring to the persecution of the Jews] within our *Volk* (and finally the mass murders) from fear or with the help of sublime self-deception or in irresponsible ignorance may have grounds for pardon [*Entschuldigungsgründe*], but we have become guilty [*schuldig*].[66]

In this brief lecture, the paradigm shift to what Wittram terms a "Christian approach to history," under the sign of a Protestant understanding of guilt, is fully evident. The basic religious orientation is reflected thematically, conceptually, and in the examples, locus of the event, and audience; likewise, Wittram's presentation of his own conscience centered on a confession of "the weakness and unfathomable nature of human beings,"[67] a phrase then immediately abstracted into a community-forming "humanity before God, who is timeless." For the lecture was concerned less with the theme of the fall itself than with the thesis of the historicity of sin and public behavior after admitting to it. What was at stake here was thus an existential question: that of the relationship between shame and honor ("honor is where human beings have their social existence").[68] Beginning with the fall of German society, it then anthropologized and universalized that event by referring to "our own depravity [*Verderbtheit*]," before turning to a differentiated consideration of different concepts of honor and ending with a mention of the "mass outlawing" and "mass murders" that took place under Nazism.

The difference between the "breakthrough of conscience" emerging in Wittram's scholarly reflection and the arguments of a historian like Gerhard Ritter, centered around the theme of national honor, may not be apparent in each author's work. But they became palpable in the framework of a direct confrontation at the Third German Assembly of Evangelical Students, held in Heidelberg in 1954, an event taking on far more than anecdotal significance in light of what has been said here. What transpired was recounted in 1999 by one of the student moderators, Werner Terpitz, in an article in one of Germany's leading national newspapers with the title (in English translation) "The Nation Is What Is Ephemeral: Students Were Already Protesting against the False

West German Consensus in 1954."[69] More than a thousand students participated in this assembly, which was organized into over forty discussion groups. It is important to note that the event produced a wave of criticism in German newspapers and on the radio, with the Heidelberg students subsequently even being slandered as "traitors." Already the preparatory pamphlet, with the title—printed in looped Gothic type—"Holy Fatherland?" (*Heilig Vaterland?*) sparked a regular storm, with Terpitz speaking of a sixty-page press echo. Following a guiding motto of "contemplation, even when it hurts," the assembly was meant to explore the roots and future of nationalism. For his part, Gerhard Ritter would see "massive protests produced precisely at the end of his talk, where he intended to offer the students hope and show them prospects. His suggestion pointing to the future, offered in a Christian sense, that the German people were perhaps led into more serious trouble than other peoples because God expected greater and better solutions from them was denigrated sarcastically as a proposal for a new consciousness of mission." The students, Terpitz commented, "were insisting that this finally be brought to an end, that God should no longer be attributed with special intentions regarding the German people." Wittram's reflections, he observed, were far more in line with both the expectations of the students and a demythologization of the "fatherland." (In any case, it was, he noted, the theologians Erwin Krämer and Heinz Zahrnt who received "tumultuous applause," not the historians.)

Evil, Its "Permanence," and
Justice for Individuals

Wittram also considered the question of the Nazi German catastrophe in cognitive-theoretical terms, as a search for its "meaningfulness in its entirety." There was more than a simple alternative, he argued, between "agnosticism, chaos, an accumulation of coincidences" and a "recognition of regular developmental processes."[70] Wittram scrutinized the "hard indisputability of the factual"[71] and declared everything as "factology"[72] that had not been hardened "in a slow process of research, critique, and control," in "a controversy lasting years or decades";[73] considering the difficulty in the 1950s of acknowledging the Holocaust as a historical theme, however, this observation has an ambivalent tenor. But if we take this "slow process" at face value, then—to use Nicolai Hartmann's phraseology—the struggle with the historical object reveals itself as the difficult achievement of the method applied to that object ("Every science . . . struggles with its objects in order to overcome [*bewältigen*] them; and this struggle is at the same time a gaining [*Erringen*] of methods").[74] The complex, sometimes verbose efforts at formulating "conceptualizations of history" and a "theory of the human being," to use two of the sorts of expression circulating in German historiography at the time,[75] make clear that within an abundance of questions concerning theory, method, tradition, and knowledge, what is really being repeatedly addressed is the underlying methodological problem of how to negotiate the relationship between history and memory—even when the terms and concepts used stem from theology. At the time, the theological conceptual paradigm for defining Protestant positions prevailed in historiography as elsewhere; Wittram himself held seminars and so forth together with theologians, for instance, a working group on "The Problem of Historical Change."[76] "Modern Protestant theology," he declared, strove to "exclude stoic and Neoplatonic distortions" from precisely those statements about human beings "gained from a biblical understanding" of them, while at the same time "including all present-day knowledge from research and experience."[77] In this way questions of knowledge and the concept of revelation, that of forgiveness of sin and the doctrine of grace, calibrated the field upon which those wishing to focus on Auschwitz had to tread. Difficult to understand from our vantage point, this also meant that the "profound concern [*Betroffenheit*] constituting the essence of faith"[78] could be rendered possible and public only in these terms. The renunciation of idealism and the effort to craft a new historical-anthropological definition of, as it was put, "the human being and history" involved a discourse of self-understanding in which one's own debit and credit were being tested: as Wittram explained, in contrast to what Karl Barth had suggested, human beings, no longer understood dualistically, were not "half good and half bad," partly damnable and partly just, but "entirely both"— although not from within but from without, "beneath the wrath or grace of God."[79]

In conversations Wittram was apparently far more open than in print, where he often was satisfied with intimating what he meant.[80] He clearly struggled to find an appropriate terminology for an "evil" in which he himself participated— voluntarily and from conviction—that would preserve his ethos as a historian without relinquishing any of his Protestant faith. In that framework, his references to "morality in history"[81] and the "unfathomability of human nature,"[82] while transparently apologetic, also represented a kind of progress, in that he was here rejecting the term "inhumanity" to define "evil" as both unhistorical and refuted by history: "Evil is not an animal but a human category," Wittram stated. "It is impossible to cleanse the human image by not admitting calculating vengefulness, capable of any atrocity, or cold delusion, indifferent to human life."[83]

Wittram's approach, we should note, was also potentially innovative because it opened the door to rehabilitating the "unwritten tragedies" and "patient sufferers," the "nameless masses,"[84] as historical subjects. In any event, his re-anthropologization of historical scholarship was a process that both generalized in its focus on the "human being" and individualized in its insistence that "no human being dissolves into a type."[85] For the sake of preserving justice, he insisted, it was necessary to render the person a conceptual starting point:[86] *the* Wilhelminian Junker did not exist, not *the* bourgeois of the ancien régime, nor, we might add, *the* Nazi. His polemic point was the unacceptability of a "personification of institutions and groups obliterating the essential difference between the factual whole [*das Sachganze*] and the personal self,"[87] a remark to be read, it seems, against the backdrop of a personal desire to remain distinct as an individual from a state, system, or party (for instance, from the Nazi version of each). Beyond this, for the retrospective historian such an approach meant, Wittram maintained, not applying any "alien normative codex to the past" but rather "persistently working toward an understanding of acting human beings from out of their own circumstances"—and only rendering judgment, "if it is not to be avoided," at those times one has called *oneself* into question. This was the only way, he asserted, of being both "procedurally proper and credible."[88]

This completed the conceptual operation making possible critical judgment of the "factual whole" without endangering the "personal self." The scholarly specialist could stand opposed to an "alien normative codex"; the moral reproaches tied to the latter were thus already removed from German historical debate and entrusted to the historian's own conscience. Rooted in a Protestant idea of repentance, Wittram's historical-philosophical venture can be summarized as follows: a critical revision of the traditional approach to history and morality, evil and its "permanence," tied to granting the individual the greatest possible amount of justice. If in the course of the 1950s the tendency was more toward such generally oriented philosophical and theological excursions and reflections, less toward ideologically hardened revanchism, this was certainly tied to what has been termed the "awareness of guilt of those who escaped" (*das Schuldbewußtsein der Davongekommenen*),[89] an awareness that Wittram spoke for in an exemplary way. Like Ernst and Heimpel, because of his own biography he took to heart appeals such as that of Elliot Cohen, cited earlier, who directly addressed the German historians in denouncing the "silence of a grave," a silence that had an "especially eloquent and baleful effect" and an "intellectual vacuum." "Where are the references to brotherly love and spiritual anguish, of self-scrutiny, diagnosis, and therapy, a restoration of wisdom?" Cohen had asked, referring to German "scholars, historians, poets, and writers."[90] But in view of the historical event in question as well as his own recourse to an increasingly popular rhetoric of Christian atonement, Wittram's efforts to address such urgent concerns could only define themselves as escapist—the real historical context was here rendered impalpable, indeed could not be confronted.

But that acknowledged, the historiography for which Wittram argued was unmistakably double sided: its anti-discursive, detemporalized, and sacrally imbued discourse also marked the beginning of a rhetoric centered on *Vergangenheitsbewältigung*, "overcoming the past." Doubtless, his use of that rhetoric reflected a conviction—in part opportunistic, in part earnest—that he was saying what others expected and wished to hear, and more could vanish than become visible behind his de-concretized metaphorical diction. Nevertheless, an off-hand comment made by the Freiburg art historian Kurt Bauch in conversation with his historian colleague Rudolf Stadelmann (until the defeat a committed Nazi) in Easter 1945 here offers helpful context. First referring to the prevailing "apocalyptic times," Bauch continued by observing that "Basically the difficulties are now only beginning. . . . How are we going to again emerge from this general distress and disgrace without denying ourselves completely?"[91] Against the backdrop of a later stage in that dilemma, Wittram's confessional efforts need to be understood, despite all their transparent failings, as contributing significantly and enduringly to the construction of a canonic historical self-understanding: a self-understanding in which Nazism was interpreted as significant for the present, representing a constantly present responsibility for individual and collective memory.

Hermann Heimpel's Historiography

Hermann Heimpel (see Figure 6) belongs firmly in the context described here, and not only because he was in fact responsible for coining and promulgating the term *Vergangenheitsbewältigung*.[92] Three years older than Ernst and a year younger than Wittram, he initiated a new form of historiographical revision in his previously mentioned speech at the 1956 historians' convention in Ulm, opening the discipline to a German discourse of *Bewältigung*, "overcoming." (Michael Kohlstruck's understanding of *Vergangenheitsbewältigung* will be helpful in the following discussion: a concern with the historical reality of Nazism that presumes an ascription of guilt to the Germans.[93]) In contrast to the first postwar years, when the discussion about revising the broad historical picture centered on the extent to which the hypertrophic concept of the nation needed revision, in the 1950s an effort began to define history and historical scholarship, events and memory in a way reconciling living recollection and scholarly method. But together with the effort, we must note that here again its realization was rendered impossible by the reality of the Nazi extermination. As Heimpel thus put it: "Presently . . . the task of historical knowledge is no longer such a liberation

from an unknown [*ungewusst*] past but inversely a replacement of lost uncon-
scious [*unbewusst*] ties with conscious scholarship."[94]

A historian of medievalism and modernity, Hermann Heimpel already
held a chair in Freiburg before 1933, and before he was thirty. In 1933, he
supported the academic upheaval initiated by Heidegger, to the best of his ability;[95] two years later he took over the chair of his esteemed teacher Siegmund
Hellmann in Leipzig (Hellmann would die in Theresienstadt in 1942). Finally
he moved to the famous old university located in what the Germans called
Straßburg, which had been developed after the German victory over France
into an elite "borderland" institution (officially a *Reichsuniversität*). After the war
he settled in Göttingen, where he served as director of the Max Planck Institute
for History starting in 1957. He was chairman of the German Historians' Association, a member of many commissions, rector of the University of Göttingen,
vice president of the German Research Foundation, and chairman of the West
German Conference of Rectors.

Although a biography of Heimpel has not yet appeared, various authors
have addressed aspects of his life. Winfried Schulze has emphasized the difficulties in passing judgment on him; Michael Matthiesen has described him as a
"fellow traveler"; Helmut Heiber as a "trendy activist" (*Konjunktur-Aktivist*): and
in an extraordinarily apologetic account Hartmut Boockmann declares full
exoneration. In 1998 Heimpel's period in Strasbourg was the subject of a talk
at the German Historians' Conference in Frankfurt, focusing on the correspondence surrounding his appointment between him and Ernst Anrich, the university's Nazi-appointed dean.[96] In the memoirs of former students, he has been
treated as a "magnet" in a pantheon including scientists Otto Hahn and Max
Planck. His pedagogic approach was, we learn, stylistically and methodically
an extraordinary experience: he exerted influence "with his entire being"; his
presentations generating downright charismatic energy. At the same time, we
find an emphasis on his "subjective" way of understanding history and rendering
it understandable,[97] and on both his "forcefulness" and the "essentially existential" nature of his presence before the students.[98] From Göttingen, Kaehler
wrote Rothfels that Heimpel was an "undisputed star of the first magnitude in
our historical firmament; I have never experienced a connection of the sort he
possesses between firm erudition and power of artistic shaping among members
of our generation."[99] He owed a great deal of his authority to a very specific
form of uprightness with which he spoke of the recent past: it was precisely the
fact that after 1945 he admitted in a "self-critical, open" way that he had not
been immune to the "threat and allure of the times" that made him credible—
this the assessment of Heinrich Schmidt (one of Heimpel's former students),
standing for many other such assessments.[100] The distinguished historian

Reinhard Rürup, at the time another of Heimpel's students, has indicated that Heimpel's references to "our guilt" or "our failure" were occasional and that the effect the references had on him were relatively general, "but in any case he was one of the very few who said something publicly."[101]

Nonetheless, a look at scattered epistolary statements of Heimpel in the immediate postwar period makes clear that in the 1950s, attempts at intellectual uprightness when it came to interpreting his own past—the basis for his postwar fame—necessitated a learning process. Heimpel had a precise sense of the problem he was encountering alongside many others: "How tough is the human will to normality, as if an old spiritual culture is refusing, for whatever reason and from whatever guilt, to accept catastrophes that have occurred."[102] As late as May 1949, in a letter to Gerhard Ritter he casually opined that so many had "gained an SA rank" like "the Virgin a child," that is, unknowingly or innocently: "Thus I don't really know. Naturally the *Reichsuniversität* was mixed up in a bad thing, and we have no grounds for excessive sensitivity. . . . After I was too quiet with the Nazis and even unfortunately once complied with them, I now can't teach and have become very aggressive with everyone. I am convinced that these latest historical reformers will have shorter lives than us." He also indicated that it would become generally difficult to distinguish "the wicked" from "the brave." "But as long as one says Europe and Gallicizes a land that in its primal ground [*Urgrund*] is German or let's rather say: Allemanic and Franconian, I will not feel I have overcome the Alsatian question."[103]

The last sentence marked a continuity with Heimpel's role and perspective in the *Reichsuniversität* set up in Strasbourg (and was, it seems, at great distance from his later "Göttingen confessions"). That perspective was articulated in an essay Heimpel published in 1941, "Research on the German Middle Ages in German Alsace,"[104] which became a kind of guiding paper for new tasks to be taken up in medieval studies at the newly Nazified university.[105] It also marked Heimpel's explicit avowal of allegiance to the Nazi state: "This empire [*Reich*] as well represents Europe's order stemming from its center. With its blood, it is defending Europe's past and future against a barbaric world that knows no past."[106] He also pointed here to the rewriting of history as unavoidable: the German *Volk*, he declared, had reached a new stage of historical consciousness through the National Socialist revolution and needed a suitable historiography adequate to this development.[107]

Now some eight years later, he mocked the "paragon of virtue"—and fellow medievalist—Gerd Tellenbach for not being able to show any appreciation "that a great, animated spirit can err in an epochal change," a direct reference to the Heidegger case but surely to his own as well in mediated fashion.[108] But the defiance at work here was in fact reactive and fragile. Although Heimpel was capable of admitting, somewhat haughtily, to "a certain elasticity regarding the feelings of others," in the late 1940s he flatly refused to furnish information about himself:

> I am not ready to have myself examined in Paris, neither regarding my character nor my relationship to National Socialism. I would see an unbearable pharisaism at work here, all the more so as in Paris we will encounter colleagues and people with absolutely no reason to reproach us with something. . . . We cannot handle the matter privately enough. In line with the nature of the matter, from association to association all too many meetings and negotiations repeatedly dredge up unpleasant things.[109]

The context for this statement was the effort to find a strategy for the appearance of the German delegation at the 1950 International Historians' Conference in Paris.[110] The refusal to be "examined" on account of his Nazi past or indeed in respect to his character, the affect-laden reference to "pharisaism," and the marking of the "private" as the only locus in which unpleasant questions could be asked were more drastic expressions of defiance than was often the case with Heimpel. But a continuity with such defensive self-assertion is manifest in his choice of autobiography as the locus of conversion and confession allowing, in this manner, a withdrawal from controversial discourse accompanied by a capacity to be present in it.

The Autobiographical Origins of *Vergangenheitsbewältigung*

As boastful as such defensive declarations may now seem, they covered over an altered sense of things on Heimpel's part. The depression from which he suffered after 1945 should be understood in this context—above all Siegmund Hellmann's deportation and death became "more and more the embodiment of a fate throwing its shadow over his own life."[111] It took some effort for Heimpel to acquire a stance of "Protestant penitence," and it was above all the extermination of the Jews that prompted him to gradually undertake an intellectual revision. His uneasy conscience is more than clear in the few fragments of reminiscence we have, for example, when in his long 1952 obituary for Hellmann he refers to his teacher as having confronted the fate of the Jews through a "deferral now inconceivable to us but that at the time was not uncommon."[112] At the beginning of that text we read: "In an anxiety dream become horrific reality that a humanist could never have dreamt of, Siegmund Hellmann died in the Theresienstadt deportation camp on 7 December 1942, abandoned by all of us, certainly lonely within the mass fate."[113] And nearly thirty years later, at an event marking Heimpel's eightieth birthday, he recalled: "My predecessor in the chair at Leipzig . . . had to die among a mass of tormented people. In Munich he had been my teacher, and I often showed him that I revered him—as long as that was no risk."[114] But frequently such confessions remained couched in very general terms, as in the following rhetorically inflated paraphrase of the concept of guilt:

> The human being lives on credit, and anyone born at the start of our century not struck by any of the arrows darkening the heavens since 1914, 1933, 1939 has eternally overdrawn his credit. He has to thankfully keep in mind that he has not yet been drawn into the depths by the millstone that the Book of Books has envisioned for those from whose mouths useless words have come. . . . Drawing our consequences we know: since we are all weak, the weaknesses of others are only pardons for our own deficits.[115]

In any event, when Heimpel gave notice of his personal bad conscience, as a historian he was in a certain sense also doing this on behalf of his vocation. Although authenticity in private, as expressed in the words on Hellmann, is indeed not the only criterion for assessing private "conversion processes," it can certainly serve to demonstrate changes in a "style of thinking."[116] In fact, in the years following 1945 Heimpel increasingly wrestled with his autobiography in the Nazi period. The historian Josef Fleckenstein reports that in the last three years of his life he frequently read the Bible in light of both his own experiences and failure in the Third Reich period and the Final Solution. Heimpel's daughter, he indicates, found Luther's *Small Catechism* (rev. ed., Luther Verlag, 1986) on her father's desk. "Many underlinings, cross-outs, and marginal comments," he notes,

> show both the intensity of the reading and engagement with the text. In its entirety the document again confirms how tormented Hermann Heimpel's grappling with the basic religious questions was at the end of his life. Already on the title page . . . he wrote: "Do I have the strength to trust in God's grace?" In the Lord's Prayer, the supplication for forgiveness from guilt is underscored, alone, with thick underlining. Alongside the statement of faith in the Almighty, the word "Auschwitz" has been inserted twice in the book.[117]

In unambiguous fashion, this double inscription, made shortly before Heimpel's death, offers a key to reflections on the semantic intertwining of religiosity, privacy, and guilt constituting the material of Heimpel's *Vergangenheitsbewältigung*. From the beginning, his simultaneous openness to historiographical science and the emotions stemming from personal experience and incrimination, at the juncture of the political, public, and private, rendered him a mediator of two discursive forms that tried to join but necessarily had to always be stymied. Here for the first time, the tendency to demonization evident in the first postwar historiographical analysis of "the German catastrophe" was replaced by an assessment centering not, it is true, on past actions of one's own person but at least on one's present relation to the events in question. In this way, personal shame could now be revealed thematically—and this paradoxically also when the grounds for this shame remained unnamed, as earlier. Here historiographical progress was tied to a form of regress. Heimpel's autobiographical path was less the staging of a conflict between the self and its environment of the sort offered by Meinecke, Haller, and Ritter than a reflection on the teleological orientation toward the present of the facts being remembered—and this for the sake of both his own memory and his own vocation.[118] This insight into the "secret power of a time-bound ordering of memory" changed the discourse about Nazism in a fundamental way.[119]

Now as previously, precisely when they were justified and also when they were perceived as honest, confessions of shame and guilt led not to a preoccupation with the theme of the Holocaust but rather to a preoccupation with oneself or else to religious ruminations couched in an expansive rhetoric. Göttingen of the 1950s was a predestined setting for this—exciting and possessing a kind of "impenetrability" at once—a quality the Germanist Walter Hinck described as "barring certain themes and questions in advance."[120] The historian Annelise Thimme (mentioned previously) has recalled a student period in Göttingen when Christianity "received a new, great chance." "Entire masses streamed to the sermons" of theology professors teaching at the university, "so that someone not arriving in time sometimes could not find a seat."[121] The intellectual historian Christian van Krockow has described the university's atmosphere in more literary terms: "When I became absorbed in Thomas Mann's *Magic Mountain*, I thought: you yourself ended up there like another Hans Castorp hearing with astonishment what the Settembrinis, Naphtas, and Peeperkorns proclaim." Something "strangely removed, almost unreal" was at work in this postwar university, "and through all the educational experiences one could almost forget what was actually being sought."[122]

The earliest demonstrable reference to "overcoming the past" was in the negative, in a lecture given in 1952 by Hermann Mau, a student of Heimpel, in which he spoke of German historians' neglected duty to "relentlessly" pursue a "spiritual overcoming of our recent past."[123] Mau had already used the term "spiritual overcoming"—*geistige Bewältigung*—in 1950, in the draft of an essay on the Nuremberg trials:[124]

> No more detailed justification is needed for stating that the most signifi-
> cant task possible is here waiting on us, above all a German task. If
> anywhere, then it is here that the discipline of history has a high degree of
> responsibility for our spiritual and political future, namely, to the extent
> that research on the ~~time~~ [crossed out in original] history of National
> Socialism has a decisive role in the formation of consciousness in our time.
> The knowledge of, which is to say, the spiritual overcoming of, its fateful
> destinies [*Schicksale*] is as important to the life of a people [*Volk*] as it is to
> the life of the individual.[125]

While quite transparent in this passage, the Protestant origins of the "over-coming" concept become even clearer in the context of an invitation to a conference commemorating the 20 July 1944 plot against Hitler, held between 15 and 18 July 1955 at the Evangelical Academy in Berlin Wannsee, with the central theme being the "liability and problematics" tied to "our history." In the printed invitation, the question was posed of whether "the shadow of our unsurmounted past" (*unbewältigte Vergangenheit*) was not showing itself "more powerfully than ever."[126] In Hermann Heimpel's writing, however, the concept not only took on more weight than in such usages, tending as they did toward cliché, but also a specific orientation. In a short text written at the beginning of 1956, he asked what expectations were for the new year, his response being a reflection about memorial days, the relationship between the state and its citizens, the question of Germany's division and possible reunification—and memory, the thematic basis for a shift from a general look back over the year to a contemplation of German history and the guilt and will to forgetting tied to it. Memorial days, Heimpel argued, forced "even those estranged from history" back "into history":[127] without "remembrance [*Gedächtnis*], namely, without accountability [*Rechenschaft*], the years are nothing. Nothing but a pile of exhausted and discarded appointment books whose entries we will very soon cease to understand. The new year demands our remembrance."[128] But precisely because the "appointments" involved here were fixed by history, they were all "in dispute," in a valuative exchange understood as a task that had become *obligatory* because of the "past twenty years" of German history.[129]

On the same page as all these citations, Heimpel seems to address the personal implications of this insight: "To the older man, facing his century's unsurmounted history may be dizzying when he considers the up and down, the apparent firmness of days of the year that still sink into forgetting."[130] What appears to be intimated here, albeit elliptically, is, again, the historian's task—an "achievement of memory" that "overcomes the danger, horribly overshadowing our present, of *forgetful forms of repression [vergeßliche Verdrängungen]*. It would be a good New Year's exercise to place together all follies, concessions to power, and weak [*weich*] reactions to the changing zeitgeist that have been expressed or seen in print over the past twenty years. For all of us, each in his own way, became guilty and have remained so, to the extent death, the lord of the last decades, has spared us."[131] Memory, then, as a form of guilt atonement, as a "clear view, undistorted by justification of the life and history of the individual and the people [*Volk*]": this alone can "heal the disease of our age," "overcome the unsurmounted past [*die unbewältigte Vergangenheit bewältigen*]. This is the only way for us, as well, to become free, although we will not be exempted from our pasts and our errors until the end of our days."[132] Heimpel could have made this appeal more credible with a disclosure of his own "weak reactions" and "concessions to power" than with a general address to others or in the indefinite use of "we." Let us note, as well, that around this time the Jewish historians Léon Poliakov and Joseph Wulf were publishing just the sort of documentation that Heimpel seemed to be calling for—a panopticon of the Nazi period but with a precise naming of names and places (this discussed in detail later); we have no evidence of any reaction on Heimpel's part to the appearance of these volumes. Be this as it may, it is clear that long before the period when a rhetoric of "overcoming" had become routine, although Hermann Heimpel's contemplative thoughts on the past themselves had a declamatory character and would have little outward effect, their "authenticating presentation"[133] projected forthrightness because it was grounded in personal conscience.

All told, the hope articulated in this text of Heimpel's was charged with ambivalence. It was hope stemming from a theological conceptual model and thus expressed in deeds of penitence, along a "path of reason,"[134] and through a salvation of memory in honesty toward oneself. "In the new year," he appealed, "let us pass through the sea of feelings and bad feelings [*Gefühle und Mißgefühle*], the ocean of dangers and fears with the keel of reason and courage. Let us expect from the new year what the new year expects of us: a life of responsibility that we take on in memory of an unfortunate and guilty history but also one rich in good—of German history."[135] Subjectively, Hermann Heimpel tried to bring together the two cultural and historiographical poles of *shame* and *guilt* emerging sequentially in the early postwar period. But objectively, following Jaspers he introduced a transformation of the historical approach to the Nazi past that involved leaving behind Ritter's paradigm of national-cultural shame and loss of honor and moving toward a paradigm centered on responsibility in guilt. On 13 November 1955 in Hannover, at a memorial event for Germany's

Volkstrauertag, its day of remembrance, organized by the government of Lower Saxony, he delivered a speech on shame that did not stop, in the usual way, at mourning for Germany's own dead killed in *Gewaltmaßnahme*, "acts of violence." Rather, he juxtaposed thoughts about a restoration of national honor with those about the damage done to it: "For men who need to speak of the dead in 1955, both mourning and pride recede before shame."[136] Heimpel here recalled not only the fallen soldiers but also the executed siblings Hans and Sophie Scholl.[137] Death, he reminded his audience, not only seized millions as "blind fate," "in war and imprisonment as a theft of life's most beautiful years," but also meant "extermination," "torment," "slow murder," "liquidation" of other millions "because they were opponents of National Socialism, or because they were Jews or 'asocials,' or, as was the term in the orders to murder the Russian prisoners, subhumans, not human beings, animals. Death met them in concentration camps and death chambers."[138]

Such words were not expected of a ceremonial speaker in 1950s Germany, and the tone of this text has properly been described as "unprecedented."[139] But at the same time, Heimpel's way of undermining apologetic discourse was in a sense to make it the starting point of his own: the text remains full of references to "the cruel victors' revenge," that is, the denazification policies of the Allied occupiers. Heimpel described the Nuremberg trials as a "landslide that followed the earthquake and buried both the innocent and guilty beneath it." Likewise, his use of terms such as "massification" (*Vermassung*) and "de-deification of the world" (*Entgöttlichung der Welt*) represented standard terms of the time for a modernization process in which a "crisis of death-consciousness" (*Todesbewußtsein*) had developed. But while retaining the old clichés, Heimpel's argumentative line followed a new path of "post-Auschwitz thinking": gas chambers, mass death, and mass murder, he suggested, rendered any traditional rhetoric (either ancient or revolutionary-modern) grounded in heroic apotheosis of patriotic death "non-transferable"—obsolete and illegitimate. During the war, "human beings were forced into death and denied honor in death as in life. This should be considered by anyone speaking ten years later of death for the fatherland."[140] In this way, conservative themes were being critically revalued by way of reflections on guilt and shame, for the sake of gaining renewed credibility in light of the Nazi crimes.

At this point, Heimpel's terminology openly applied autobiographical self-reflection to a politically motivated interpretive struggle. But in postwar Germany, the idea of coming to terms with or overcoming the past was never separable from that of finishing with it, which rather lay at its inception. In this text and elsewhere, we find insight into the necessity for reflection and responsibility for the past *together with* longing for liberation from "history," remainders of defiance and refusal.[141] This is the case as well with Heimpel's volume of essays treating "the human being in his present," which he describes as the conceptual continuation of his memoir of childhood.[142] Here the introductory chapter, from which the title is derived and which expresses an intention to reconcile history and the present, is of special significance, representing a theoretical effort to understand actuality and continuity not as opposed concepts but as emerging from each other. This foreword begins as follows:

> Whoever remained spared, like the author, in the destinies [*Schicksale*] of his people and time has all the greater a duty to reflect. If he dares to admonish . . . and recall the upheaval of 1945 and the opportunity it provided us for contemplation [*Einkehr*] and a new beginning, that openness of the heart, so easily lost, at the borderline of orders and regulations, then all criticism is first of all self-criticism, admonition of oneself. If he puts forth the question of why the historian commits himself so readily to success, why the humanities are so unprotected against the menace and temptation of the time, he must first remind himself and others that he allowed such a process to take place with himself.

Despite the passive construction of the last part of the above sentence, more strongly manifest in the original German (*daß auch er solches an sich geschehen ließ*), it arguably contained more than humbleness and contemplation. It arguably also contained a certain threatening undertone. For read out to others, the equation of criticism with self-criticism conveyed something mitigating or de-escalating. Concerning the continuation of his career after 1945, Heimpel had a clear opinion: "As long as our guilty generation is needed, the guilty person must dare to act as if he were not guilty when placed somewhere where action is needed."[143]

Die halbe Violine:
Augustine as Model

Die halbe Violine (The Half Violin), Heimpel's account of his childhood,[144] has been described as a "picture and cultural document of the bourgeois age" in Germany, with a positive emphasis placed on just what continues to make the book's reading difficult: its tendency to ennoble and transfigure the subsequent decline through the "conciliating patina of the past"—this the enthusiastic commentary in the *Historische Zeitschrift*.[145] As it happens, virtually all the various academics and historians who reviewed this memoir or spoke of it retrospectively shared such enthusiasm, while more or less entirely passing over its crucial subtext: the past-defined depths and shadows. To summarize the rest of this reception: Heimpel's Göttingen colleague Kaehler referred warmly to the book's conjuring of the atmosphere of a period "that it is now customary to unjustly disparage."[146] The pedagogue Herman Nohl praised the book fulsomely and unequivocally for, among other things, its "descriptive iridescence" and "entirely original" qualities.[147] The historian Heinrich Schmidt greatly admired a "sequence of present tenses," for Heimpel had narrated from the perspective of prevailing consciousness, not from that of the retrospective analyst.[148] (Elsewhere Schmidt would indicate that the book had been one of the "most moving life experiences" of his student period, opening up a possibility of "grasping life even in the forms in which it appeared and was expressed after 1945 . . . as of equal worth to forms of the past [*die Vergangenheiten*] and like them 'directly tied to God.'"[149]) Heimpel's students Boockmann and Fleckenstein both generally saw the book as an attempt at gaining self-assurance in a time of collapse:[150] not a false analysis, but one bypassing what type of self-assurance was involved here, how the process was undertaken, and the function it was accorded by Heimpel.

In fact, although not immediately apparent, a subtext of guilt and shame, history and the present are tightly interwoven into Heimpel's narrative. He himself referred to the book, more accurately than his reviewers, as a study of "childhood time and historical consciousness";[151] it is the case that rather than simply presenting the reality of various "presents"—his later theoretical formulation—it also illustrates the conviction, on which he would later elaborate, that history and the present exist side by side, that forgetting will necessarily develop into a political danger, and that the present begins "with the last constitutive event, namely, an event determining one's entire existence."[152]

In this memoir, then, we are offered not only "immediacies of life" and "the gleam of mother of pearl" (the descriptions are respectively Schmidt's and Nohl's) but also their loss. In short, the text takes on the basic question of how a generation such as his own, saturated in high bourgeois values, could serve as a pioneer for Nazism. In a narrative forming what amounts to a highly reflexive *Bildungsroman*, a novel of gradual enlightenment or educational formation, Heimpel repeatedly plays on variants of "homecoming"—the word was also originally intended as the book's title. In effect, in the context of the Protestant penitence of a theorist of remembrance, the material for an autobiography set in Munich at the start of the twentieth century also serves as a postwar mirroring of Augustine's *Confessions*.

Both artful and pretentiously written, the narrative evokes years of Edenic childhood happiness before the Great War—a world of familial order, certainties, vacations in the mountains, and the ritual of violin lessons. Heimpel considers these things in terms of loss, in a style of steady melancholy: "A world went under."[153] It becomes increasingly clear that in the growing child (reported on in the third person, and under the fictional name "Erhard Stengel"), Heimpel is examining experiences that distinguish history, as a temporal dimension with depth, from progress, technology, and acceleration: "There was no talk of history in the Stengel household. The past was finished. A good thing. Father hated files and old letters, all too many memories, junk and dust. . . . As long as it contributed nothing to progress, Father tended to consider the past with a touch of irony."[154] The son's enthusiasm is of a very different nature: "Finding one's own in the other, the present in the past, what is trusted in what is alien, history, time, reconciliatory time."[155] Consistently, the historian brings together the image of his hometown, Munich; the return there through the writing of his text; and the Christian intensification of this idea in the homecoming metaphor. After having lived, after the "turmoil" spread over the world by human beings, he longs for the old homeland. He then begins his "wandering" toward childhood and youth: "The spirit opens the way home through memory. What is a human being? The human being is the being with memory. Angels have no memory since they see God. Human beings have memory because they know of God and do not see him, but are on the way. Their ways are ways home to themselves, namely, to their origin, there where they are really at home, namely, with God."[156] This definition of human existence as a form of mnemonic existence, within which every memory functions as a reminiscence of guilt, which is to say a turning away from God, thus becoming a short stage on an imagined return home, is dominated by a verbal field composed of fear, guilt, and forgiveness that culminates on the last page of the book. It ends with an observation about the connections between life and guilt. Here Heimpel notes gloomily that "all fear that can ever be . . . was already once found on Munich's streets, all unity and all forgiveness. All guilt as well was already anticipated at the age of seventeen, all departures, for guilt sits in departures, every locomotive throws an accusation at us."[157]

The evidence for reading this memory-text's movement from a childhood idyll to the theme of guilt as Heimpel's self-commentary on the Third Reich is not to be found in the text's conditions of origin alone, or, say, in the context-free, hence striking, evocation of an accusatory locomotive, pointing us toward deportation trains to death camps. More decisive support for this reading is offered by an unpublished final four-page chapter in which Heimpel offers an eyewitness description of Hitler's 1923 putsch in Munich; these pages would only be published, separately, over a decade later—they would not even be incorporated into new editions of *Die halbe Violine*.[158] Under the title "Traum im November" (Dream in November), Heimpel here imagines an extraordinary scenario fusing real history with apocalyptic vision, information about himself, and unconvincing justification. Although absent from his memoir, only this half-parodistic, half-apocalyptic narrative within the radius of 9 November 1923 shapes it into a satisfactory whole. As Heimpel here presents things, neither place nor time retain the "innocence" of a child's paradise: Munich emerges as the location of the first Nazi arrival on stage; in retrospect 9 November bears the double significance of the putsch in 1923 and the November pogrom of 1938. Heimpel at this point describes the insecurity of a twenty-two-year-old student whose capacity for judgment has no chance against the weight of political beer-hall rhetoric:

> Erhard sat over his beer mug feeling the respect he was accustomed to when facing the deliberations of knowledgeable men, of officials. He was full of goodwill and made an effort. Maybe today the political quality would emerge that he was bound to by his studies, the political sense they're always demanding now, doubtless properly. Correct. This too correct now. And again: correct. Maybe it's all correct? The speaker only makes statements he's thought about carefully. But maybe much is correct and the whole thing false.

But such qualms are defeated by his own efforts at impartiality:

> Much indeed seemed doubtful—but what is doubting behind a beer mug against conviction behind a lectern? You educate yourself—and Erhard educates himself constantly—to listen: become absorbed in the lecture, follow words and reasons. The meaning will be understood only by those prepared to believe: critique before interpretation is bad craftsmanship; the inverse is correct—you learn as much through your documents and chroniclers.

It is, in fact, the academic discipline of history that seems to rob the narrator of judgment in listening to Kahr, Ludendorff, and Hitler ("the new man wearing the confirmation boy's outfit"):

> [As with] the question of dating . . . reasons and counter-reasons appear. . . . But perhaps it is already sufficient to try to heal history [*Geschichte*] with this conciliatory common sense: such luck refining history [*Geschichte*] into *Historie*. [This is apparently Heimpel's citation—its terms in any case erroneously inverted—of Heidegger's distinction between authentic temporality, *Geschichte*, and inauthentic or natural time, *Historie*.] Perhaps that

suffices; perhaps it is more than a simple conclusion. . . . But we must not be content with this. History [*Geschichte*] is necessary, interpretation and critique. Pay attention and apply that. Oh how laboriously it is all connected. First date, then evaluate. First understand, then judge. Medieval and modern history. And then when you came that far and saw the connections, action would finally follow. Oh how long is this road—is there one that is shorter?

At this point Heimpel, who in 1933 took the "shorter road," has his alter ego Erhard face flags, "wild gestures," and torches in a dream. He stands in the university library's reading room under the inscription *favete linguis*, and sees his Jewish colleague and friend from his Freiburg student period, Arnold Berney, together with his teacher and model, Siegmund Hellmann, appear in a slowly beginning conflagration that swallows up the library's historical works: "Oh God, November isn't yet finished." Everything is destroyed in the midst of clouds of smoke and showers of sparks, "fire-wind" and roaring noise: "The library gyrates. . . . Here's icy air, no roof. Rainwater has settled beneath the rusty balcony. . . . Then comes silence. *Favete linguis*." At the end of Heimpel's disturbing dream-vision—as strong in its own way as Elias Canetti's in *Auto-da-Fé*—we have the sentence: "A time is probably coming in which not being dead is a reproach."

As a medievalist, Heimpel was naturally familiar with the motif of a burning library as the symbol of the end of the world. But in the cited sentence and the scene of which it is a part, if we wish to really move past the level of simple lip service to a moral catastrophe onto the level of Heimpel's approach to *Vergangenheitsbewältigung*, we must take account of an important and quite transparent intertextual dimension. We are perhaps pointed there more directly in a sentence from another of the historian's texts, concerning "thoughts on the self-stocktaking of the Germans," published in 1954: "Memories leap above the backwater of history like cold fire and jump upon people: at one time friendly, then frightening, often awaking shame."[159] Hovering in this sentence, in the question of shame and guilt inscribed in the images of the library in flames and the return of murdered Jewish colleagues, are Augustine's "confessional recollections." In the tenth book of the *Confessions*, Augustine interrupts his self-accusation to inquire into the sense and purpose of his text—the point where he lays out his much-cited theory of memory. Central to this theory is what Harald Weinrich has described as an "asymmetry between human forgetting and divine remembrance."[160] Already for Augustine, "remembrance" refers to the present, takes in "personal self-assessment," a linkage presented by Augustine as a kind of "homecoming." This basic idea joins the realms of "guilt" and "forgiveness"

in that human beings' falling away from God is manifest as guilt through forgetting, while divine forgiveness of human sin is apparent not as its forgetting
but as a recollection of the sinner. If God is invisible, but what is most inward in
a human being, thoughts and memory, remain accessible to him through the
grace of forgiveness, then he can be sought out there: "Not with the voice's
sounds, but only with the soul's words and in the outcry of thoughts."[161] This
path of Augustine—followed, it seems, by Heimpel in his own way—is a return
to God, forgivingly rewarded the sinner by forgetting, since God always recalls
the one who has sinned.

Unwritten Books:
On "Knowledge and Its Ascesis"

The guilt question permeating Heimpel's images of his academic vocation's
destruction, an event unfolding in view of returned former Jewish friends and
teachers, was a way to reflect on recent history in its totality. The historian put
it as follows in a 1962 interview with Wolfgang Berkefeld: "Now the murder of
thousands upon thousands belongs to our history."[162] Reflecting of Heimpel's
struggle to come to terms with that fact, his historiography and a private
"working through of the past" were joined in what he termed "knowledge and
its ascesis": a citation, as it happens, of Jakob Burckhardt's "last word" as a
historian.[163] Outwardly, both the knowledge and the ascesis were presented as
an attempt to newly conceive German history. In the final sentence of his interview, Berkefeld expressed the plausible opinion that such a general history,
anticipated for years, would emerge in the course of a continuation of the
memoirs (planned under the title "Die zweite Violine"). In both projects, as a
historian both of himself and of twentieth-century Germany, Heimpel would
have had to treat the Weimar Republic, the rise of the Nazis, "racially" grounded
antisemitism, Hitler's war, and the annihilation of European Jewry as official
history and autobiography, research *and* memory. He would, in other words,
have had to insert the authority of the specialist into his autobiography's second
volume and the authenticity of the eyewitness into a *German history*. He abandoned both projects.

   In 1997, on the basis of Heimpel's lecture manuscripts, Ernst Schulin
demonstrated the close connection between Heimpel's intentions and the
failure to realize them. On the one hand, Heimpel was certain—particularly as
a medievalist—that "German history, even the history of National Socialism,"
could not be written "as a history of the devil." All history of human evil, he
believed, stood under the question of how evil made itself useful to good. But
on the other hand he grappled with the question of "the meaning of a German

history to which Auschwitz and Belsen now belong to the same extent and as irrevocably as the history of Aachen and Wittenberg." Here as well, "knowledge and its ascesis" emerged victorious: the relevant lecture remained unpublished.[164] But his audience heard a historian wrestling with tears and a failing voice as he spoke from his lectern tersely and tonelessly about the war, the Final Solution, and the collapse.[165] Schulin offered an apt assessment: "For listeners like myself, although the lecture would remain in memory, already at the end of the sixties I was thinking: how historical [*historisch*] would a book by Heimpel on German history now seem, if it existed; how outdated, how typical of the fifties!"[166]

Heimpel's concluding response to his question about "Auschwitz and Belsen" was that while history sometimes spared the guilty and not the guiltless,

> the sun, which shines on the just and the unjust at once, does not illuminate the dead. This is the first meaning of German history and all history: consideration of the living, those who got off undeservedly but also simply those still not dead, for the dead who could still be living as rightfully as ourselves: they are owed no self-accusation or humiliation of the German people but a spiritual overcoming of German history. The meaning of history amounts to something simple: . . . It lies in the current passing from the history of what has happened to the history of what is happening. . . . The present is the realm of freedom [*Reich der Freiheit*], namely, the space for a form of action that is saturated for us with responsible memory— with memory of German history.[167]

The mnemonic theory of "responsible memory," the critique of a present lacking history, the guilt-centered historical theory, and the explicit historiographical turn to "overcoming the past" were articulated by Heimpel, a reader of Maurice Halbwachs,[168] not only autobiographically but also in methodological texts, as a "question of meaning" (summarized as "history after 1945? Why 1933?").[169] This led to the conception of a "mnemonic theory" involving a reflection over the relation between memory and forgetting, introducing the effort to understand and explicate the distance from the Nazi past: "Historical scholarship [*Geschichtswissenschaft*] is the scientifically disciplined conscience of human beings."[170] Key concepts for understanding both "memory" and "forgetfulness" were, alongside acceleration (the "too much" of history), above all "guilt" and "conscience": those life-retaining forces available for the present emerged from the "capacity" and "inclination" to forget. Heimpel thus opened a speech given in 1959 for the state of Lower Saxony as follows:

Let us begin with one observation: our memory is growing weaker; we are inclined toward forgetfulness; we live in nothing less than a condition of paralysis of memory. Forgetfulness is the price human beings pay for having subdued the earth. Forgetfulness comes from speed [*Geschwindig-keit*]. But not only speed makes us forgetful. Rather, we also forget history because we have experienced and have to experience all too much history. For the sake of survival, human beings are inclined and have the capacity to forget. And especially the guilty—we guilty—do not like to think back. That is a barrier between us and the past—the guilt barrier that our fore-fathers did not know. . . . Pathos and simple sympathy have been lost: through speed and guilt.[171]

With "speed," *Geschwindigkeit*, Heimpel basically meant what Carl Schmitt meant with "acceleration," *Beschleunigung*: modernization. His reflections in this text reveal a completely unreformed resentment—coached in the standard rhetoric of its tradition—regarding putatively dissolutive aspects of modern-ization such as consumption and commercialization, urbanization and indus-trialization, demands for social-economic equality, and nontraditional morals. In any event, more central in our context is his idea of a "guilt barrier," which as a barrier between the past and the present makes clear that the "past" Heimpel is referring to is not the Nazi past, a reality that is signified with the image of the barrier itself.

That reality is defined as doubly problematic. On the one hand, it is tied to the theme of "guilt," hence to the very heart of postwar German discourse. On the other hand, within it the relation to the general past is an altered one, with Heimpel, as a medievalist, bringing a closely related question into play: whether every look at the past must be passed through the needle's eye of the horrific re-cent events. A "naive approach" to history, he insisted, was no longer possible— neither outside scholarship nor, especially, within it. Indeed, such scholarship played a direct role in a "natural relationship with history" having become more difficult if not impossible.[172] "The unparalleled present," he continued, "pushes the past back further for our generation than for earlier generations, makes the past fully past. The unparalleled present makes the past uniform, in a way removes its temporal organization; it creates those simplifications [*jene Simplifikationen, jene Vereinfachung*] . . . of history that are almost an annulment of history for the feeling of those who are living."[173] How was historical scholar-ship meant to react to this? How was "historicism" to be newly understood after its end? That scholarship, Heimpel argued, fulfilled its task "when it over-comes [*bewältigt*] time as present in regulative thinking [*ordnendes Denken*]," that is, when it became more "historistic" (rather than less historical), understanding itself as the "memory of human beings."[174] Having thus used the "overcoming" concept to define the task of a conservatively understood historiography, Heimpel continued with a series of related, quasi-Heideggerian observations:

> History [*Geschichte*] as science, *Historie*, does not alter the world. It is the memory [*Gedächtnis*] of human beings. . . . To have memory is more than drawing lessons from history. To have memory is something inherently human. In this way history is a portion of humanity. Memory [*Erinnerung*] of past times already gives individuals their actual depth, their actual human nature: historical memory [*das historische Gedächtnis*] extends human life beyond its physical lifespan. Memory is tradition but not, to be sure, unconscious tradition like that of old estate society; rather it is conscious tradition, not prejudicial prejudgment [*Vor-Urteil*] but judgment [*Urteil*]; tradition is thus not bonds but freedom: the freedom to step out of the accidental contemporaneity [*Zeitgenossenschaft*] of those living with us into the contemporaneity of the past.[175]

This exposition of the tasks of contemporary German history following the German catastrophe culminates in the sentence "history is an overcoming of the past." It is important to keep in mind here that at the time the present associational matrix of the *Bewältigung* concept did not exist—indeed, as suggested Heimpel was the most important protagonist of the concept's establishment in historical-political discourse. But we must not overlook the fact of the particular accent Heimpel was placing on it: "overcoming the past" means precisely *not* a preoccupation with the Nazi period; rather, it is meant to suggest that historiography can offer, as he put it, "freedom from history"—that it can bring about reconciliation and a purging of the burdens of conscience:

> To the denoted task of historical scholarship, overcoming time as present in regulative thinking, we could add a second duty: freeing human beings from their dark contingencies, from resentment and taboo, from the law of pressure and counter-pressure, from action and reaction, from partiality, rage, and an unpurged conscience: History is an overcoming of the past. Historical scholarship offers freedom from history [*Geschichtswissenschaft verleiht Freiheit von der Geschichte*]. History would thus be not only the life-extending but also the reconciliatory memory of the human being.[176]

This anthropologically derived function of historiographical labor, Heimpel concluded, would be hard to legitimate with traditional standards of objectivity.

It was thus only logical for Heimpel to here essay a redefinition of "objectivity," which was now marked off from mere "correctness," *Richtigkeit*, as part of a plea for the historicity—the term understood in Heimpel's particular sense—of memory that sounds eminently modern: "Historical objectivity [*historische Objektivität*] is the striving to grasp the alien partner of one's own history [*der eigenen Geschichte*] not as an object but as a subject." What was at stake, Heimpel insisted, was understanding "historical objectivity not *for* history but *from* history": an approach pointed to "from the experience and complicity of one's own time."[177] He offered the Germans and the Poles as his example, "a rapprochement in a struggle with oneself, with the other, about the others." At this point Heimpel referred to the thousands of pages of documentary volumes kept at the German Federal Ministry for Expellees, through which professional historians had constructed "a memento of German suffering, memory of the expellees, warning to those who were spared":

> But this German consideration of the matter does not suffice. Whoever reads these documents also reads them with an awareness that injustice and atrocity, inflicted on Germans, are not only actions [*Aktionen*] but also reactions to campaigns of expulsion [*Vertreibungsaktionen*] that are our burden. The necessary balance will be produced by the planned documentary volume placing the expulsion of the Germans in its European framework; until its appearance consulting the just-published, calmly written book by Alexander Dallin . . . suffices.[178]

The supplementary volume Heimpel referred to here never saw print; the book by Dallin, which can be considered the first historical study of the German war of extermination in the East, received scant attention in Germany at the time.[179] In any event, Heimpel was one of the few public figures to offer a critique, however carefully expressed, of the project on the German expellees, one of West Germany's most ambitious postwar historical projects; and he arrived at this critique by reflecting on the function and functioning of memory, through both insight into the plurality of "memories" and a recognition that "a new present" shone "new light on the past."[180]

At play here was a mix of fundamental reflection that Heimpel tried to articulate as a German,[181] methodological innovation he was calling for as a professional historian, and, as a private person, a feeling of shame that he allowed to show through. In this text as well, "naive consideration of history" had to be faced up to since "what is human is no longer self-explanatory."[182] An "experience of one's own inhumanity,"[183] indicated Heimpel, was grounds enough to confirm an "anthropological turn in history": "The historian is referred more

strongly than earlier to the express question of what a human being is. He looks
for the answer by asking what a human being was," and this not only in the
sense of either universal history or prehistory but with a conscious view of recent events: "Should we forget our own experience and in this way not transmit
it? Should we take our own experience with human beings to the grave instead
of attempting to use that experience to understand the past?"[184]

Manifest in such questions and formulations, Heimpel's efforts to avoid
separating memory from history were what gave him a special role in the context of German historiography of the 1950s. The "unparalleled" nature of the
times, he wrote,

> demands that we think historically [historisch]. The inclination of modern
> society to forget the past prompts historical scholarship to be the memory
> of this society. The weakening of a natural relationship to the past must
> summon us to generate this tie through reflection. . . . Nietzsche's position
> has been reversed. Nietzsche saw his age suffer from an excess of past re-
> called by scholarship and demanded productive forgetting. Our age risks
> suffering from a lack of remembered past. . . . Only knowledge about the
> horrors of the past will allow us to look directly at future horror, in order to
> hold it at bay.[185]

For Heimpel, "historical consciousness" was thus the same as "historical
self-consciousness"—the reason for the compulsion to offer an autobiographical reckoning. But it was also one reason for Heimpel's adherence to the
academic-political conservatism of his time. Despite all revision and innovation,
it was essential for him not to neglect the traditional themes of scholarship,
since like all other scholarship, history lives in two realms. It is simultaneously
open to the world and unworldly, lives from ongoing events but just as much so
from continuity: the continuity of one's own past and that of research. Undis-
turbed by the dictate of one or another present, this research is repeatedly referred to the simple, calm, and lengthy clarification of objective connections and
causal questions.[186]

Heimpel moved to his speech's end with the following plea: "Let us never
abandon continuity. History, inflamed by demands of the present, is nonetheless
also in turn a calming of this present; it is human memory that not only recog-
nizes and understands but also reconciles."[187] Hence by grasping reality historically, the historian serves the present: "We answer our opening question, whether
historical scholarship does justice to the demands of the time, with a distinct
yes. But we bring to mind: not only is the past in debt to the present, but the

present also has a duty regarding the past, the task of memory, presided over by the historian. Memory renders human beings human; in this sense history and historical scholarship are elements of being human."[188]

Against "Emotions from Göttingen"

Discourse about "overcoming the past" was a conservative invention of the 1950s stamped above all by its defensive character. But this mildness had its reasons: not the confrontation with the "past" but the "arrival of the present" was meant to alter the writing of history. In this respect, while in this chapter the "Protestant penitence" of a group of postwar German historians has been scrutinized in terms of its accomplishments, innovation, and function, that penitence also had possibilities of semantic twisting, trivialization, and the sublimation of self-justificatory strategies at its disposal. Remorse, repentance, and shame could thus grow from a need for reconciliation, become over-whelming, and culminate in a "parallelizing" stance or sentiment, to the effect that mutual recriminations were *really* to be avoided. When in 1958, in a conver-sation with a businessman in southern Germany, Auschwitz survivor Jean Améry heard a "confession" that the German *Volk* no longer bore a grudge against the Jews, he began to understand that this sort of aggressive reconciliatory scenario could be faced only with his own resentment and its explication.[189] The differ-ence between the desire for autobiographical confession and a refusal in the same period to offer personal information officially and when asked may seem a contradiction but is in fact an essential part of this discursive structure. The above-noted Tübingen theologian Helmut Thielicke, a thorn in the eye of the occupying authorities in his fanatic opposition to denazification,[190] encapsu-lated the mentality of this dimension of "Protestant penitence" in straightaway rejecting the Allied questionnaire procedure from a sense of national honor — and on grounds grotesquely distorting political proportionality: the question-naires, he explained, "were based on a collective condemnation that could only be avoided through complicated and degrading acts of self-justification. Count-less innocent people were locked up for years without court decision, indeed without even suspecting the reason for their arrest." But as was the case with the approach taken by Heimpel, Wittram, and Ernst, Thielicke's stance actually had biographical-theological sources: "In this manner all moral appeals and all attempts at 'reeducation' were inherently implausible, and I saw with deepest horror how unknowingly and against what was desired the poisonous seed of a new nationalism was being sown and how it had already begun to sprout in many hearts during the time in the camps [*die Lagerzeit*] — in hearts nevertheless ready to bow before the rod of divine punishment."[191] Following Thielicke's logic, nationalism and obduracy were manifest *results* of reeducation, not the reverse. "Hearts . . . ready to bow before the rod of divine punishment" were not to be burdened with superficial and annoying questions such as whom a person had voted for in the thirties and whether a person had been a party member. This defiance was an answer to the contempt quite often confronting the confessing and atoning historians. For example, the theoretical-reflective work of Heimpel and Wittram, together with that of Heuss, published in short intervals throughout the 1950s, would be bitingly denigrated by Theodor Schieder as "seething emotions from Göttingen" (*Göttinger Wallungen*).[192] This corresponded fully to the "heroism of silence" regularly cultivated in certain circles. In this respect, for right-wing intellectuals in postwar Germany, the name "Eugen Kogon" stood for everything they rejected. In November 1949, Rudolf Diels thus wrote to Carl Schmitt of the "rémoulade of remorse, atonement, impotence, and self-mutilation" into which Schmitt might well "toss some stone-hard formulations," so that "the saltless broth of the Kogons [splashes] into their eyes."[193]

The borders extending to the extreme right spectrum were in fact flowing, the theologically framed defiance of historians such as Heimpel and Wittram stubborn and, along with self-pity, widespread. Nevertheless, the differences at work here were more meaningful than points of contact. Not least of all because of greater knowledge we now have about Schieder's role in the Third Reich,[194] clarity in one respect is important: despite its one-sidedness, described here, and in face of the "laboratories of self-assertion" of which Dirk von Laak has spoken in reference to right-wing intellectual circles,[195] the "public display of remorse" so often denounced on the right was a necessary first step on the path to openly addressing the Nazi genocide.

4

"How Difficult It Is
Not to Write Powerfully
about Auschwitz!"

*The Early Years of Munich's Institute
for Contemporary History*

Controversies about the Early History of the IfZ

In 1999, on the occasion of its fiftieth anniversary, the Institut für Zeitge-schichte published a festschrift describing both its own founding and the develop-ment of research in contemporary German history in postwar West Germany.[1] In the festschrift, we find references to the difficulties emerging in the early postwar phase of both the discipline and the institution. But first and foremost, we find a sustained argument that from the start, West German historians in general and the institute in particular showed a commitment to research on "Auschwitz." That the theme was suppressed was, we are informed, simply an often repeated "fable" (*Mär*); that "nonsensical assertion," IfZ director Horst Möller asserts in his look backward, needs to be "refuted."[2] Hence instead of exploring the difficulties confronting German historians after the Third Reich's collapse, Möller praises "the institute's planning at the time and its detailed dis-cussions in the board meetings."[3] Already in 1951, Möller explains in reference to files from the early 1950s, the fate of the Jews was inscribed in the institute's research plans. Both a "chronology of persecution of the Jews with exemplary documentation" and "accounts of Jewish humanity" are to be found as plans in the files; hence he sees both as confirming his thesis.[4]

But this conception of how things stood must not only be balanced by far more critical assessments, for example, by Sebastian Conrad's sharply negative account.[5] Rather, it is also contradicted by the same documentation that Möller cites from the early phase of the IfZ. Conrad mainly focuses on the idea of a "German perspective" aimed at foreign "ignorance" he sees at work in key texts by authors of the time. He speaks of German contemporary history of the 1950s becoming an "island" after the Germans, forced to concern themselves with the catastrophe of the immediate past, delegated the task to a non-university research institute in order to have, so to speak, nothing more to do with it. But the material in the institute's own archives reveals a far more skeptical awareness of the possibilities and limits of one's own research than what is suggested in the 1999 institute festschrift. For example, in 1952 the institute's first director, Hermann Mau, showed more thoughtfulness in indicating that he and his colleagues were aware they would not be able to fulfill their role without stronger general participation by German historians and the universities, and that the IfZ had to be protected from a false impression it could "spiritually [*geistig*] overcome the National Socialist past alone and, so to speak, representing German scholarship."[6] Such a differentiated view of the context of one's own work indicates that already at the time of the institute's founding, the possibility of actually carrying out all the tasks that were its raison d'être could be easily overestimated. In 1947, we thus already find Bavarian minister of state Anton Pfeffer suggesting seven research sectors and twenty rooms for archives and the library.[7] But there is no reason to retrospectively duplicate such overestimation—this time with an apparent sense that the Munich historians not only had an exaggerated task but in fact fulfilled it with total success. The documents presented by Möller in no way show "how it really was"; the two plans were never published. Beyond this, and of basic importance, to cite an "account of Jewish humanity" without indicating whether this in fact had anything whatsoever to do with the genocide of the Jews is in itself highly problematic.

Let us now consider the approach to the genocide really taken by the IfZ in its early days, using the institute's own archival material, to the extent it allows a reconstruction of decisions taken at the time. What I wish to do here is focus on forms of presentation and their scope and limits, not to essay a purely quantitative look at the problem, for instance, one that counts bibliographical entries since the 1950s and displays the number of copies of *The Diary of Anne Frank* sold in West Germany until 1981 to generally refute the thesis of postwar repression of memory—as, quite astonishingly, does Möller.[8] A failure to examine both the problems guiding the period's research and its prevailing cognitive interests cannot do justice to the ambivalence inherent in the relationship between research and memory at the early IfZ. At the same time, the following discussion will take due account of the fact that in their historiographical practice, those at the institute began as an "outsiders' guild,"[9] a practice forming a contrast to the contemporary German history being generally written within the universities.

The Early IfZ Confronts Legitimation Pressure

In 1955, Paul Kluke, the second director of the IfZ, wrote as follows concerning its program:

> We certainly do not wish to champion the thesis of a German collective guilt in a juridically palpable way or gauge this guilt before an international tribunal in a precise dosage of evidence and punishment. But twelve years' worth of deeds remain, terror and homicide, cold-blooded murders according to the roster declared lawful by the minister appointed guardian of the law, the industrial annihilation of millions of innocent people, and contemporary history itself has to concern itself with these deeds. In doing so it shakes off the reproach of dirtying is own nest. That has occurred through the deed itself, not through the conduct's retrospective explication.[10]

Such comments now sound superfluous, since there is no longer any question about whether and on what basis historians should concern themselves with Nazi annihilatory policies. But along the path of the slow reestablishing of contemporary history as a discipline in West Germany of the 1950s, the Nazi mass crimes represented the greatest obstacle for establishing an institute that had to steadily worry about both its political recognition and financing: its money was granted year by year by a board that had representatives from both the federal government and the various West German states. Hence the historians saw themselves facing constant mistrust and a need to overcome the reproach of "dirtying" the integrity of the nation. Kluke's reference to a precarious relationship between "the deed itself" (*die Tat selbst*) and "the conduct's retrospective explication" (*eine nachträgliche Erörterung des Tuns*) reflects a knowledge of such difficulties, resulting from the political and financial dependency of one's own work and a general "defensive mentality" of the postwar West German public.

In this context the claim to pursuing "meticulous objective scholarship" could have downright threatening undertones. For a long time, reported the *Stuttgarter Zeitung* in 1950, "differences of opinion have broken out over the question of whether objective research is endangered when individuals who have been politically persecuted too strongly and do not have a specialized background are brought in for the work."[11] Naturally, the author added, a "camp specialist" was needed here, but in general it was understood "that recent German history" could not "so to speak be assessed with denazification-court standards."[12] Even in the press's reflections on the matter, the dilemma was clear. It was in the end politically inopportune to neglect the concentration-camp theme, but on grounds of scientific objectivity, the voices of those who had been "politically persecuted too strongly" had to be kept from dominating. For those voices would simply impose the standards of denazification on recent German history—this the mistrust articulated in the newspaper piece. In their public expression, such expectations regarding the future IfZ make clear the historical-political balancing act that would be needed to get the institute under way.

In his retrospective look at the IfZ's beginnings, Hans-Dietrich Loock, for some years a researcher at the institute, may well have expressed the situation most pointedly at the start of the 1970s: "Auschwitz offers the strongest resistance to contemporary history's emergence."[13] How is this resistance, identified by Loock at twenty-five years' distance with a view to the institute's beginnings, itself to be understood? What findings take center stage if we make our starting point the skepticism accompanying the IfZ's twenty-fifth anniversary rather than the uncritical evaluation accompanying its fiftieth? Can we find a more empirical basis for describing the problem than diverging perspectives of those immediately involved, on the one hand, their institutional heirs, on the other? Was there indeed serious descriptive and theoretical work on the Holocaust at the IfZ in its early phase, and if so on what documentary basis, in terms of which problems, and in what form?

A Policy for the Past: Sobriety and Distance

Contemporary history is inherently codetermined by those experiencing it: this is Lutz Niethammer's observation,[14] reflecting a wish to integrate rather than exclude the interpretive battles played out on the field of that history, which Niethammer defines in terms of a "slow and approximative" process "from the outside to the inside, which piece by piece, and in a rarely completely attainable way," divests the "protective secrecy granted authority" of both its "public self-presentation and legitimation," or at least, Niethammer adds, "subjects it to scrutiny."[15] Contemporary history has these qualities, he argues, even when it stakes an explicit claim to objectivity. At the IfZ, the ideal of "objectivity" and evocation of "distance" formed a paradoxical starting point for historical work whose approach was meant to be demonstrated through use of the most prevalent form of scholarly speech-regulation available. Scholars of the older generation formulated critiques of this stance reflecting different forms of labor of memory; Hermann Heimpel thus underscored, as we have seen, the need for a new assessment of German history born "from the upheaval," while for instance Karl Otmar von Aretin argued that it was "nonsensical" "to try to describe the most recent past purely positivistically and without valuation," that the truth of that past could not be generated "solely from a chemically purified alignment of facts."[16] It is telling that in the founding years of the IfZ, when a research program had still not crystallized, it was eighty-year-old Walter Goetz (1867–1958) who emphasized, in pedagogical diction in a memoir, that the time of the Third Reich had "to be thoroughly researched so that the nation knows how it reacted in the twelve years of National Socialist rule," and above all that the nation bore "a certain guilt for this deepest descent of German history."[17]

But such memoirs hardly conveyed the scholarly ideal of the IfZ—quite to the contrary. In Munich the interest was in research not on "guilt" but on "causes," not self-enlightenment concerning the "deepest descent of German history" but knowledge of the structure and course of the Nazi system. Distancing itself from a form of reasoning aimed at general conclusion, the historiographical discourse over Nazism and German history between 1933 and 1945 "scientificized" itself at the institute, with the emergence of a new set of evaluative criteria. The Archimedean point of interpretation was no longer the proud heights of German history *before* Hitler but information from documentary sources culled in view of objectivity. Because of the dignity, inherent in scholarship, which this guideline possessed, and because of its general self-evidence, it has been scrutinized far too seldom, although the concept of objectivity is not infrequently appropriated by those simply wishing to marginalize other perspectives on an issue. In this respect, Hans Günter Hockerts has suggested that "the concept of objectivity be removed from circulation" whenever it creates an impression that "contemporary history can leap out of the stream of time and observe and judge it from a firm, that is precisely 'objective' bank."[18] In the context of the early IfZ, we thus find Theodor Eschenburg, alongside his Tübingen colleague Hans Rothfels the guiding spirit at the *Vierteljahrshefte für Zeitgeschichte*, founded at the institute in the 1950s and presently still the most important German journal of modern history,[19] praising Konrad Heiden's history of National Socialism,[20] written *before* the author's flight from Nazi Germany, because he was here "forced to take distance," hence to treat, with "great objectivity," the "positive side of National Socialism," the "inadequacies of Weimar democracy and its parties," and the relationship between Nazism and

Bolshevism.[21] (Notably, these formulations appear in a book by Eschenberg treating the "tasks of contemporary history," hence historical method, and staking its own claim to scholarly objectivity. But works with such arguments were in fact legion.[22]) For Eschenburg, Heiden's works on the Third Reich written after his flight lack "the impartiality" found praiseworthy in the earlier book: "Abroad there are forces standing all too greatly under the influence of memory of the recent past, while many Germans would like to see the period simply extinguished. Conflicts emerge from this overvaluation and undervaluation, because both those clinging to memory and those tossing it aside cannot achieve a distanced consideration and judgment of the lived past."[23] In its words on "overvaluation," this statement contains what might be considered the new research institute's basic principle regarding the past in the 1950s and early 1960s—a principle opening up criticism of above all works emerging outside Germany, very often by emigrants, many of them German Jewish. Although the core of the early IfZ's stated method involved an evocation, questioned by no one, of objectivity and distance, frequently this meant nothing more than, precisely, the non-questionability of one's *own* temporal and geographical proximity to what was being analyzed, with the plausibility and coherence of one's own experiential perspective being the decisive factor.[24] This standpoint contains a contradiction displayed in numerous similar texts from this period, all expressing an effort to define contemporary history according to the idea of a historical scholarship that was "sober, upright, close to reality."[25] On the one hand, there were references to the significance of a contemporary status allowing recognition of possible connections and an avoidance of an "isolating consideration" of individual events—the tendency of many born after the events. On the other hand, there was considerable investment, itself stamped by pathos, in demarcating "distance," "objectivity," and a "sober viewing and judging" from an "emotional," "emotion-laden" history "with its irredeemably confusing effects."[26] Contemporary history was to be written "really out of one's own experience and at the same time with distance."[27]

"Laocoöns in a Struggle with Rolls of Microfilm"

The problems inherent in various statements emerging from the early IfZ cannot really be understood without juxtaposing its official and nonofficial approaches to memory. For although this center of empirical research also had a duty to convey its work to and help educate the postwar German public, its ethos was research, not *Vergangenheitsbewältigung*, "overcoming the past." From the start, the term was what Hermann Graml has described as a mocked "nonword," *Unwort*,[28] at the IfZ. In a letter to H. G. Adler, Hans Buchheim made jokes about the term, noting, "At my desk, I am trying to process [or: come to terms with (*aufarbeiten*)] the 'nonprocessed past' [*die unaufgearbeitete Vergangenheit*—another expression so common in postwar West Germany that it had become a cliché]."[29] Nevertheless, regardless of the mockery that the term *Vergangenheitsbewältigung* incurred, Hans-Dietrich Loock, for instance, recalled those at the IfZ allowing themselves to be "elevated" by it,[30] thus pointing to its key conceptual role in the institute's late 1950s West German boom, in particular after it called attention to a plague of swastika scrawling afflicting the country. Hence while there was determined resistance to the pathos and rhetoric of a "complicity of everyone in general guilt," researchers remained in that radius, both as personalities with their own memories of the past and in the context of one's own present with its themes, questions, and answers. (We can here compare the concept of a "third way" that Hermann Mau felt the institute needed to follow, complicity here being confirmed and argued against at once.)

In this way, what emerged was not only demarcation but also affiliation, with various argumentative models taken over seamlessly from the available historiographical tradition. This situation notwithstanding, in 1962 in his biography of Goebbels, Helmut Heiber, who himself constantly referred ostentatiously to the soberly objective criteria involved in research on contemporary history, could present the thesis that young Goebbels' interest in Latin demonstrated "the—strictly speaking—un-German, Romanic character of his being."[31] To be sure, "radical research on conscience" was rejected, but from our own perspective many arguments seem to have functioned as sedatives for both a collective German conscience and that of the individual researchers. They subscribed to a "faith in science,"[32] but quite often this simply involved a defense of national self-images using other means. There was a desire not so much to collect questions as to offer answers. But above all researchers were "first sent to the archives. . . . In our searching we encountered neither guilt nor development, but rather sources. We were suddenly no longer Atlases but rather small Laocoöns in a struggle with rolls of microfilm. But taming the documentary snakes—that was hard work. . . . The moral impetus became concrete: it was related to the proper processing of the documents."[33] As Loock's cultured analogy with the futile struggle by the Greek mythic figure Laocoön to overcome the snakes killing his sons suggests, the question of the standards for proper historical knowledge could only—in opposition to the approach of Heimpel and others—be answered through the "laborious business of historical research."[34] That was the reality and universal foundational consensus at the IfZ; writing in contemporary history "could not be produced in any other way."[35]

But this self-image rested on an ideal resulting from the fact that there was both a desire to avoid ongoing interpretive conflicts and a need to build, as suggested, on the primary reality of lived experience. What was propagated was the "coolest, most objectivized, scientific description of the events," from well-grounded mistrust of every form of postwar propaganda and mass journalism,[36] but despite all the "file fixation [*Aktenhuberei*]" they had found no distance, for the "destruction of the recent past involuntarily continued to affect us."[37] As young men, institute members had saluted the swastika "without resistance" (something Loock found disconcerting in his 1970s retrospect),[38] fought and been wounded, survived years as POWs. Both Buchheim and Thilo Vogelsang had been gravely wounded; Heinz Förster, the IfZ's first managing director, had fled from a Polish POW camp; and Helmut Heiber had spent years as a prisoner in Yugoslavia.[39] But, Loock indicated, "this half-understood continuity of everyday life did not concern us."[40] Or the researchers defined themselves as "indeed concerned [*betroffen*], but hardly burdened [*belastet*],"[41] enlightened people who held talks in schools of continuing education, teachers' associations, state offices for political education, and Protestant academies—"they all invited us, either individually or the entire lot . . . precisely 'coolly objectivizing' and 'scientific'"[42]:

> I still recall a conference of the Lower Saxon Landeszentral für Heimat-dienst [State Central Office for Service to the Homeland] in Spiekeroog. There was time between the talks and discussions. We walked along the beach and through the dunes, often together with course participants, who sometimes had followed our speakers with interest. . . . The old teachers spoke slowly, reflectively, even a bit shyly. One said—and we noticed it was meant to sound casual—"I was in the party." The others simply nodded. And then it came: the lifetime confession and the only half-pronounced request for absolution. There it was, the feeling of guilt, the desire for *metanoia*—and there it was: the belief in science. They confessed to us young whippersnappers, us ordinary soldiers [*Landsertypen*], because we were scholars, because we had studied the subject. . . . We did not condemn but gave out absolution. . . . We had taken on the presumptuous role of the popular educator and confessor. But did we have another way? We proceeded uncertainly, stumbled over ourselves, learned from every stumble, and learned from the old teachers that the past cannot be overcome. . . . Contemporary history emerged in this way as well.[43]

In this memoir, at the neurological point of postwar West German history, Loock tried to identify the historical locus of his own research. It was a time of "faith in objective scholarship," of the historian's "role" and the "misuse" of authorities and books, for instance of *The German Opposition to Hitler*, of which Hans Rothfels had "so magnificently reported to the Americans in 1948." "How we misused this book"—again Loock—"and its object. We merely stored facts [*thesauriert*]. On 20 July the safe was opened. And then the resistance was radiant, sweating morality. We stuck ever more resistors in the safe."[44]

Research Mission and Unofficial Memory

The IfZ's ambivalent and contradictory perception of the Nazi persecution and extermination of the Jews is also manifest in board discussions. Even a look at the new institution's christening points in that direction: in the late 1940s, hence before the founding meeting of the IfZ, its future name was still unclear; so was, completely, the course to be taken between research, on the one hand, and memory in the service of political guidance, on the other hand. As recorded in minutes of a preliminary meeting of the board at the end of May 1949, founding director Gerhard Kroll, for example, deemed the name chosen "at the time," Institut zur Erforschung des Nationalsozialismus (Institute for Research on National Socialism), to be "an unfortunate one. It would not be practical to establish a monument to National Socialism in this form"[45] (see Figure 7). He then suggested both the future name, Institut für Zeitgeschichte, and Institut für jüngste deutsche Geschichte (Institute for Recent German History), in the process underscoring both a scholarly-scientific refutation of "reports on National Socialism in the form of dime novels"[46] *and* an enlightening-educative mission. A month later, in a letter to the future institute's directorship, West German president Theodor Heuss indicated that he felt it would be "useful"—*zweckdienlich*—"to have the term National Socialism appear in the name. That certainly has a repellent and attractive quality at once." But perhaps, he suggested, "the National Socialist epoch" could replace "research on National Socialism," "because that way the effects are more strongly included." A few experiences, Heuss added, had shown that with retention of the term National Socialism it was easier to reach material in private hands than with the more general name, "through which only scholars feel themselves addressed."[47] But already in the founding meeting in September 1950, Kroll—at the time still director—pushed the board members to agree "that the institute be allowed to have (for telephone purposes) the subtitle 'Institute for Contemporary History.'"[48] The decision to use the alternative to the planned name took place in a few steps. In May 1952, the suggestion was made to conflate the two possibilities in reverse order, which is to say "Institute for Contemporary History (German Institute for the History of the National Socialist Period)," but with the comment: "It was decided that the present subtitle gradually be removed so that the institute's future official designation will be Institute for Contemporary History, Munich."[49]

Wolfgang Benz has described the conflict between "politically thinking officials" and the "scholars in the historical sciences" as not, in the end, a conflict between conservative or reactionary and progressive forces:

> The majority of the protagonists in both camps were conservative, but [those in] one camp had sat in concentration camps during the Nazi period, as had State Secretary Hermann Brill, or else had done forced labor, as had State Secretary Walter Strauß, while on the other side, that of the professors, too many had leaned toward the power-political goals of the regime. And one camp was interested in social enlightenment and a utilization of historical research, the other in defending its ivory tower.[50]

Against this backdrop, it is clear from the preliminary meetings of the future IfZ's board that in its planning stage, the goal of the institute was in fact by no means research alone, but rather a mix of enlightenment and rehabilitation. At that point, the future mission seemed clear: "This institute is not to have the task of writing a seamless history of National Socialism. . . . That history itself is a matter for the historians. But the institute has a publicistic task to fulfill."[51] At the beginning of 1949, Brill could even underscore the urgency of founding the institute by pointing to an "extraordinary" growth of antisemitism and public "indifference to and distaste for the Enlightenment."[52] And in the same meeting, among pressing potential projects and themes to be considered, "Hitler and Bayreuth" took first place, followed by "2 May 1933—takeover of the unions"; in third place was an examination of the finance ministry's files.[53] At the same time, there was a great desire for, in Hessian state secretary Brill's words, "an opportunity to be given German scholarship to rehabilitate itself before the international public, in order to regain the world's respect."[54] This strategy of German self-rescue through scholarship was also evident in the first year's choice of themes and projects. In the founding meeting of the "German Institute for the History of the National Socialist Period" on 11 September 1950, in which West German president Theodor Heuss participated, at the suggestion of none other than Eugen Kogon, agreement was reached "that at least one member of the board must be an acknowledged specialist in the German resistance,"[55] clearly a reference to Rothfels. There was also a proposal to establish six independent "units" (*Referate*), treating, respectively, the historical-political events, economic and social history, cultural history, military history, legal history, and finally, as another autonomous unit, the "German resistance movement."[56] In the same session, the following list of thematic proposals was meant to serve as a basis for a working plan: (1) "The work of the Scholl siblings"; (2) "the Reichstag fire"; (3) "Bayreuth and Hitler"; (4) "Moeller von der Bruck/*Tatkreis*"; (5) "the events of 30 June 1934"; (6) "Kristallnacht"; (7) "Documents on the preliminary history of 20 July 1944"; (8) "the Fritsch crisis of February 1938."[57] This meant, Hans Buchheim comments retrospectively,

> that everything not personally experienced or observed was absent from the research program. In the consciousness of contemporaries from our century's fifth and sixth decades, what presently clearly represents the horrific reality of the Hitler tyranny, indeed to an extent stands at the center of work on the National Socialist period, so that one's view of the multiple layers and complexity of the total phenomenon threatens to be distorted, lay in a gray zone—apparently also for members of the board, who had all been established opponents of National Socialism, in part also victims such as Hermann Brill and Eugen Kogon. Even when attention was turned toward the crimes against humanity, they were not present under the names of Auschwitz, Sobibor, Treblinka, Majdanek but rather merely under "Buchenwald" and "Dachau." Did these contemporaries know what happened when they feared it was so and hoped it was not?[58]

In short, the main emphasis lay on resistance, with the German perspective being manifest in the choice of themes, even the sixth one. A half year later, the expanded thematic plan was presented by Mau; the persecution and extermination of the Jews was now not even present. Instead we find "Hitler's time in Vienna and Munich"; "the sociology of the National Socialist Workers' Party before 1933"; "occupation policies and national resistance in the Balkans"; "the Brauchitsch and Halder circles"; "German industry and the rise of the National Socialist Workers' Party."[59] In this meeting, Gerhard Ritter initiated a wide-ranging discussion of the "German resistance," with due attention paid his own book in preparation on Goerdeler. That an awareness of the historical-political exclusionary function of the resistance theme was present is revealed in a remark by Brill, as noted in the minutes: "other themes" had to be dealt with

> whose importance was in no way secondary to those named, but for whose public treatment nothing had yet been done. On moral grounds, above all the victims among the Jews are to be thought of here. A description of this complex is easily realizable on the basis of documentary reports from the ghettos, e.g., from Smolensk and Vilna, each of which recorded the course of the events until shortly before the decease [*Ableben*] of the author.[60]

Ritter's Goerdeler book was published. A description of the events in the Smolensk and Vilna ghettos, described by Brill as "easily realizable," never appeared.

The Rejection of Reitlinger and Sontheimer

Looking back, the extent to which the themes of "resistance" and "persecution of the Jews" were mutually balanced in the early institute is very clear. Often one theme was presented simultaneously with the other or else in implicit argumentative delimitation. According to a decision of the board, the Bundeszentrale für Heimatdienst (Central Federal Office for Service to the Homeland) would be offered both themes at once;[61] in the board minutes, the strategy of "thematic balance"[62] appears downright aggressive. When it came to the Holocaust itself, however, a direct and concrete addressing of the theme was avoided. In 1954, a decision had to be reached about how to deal with a book by the British historian and man of letters Gerald Reitlinger, *The Final Solution*. This book in fact represented the first general account of that genocidal campaign. The argument *not* to translate it may seem astonishing; the argument certainly underscores the issue's explosiveness. The institute's main interest, it was pointed out, lay in its own project of a "general documentation of the Third Reich's policies toward the Jews [*Judenpolitik*]"; also cooperation with London's Wiener Library was being planned, and such a translation "would destroy this plan." Instead, Hans Rothfels declared himself ready "to undertake a review of Reitlinger in the form of a brief contribution [*Miszelle*] [in the *Vierteljahrshefte für Zeitgeschichte*]."[63] The *Miszelle* did not, however, appear. For many years in West Germany, Reitlinger's book would be considered not so much a contribution to history as "the most fearsome accusation leveled against the National Socialist state that has ever been written." De facto this praise was backhanded.[64]

Under the IfZ's new director, Paul Kluke, the line taken up to that point was somewhat corrected, although not fully abandoned. Kluke considered "treatment of the Jewish policies of the Third Reich" to be a "pressing" task, and he placed his hopes on "Dr. [Hans] Lamm, returning to Germany with a grant from New York."[65] On the list of future planned projects, we thus find *Kristallnacht* replaced in the mid-1950s by "antisemitism, racial legislation, and the so-called solution to the Jewish question"—and this even number 2 on the list.[66] In this modified research context, two things are nonetheless evident: first, that with the planned "publication [of work] on the destruction of German Jewry" (for example, in collaboration with the Wiener Library), a blocking out of the momentous Eastern European and general European dimension of the mass extermination persisted—together with an insistence that Nazism was to be studied "not only starting with its German premises, but also with those that were both European and global";[67] and second, that "less the political responsibilities than the human tragedy" would be the focus of the Holocaust's treatment, as explicitly stated in the board minutes.[68] Plans to determine historically precise figures regarding the extermination were recorded in January 1960 as follows: "Dr. Krausnick explained that the study had already begun and that the Federal Office of Statistics was ready to cooperate. The difficulty lies in the facts. Exact numbers will never be possible since the mass of gassed people was not registered. We will need to expect a possible difference of 1–2 million people. We might, however, be able to arrive at a minimum number; but this will not yet have refuted the figure of 6 million." In any event a precisely calculated minimum number would then be available that could "lead to a well-grounded estimation of the actual number of victims."[69]

In the second half of 1956, twenty-six thousand dollars arrived from the Rockefeller Foundation, intended to help fund two years of research "on National Socialist policies toward the Jews and on occupation policies during the Second World War."[70] In any case the minutes record an insistence that "at present it is not easy to find suitable researchers for this." The research was "not only to be expanded in the direction of *Judenpolitik* and occupation policy, as planned for the Rockefeller funds, but there should also be an effort to examine changes in the Third Reich's justice system and its economic and financial policies."[71]

In the mid-1950s, the Weimar Republic period was still part of the present of historians at the IfZ—part of their lived experience, for some of them the determining years for their education and career plans. In Freiburg, Kurt Sontheimer, then assistant to the political scientist Arnold Bergsträsser, was studying forms of antidemocratic thinking in Weimar Germany.[72] Kroll now openly tried to neutralize the anticipated objections to Sontheimer's research plans, emphasizing that the author was in no way denying the "political, economic, and constitutional burdens of the Weimar state," that he did not intend to render politics "into a literary-historical matter," and that he did not proceed according to authors but rather systematically, in order to avoid giving his description "for instance, a denunciatory character." Nevertheless, in the ensuing discussion the project was rejected because the theme was "not significant enough" "and it is more important to treat the social substrate upon which such ideas can develop. It was also pointed out that such a study could heroicize such scribblers and remove them from deserved oblivion."[73]

At the IfZ, then, there was a very conscious process of deciding what was to be remembered, what forgotten. In October 1960, when Hans Herzfeld's and Werner Conze's evaluations of Sontheimer's manuscript were ready—

Sontheimer had meanwhile succeeded in having it accepted as a habilitation thesis in Freiburg—the reservations in Munich again came to the fore: Conze criticized "a lack of a will to understand"; Rothfels opined that the author merited the reproach of being "somewhat 'too complacent'"; and Herzfeld observed that through an "omission of Weimar's left-wing opponents," the book's title was not justified, but the fact "that it had not sensitively followed every turn of the [period's] intellectual-political thought and intentions in his view simply represented a characteristic position of the younger generation of historians in general, a position that had to be recognized as such."[74] It was now decided that an additional evaluation would determine things. This came a year later, from Otto Heinrich von der Gablentz together with a fourth evaluation from Hans Kaufmann. As the institute's general secretary, Helmut Krausnick hoped for a compromise, but this turned out impossible. Above all Kaufmann's vehement rejection—in his view Sontheimer revealed an absence "of any capacity to scientifically analyze the material of his theme"—was decisive in denying "release of the manuscript" for institute publication, in face of von der Gablentz's milder "methodical" reservations "against, as it were, a free-ranging ideological history without consideration of the social and political preconditions."[75] (At the same time, Gablentz defended Sontheimer against Kaufmann by referring to his other publications.) For his part Herzfeld, although repeating his personal opinion that tolerance should be shown the younger historians' generation, now confirmed that the methodological objections "could not be resolved through revision."

This rejection by the institute board was accompanied by unanimous acceptance, as "especially valuable," of Thilo Vogelsang's completed manuscript on the Reichswehr (the Weimar-period German army), the state, and the Nazi Party (the reviewers were Herzfeld and Rothfels), on grounds of its "much more positive line regarding the Reichswehr and state." The motives and conceptions of Chancellor Kurt von Schleicher were, they indicated, much more extensively documented than previously, "so that it can be said that the definition of Schleicher as nothing more than a politician of intrigue and ambition has been convincingly refuted."[76] Hence at that time in the IfZ, a book looking relatively kindly on democracy's undertaker in the last days of Weimar was favored over Sontheimer's critical account.

On Problems in the Definition of *Zeitgeschichte*

In respect to both theory and empirical research, Hans Rothfels made a greater mark on postwar West German contemporary history—*Zeitgeschichte*—than any other historian.[77] He wrote, as we have seen, the pioneering book treating the German resistance; at the start of the 1960s, he was still in a position to forceful claim that on the basis of the previously mentioned work with the Wiener Library and its "material about the help offered Jews by Germans . . . the problem" could be illuminated "for once from this side as well."[78] But Rothfels' "elastically broadly conceived concept of *Zeitgeschichte*"[79] also garnered praise and was influential over many years. He defined the year 1917 as the great caesura, thus rendering the Russian Revolution and America's entry into the Great War as a focal point of his and his colleagues' historical theory. He hypostasized the German historians' professional interest in the "world civil war" of ideologies, the events in Germany between 1933 and 1945 here emerging as in effect a detail in a larger, more fundamental design—one excerpt from an age of upheavals and crises extending into the immediate present. And he called for making "the structural and essential elements [*das Strukturhafte und Wesenhafte*] of an epoch oriented in many respects toward totality"[80] into the historians' central research goal—and not, precisely, the history of the experience of individuals and groups. At first glance, we might see this experience as being addressed in Rothfels' much-cited dictum of *Zeitgeschichte* as taking in the "epoch of the *Mitlebende*"—those living together, in the present; but with his denigrating warning against "presentism," the dictum was basically no sooner pronounced than revoked. Likewise, in considering the statement we should keep in mind the warning—its gist often repeated subsequently—of Rothfels' student Werner Conze that Rothfels "brought his own bitter life experience into his work in *Zeitgeschichte*, objectivizing it in his methodologically and otherwise precedent-setting introduction to [the first volume of] the *Vierteljahrshefte für Zeitgeschichte*," Conze's reference here being to Rothfels' essay on "*Zeitgeschichte as a* calling." The statement is, in fact, the opposite of what was the case: Rothfels promoted themes he had *not* experienced; and as we have seen, he banished his own experience of antisemitism, expulsion, and emigration from what he considered legitimate scholarly discourse.

Even at that time, *Zeitgeschichte* could have a very different conceptual grounding—something clearly spelled out in the argumentation of Eva Reichmann, for whom the discipline involved at once a "political and moral calling." At the center of Reichmann's work, we thus find, as she puts it in her essay of 1964 on "*Zeitgeschichte* as a political and moral calling," "genocide, the intentional extermination of entire national groups, not caused through military action and using all of technology's achievements." "In enumerating the horrors that have come over us," she argues, "in order to avoid any lack of clarity we need to accept a hierarchy: there have been many revolutions and wars in the course of history, as well as injustice and persecution. In our age only one term had to be newly coined, because the phenomenon it designates did not exist before."[81]

Although Reichmann avoided any explicit dissociation, her essay has to be seen as a direct response both to Rothfels' programmatic and incomparably more influential essay inaugurating the *Vierteljahrshefte* and to the orientation Rothfels established, dominating West Germany's professional historical circles. Inversely, in his foregrounding of the historian's mission as research on the modern "age of crisis-ridden upheavals," the geopolitically "universal constellation," Rothfels emphatically—if implicitly—rejected any definition of the contemporary epoch as one where, in Reichmann's words, "it could transpire that together with men, women, and old people, unfathomably inconsolable streams of children entered the death march to the gas chambers."[82] Rothfels did refer to the "urgency" of research on contemporary German history, with work on "the National Socialist phase" proceeding "with all energy," but while speaking of "discarding of any apologetics," he here also spoke, in the same breath, of a rejection "of all tendencies to self-debasement."[83] He was concerned more with "a theory of our age" in the conservative sense of Hans Freyer than with knowledge and acknowledgment of what had just taken place.[84] (In his book offering a "theory of the present age," to be published two years after Rothfels' essay, Freyer would offer a long reflection on the "civilization mechanism," the "secondary system," rationalization, and the "spirit of the machine," articulating—as would Heidegger in his own conceptual realm—an aversion to modernity moving into postwar West Germany from the prewar "Conservative Revolution."[85]) Speaking more generally, it is clear that while in these early postwar years at the IfZ, a battle raged around it over the justification and very existence of *Zeitgeschichte*, even its champions did not incorporate the Nazi genocide into the discipline's definition. And a historian such as Eva Reichmann, recalling the Holocaust a decade after the inception of *Zeitgeschichte*, would be written off as representing an outsider's, Jewish-particularist perspective— certainly not one reflecting the historian's calling. The research maxim was centered not on the unprecedented nature of what had happened in relation to its sociohistorical and ideological causes but on a "solidarity with the past that was never truly thought through to its end."[86]

Furthermore, it can also be shown that the opponents and defenders of *Zeitgeschichte* were in precise agreement on one basic point: that the dimension of memory, as a troubling dimension, was intended by those in the discipline to be as small as possible, and that as a corrective of memory the dimension of research was intended to be correspondingly large. Those generally rejecting *Zeitgeschichte* were skeptical concerning that possibility, while its champions proceeded, optimistically, to demonstrate their pursuit of "objective *Zeitgeschichte*."

In the words of Fritz Ernst, the imperative was learning "to consider one's own past from the outside."[87] In any books, essays, reviews, and smaller pieces from that period, we find the approach to twentieth-century German history marked by reflections about the possibilities and limits of memory and about the "characteristically tense relationship" between proximity and distance at the heart of historical scholarship, with the latter pole representing its sine qua non. In the words of Karl Dietrich Erdmann, referring to that scholarship: "The closer the object is that it wishes to approach, the more it is duty-bound to attain distance."[88] The turn to the immediately past and burning themes tied to it thus began with a process of "reality-distancing," even for those who had begun, practically and theoretically, to do research on *Zeitgeschichte*: "time was laid between individuals and the events,"[89] Erdmann himself speaking of an "emergence of distance though the questioning process." Where no spatial distance was possible, and no temporal distance yet available, distance had to be achieved through one's scholarly stance: "When the historical object still concerns us so closely that yesterday may seem today and we still stand in the middle of the tumult, then the distance demanded by the historian is distance from himself. . . . But the path to gaining distance is taken through a conscious process of questioning."[90] Hence questions of historical scholarship were here directly defined in terms of a "distancing process" abstracted from personal memory and battles of memory, which is to say as the simulation of a fifty years' time span: the span "needed to bring an event to historical maturity."[91]

If we contrast these efforts at proper distance from the history of one's own time with the consideration soon paid at the institute to possibly extending its *Zeitgeschichte* past 1945, the opposition between conception and practice becomes evident. The question—which was apparently not seen as colliding with the heuristic problem described earlier—was heavily debated: "As chairman of the board, Ministry Director Hübinger pointed out that if the institute took up the period after 1945, it should expect the reproach of having turned away from its actual, original research on National Socialism"—a question Hübinger saw as needing clarification not only in terms of principle but also pragmatically, in terms of financing by the federal government: "As much as he recognized that the concept of *Zeitgeschichte* also took in the time after 1945, it was his duty to draw attention to these possible consequences. Professor Litt supported this viewpoint, emphasizing how important precisely this particular work of the institute on the National Socialist period was. Any distraction from this task was liable to weaken the sense of the institute."[92] On the other hand, above all Krausnick, Herzfeld, and Rothfels argued to the effect that actually no "specialization in National Socialism" was desired, countering the charge of "certain circles" that ascribed to the institute a "one-sided *Zeitgeschichte*," thus "trying to discredit" the institute "in its scholarly credibility."[93] If the institute were to remain a living center of historical scholarship, it would be impossible to "restrict it exclusively to National Socialism."[94]

Questions regarding both periodization and the general historical areas to be covered at the IfZ were again raised in the 1960s; the basic problems returned persistently. For example, a board meeting held on 11 March 1964 saw formulation of the following convictions: now as previously, National Socialism had to be the institute's primary research focus. But that movement was "finally not to be assessed as the logical crowning of German history, but rather represented a kind of 'state of emergency' [*Ausnahmezustand*] taking up a limited period within *Zeitgeschichte*," so that "an elastic explication" was possible of what *Zeitgeschichte* was meant to be.[95] In this context, Rothfels had his own distinct plea: as was already long-since standard in the *Vierteljahrshefte*, because of the reproach from a certain side that the institute had no mission other than "rummaging in guilt," it was nothing short of "tactically mandatory" to carry the work beyond 1945. *Zeitgeschichte* should not prescribe itself "any fundamental temporal barriers."[96]

Critique from the Right:
Armin Mohler versus Hans Rothfels

In these years, it turned out that what Rothfels here viewed from a "tactical" angle, reflecting a sense that flexibility was called for by those leaning "right," would develop differently. During the so-called Hoggan affair, centered on the revisionist historical theses of the British author David Hoggan concerning the origins of World War II,[97] the "National Conservative" intellectual Armin Mohler provoked Rothfels in a thoroughly direct manner. The quarrel between these two figures was prompted by the clear rejection of German historical apologetics that Rothfels had voiced at the German historians' conference in Duisburg in his function as chairman of the German Historian's Association. Likewise, in 1963 the IfZ had organized a conference at the Tutzing Academy for Political Education on "unease at contemporary history" (*Unbehagen an der Zeitgeschichte*), the main focus here being on articulating a rejection of Hoggan's book and ideas.[98] Hoggan's basic argument was that in the 1930s, British diplomacy had engaged in warmongering, with World War II's origins lying in a British political "attempt," in his words, "to exterminate Germany" (*Deutschland zu vernichten*).[99] The book's foreword even spoke of a refutation of a "second war–guilt lie," referring to the book as an example of "sober critical documentary research," and of the book's importance as the "only psychotherapy" that might "help Germany to inner freedom in the complexity of its postwar ties and penances [*Bußen*]." In May 1964, the book would be awarded the "Ranke Prize" in Germany by the dubious "Ranke Society." In the conflict with Mohler—who at the beginning of the 1960s had already demanded the closing of archives containing material treating the recent past[100]—Rothfels' own conceptual premises were clearly profiled. Where, for example, Werner Conze treated the basic problems at work here in a remarkably deferred way, postulating a methodological principle that all questions were allowed if scholarly freedom was to be preserved, Rothfels was much more clear-cut.[101] In his exchange with Mohler, he confronted not only the book but also the question of sense and nonsense in work on the past in general. In this context it becomes clear that the right-wing reproach that, as formulated by Mohler, "overcoming the past" was being "borne on the back of all Germans"[102] encountered a Rothfels different from the emigrant who returned to Germany immediately after the war. (In this respect Mohler's diplomatic epistolary compliment is worth citation: "In any case I always think back with gratitude to the way you formed a counterweight, in your return from the United States and the subsequent years, to your colleagues who remained in Germany, so many of whom wanted to throw all history overboard in panic."[103])

But at the same time, the exchange of letters reveals Rothfels' highly vital conservatism, whose anti–right wing stance nonetheless illuminates transformative processes within his own position. At the beginning Rothfels—who in his own words was "more than sick and tired of the case"—repudiated Mohler's article in *Christ und Welt*, Mohler's assertion there that Rothfels had "lost his nerve" at the historians' conference, and his reference to, as Rothfels described it, "my insertion into the vortex of emotions and latent hysteria, indeed among the national masochists."[104] He had, Rothfels indicated, refuted Hoggan unmistakably but in restrained form: "You [to the contrary] believe that it should have tactfully been said 'how moving that as a foreigner with no obligation in this respect you make yourself "unpopular" by describing us as less bad than we actually are.'" But that was too much for Rothfels: "In the first place it is not a question of us but of Hitler and his regime. In the second place Hoggan is not rendering himself at all unpopular. I cannot imagine that you are unaware what is here at play and what circles are involved. This has nothing to do with revisionism in the style of the years after the First World War."

Rothfels suspected that Hoggan's toadies stemmed from "various cliquey circles of mostly old, established Nazis." Mohler's "caricature . . . of research in contemporary history" positively infuriated him, above all Mohler's "catchword of 'national' contra 'national-masochistic' historiography"; this awakened "the most nasty [*Übel*] memories." In his reply, Mohler felt called upon to remind Rothfels that "every statement on contemporary history" had direct political consequences and led to "payments of tribute, denigrations of German provinces and capacity for political action, etc."[105] These "armaments against the Germans as a whole," Mohler opined, were promoted through a "'*Zeitgeschichte*'" hiding itself "behind its great name and misusing its name," automatically leading to "the hour of the Russians." "You will then probably be in Chicago while I will have to remain here with my swarm of children," Mohler then predicted, thus giving free play to his antisemitic resentment. Although Rothfels replied again, this was only to end the correspondence—and to do so with palpable hurt and anger: although Mohler's "view that the final winners will be the Russians" was not so off-base, he and his historian colleagues were not responsible but rather a "National Bolshevism" à la Mohler. Rothfels now stated bluntly that he found "the characterization of *Zeitgeschichte* as national masochism an infamy." And then he added the following self-defense against Mohler, highly telling in what it reveals about the conceptual tensions at work in his own passionate premises: "My efforts, and those of many others, are aimed precisely and it seems to me not without considerable success at bringing about international recognition of the distinction between Germans and National Socialists."[106] To which Mohler replied—together with a clipping from the same day's *Frankfurter Allgemeine Zeitung* reporting on a notice by the East German ministerial council that it intended to collect Nazi documents demonstrating war crimes and crimes against humanity—that "*Zeitgeschichte* can be not first and foremost a science but only a *weapon* (including for suicide)."[107]

In the archives covering the institute's early phase, we find frequent references to the serious difficulties involved in establishing a research center focused on critically scrutinizing what had just taken place. As we can observe, for example, in Ritter's skepticism, the trailblazing role the institute here took on rendered it suspect within Germany's universities, but the situation in this respect should not be exaggerated: the manner in which the early IfZ produced knowledge of the past was soon well suited for soothing such prejudices by chaired professors. Already at the 1951 historians' conference in Marburg, sections on "problems of *Zeitgeschichte*" and "sociology and history [*Historie*]" were institutionalized as historiographical innovations, with the public "at home and abroad" being presented, as Hermann Heimpel, president of the Historians' Association proudly noted, with a "history [*Historie*] as political science that has its ear to the present."[108] Here as well, what carried the most weight was concern for avoiding misunderstandings—and for finding the right style to that end. The head of the relevant conference section, Heinrich Heffter, observed earnestly that "the path of professional historical research in *Zeitgeschichte* must pass between two cliffs, aversion [*Abneigung*] to touching on those fearful things in any way and fear of having to amend [*revidieren*] political prejudices that have formed since 1945." Heffter here described the dilemma precisely, and it is hardly surprising that he recommended "objectivity" and "justice" as the means to confront the difficulties.[109] Let us now look more closely at the nature of this "objectivity" and "justice" in research on "fearful things."

The IfZ as Expert Authority before the Law

For the image of Nazi genocide shaped at the IfZ, the years between 1958 and the mid-1960s represented a striking caesura. In this period, the European dimension of the murder process was slowly assimilated conceptually into the institute's work—a change above all constituting a reaction to public debates. Between 11 April and 15 December 1961, the trial of Eichmann in Jerusalem kept the German public breathless, with over eight hundred articles about the organizer of the "Final Solution," his interrogation by Israeli prosecutors, and witness testimony appearing in the *Frankfurter Allgemeine Zeitung*, *Frankfurter Rundschau*, *Süddeutsche Zeitung*, and *Die Welt* alone. When the Israeli journalist Amos Elon visited the IfZ, he made an observation addressing a generational change in a casual, unspectacular way: Thilo Vogelsang, an institute board member, sat in his office "beneath a huge map of Europe registering Nazi concentration camps and death camps."[110]

Several years later, we find Helmut Krausnick insisting that a documentation of the persecution of the Jews has to take in "the execution of the so-called Final Solution, throughout Europe."[111] There can be no doubt that the many expert reports prepared by the institute for trials involving Nazi crimes, together with publication of the memoirs of Auschwitz *Kommandant* Rudolf Höß, were what led to such insight. But another factor manifest in the board meetings is appreciation of an altered relationship between history and memory. We see this, for example, in the call for "greater general impact" by the institute and its "need for *publicity*" (the latter word in English).[112] In the case of the expert reports, the approach taken was conceptually defensive; in the case of the Höß text it was far more offensive—one more reason to understand the 1958 publication of this text, in particular, as marking a sea change in West Germany's public discourse about Auschwitz.

The IfZ's expert opinions were published by its own press and in small quantities, a practice criticized by board members, who raised the question of why a "weighty sign of the institute's internal work" was "not taken up in the official series Quellen und Dokumentationen." They in fact had come to find "the argument of considerably lower pricing" somewhat irritating.[113] The first volume appeared in 1958, the second in 1966,[114] the authors being Broszat,

Buchheim, Heiber, Graml, Hellmuth Auerbach, and, as additional contributors in the second volume, Vogelsang, Loock, and Hans Mommsen. The first volume was a selection from the 150 assessments and responses to inquiries prepared annually at the institute in its early years (later the number would increase steeply); the main focus was on the "many measures of persecution taken by the National Socialist regime." In his foreword, Paul Kluke described the volume as a "pioneering" reference work, despite its "fragmentary development and "provisional results."[115] The volume, he explained, addressed "difficult factual questions" and contained a section about the "persecution of the Jews in Germany" and another about that of the Jews "abroad," together with other sections about the police and paramilitary organizations. Sometimes documentary evidence and excerpts were simply presented together, and sometimes a report was the size of a small full-length study, as was the case with Broszat's eighty-page description of Rumania's policies toward the Jews.[116] Despite the institute's rejection of Reitlinger's work, and of that of both Léon Poliakov and Joseph Wulf (to be discussed in detail later), in this period it was forced to have intensive recourse to all three historians—something we particularly see in the second volume's frequent citations.[117] That volume also confronted the problem of the history of the Third Reich's influence, considering two radical right-wing West German publishers: the Druffel Verlag and the Hünenburg Verlag of Friedrich Spieser.[118] Although in his foreword Kluke voiced the hope of offering "information for teachers and journalists" and "reading for those interested in history,"[119] both volumes remained quite unknown. At the same time, as Andreas Hillgruber observed in his review of volume 1, they documented the historian's difficulty in face of juridical inducements to weigh "individual cases of guilt and responsibility."[120]

Auschwitz from the Perspective of Höß

A juncture between research and communication with the public was first announced with publication of the text by Auschwitz commander Höß—a project discussed by the board at the beginning of December 1957. Because of its explosiveness, it was approached differently than earlier projects and would indeed have enormous resonance inside and outside West Germany.[121] Hermann Brill's sentiment that, as he explained to the board, "he could not reconcile himself to the thought that the institute intended to publish the written outpourings of a mass murderer" failed to hinder publication—or the publisher's strategy to contact the public through advance serial publication in the papers, together with its early plans for a paperback edition. The backdrop to this was, in part, a slow change in the general picture of the perpetrators. In that altered

framework, Höß's Auschwitz memoir, which the *Kommandant* had furnished
with the title *Meine Psyche*, conveyed an impression of being not so much the
"outpouring" of a madman as a source with, as the meeting's minutes put it, an
"in many respects representative character from which we see that the crimes
of the Hitler state were certainly not committed only by criminal types in the
usual sense."[122] After the volume appeared, its significance was quickly recognized, both publicly and in the IfZ, as, to cite the board minutes from April
1958, "a document going far beyond the circle of the historian's interest." Not
only the "numerous facts it contains on policies regarding the extermination of
the Jews" but above all the "idiosyncratic mixture of sentimentality and frivolity"
led "into a central problem of the National Socialist period"; in this context there
was a suggestion of using the (eventually rejected) title *The Path to Auschwitz*.[123]
According to Martin Broszat, the volume's editor (see Figure 8), the text served
as "evidence," "for despite all other evidence, widespread doubt still exists facing
the fact of Auschwitz and the murder of Jews in the gas chambers." Or, he remarkably added, at least there was a "very unspecific knowledge, a knowledge
not sure of itself." As Broszat saw it, by forcing a "confrontation with the most
abysmal inhumanity," the publication could and should contribute to the catharsis that is an imperative for national self-respect following the epoch of the
Third Reich.[124]

The public resonance was itself remarkable. The publication of the Höß
memoirs can certainly be considered one of the earliest examples of scholarly
discourse about "Auschwitz" in West Germany—this years before the Eichmann trial in Jerusalem and the so-called Auschwitz trials in Frankfurt.[125] The
tenor of the commentary conveyed astonishment that Höß exemplified the
"phenomenon of National Socialism";[126] in general it was clearly oriented
toward Broszat's introduction,[127] emphasizing that Höß was in fact, as Walter
Hähnle put it, "no perverse sadist" or "one of those degenerate [*verkommen*] brutal
types [*Brutalinskys*],"[128] until then the types viewed as capable of horrendous
crimes. Hence for Gottfried Vetter, although consciousness had to struggle "to
classify Höß as part of the human species"—this his articulation of a widespread unease—with closer consideration "the uncanny phenomenon" dis-
solved "in an almost banal way, but one no less uncanny as a result." For Höß
was no "degenerate [*Entarteter*] in the machinery of death, but the type of the
'executive official,'"[129] and again in Hellmuth Becker's words, not one of the
"rowdies" [*Schlagetots*] but rather "a man who in his disposition could have lived
among us."[130] And an anonymous writer expressed his own unease as follows:
"The case shows how much deeper and confusedly the roots of our calamity
[*Unheil*] reach."[131] Höß, Günter Hönicke similarly observed in an essay for
Norddeutscher Rundfunk, was no asocial mass murderer by birth but rather a

careerist, with the apogee of his career coming together "with the deepest debasement [*Erniedrigung*] that can be recorded in human history."[132] Another anonymous writer confirmed that not only Höß's deeds were shocking but also his "horrid-pedantic [*grausig-pedantisch*] language."[133] One exception to the thrust of such commentaries was offered by "H.L." in Stuttgart's *Außenpolitik*, in a piece arguing that the phenomenon was "not something specifically German."[134] But in general the form of Höß's memoir was perceived as confusing in light of the horrendous deeds, with emphasis placed on a mentality expressed in what Werner Jochmann accurately termed a style of "sober practicality [*nüchterne Sachlichkeit*]" distinguishing the text. "Were those who acted in this way still human beings?" Jochmann asked rhetorically. "Do we not rather encounter social outsiders, brutes [*Rohlingen*], sadists, or criminals?" The answer was in the negative: "Desired were robots for fulfilling duty, men like Höß. In them we encounter human beings with average gifts, by no means wicked, loving order, and pedantically conscientious."[135]

What Helmut Lindemann termed the "split of moral consciousness" and unshakable "feeling of rectitude" exemplified by Höß had led to a new form of reflection about "the horror of Auschwitz": "as grotesque as it sounds, he was aiming for a humane form of mass murder."[136] What had been discovered both on a broad journalistic level and in the general scholarly studies of Nazism that were now appearing[137] was "the gas chambers as a tool," the "everyday" nature of mass executions[138]—Paul Noack here took up the phrasing of Broszat—and what Erdmann referred to as the "entirely impersonal qualities" of the extermination process,[139] the latter point often made with a zeal that now seems somewhat hasty. In any case, Becker's widely shared prediction in his previously cited article that the Höß book would "play a decisive role" in West Germany's processing of the past turned out to be accurate.

At the same time, both the experts' reports and the Höß memoir, together with the success of the two projects, did not amount to a needed focus on the victims of the Final Solution. The extermination of the Jews remained a theme treated with reticence. The chain of decisions leading in 1965 to rejection of Erich Kuby's proposed project for a comprehensive two-volume documentation of the persecution of the Jews in Germany can no longer be reconstructed. Becker reported conversations with Kuby in which he voiced his desire to write a "political-pedagogical book" compensating for the lack of adequate documentation of this sort, since an "aid for social studies instruction" was needed; Rothfels sharply rejected the idea. As the minutes report it: "Documentation for general political-pedagogical purposes isn't really an IfZ thing and is already on hand" (a remark referring to Wolfgang Scheffler's earlier book on "persecution of Jews in the Third Reich," which appeared in 1960). In Rothfels' view, "it was hardly possible to burden members of the IfZ with this additional task." But because the persecution theme had meanwhile become differently coded, there was a real desire to help shape a picture attracting ever-more interest. Hence according to the minutes, if Wolfgang Scheffler was prepared to now produce a more comprehensive documentation than the earlier one, there was a willingness to work with him, "as long as no excessive burden results from this." But, we read, "because of the [public] effect, the IfZ would, absolutely, . . . have to be present in the background."[140]

H. G. Adler and the IfZ

The IfZ's relationship with the Prague-born Jewish historian—and Auschwitz survivor—H. G. Adler represents a special chapter in its postwar history. Over time, Adler's cooperation with the institute became a highly precarious business. In 1959, "winning Dr. Adler for a special study involving the theme of persecution of the Jews in the framework of the research project supported by the Rockefeller Foundation on occupation policies and those toward the Jews is especially welcomed by the board."[141] And his detailed book on Theresienstadt was praised at the IfZ as "outstanding."[142] First contacts had been initiated in the mid-1950s, with a visit by Adler to the institute in May 1956. The idea soon occurred to the Munich historians that Adler could be something like a consulting expert on questions regarding the camps and deportations, "to the extent that we ourselves cannot say anything or only insufficiently . . . since you certainly would be able to help us further."[143] Adler responded by pointing to the International Tracing Service in Bad Arolsen but also gladly agreed to cooperate.[144] And in autumn 1958 the institute asked him whether he would accept a commission to write "a work of your choice" in his "thematic area."[145] Adler and Buchheim now began a regular correspondence and smoothly unfolding cooperative work. The correspondence repeatedly reveals differing positions, Adler thus emphasizing the Wehrmacht's "incrimination" through both "simply observing atrocities" and "its own atrocities," which were "even worse [*ärger*] then generally thought" (an insight only achieving widespread—if initially grudging—public acceptance in Germany in the late 1990s as a result of the highly controversial traveling exhibition "Crimes of the Wehrmacht").[146] On a separate level, but in its own way just as tellingly, he referred to "small linguistic objections where the Nazi language has not been sufficiently overcome" in Martin Broszat's book on Nazi policies toward Poland, a book he otherwise praised.[147] All told, Adler viewed himself at this time as a "friend" of the institute.[148] He assured Buchheim of the "affinity" between the latter's reflections on totalitarianism and his own; Buchheim in turn, for instance, thanked Adler for his suggestions regarding relevant literature.[149] Both men agreed that Reitlinger's work was to be rejected; Buchheim flattered his colleague by indicating that Adler's book on Theresienstadt should be read rather than Reitlinger's ("But if someone simply screams very loudly and absurdly, than attention by the public is a certain thing, however dilettantish his work. Solid, authentic knowledge has much more difficulty gaining attention. Why in fact does the intellectually normal consumer [*der geistige Normalverbraucher*] read Reitlinger and not Adler?").[150]

The two men were in equal harmony in rejecting Hannah Arendt's *Eichmann in Jerusalem*. In a board meeting, Karl Dietrich Bracher had suggested that a piece on the controversial report be published in the *Vierteljahrsheften*, and Rothfels had urged that Adler be convinced to himself write a short piece on the Jewish councils.[151] Krausnick asked Adler about this,[152] and he declined, instead recommending Otto D. Kulka and indicating that Arendt's book needed "dismissal" [*Abfertigung*]. The "professional dilettantism of the author" had to be demonstrated; her book was crammed with errors. Adler even reproached her for manipulating the fact: she had "no clue" and concocted "a poisonous brew" out of her opinions.[153]

Even after leaving for Bonn, Buchheim, who at the time was one of the "special examiners" responsible for testing former SS members for eligibility to join the West German army,[154] would remain Adler's main interlocutor at the IfZ until the collapse of cooperation between the latter and the institute on Adler's major project on the deportation of the German Jews, *Der verwaltete Mensch* ("The Administered Man"; the book would finally appear in the 1970s). But the friendly tone of the correspondence between them was one thing, relations between Adler and the IfZ itself another; these relations were marked by increasing troubles, in part certainly grounded in mistaken expectations on his part regarding the institute following the promising start. We thus find the *Vierteljahrshefte* rejecting Adler's essay on the sociology of the camps in 1958.[155] The deportation project was itself grounded in contacts with the institute beginning that same year. At the beginning of December Adler was referred to a collection of sources said to contain all the files concerning the deportation of the Jews from Lower Franconia. He immediately turned to Buchheim, expressing interest in signing a contract with the IfZ for "research on the deportation complex precisely from the Gestapo's standpoint."[156] When Buchheim had not answered after six weeks, Adler asked again; Buchheim answered at the beginning of February 1959, explaining that the inquiry was causing him "headaches" (*Kopfzerbrechen*) and he considered Adler's letter "first of all to be private." In principle, he explained, as the IfZ's director Krausnick had nothing against such cooperation, but the suggestion had to be "as concrete as possible."[157]

Adler then clarified his proposal in an additional letter[158] and received written permission to do the research in turn for an honorarium to be paid from special institute funds: "We know," wrote Buchheim, "that in your work we find exactly what we are always striving for: a connection between exact individual research and perspectives that illuminate larger contexts and more general problems."[159]

This was precisely what Adler intended; the dimensions of his project were remarkable. He expressed the hope of "furthering research beyond the position it has reached with Hilberg":[160] "From the Würzburg Gestapo files," he observed, "we can study the technique of deporting Jews from the 'Old Reich' systematically and in every essential detail; and it seems very important to me that we can do so from the official perspective not only of the Reich Security Main Office but also of the other participating state and regional authorities."[161] What he had planned was a "general overview of the deportations from the 'Old Reich,' perhaps with reference to all of 'Greater Germany.'" What remained open was whether this was to be a documentary work or a general description, but Adler promised (and this would, of course, have been crucial for the institute) to in any case preserve a "very strict and unemotional" tone.[162]

This work turned out more difficult than any of those participating had imagined. For Adler the research arrangement was becoming an increasing burden, so that by the end of February 1961 he had begun "to regret having obliged myself contractually;"[163] a month earlier he already could indicate that "to be honest" he felt himself "duped" [*genasführt*]:[164] there was no cooperation from the Würzburg authorities, no offers of assistance from the IfZ. He did express appreciation for the "willingness to help" shown by Herr Hoch, the IfZ's archivist, who seems, however, to not really have made the project his own responsibility. Adler summed things up in an expression of concern to Heinz Förster that the project could remain a "miserable patchwork."[165]

In December 1961 Adler offered Anton Hoch an assurance that in any assessment of the documents for which he gained permission, he would be ready "to disguise any personal connections that the authorities wish." "I am only concerned," he explained, "with precisely understanding processes in their functioning and then with describing them in a study of a purely historical-sociological nature. Individuals do not concern me and need not be afraid."[166] With time, Adler—in general a remarkably conciliatory man—expressed his helplessness in an increasingly tormented manner. With a response from the authorities never coming, he was becoming convinced he would not be able to honor his contract. The feelings of loneliness intensified. In his words to Buchheim: "My isolation is in any case bad; it has only worsened in the last two years and often I ask myself for what good and for whom are all my activities, scholarly or artistic."[167] But he did not so much hold his colleagues in Munich responsible as despair at the country and at a German government that

> is not ashamed to suffer a Herr [Theodor] Maunz [the reference is to a
> Nazi jurist who remained highly influential in postwar West Germany] as
> a member but evidently cannot allow a Jew to look at papers from the
> Second World War that concern Jews. This Jew may simply be interested
> in knowledge and not exposing blackguards [*Lumpen*]; he may have even
> offered a written assurance that he will remain a Jew and should recognize
> that he is not to get mixed up in any matters involving old Nazis and their
> patrons. Camp and Gestapo functionaries can perhaps be sacrificed,
> but for heaven's sake "honorable" officials have to be spared potential
> annoyances.[168]

But there was also growing estrangement from the institute. Still cautiously, "Adler confided to Buchheim that "unfortunately," he could "not fail to gain an impression that whatever the reasons, people do not wish me to historically penetrate and illuminate those connections expected of me by the IfZ—after all a state institution."[169]

In the same period, Adler asked the institute to offer Hermann Langbein— a former Communist resistance fighter, Auschwitz survivor, and founder of the International Auschwitz Committee who had been active as a publicist over the past decade—some professional perspective, on the grounds that "the phenomenon of Auschwitz has hardly been touched on by researchers, and we certainly agree that such research has now become timely."[170] Adler made the concrete suggestion that Langbein be asked to research the "office of the chief SS doctor for Auschwitz" and "members of the SS in the Auschwitz concentration camp": "This would contribute to a typology of the camp personnel extending from the leading functionaries to the SS guards." In this letter, Adler also spoke explicitly, in reference to chief Auschwitz doctor Eduard Wirth and SS *Oberscharführer* Wilhelm Boger, head of the "flight, theft, and manhunt" department of Auschwitz's political section, of an "entanglement in guilt" by "originally thoroughly well-meaning men who wanted to help the prisoners" but who turned into "mass murderers" and "sadists."[171] The answer he received from Buchheim spoke volumes: the institute lacked the necessary money and had other thematic focal points; rather than undertaking a research project, Langbein would preferably record "his experiences and insights in the form of a witness account." "We would be delighted," Buchheim added graciously, "to receive a detailed report on Auschwitz from an authority [*von einem Kenner*]—a report that in a certain way would represent a counterpart to the memoirs of Höß."[172] (Perhaps to Buchheim's surprise, Langbein declined the offer. He wished, as Buchheim himself would explain, to prepare a study, not a "witness account.")[173]

Seven years after the IfZ signed its contract with Adler, it was felt, as Helmut Krausnick explained, that belief in the success of his documentary project had been mistaken. In the course of the past years, he had been very ill several times (and had even asked the IfZ to help him cover operation and hospital costs on several occasions),[174] had parallel working projects that were needed to earn his keep, and thus required far more time than had been agreed on. He had also altered his main area of focus, having become steadily more interested in the "processes surrounding the act of deportation" itself.[175] And not least of all, he had gone well beyond the agreed-on length of the manuscript, as he had informed the institute at the end of 1964.[176] For these reasons, his request for a contract extension was denied. In 1965 he submitted two parts of his book. Although Broszat and Vogelsang corrected the manuscript,[177] the sense of commonality had been broken. In his book's introduction Adler put it as follows: "There was little applause; my tome [*Elaborat*] did not correspond to the conceptions of the competent gentlemen on either scholarly or stylistic levels. Our paths thus separated."[178] The evaluation of Hans Herzfeld and Ernst Fraenkel based on the manuscript's first four hundred pages was "very critical," their conclusion being, again as Adler put it, that the results did not correspond to "the fostered expectations."[179] The suggestion that the manuscript be published as it was in the institute's own series was rejected; it was simply returned to Adler "for your own utilization." What was lacking in this "very personally colored product," his colleagues observed, was a "noticeable disparity between analysis and appraisal of the material," together with a systematic examination of the older literature.[180] In addressing the "strongly subjective components" of the book—while also arguing for its publication and asking that the "materially unfavorable position of Dr. Bracher be considered"— Bracher pointed to the core of the problem that the IfZ in fact had with it: that "Adler was not only engaged in scholarship" but also had been "a directly participating contemporary [*unmittelbar beteiligter Zeitgenosse*]."[181] The institute's view of the book as not being classifiable, to cite Hans Herzfeld, "either as a documentary or a research publication" meant that as in similar cases, it posed strategic difficulties for research policy. With no one really knowing how to proceed, a consensus was formed to publish the book "on the grounds of popular education," with, to be sure, "the recommendation and support of the institute," but by an outside publisher.[182] Adler's own summation was bitter: his book "had been written without help from the scholars or sponsorship from the powerful"; he then cited an English man of letters to the effect that he had not written "in a mild restrained style, nor protected by academic life," but rather "in the middle of sorrow and chaos, illness and care."[183]

The IfZ's "Auschwitz Report"

In the middle of the singular history of Adler and his book came the two-volume expert report submitted by the IfZ for the Frankfurt Auschwitz trial, *Anatomie des SS-Staates*.[184] Although the trial opened in December 1963, its preparation extended back to the 1950s; without any doubt, it marked a key point in the historiography of Auschwitz.[185] Contributions to *Anatomie* included Helmut Krausnick's discussion of the persecution of the Jews, Hans-Adolf Jacobsen's of the so-called Commissar Order, Martin Broszat's of the concentration camps, and Hans Buchheim's of the SS. These studies had a significance that would be long lasting; Broszat's essay, for example, was assessed by Christian Meier thirty years after its appearance as "the foundational essay on the theme," and Ulrich Herbert described the report as "a first highpoint" whose sober and impressive analysis had "marked and defined the state of knowledge of Nazi extermination policies for decades" and whose level of scholarship would not be matched for a long time.[186] Nevertheless, Robert Gellately's assessment in 1992 of *Anatomie* as "too successful"[187] was also on the mark; the quick fame achieved by this "standard work" seems to have had a paralyzing effect on subsequent research. But the two volumes' contributions themselves revealed a concrete limit, focusing on a description of the Nazi state's highly complicated "framework of action" rather than what Jens Banach has termed "the factual application of power."[188] It is also the case that the volumes generally represented, as Irmtrud Wojak has observed, a somewhat precarious "fusion of history and criminology"[189]—two very different realms coming together in postwar West Germany in a concept of *Vergangenheitsbewältigung* that took in everything somehow having to do with Nazism.[190] Acknowledging this reality should of course not amount to "a process of inappropriate moral censure."[191] Rather, the purpose of analyzing the historical locus of *Anatomie* and other such historical achievements must be to illuminate a key contemporary juncture between research and memory.

In the case of the IfZ expert report, the juncture found its form in the court's confrontation with the historical situation that was being addressed. Through Buchheim's foreword to the two volumes, which encapsulated the institute's premises, what was meant to be a professional assessment took on a different, conceptual dimension. Elsewhere Buchheim had already warned against settling the theme of Nazism and the SS in a "tense field of accusation and defense" and allowing the image of both to become unhistorical through a "mixture of commentaries in the realm of constitutional and criminal law." Buchheim thus emphasized that "the historian, facing other responsibilities than the judge or lawyer, is not allowed but compelled to dispense with categories of accusation and defense and disregard personal 'cases.'"[192] The historian's true task was first to consider the "particularity of the total picture" and second to further an understanding of causes.[193]

In the first volume of *Anatomie*, Buchheim introduced his study of the SS as the Third Reich's "instrument of rule" with a kind of abbreviated reception history of the Nazi crimes. He here distinguished two groups who in his view revealed two different approaches to the crimes, with each group ignoring contexts and revealing both particular interests and a necessarily distorted perspective. He began with an oblique reference to a passage in Kogon's *SS State* where Kogon asserts that "The concentration camps are one of the horrible facts around which German conscience would have to circle. The nation [*das Volk*] wishes to hear nothing more of these facts."[194] For Buchheim, "The camp crimes and mass murder of the Jews were specific elements of National Socialist rule. For many people, this context is forgotten, and this for very different reasons. For some, for example, concern with the Third Reich is reduced to the name Auschwitz; their thoughts circle around the fact that hell became historical reality. Nevertheless, they here lose touch with the historical whole."[195] As Buchheim saw it, this group was marked by disinterest in "the intellectual and political premises" of a deed it simply tied to "general moral and cultural-critical considerations." The other group, for whom, he indicated, "the crimes are an erratic block" standing "disconnectedly [*zusammenhangslos*] in that segment of German history," "has nothing essential to criticize in the policies of the Hitler period" "aside from the most blatant crimes."[196]

Buchheim's placement of such highly disparate groups alongside each other as suffering from dialectically related cognitive deficits is highly telling. The "nevertheless" with which he begins the last sentence in the preceding excerpt indicates that although understanding the argumentation of the first group, clearly the group constituted by Nazism's victims, he considered the argumentation inadequate. The other group, composed of those who generally supported Third Reich policies without, at present, feeling responsible for "Auschwitz," was, transparently, the large group of West Germany's *former* Nazis. Buchheim here sought to describe a "reality of the Hitler regime"[197] standing against *both* ex-Nazis and their victims; "understanding Auschwitz" thus in turn meant a refusal to follow the viewpoint of either those who aporetically *centralized* the crime or those who apologetically *marginalized* it. To reiterate, neither a reproachful "circling around" nor an irresponsible evasion was, for Buchheim, a suitable way of answering the question of the connections "between this political form of rule and ideological mass crime."

Even in the choice of title, *Anatomie des SS-Staates* was closely linked inter-textually with the German version of Kogon's *SS State*. The subtle simultaneity of appropriation and correction can be interpreted as a "compulsion" to compromise resulting from the context of the IfZ report's emergence. The at the time most important German book about the mass crimes was developed for use in a trial of accused perpetrators at Auschwitz; at the trial, it made it easier to decide that a process of genocide carried out along principles of labor division was to be principally interpreted in the framework of "abetment." The ethos of the report's two volumes was encapsulated programmatically in a positivistic exclamation by Buchheim: "How difficult it is *not* to write powerfully about Auschwitz!"[198] Against such an intentional backdrop, a turn back to the question of memory illuminates a second, less manifest level of the Auschwitz report's meaning, running alongside its singular position in research on the Third Reich. For precisely when we focus on Buchheim's way of viewing the crime against the Jews, the presence of a past-centered political agenda becomes evident in the report's two volumes, and in other contemporary books on Nazism and Auschwitz as well, so that in the end they can be understood as books written specifically *against* another, real and potential approach to that theme.

To take the most obvious case in our context: both Buchheim's general study of the SS and—even more so—his discussion of the relationship between orders and obedience in the report's second part were clearly intended as a foil not only to Kogon's work but also to a lesser-known work, Gerald Reitlinger's *The SS: Alibi of a Nation, 1922-1945*, which first appeared in English in 1956, hence a few years after his *Final Solution*, and the following year in Germany in a translation whose subtitle was all too typical of the time: *Tragödie einer deutschen Epoche*.[199] The main title of the original English edition articulated a very different program. For in his book, Reitlinger, who already had a name due to *The Final Solution* (as indicated, a pioneering work), was arguing that although the SS was indeed horrible and powerful, this was not to the absolute degree of its frequent depiction in Germany, where it thus functioned as a kind of "devil *ex machina*." In a sharp corrective to that self-serving myth, Reitlinger underscored the SS's role as part of a larger criminal network composed of the German army, the Nazi German bureaucracy, the regular police, and countless numbers of fellow travelers working together with active and aggressive Nazis.

In a vehemently critical review of the English edition, Buchheim now reproached Reitlinger for passing a "distorted" judgment and directly warned against publishing his book in German.[200] In Buchheim's view, Reitlinger had concluded that "the entire German *Volk* . . . was simply evil." The book even sometimes operated, he suggested, on the "level of neo-Nazi pamphlets," above all in Reitlinger's "distorted picture" of the German resistance. Tellingly, Buchheim also found fault with the book's neglect of organizational structure and its systematic orientation toward "political developments" within Nazi Germany. Buchheim's own study countered that orientation through an emphatic underscoring of its own cognitive interests. As he explained it, "There is less reference to the particulars of what the SS did, more to how the power apparatus formed from a unification of SS and police developed and functioned; in other words: how totalitarian rule was exercised in everyday practice."[201] Hence whereas Buchheim perceived the SS in a framework of *totalitarianism*, Reitlinger presented the organization as the symbol of a *society* that used its help and that of other organizations to plunder Jewish property and first ostracize and expel, then exterminate the Jews, a scholarly approach that in Buchheim's view was "distorted." In Reitlinger's book there is, he indicated, no trace of a "probing confrontation with the problem embedded in the theme," since "he simply has no desire to pose the question of how a people could implicate itself in such guilt, but simply condemns, makes the SS into the prototype of our nation." Reitlinger was, for Buchheim, "incapable of seeing through the confusing perversion of good and evil characterizing the history of the National Socialist period"; he had not examined Germany's intellectual-political developments over the past several decades closely enough to offer a balanced assessment.

In a key passage of a summary of his book's main arguments, Reitlinger transgressed a German taboo. The postulate—transmitted to the Allies, he explained, by "German emigrants in the postwar trials—that "the SS was a state within the state, only responsible to itself, a terror to the German officials and the power that drove them to tyranny and cruelty,"[202] seemed too simple to him, not reflecting the Third Reich's reality: "Most people overlook . . . that even the Gestapo could not act independently and depended on cooperation from many circles of the German bureaucracy." And further:

> People do not want to acknowledge that the enormous machinery through which more than four million Jews were torn from their apartments in order to perish in often distant concentration camps, ghettos, and gas chambers, could not have been steered by a single obscure Gestapo department, that it could not have been kept completely secret and not at all set in motion without the cooperation of special departments of the Ministry

of the Interior, the Ministries of Transportation, Finance, and the Economy, the high command, the Ministries of Labor and Armament, and above all the Foreign Office.[203]

The objections Buchheim raised to Bertrand Russell's overview of the Nazi crimes in his 1954 book *The Scourge of the Swastika*, published the next year in Germany as *Geißel der Menschheit*,[204] were similar to those raised against Reitlinger: the author had "hardly" inquired "into the historical background or 'how it could have been possible.'"[205] Instead "we find one atrocity listed after the other. . . . The most horrible truths are mixed gaudily with evident half-truths and falsities and pronounced horror stories, so that even with the best will the reader cannot gain an impression that the author was concerned with being objective."

In this period in Germany, the German historians defined what was "objective" in respect to the SS and death camps and what was not "objective." And they often did so in explicit rejection of the "engagement," "testimony," and "pathos" of Jewish and other historians confronting the moral atrocity of what had taken place. In the following chapter, we will see how this rejection played itself out in face of the life and work of the Polish Jewish historian Joseph Wulf.

Research without Memory

Any "balanced" assessment of the early history of the IfZ will be inherently ambivalent. On the one hand, in light of what the institute faced at its inception, and of the fact that rather than having useful historiographical traditions at its disposal, the traditions it had needed to be kept at a distance, it would seem that the cited positive self-description by Möller was quite on target. A range of research and publications that was unavoidably time bound but still impressive both quantitatively and qualitatively, beyond that a successful establishment of the historical facts and issues it addressed within both German historical scholarship and public awareness, represent two achievements refuting the IfZ's nationalistic and apologetic critics in the early postwar period. In this way, the institute's development in the 1950s cannot be considered separately from the emergence, after a long struggle, of historical research on the Nazi period and the Holocaust as an established discipline within the Germany university system.

At the same time, the deficits of the institute's work in the first fifteen years are also clear: structural weaknesses such as the political dependence on federal and state donors and the dominance of a perspective shared by retired generals and professional administrators on the board; a faith in authority of responsible parties at the institute that surfaced in interviews with former Third Reich officials. There were also naturally individual limitations and errors, even blunders such as the particular history of the publication of Hitler's "table talk" and its impact (discussed later) or the resentment shown toward critical studies of both the ideology of the "Conservative Revolution" and social Darwinism.[206] Such misjudgments, and worse, would have to be duly weighed in forming a full picture of the institute's scholarly production in this period; the picture thus coming into focus would likely be of a historiographical avant-garde whose opposition came less from official quarters than from Germany's academic historians themselves, and whose temporal limitations do not diminish the gain in both knowledge and reputation that the IfZ represented for the postwar German historical discipline.

Nevertheless, neither foregrounding the positive accomplishments nor pointing to their limited scope, and certainly not establishing a "golden mean" between the two options, does justice to the problem emerging in this discussion: that what was being promoted in the IfZ's early years amounted to research without history, at times even directly against history. The disparate facets of the historians' own memories were not dynamically rendered into research-guiding questions, and the same historians failed to draw on the memories of academic outsiders—many but not all of them of German Jewish origin—who viewed the Holocaust as by rights at the core of research on Nazism. The spotless account presented by the institute in 1999, explicitly and vehemently, of its early work on "persecution of the Jews" and "extermination of the Jews," on the occasion of the IfZ's fiftieth anniversary, made a massive detour around the published research of the intervening decades. This was far more than an error of detail: through the IfZ's conceptualization of the Third Reich from a strictly German perspective, an image of the Nazi period was established in Germany that precisely did not reflect the historically central significance of the regime's exterminatory policies but rather presented a narrative of the seduction and subjugation of the German *Volk*, from the perspective of the regime's fellow travelers.

As presented as late as 1999, the institute's self-understanding involved a scornful denunciation of "memorial day historiography" and a "compulsion to remember" as a "massage for consciousness," while attempting to assign the institute the oppositional role of maintaining "discursive hygiene" in the realm of contemporary history.[207] This self-understanding would have been far more credible if the IfZ's own memory of itself had not been so thoroughly elided—above all, its memory of the approach taken to outsider Jewish historians, which is to say to Reitlinger und Adler, but most tragically to Joseph Wulf, whose conflict with the institute is at the center of the following chapter.[208] Hence however unreflective and redundant, Hans-Peter Schwarz's praise of the early IfZ's professionalism and rationalism in the jubilee volume's introduction, of the institute's orientation toward empirically verifiable knowledge and "internationally recognized standards of objectivity,"[209] does not so much call for refutation as for simply being applied to the history of the institute's own research. Something else does, however, need to be left behind as historically untenable: the juxtaposition, in the postwar West German framework, of a "still inadequately enlightened public disposed toward repression," on the one hand, and the "objective documentation of and research on National Socialism," on the other hand. Particularly in regard to the Holocaust, the self-image of a historical upholding of a special mission, the introduction of "the unvarnished, objectively verifiable truth about the Third Reich"[210] to public discourse and in the face of public resistance, is refuted by the contents of virtually every book by a German historian published between 1945 and the early 1960s.

The historical-political distaste for the criterion of memory, in the sense described in this book and revealed in strikingly recent self-descriptions of the IfZ, had an outdated tenor not least of all because in the intervening decades institute members had themselves critically scrutinized the relationship between their own experiences and memories and the institute's official research program. In the previously mentioned far more modest and self-critical assessment offered for the institute's twenty-fifth anniversary, we thus find a direct confirmation that the entire postwar period was marked by an inability to produce a general study of the annihilation of Europe's Jews.

In his cited memoirs of 1975, Hans-Dietrich Loock refers to the famous scene in which Willy Brandt, postwar West Germany's Social Democratic chancellor, fell to his knees in Warsaw before the monument to the ghetto revolt: "That was no overcoming of the past, but rather its acceptance—something of which scholarship is incapable."[211] And he poses the rhetorical question of whether the historian's task was, indeed, simply to do research or whether remembering was also appropriate. He answers his question as follows:

> Historians may in any event remember; and in remembering the emergence of *Zeitgeschichte*, they may move back to the time that *became* that *Zeitgeschichte*. I still see us—as if it were yesterday—a small troop of "working men" on the camp's parade ground, standing around the *Oberstfeldmeister*. He told us that autos had been built into which exhaust fumes could be pumped and that Jews had been stuffed into the autos and killed in that way. He finished with the sentence: "Now we have better methods." He apparently had not expected our reaction. First a muffled cry of indignation

that could be felt in a downright physical way. And then a loud cry, half uncontrolled and half calculated: "That's unworthy of a National Social-ist!" The next day I was assigned to external work and only stepped into the camp again when we were released from labor duty. . . . That is no special story. Nothing happened, and I had a nice day all the remaining weeks. But history [*die Geschichte*] ate into my memory.[212]

In the late 1950s, the IfZ was characterized far more by research on the past than by memory of it. As we have seen, through the studies of Helmut Krausnick, Hans Buchheim, and Martin Broszat, in this period knowledge of the extermina-tion and camp system became part of the canon of modern German history, and the research of these historians remained authoritative for decades to come. In contrast, memory—as surfacing, for example, in the autographically localized moment when Loock received information about the extermination of the Jews—remained personal, secretive, and nonscientific. The first wide-ranging descriptions of the Final Solution were presented, initially to the courts, then to the public, with the "technical exactness of the historian," and with a "hiding of one's own indignation in footnotes."[213] The extermination of the Jews was, in fact, not conceptually grasped, not perceived as a unique event. In this way, to once again cite Loock, the "extraordinary was settled within ordinary circumstances."[214] It thus became *Zeitgeschichte*: "Only *Landser*," which is to say Wehrmacht privates, "could be barefaced enough to make a start," Loock ob-served, self-critically and ironically, and to his enormous credit.[215] But in the following pages, I would like to pose the question of whether it was really only *Landser* who made the start. Framed by key events catalyzing the German public's growing capacity to articulate—and not simply evade—its recent past, the focus here will be on documentation as a principle, in relation to one out-sider in particular: Joseph Wulf, one of the few knowledgeable "competitors" in the early days of research on *Zeitgeschichte*, hence for some years nothing less than a one-man counterpart to the IfZ.

5

"Prehistorical Excavations" and "Absolute Objectivity"

On the Travail of the Polish Jewish Historian of the Holocaust Joseph Wulf

The "Documentary Principle" . . .

The early 1950s saw publication of the West German paperback edition of *The Diary of Anne Frank*—a book that quickly became the nation's Holocaust document par excellence, a classic that probably remains unsurpassed there in terms of both its iconic qualities and the needs fulfilled by its reception. Having first appeared in Holland directly after the end of the war, the diary was translated into German five years later but initially was mostly ignored.[1] But after the diary's theatrical version met success in Germany, sales quickly rose: nearly 750,000 copies of the paperback between 1955 and 1960. Around two million people saw the play, which had a total of two thousand performances in all the country's major cities; twice as many spectators saw the movie version, which came out in 1959.[2] When in March 1957, as an introduction to Germany's "week of fraternity," the head of Hamburg's press office, Erich Lüth, offered a "voyage of memory" to Bergen-Belsen, instead of the expected eighty young people over two thousand showed up, and a procession in buses and cars began: "In long columns," the Berlin *Tagesspiegel* reported, "the young pilgrims filed past the field of graves where Anne Frank rests in an unknown location."[3] On the play's opening nights in Berlin, Düsseldorf, and elsewhere, the theatergoers silently departed "in stricken commemoration of death."[4] And a reporter for the American journal *Der Monat* who had become interested in the "curious triumphal procession" of both the book and play[5] received astonishing spoken answers to a survey he initiated of responses to both. Older people faulted things being seen through "American glasses" ("It was never like that in Germany") and felt reminded of their own fate ("We ourselves lost so much!"), or they warned against youth being "weighed down" with "snow from yesterday." Younger people expressed opposite views that were just as revealing: they were shaken but, as the interviewer explained, recognized precisely "the prototypical young person" in Anne Frank. "Young Germans are discovering their own situation in the borderline situation" is how he put it:[6]

> In the eyes of most of the young theatergoers, the political basis of the tragedy has shrunk to a "historical backdrop" that remains too alien, distant, and incomprehensible to be really interesting. Not dissimilarly to the political conflicts leading to the arrest and execution of [Schiller's] Maria Stuart, for the great majority of youthful theatergoers National Socialism and the persecution of the Jews simply remain odd, second-rank external circumstances for the personal tragedy of their female hero. Even after the evening at the theater, the practice of German National Socialism remains a book with seven seals that they feel no need to open and understand.[7]

Gerhard Schoenberner likewise spoke of a paradoxical "burning interest in secondary questions," noting that in the diary itself "the persecution of the Jews is only treated indirectly."[8] In respect to the play, what did generate great excitement was a competition for the role of the main character—a remarkable carnival-like event, including large billboards with fashion ads for "Anne Frank skirts and blouses."[9] There was irritation at the use being made of this document of Nazi persecution: "The public likes being moved by a young girl's diary but wants to know nothing about the system of gas chambers."[10] But when asked, most *Jewish* Germans declared that they had no desire to see the play since it would evoke painful memories. As Norbert Muhlen noted in his article on the German Anne Frank mode, a reader's letter from a Jewish woman who had emigrated from Tel Aviv responded to the discrepancy between that mode and the historical knowledge avowed by most Germans by demanding a stop to "these Anne Frank performances," which amounted to "sugar water!" and "half the truth." (She then supplemented the young girl's interrupted diary with a long citation from the account of Anne Frank's friend Lies Goosens, who had seen her once again in Bergen-Belsen.[11])

The play was without a doubt a "German" play for Germans of the 1950s, whatever their age. *The Diary of Anne Frank*, when not being belittled as expressing the ideology of Jewish American "best-seller manufacturers,"[12] was suitable for intimate identification and personal rapprochement, as much as to pathos-laden hyperbole and a kitschy longing for reconciliation that, when expressed by a young girl, could be met with gratitude. For Germans, the diary represented "the truth . . . nothing but the truth, the entire truth."[13] The 1955 paperback offered instructions for reception on the front cover: "I believe that human beings are good at heart"—precisely the sentence that could close the gap between general moral avowal and a specific desire *not* to know. Eva Reichmann, herself astonished that something could be brought about through a child "that was impossible through documentary proof, reproaches, and accusations," turned directly to the theatergoers in the April 1957 program published for Essen's theaters. People should not isolate and sentimentalize Anne Frank's fate, she warned—not forget that being shaken only constituted a start. What they needed to ask was *why* the child had to die, and they needed to gain a clear sense of the political events leading to the extermination. All of this was more difficult "than taking the child Anne Frank into one's heart and crying about her." "It is easy," Reichmann observed, "to be moved by a good piece of theater; and a nearly self-satisfied sense of well-being results from the emotion involving an event that it is nigh common courtesy to turn away from indignantly."[14] In any event, in Germany people continued to read about the prehistory of the extermination of the Jews in a text written by a "child who knows nothing and understands everything"[15]—against the backdrop of German longing for innocence, this offer of identification was highly tempting.

. . . and Its Historical Problems

For the early period of Germany's confrontation with the Nazi past, Anne Frank's diary was only the most prominent example of the "documentary principle," which held a position that has hardly been examined. While what was tentatively referred to as such a "principle" had a special meaning for that period, the principle's resonance has moved well beyond it, even manifesting itself steadily and in illuminating ways in the 1990s: for example, in Walter Kempowski's "Echolot" project, a "collective diary" assembled from disparate sources for Germany in January and February 1943 (1993, 1999); publication of the Nazi-period diaries of the German-Jewish Romanist Victor Klemperer (1995); and, arguably most importantly, the controversial and influential traveling exhibition organized by the Hamburg Institute for Social Research, "War of Annihilation: Crimes of the *Wehrmacht*, 1941 to 1944" (1995–1999). Each of these examples thematically addressed the persecution and annihilation of the Jews, and each was either more or less strictly source material (or compilations) or at least conceived along documentary lines. And through the power of something akin to everyday authenticity, each gained a significance going far past a specialist framework, catalyzing intense public debate.[16]

At the end of the 1950s, Walter Anger, editor of an early documentation of the Third Reich's history,[17] explained his method in a way that was still very naive but that involuntarily got at the heart of the problem: "Every assertion is . . . proven by documents."[18] In relation to the Third Reich, procuring documents was not a problem, but the claim to objectivity projected onto the material was one. Walther Hofer would proceed far more aggressively in his well-known—and still widely read—documentary collection from the same period,[19] even introducing the volume with the following statement: "In most cases the question of objectivity, repeatedly posed precisely in connection with the scientific treatment of problems of contemporary history, . . . offers its own resolution. Whoever presents the object of the description itself in a documentary way or allows it to speak is by definition objective."[20] The solemnly positivistic conviction at work here underscores its own premises: that the printing and dissemination of "documents" constitutes an, as it were, metahistorical act following fully different laws than those usually at work in scholarly labor. But as noted in relation to *The Diary of Anne Frank*, such texts, found, presented, debated, and with their strong cachet of documentary authenticity, in fact have their own communicative structure whose deciphering can be of considerable interest.

In this regard, roughly a quarter century ago, Hans Mommsen indicated that for West German research it seemed "understandable that the initial preference was for documentations and source editions"; in this way he suggested a pragmatic and systematic scholarly decision, made according to long-standing traditions of the discipline in proper working sequence. But with some scrutiny the question of where "source editions" begin and where "documentation" spills over into commentary emerges as an extremely convoluted interpretive struggle. The line between "source" and "commentary," "National Socialism" and research on it, is by no means always clear cut.[21] The problem is naturally all the more present in texts written by Nazi perpetrators. When the memoirs of Alfred Rosenberg, written in the Nuremberg prison, were first published in 1947, they had the title *Portrait eines Menschheitsverbrechers* (translatable rather awkwardly as "Portrait of a Criminal against Humanity"). A few years later the volume reappeared in shortened form, this time named simply *Letzte Aufzeichnungen*—Last Notes—and supplied with a polemical commentary. By contrast the edition of 1955, published by the radical right-wing Plesse Verlag in Göttingen, was complete but unannotated. The change had a meaning—as Hans Buchheim noted, "a complete lack of commentary" was "also a commentary."[22] The backdrop of this remark was an interpretive struggle between a postwar historiography just taking shape and versions of the past by those who had participated in it: not only tamed "sources" but high-profile accounts and committed interpretations serving as competition to scholarly history. The plethora of popularly oriented apologies, representing a genre of their own, had to first be separated from texts ennobled as "sources" and one's own scholarly interpretations, and this task could not always be realized through a simple consignment to oblivion of the sort meted out to a pamphlet by the Nazi war criminal Julius Lippert, which had been published by the Druffel-Verlag. (In this case, the *damnatio memoriae* had first been called for by Buchheim in 1955 — "Here a Nazi of the worst sort has produced a self-portrait that really deserves a *damnatio memoriae*" — then carried out a year later in the form of confiscation by the state.[23])

In an essay published in 1998, Harald Welzer interprets Albert Speer's famous memoirs and diaries as the prototype for a kind of "anticipated retrospection" (the term is borrowed from Alfred Schütz): life in the "mode of future two," or a historiography of one's life written during one's lifetime. In Welzer's view, the historical consciousness of Speer, Hitler's architect and armaments minister, who successfully presented himself and was marketed for many decades after the war as the Third Reich's "model architect" and "model minister," and also as a "model defendant" in Nuremberg, "model inmate" in Spandau, "model witness" in his publications, and finally "model atoner" of the late postwar period, can be understood to involve a sustained and megalomaniac focus "on the future of his past": a focus not appearing all that peculiar against the social-historical backdrop of the 1950s. What was in the end at play here, Welzer sums up, was the "endurance of delusions of grandeur after their factual rebuttal."[24]

For the postwar historians, the struggle over memory needed nothing more urgently than clarity. The sort of ambivalent accounts by ex-Nazis such as Peter Kleist's *Auch Du warst dabei* (You Were There as Well) from 1954 revoked an essential consensus that a uniform, consistent division between "National Socialism" and its opponents was possible. "Distortions," "incomplete information," "ambivalences," and "cynical euphemisms" were perceived as the "product of conscious malice" and as a "falsification of German history" — the terms are Buchheim's — that could be "unobjectionably condemned." But the vehement rebuttal had motives extending past the scandal at hand, for it was also necessary because Kleist's titular address to his readers could not be as easily refuted as the apologetic passages in his text.[25] (After the war Kleist was able to present his ideas at conferences "meant to promote human understanding between former followers and opponents of the National Socialist regime." Buchheim reports on an "intense confrontation" between Kleist and some listeners who were horrified by his "coldness and human indifference," but who in the end were ready to accord him "subjective truth in a kind of attestation of honor."[26])

In the 1950s, the perspective of the perpetrators not only circulated in the form of radical self-exculpating literature published by obscure presses. To a much stronger degree, through historians' commentaries, classifications, notes, and evaluations, it also left its mark on the presentation of events in texts defined as "sources." The term Welzer uses for the process is "deferred historiography":[27] texts defined as testimony and characterized by being meant to answer questions—but with the questions and answers furnishing the cultural framework within which the testimony is understood.

"Hitlerism" in Hitler's "Table Talk"

The earliest documentary publication of the IfZ—in fact, the first of its publications period—here serves as a good example. This was an edition of *Hitlers Tischgespräche* (Hitler's Table Talk), edited by Gerhard Ritter, who in his foreword emphasized that he wished to "neither accuse nor defend" the dictator, "neither damn him nor glorify him," but rather to "show how it really was."[28] Publication sparked a regular scandal, conjured up by the Munich historian, who had incessantly called for objectivity in treating the past and justice vis-à-vis German history in particular, and threatening to squander the institute's chances for credibility.[29] There was an ambivalence to Ritter's behavior also evident in the text's prepublication in the glossy weekly *Quick*, with the series' trivialization being made amply clear in headings extending from "Hitler and Kings" to "Hitler and Women" and onward to "Hitler, the Antichrist."[30] Ritter disputed any knowledge of plans to publish in the journal. It in any event seems a striking irony that precisely in the IfZ board meeting that discussed how "the description of the history of the National Socialist period by unbidden people with dubious tendencies in the illustrated press" was to be averted, he himself cited the "table talk" project as urgently needed "to confront the danger of things being trivialized by the journalism that is emerging."[31] As indicated the institute, which in this case Ritter dominated and which unanimously accepted his suggestion,[32] fell into both scholarly and political discredit through the publication as a whole and the prepublication in particular.[33] As State Secretary Walter Strauß explained, shortly before the volume's appearance, "the Federal Chancellor expressed his strong perplexity over this"; viewed politically, "in connection with the attacks on its first publication, the institute's existence is at stake."[34] Bavarian first minister Hans Ehard also reacted sharply in an article in the *Bayerische Staatszeitung* of 11 August 1951, after which the institute's board directly criticized the prepublication, Ritter's foreword itself, his thematic division of the material, and the numerous subheads in the manner of a "Goethe breviary."[35] But for the board, what was decisive was the absence of any commentary: "The preface of Prof. Ritter does not speak out clearly enough against Hitler, and Picker's foreword is simply superfluous," but a commentary was needed for at least two thirds of the book.[36] There was general astonishment over "the extent to which Prof. Ritter . . . underestimated the importance of a scholarly commentary."[37] At the same time, the board did not accuse Ritter of scholarly incompetence, but spoke simply of a "tactical mistake";[38] indeed, for Hans Rothfels what was at work here was "a certain neglect of particular psychological dimensions."[39] Still, in January 1952 a decision was reached to encourage Ritter to leave the board.[40]

For its part, Ritter's foreword suggested a defensive strategy from its first sentence. He expressly affirmed dispensing with a commentary, despite an awareness, as he noted, of "the danger that uncomprehending readers will take Hitler's most brazen assertions at face value because they were delivered in such a self-sure way."[41] From our present perspective the naïveté with which the Freiburg historian laid claim to a standpoint of "truth" and objectivity "beyond accusations and defense, damnation and glorification"[42] is highly remarkable. The naïveté lies in an unhesitating presentation of Picker's material in three different respects. First, Hitler was pronouncedly trivialized *both* in the "table talk" and in Ritter's foreword. What emerged in both, in Ritter's own earnest words, was "a well-rounded, truly vibrant [*lebendig*] image of the entire person."[43] Ritter thus highlighted Hitler's humor as much as his love of animals. And there was an equally trivializing uncritical reproduction of opposing stereotypes such as that of the "magical spell" the dictator cast on his audience, his "seductive" and "truly demonic" qualities.[44] (Institute director Mau himself vehemently defended just that point: "Evil," *das Böse*, was by no means recognizable as such in all in its manifestations; precisely that rendered it dangerous and uncanny: peaceable Hitler, "in conversation about technology, dogs, women, or art, stands in no contradiction to the Hitler of the hate-filled, violent, bloodthirsty monologues." Both facets belonged in the differentiated picture "that it is the historian's task" to produce.[45]) Second, the comparative possibilities that Ritter raised were oddly artificial. He thus compared all of Hitler's table talk to Luther's, contrastively referred to Bismarck's informality in the German military headquarters in 1870–71, and believed he could see an echo of stoic philosophy in Hitler's fatalism.[46] At one point, Ritter posed the question of whether Hitler was being done an injustice "when his appearance is seen as somehow operatic"; at other points he supplied the self-stylizing dictator with even more literary panache, with fanaticism gleaming "uncannily from

Hitler's eyes" and readers of the "table talk" feeling themselves transported to "Klingsor's enchanted garden." But the naïveté's third and most crucial dimension remained the drastic historiographical abstinence, often echoing the numerous, by no means innocuous clichés from Picker's own foreword,[47] accompanying Ritter's inflationary rhetoric regarding the significance of his documentary source: this abstinence was conveyed in a mere paraphrasing of Hitler's remarks over pages written in the historical present. In this respect, the form that Ritter's own resistance took to the document he praised as an "everyday source" is especially striking. Rather than trying to incorporate the text into his own scholarly interpretation of Nazism, he described it as a confirmation of opinions expressed earlier in the preface: as reflecting demonism, the "barbarism of mass humanity" or "technicized barbarity," and finally a "fatality" (*Verhängnis*) of person and nation, the latter allowing "itself to be seduced by him and that now—long since having become a tool of his will to power—had to bear the entire burden of responsibility for his rule."[48]

It would be Hannah Arendt who took vehement public exception to the volume, seeing it as a "more misleading than illuminating document"[49] with, in its published form, a "tendency to glorify the great man" that she blamed on Picker, Ritter, and the IfZ: "Since all commentary has been dispensed with, the free, unopposed word has been left to Hitler, just as in his lifetime."[50] The text, she indicated, was nothing short of "propaganda for Hitler" and "assistance to German neo-Nazism," however involuntary; one would hope that the IfZ would learn from its "blunder" and from the "so suspicious popularity of this 'source.'"[51] Arendt's indignation homed in on the "ambivalently undecided" core of the published volume, on Ritter's protestations "in an afterword set in the smallest possible print," and on "certain subheads" insinuating a "difference between Himmler and Hitler" (the "uncritical publication of his propaganda speeches at table will in any case serve to support the historically completely unfounded fairy tale of the 'good' Hitler who knew nothing of 'bad' Himmler's deeds").[52] Instead of positivistically and pedantically beating the dead horse of the dictator's militarily "inessential errors," what should have been demonstrated was the "essentially mendacious nature of the talks"—this especially the case, Arendt added, in view of the "'eradication' of the Jews and eastern peoples." For while Hitler was still chatting away in his "table talk" "about suitable areas of settlement for Jews and the possibility that even Jews were decent people," since the summer of 1941 those groups were being shot to death by the hundreds of thousands.[53] Hence for Arendt as well, both the Hitler document and its presentation encapsulated the problem of deferred historiography: the document had been edited by someone "who is not aware that a historical-political source is determined by the moment in which certain things are said to a certain audience." And she described the German "audience" of the time rather bluntly: as stamped by "a striking lack of enlightenment."[54]

Soon after its publication in 1951, *Hitler's Table Talk* was removed from circulation, to be published anew outside the IfZ a decade later. The first edition's connection with the IfZ was not mentioned.[55] The organization according to subject and theme that Ritter had still preferred was done away with and the passages omitted in 1951 restored. Now the military historian Percy Ernst Schramm, who taught in Göttingen, took on the material's classification, assessment, and interpretation, initiating a "medical explication of the 'Hitler case,'" which was to be handed over to psychologists and psychiatrists for whom, in Schramm's words, "historians must be limited to the role of assistants."[56] Such restraint is remarkable considering that perhaps no other historian had been so personally close to Hitler as, in fact, Schramm. It is true that in the Third Reich's early years he looked down with elite distance at everything petty-bourgeois in Nazism. But Hitler's foreign policy always had his wholehearted admiration, and he joined not only the SA in 1934 but the party in 1937. During the war, he was for some years the official staff diarist of the German High Command, serving under General Walter Warlimont, hence part of the Wehrmacht's inner circle.[57] After the war he published several books based on this intimate perspective.[58] But when it came to explaining Hitler, he preferred focusing on a demonically pathological essence to any sort of serious historical research; indeed history was here reduced to pseudo-explanation—the aim being, from our present perspective quite transparently, to accommodate Schramm's picture of his own "neutral" official function. In referring to Hitler as "the great 'X'"—*das große "X"*—Schramm was thus referring to what he wished to have understood as a mysterious, demonic, by implication irresistible "substance" to the dictator's "being"—*die Substanz seines Wesens*. But the reality was more banal and shabby: Schramm was merely one of many willing followers. In any event, although in his presentation of an effort to fathom such a substance Schramm capitulated as a historian, in making use of his own biographical proximity to Hitler's personal doctors Brandt and Hasselbach to gain information, he was not at all dispensing with interpretation.[59] His interpretive effort ended with an indication that "there were so to speak several Hitlers": that presumably located behind the various external forms was the "uncanny Hitler," and behind that the "ultimate Hitler," to be grappled with by physicians.

For Schramm, then, the "fact of Hitler"—*Faktum Hitler*—represented a "vacuum," a "borderline case of human individuality."[60] But as suggested, the thesis of Hitler's "double-faced and enigmatic" nature[61] is a transparently apologetic construction; as the "actual face" of Hitler, the dictator's "Medusa's face," Schramm explained, would, once seen, have even turned his most fanatic accomplices ("members of the round table") into stone.[62] It thus became clear that no normal mortal could resist a man with such demonic powers. As for Hitler's rabid antisemitism, for Schramm this was a mere "tick" resembling that of a medieval man who "sensed the devil everywhere." In this way it simply represented, Schramm was suggesting, one aspect of the dictator's general "social and weltanschauung-based ressentiment." Hence in Schramm's picture Hitler behaved as enigmatically, irrationally, and pathologically toward the Jews as he did toward the church, the worldly administration, jurists, professors, the middle class, and royalty.[63] In his preface to the *Table Talk*'s new edition, Schramm in fact referred to the mass murder of the Jews only once: in the face of Hitler's atrocities, he observed, everything "that a Genghis Khan" ever ordered seemed small; they could only be compared to "what happened during the Russian Revolution and Stalin's violent rule."[64] Consequently, any attempt to "somehow intellectually-historically locate the Hitler problem within Germany's development" amounted to nothing but "botched method" and falsification.[65]

In light of the basic historiographical problem informing the first edition's withdrawal, Martin Broszat's expressed recommendation of this "source" for teaching contemporary history a few years after the event seems almost like pure defiance. As Broszat put it, "With the help of Hitler's table talk, it is possible to move directly to Hitler's essential characteristics"; "despite the loud critique of their publication"—this certainly constituted Broszat's tacit reference to Arendt—the talks represented "without a doubt one of the best sources for approaching Hitler's unadorned essence." Critique of the documentation, he insisted, was both "naive" and "deviant."[66] As we will see later in this chapter, starting in 1957, although the issues in play were far more complex and the stakes were higher, the same general stance toward "sources" and the need for their "unadorned" or interest-free interpretation would inform Broszat's objections to the Holocaust historiography of Joseph Wulf.

The Gerstein Report (1953)

Located in the first volume of the *Vierteljahrshefte für Zeitgeschichte*, the documentary appendix eventually known as the "Gerstein Report" was, in Hans Rothfels' words, a "witness report on the mass gassings."[67] Introduced by Rothfels, the document has an intensely ambivalent texture; in the context of the IfZ, its publication introduced another episode of "how it really was" discourse whose problematic nature only becomes evident with close consideration. Kurt Gerstein (1905–45) was an SS *Obersturmbannführer* who was found dead in his cell in the military prison of Cherche-Midi in Paris on 25 July 1945; he brought together in one person the physiognomy of a perpetrator and victim. Beginning in 1933, he was a member of both the Nazi Party and the Confessing Church; in 1936 he was dismissed form the civil service and in 1938 from the party. Following the euthanasia-defined murder of a relative, Gerstein tried to disseminate information about the murder of mentally ill persons, justifying his entry into the Waffen SS in terms of an intention of learning more about the background to this. On the one hand, since 1942 he held the position of section leader for "technical disinfection in health technology" in the SS, being responsible for the requisition of Zyklon B gas. On the other hand, his reports from Treblinka and Belzec in August 1942 and their distribution to neutral countries abroad was one of the most spectacular acts of resistance from within his milieu. Years after his death, the Tübingen denazification court continued to classify him as an "incriminated person," on the grounds that "in view of the horrific degree of the past crimes" he could not be judged free of responsibility for them: "The court is of the opinion that the concerned party did not do everything of which he was capable."[68] But on 20 January 1965, Gerstein had his name cleared by the minister-president of Baden-Württemberg, Kurt Kiesinger. He had, the announcement read, "made every effort to actively resist the National Socialist tyranny."

Simultaneously with the IfZ's publication of the Gerstein Report in the *Vierteljahrshefte für Zeitgeschichte*, the *Frankfurter Hefte* received permission to print it as a "reminder of gladly forgotten or—even worse—suppressed events." It is telling that in this case the text was supplemented by excerpts from an eyewitness report by Jankel Wiernik, a Warsaw Jew forced to work in the Treblinka *Sonderkommando* starting in August 1942 and who managed to escape during the famous revolt by Treblinka's inmates in August 1943. The full report had appeared in English and Yiddish; Heinrich Böll was responsible for Eric Joseph Cohn's German translation.[69]

Historians have assessed Gerstein's report in very different ways. Published in 1967, Saul Friedländer's book *Kurt Gerstein: The Ambiguity of Good* is the most extensive consideration to date of the report and what it reveals about Gerstein as a prototype. The book's title underscores its conceptual relationship with Hannah Arendt's report from Jerusalem over the "banality" of Eichmann's "evil": for Friedländer, the "unique character and unusual significance" of Gerstein's case lies in the "complete passivity of the 'others.' If thousands or merely hundreds of 'Gersteins' had been present in Germany . . . , then tens of thousands of Jews would certainly have been saved by precisely these 'official' accomplices of the regime."[70] Friedländer is doubtless accurate in characterizing his subject as being acutely aware of the danger of being mistaken for a monstrous criminal through the stigma of having joined the SS. The ambivalence at work in that self-image, and the "loneliness of his actions," rendered his story into that of the "tragic fate" of participation and separation that was potentially emblematic of a certain *general German* self-image. (In this respect, it is illuminating that in the intense debate over whether to erect a central Holocaust monument in Berlin in the 1990s, the figure of Gerstein played a role—albeit marginally— in the defense of the universalistic suggestions of the theologian Richard Schröder, for example, that the monument should read "Thou Shall Not Kill!"[71]) But with his observations here Friedländer has arguably only addressed one part of the problem by too closely sticking to Gerstein's sense of things, thus making the tragic dilemma of being caught between being, as it were, in a state of guilt and desiring to maintain basic norms in the center of his essay. In fact, Rothfels' introduction to the report in the *Vierteljahrshefte* points to something lying outside the framework of such a dilemma and endowing the "Gerstein Report" with an appellative framework: the historian's justification for its printing not only foregrounded the absolute secrecy maintained about the mass gassings that the report refers to but also underscored, with Gerstein as an example, the distinction between "the Nazis" and "the German *Volk*."[72]

Rothfels discussed the report at considerable length, concluding that the "crass material"—*Kraßheiten*—it contained "and that one resists accepting" manifestly inculpated not "the man who observed it but rather the events themselves and their actors."[73] These "events," namely, the mass gassings in Belzec, Treblinka, and Majdanek, were, in the words of Odilo Globocnik, cited by Gerstein at the very start of his report, "one of the most secret matters that exists anywhere at present; you could even say the most secret. Whoever speaks about it is shot on the spot. I heard that only yesterday two loudmouths were shot."[74] Against the backdrop of this fact, there is, to be sure, something undeniably odd about someone who had been thrown out of the party and had an internal sense of being a resistor nevertheless being an intimate eyewitness to the horror. It seems likely that this was a strong motivation for Rothfels citing voices referring to the "mastery" of Gerstein's "camouflage," on the one hand, the "constancy of his inner nature [*Wesen*]," on the other hand.[75]

Joseph Wulf and Léon Poliakov:
The Earliest Documenters of the Holocaust

The trap at work in the documentation I have discussed was equating the perpetrators' viewpoint with genuine historical explanation; in the process, their pronouncements became almost "scientific." On the other hand, victims' statements merely had to be deemed reassuring in tone and substance, as was the case with Anne Frank's diary, for these individuals to be appropriated into the broader social consensus. In these cases it was less the "scientific" nature of the discourse, more its "authenticity," that cast the documents in a light favored by the times. An anticipation by the sources of what people really wanted to say is a widespread phenomenon of the 1950s in the context of the "clean" Wehrmacht, the war in the East, and the genocide of the Jews. But inversely, the documents documenting the Final Solution, the massive participation in it, its preliminary steps, and its consequences were rejected, devalued, and relativized by a guild of professional historians who were otherwise inclined to fetishize documentation. For in this period, the actual documentary work on the Holocaust was being presented by two Jewish scholars, Joseph Wulf and Léon Poliakov; in 1959, it would appear in a volume titled *The Third Reich and Its Thinkers*. Their difficulties in facing an indifferent, shamed, and silent majority society were fundamental: *they* had to demonstrate their credibility, objectivity, and renunciation of revenge—a situation leading in this documentary work to particularities of a compositional, rhetorical, and metaphorical nature that will be addressed below.

In 1960, in a review of the two authors' *The Third Reich and Its Thinkers* that remains breathtaking in its shamelessness, Armin Mohler reproached them to the effect that both this book and their previously published "tomes" (*Wälzer*) were simply a "nuisance" (*Unfug*) and in any case "a kind of address book for the continuation of "denazification." Serious scholarship played no role here, because the "historian's first duty, to view the individual fact in its general context," had been violated: "I am unaware of the biography [*sic*] of the editors, but it is hard to imagine that they have direct experience of a totalitarian state." The book's title, Mohler indicated, would "in honesty" have to be "A Compilation [literally, *Florilegium* (*Blütenlese*)] Concerning the Cultural Policies of the Third Reich, selected from the Nuremberg documents and the archives of the Centre de Documentation Juive in Paris." (Poliakov had co-founded that archive, together with Rabbi Isaac Schneersohn, in Paris in 1943.)[76]

The documentation of Poliakov and Wulf had begun appearing in short intervals starting in 1956; being the first effort to describe the annihilation of European Jewry, it had drawn some attention both inside and outside Germany. Along with *Das Dritte Reich und seine Denker* (hereafter *The Third Reich and Its Thinkers*), it comprised the volumes *Das Dritte Reich und die Juden* (hereafter *The Third Reich and the Jews*) and *Das Dritte Reich und seine Diener* (hereafter *The Third Reich and Its Servants*); the final volume, *Das Dritte Reich und seine Vollstrecker: Die Liquidation von 500,000 Juden im Ghetto Warschau* (hereafter *The Third Reich and Its Executioners*; subtitle: The Liquidation of 500,000 Jews in the Warsaw Ghetto) would be authored by Wulf alone.[77] In contrast to what some of the titles suggest, all the volumes approached the Nazi extermination process directly, in the authors' own words, "as necessarily emerging from the problem we are treating. The National Socialist way of thinking itself led there."[78] And they focused on the process both in a differentiated manner and in painstaking detail.

At the time the volumes in question were appearing, the term "Holocaust" was not yet in circulation. At a distance of more than five decades, it is clear that this ambitious project was not only courageous and innovative but would exert a long-term effect only possessed by books defying fashion. What distinguished the project was nothing other than precisely an intense concern with and focus on the "general context" that Mohler wished to deny it. Both Wulf and Poliakov had more than ample "direct experience of a totalitarian state." As a child, Poliakov had fled with his parents from St. Petersburg after the Bolshevik Revolution; in 1940 he fled from a German war-prison camp, joined the resistance, then playing a pivotal role in organizing French Jewish resistance to the Nazi extermination efforts. He lost his entire family during the Holocaust.[79] Wulf spent 1941 to 1945 in ghettos and concentration camps and bore the Auschwitz tattoo number 114866; after he regained his freedom he promised himself that he would make the Third Reich's history his only concern "to the end of my life."[80]

Joseph Wulf (see Figure 9) was born in 1912 in Chemnitz into a prosperous Jewish merchant's family.[81] Starting in 1917, the family lived in Krakow, where Wulf would later begin his studies of both Jewish thought and agriculture. Although he did initially continue his studies in the former field in Nancy und Paris, despite his father's hopes he did not become a rabbi, instead deciding to become a writer. In 1934 he married Jenta Falik-Dachner; soon he had to have both his wife and son hidden from the Germans with Polish peasants. Wulf himself joined a Jewish resistance organization, was caught by the Gestapo, interrogated, and taken to a camp; he only managed to escape on one of the notorious death marches organized in the spring of 1945. His wife and son survived the war, but most of the rest of his extended family was murdered, his father in the Plaszow camp in Krakow; his mother, mother-in-law, and her small daughter in Belzec; his brother while being transported to Auschwitz.[82] Already in February 1945, Wulf helped found the Jewish Historical Commission in Poland, which published thirty-one documentations concerning the Third Reich in the two years before he left the country. In the postwar period he lived in Stockholm, then Paris, where he worked as a newspaper correspondent, co-founded the Centre pour l'histoire des Juifs Polonais, and became acquainted with Poliakov. In the 1950s he returned to Germany and lived with his wife in Berlin.

When the first volume of the documentation of Wulf and Poliakov was published in 1955 by Arno Scholz's left-wing Arani Verlag in Berlin, it marked the breaking of a West German taboo; in particular a documentary excerpt bearing the signature of Konrad Adenauer's political advisor Otto Bräutigam sparked an extraordinary national and international press reaction. (Bräutigam, who would accompany Konrad Adenauer on his famous trip to Moscow,[83] had been director of the section on "general politics" of the Reich Ministry for the Occupied Eastern Territories; the citation in question reads: "Through word of mouth, clarity may well have meanwhile been reached in the Jewish Question.") The volume was not a best seller. Nevertheless, "everyone praised the book with words such as 'an important work,' 'a very useful book.' Some even referred to it as a 'classical documentary work,'" Wulf would bitterly comment two years later, his point being that such elevation to "classic" status was no realization of his own intentions.[84] In total, his "prehistorical excavations," as Wulf ironically put it,[85] were received in part "positively-neutrally,"[86] in part "peeved [verschnupft]."[87]

Today the documentary volumes are either dutifully cited in specialized bibliographies or entirely overlooked.[88] In any case, the fact that the volumes are not cited, hence apparently are not consulted or used, indicates that their innovation and singularity are consistently not recognized. This seems to represent something like the later culmination of the nearly entirely negative response by the West German historians to the volumes when they first appeared: the typical response was sneering at "the excess of citation-laden margins," denigrating "the hardly meaningful headings" as unscholarly,[89] when there were any comments at all: the volumes were ignored in both Theodor Schieder's *Historische Zeitschrift* and in the scarcely less important *Geschichte in Wissenschaft und Unterricht*. Wulf's documentation concerning Martin Bormann was qualified by Max Braubach in passing as "an in any case highly illuminating material collection."[90] All told, the friendliest reception came in a review of *The Third Reich and the Jews* by Hans-Günther Seraphim, then offering in Göttingen what seems to have been the first academic course in Germany treating the genocide of the Jews, a course making "modest" use of documentary evidence.[91] Seraphim himself, however, insisted that the book did not fulfill "the demand for a scholarly history of the National Socialist regime's policies toward and persecution of the Jews." This, he insisted, still needed to be written.[92]

The First Controversy between Broszat and Wulf

Martin Broszat (1926–89) belonged, like Buchheim, to the younger generation working at the IfZ, and like Buchheim, his reaction to documentation of Nazi crimes by Jews was downright allergic. Concerning *The Third Reich and Its Servants*, he objected that, despite his "painful shame," the book was polemical and "nonscientific."[93] The editors, he explained, had "foregone the ultimate precision of scholarly [*wissenschaftlich*] editions," with the question being raised "whether the present documentary collection" corresponded "to the requisites of exhaustiveness and methodological circumspection in respect to selection, organization, and themes." Such documentation, Broszat continued, in particular an "ironic tone" having a "merely journalistic" effect, perhaps was appropriate for "stubborn deniers of facts" but abandoned "the distance of scientific-historical [*wissenschaftlich-historisch*] documentary publications," blocking rather than opening the way to a "deeper grasp of the historical material." At this point Broszat turned to legal metaphors: What the documentary collection "demonstrates is the impossibility, applicable to all political white papers [*politische Farbbücher*], of offering a precisely formulated proof with documents *alone*, which is to say without their critical processing. Documentation inevitably becomes a plea."[94] "Proof," "plea"—the word choice, the "white paper" context, the rejection of the work of Poliakov and Wulf in general—all this revealed Broszat's conviction that a description of the extermination of the Jews could not be left to Jewish survivors. The argumentation becomes even clearer when Broszat's objections focused on the photographic material included in *The Third Reich and Its Servants*, which he viewed as "without verbal-logical conceptuality [*ohne sprachlich-logische Begrifflichkeit*]," hence exposed to the "danger of suggestive persuasion." This applied, Broszat explained, even more to photos than to film, the "static duration" of details cut away from their environment rendering the photos' contents into "something ecstatic-symbolic and suggestive," and doing so with images that were "already inherently pathetic": "The documentation then succeeds only through excessive impact; it allows no place for consideration and control. Precisely because National Socialist journalism [*Publizistik*] made use to such extent and so unthinkingly of the seductive medium of suggestive pictorial effect to both fan enthusiasm and inflame enmities and hate, the historical-intellectual [*historisch-geistig*] examination of the National Socialist period should find a better means." And in fact, as H. G. Adler put it more in admiration than critically, the authors had assembled an ungainly [*ungefüge*] primer of the atrocious," a "ghostly vortex [*Gespensterwirbel*]" from which readers could only distance themselves through "flight."[95] Here "the German reader is presented verbatim for the first time with the most important documents concerning the history and execution of the policies toward the Jews of the National Socialist state."[96] In their presentation, Poliakov and Wulf were provocative in a broad range of respects: in their sense of symbolism, their photos, the documentary collection in general, and various comments. Even "terrible things" were "sometimes easily explained," they observed.[97] Although his approach was attributed to reductionism, irrationalism, and unrestrained emotion, it was in fact strongly in debt to something like a pathos of the concrete: "In our century," Wulf would remark in a separately published, short documentation of the press and radio in the Third Reich, "one could almost say the camp inmate grasped the character and goal of the concepts of freedom and public opinion far more concretely than the thinker"[98]—the basic point here running directly counter to Broszat's call for "a scientific approach" (*Wissenschaftlichkeit*), "rational conviction," "systematic work" (*Systematik*) by those who "had to suffer under the rule of National Socialism": "When elevated to a principle, bitterness and sarcasm" could "be no help in historically deciphering the phenomenon of National Socialism."[99]

As we have already seen, Poliakov and Wulf were not the only researchers to have devoted their writing to the Nazi Final Solution and to have for that reason waited fruitlessly for public and professional recognition: this was the time when Gerald Reitlinger's descriptions of the genocide and the SS apparatus were being reproached by Hans Buchheim for "completely lacking understanding and respect for the entire German anti-Nazi resistance movement," when material from Reitlinger's books made its way into a poem of Paul Celan[100] but not into Germany's historiography, and when Raul Hilberg could find no German publisher for his encyclopedic study *The Destruction of the European Jews*. As things stood, only a handful of outsiders, among them a high percentage of autodidacts like Wulf, were then willing to engage in what Hilberg termed a "revolt against silence."[101]

But what were the special characteristics of the documentation of Poliakov and Wulf? What was the idea of Nazism, the Nazi perpetrators, and Nazism's relation to Germany upon which their volumes were based? How did the two authors thematically address the process of genocide? What problems did they pose, and what form of metahistorical reflection informed their work?

The Holocaust in Poliakov and Wulf

In contrast to the overwhelming majority of West German historians, Poliakov and Wulf placed the German destruction of European Jewry at the center of their interpretation of Nazism. They described the Holocaust as a "technique" placed "in the service of a methodological denial of life," and similarly to Hannah Arendt they spoke of an "industry," of "mass murder as a goal in itself":[102] "A completely new industry emerged with all the trappings—main centers Auschwitz, Treblinka, and Sobibor," the "complicated machinery" functioning "in no other way than would be expected from German organizational capacities."[103] The decisive problems and thematic fields informing the past twenty years' research were already evident in the work of these two authors, albeit tacitly in the form of choice of documentation and organization, together with the very limited commentary. They spoke of "robbery and plunder" with a directness worlds removed from the metaphysical constructions of guilt manifest in the writings of Heimpel, Wittram, and other luminaries of the postwar West German historical scene. The process described in the first of the five chapters of *The Third Reich and the Jews*, they explained, placed its stamp on all phases of the tragedy[104] and took in all social strata from which the perpetrators had emerged. The process was one of *both* "organized robbery" and "shameless plundering," "corpse stripping."[105] They found it no contradiction at all to together treat the behavior of business leaders and SS officers, "merchants, doctors and other academics," on the one hand, and individuals "fighting in the East" who would quickly send "rings or watches seized from Jews as gifts to their brides and children," on the other hand. But despite the precise details involved here, they kept a steady focus on the more general dimension of events: the "decisive" element of the mass murder was not this tragic nexus between "Jewish misfortune" and a broad public interest in the "large-scale Aryanization program." "Profit-seeking" and "self-interest," the authors argued, at least had "a meaning that can be derived from known human qualities and can be harmonized with them." The "decisive element" was, to the contrary, "the absolute senselessness of someone running amok."[106] Accordingly the authors gave the volume's second and most extensive chapter the simple and drastic title "Exterminate, Exterminate!" (*Ausrotten, ausrotten!*).[107] In the subsequent volume on *The Third Reich and Its Servants*, Wulf and Poliakov put it as follows: death "was a horrific [*entsetzlich*] goal in itself, not only a ghastly [*grauenhaft*] means to reach a certain goal."[108]

But perhaps the authors' comments on the relation of the Germans to the extermination campaign represented this documentary project's most provocative aspect. "They served all too well"[109] could be the motto of one of the central arguments at work in all the volumes. In a sense this could be read as an anticipation in the 1950s of Goldhagen's controversial thesis of "Hitler's willing executioners," but the analysis of Poliakov and Wulf was actually grounded in the *inverse* problem of the centuries-old "extraordinary streams of spiritual energy" characterizing the relationship between German and European Jewish history.[110] The hiatus between that and the separate historical reality of Germany as the source of "a complex of industrial murder new to our civilization"[111] is a foundational contradiction inscribed as a subtext in this documentary collection, rather than being consigned to silence through a universalized concept of antisemitism. Later, in his "press and radio" book, Wulf countered the prevalent inflated fixation on the totalitarianism of the Nazi system with the passing remark that in the end, every form of totalitarianism was based on a "hysteria of power."[112] In this period as well, he would repeatedly underscore the personal and intentional side of the murder process, for instance, referring to "hostility to reason" and a loss of "objectivity and integrity"—and to a murderously "philistine," "petty-bourgeois" sense of the world (*Banausengemüt*; *Spießersinn*).[113] Nazism, he conceded, had "in any case" powerfully intensified "the super-absurdity [*Superunding*] of totalitarianism, folly."[114] But what characterized it most strongly alongside cruelty and hate were thoroughly "German" factors: "diligent industriousness" (*emsige Betriebsamkeit*), "assiduity" (*Beflissenheit*), "efficiency most valuable for life" (*lebenswerteste Tüchtigkeit*), "factual knowledge," and a fulfillment of one's duties."[115] Within this framework of dutiful and efficient industry, Wulf and Poliakov suggested, the Third Reich's "executioners" needed countless "servants," who alongside their duties "had to be familiar with the problem that has entered history as the 'Final Solution.' The present documentary collection thus makes irrefutably clear their behavior in respect to this greatest of all crimes of National Socialism."[116]

The authors here properly distinguished "entirely private attitudes regarding these things," hence whatever antisemitic motivation the various individuals involved may or may not have had, from the functioning of Hitler's *Judenpolitik*, the "approach they took . . . as responsible officials within their areas of competence," hence their actions in themselves.[117] In the latter respect, those individuals "pitifully failed," whatever "they may have felt in their deepest hearts." For Poliakov and Wulf, the "most immense tragedy of our century" was a German tragedy, carefully planned and smoothly functioning "without any hitches."[118]

In the approach they took, Poliakov and Wulf centered on entirely other perpetrators than those perceived in West German society. The "connection between diplomacy and Auschwitz," they insisted, was "surprisingly close," the local authorities intimately involved, an outer appearance of rule of law maintained. They used strong images to describe a past reality emerging from the mass of filed documents they had seen: "The diplomatic delegations in France, Hungary, and Rumania" developed into "spinning rooms in which the Norns spun the fate of the Jews in each separate land." They even spoke of the diplomatic service's "pleasure in combat" (*Kampflust*) against the Jews; and the combat's "enthused pioneers" (*begeisterte Vorkämpfer*) are named (Franz Rademacher, director of the German Foreign Office's "Jewish Department"; Eberhard von Thadden, advisor on "Jewish matters" to Foreign Minister Ribbentrop; Undersecretary of State Martin Luther, specialist on variations of the "Jewish Question" in different foreign states); and these figures were distinguished from the "more phlegmatic contestants."[119] In any event, Wulf recognized and, in highly non-metaphysical fashion, spelled out the historical reality of the tension between "racial mania" and "the machinery of annihilation"[120]—yet another insight that nearly guaranteed a lack of scholarly success in West Germany of the 1950s. Only other outsiders saw clearly what made the Wulf and Poliakov volumes extraordinary—for instance, H. G. Adler in London, who devoted longer radio reviews to each of the volumes. In this documentation, Adler explained, "the infection of the different branches of civil administration and the Wehrmacht by National Socialism's evil spirit [*Ungeist*]" was clearly outlined, its wartime scope "gaining ever-more eerie dimensions because far too many responsible parties displayed no scruples about participating in the crimes or were merely indifferent, or else let the crimes have free reign through inertia, while too many others could not decide on courageous resistance, opting instead for simply looking away, more or less disgusted."[121]

Alongside the German Foreign Ministry, those whom Poliakov and Wulf tied to "racial legislation," "zealous service," and simple "obsequiousness"[122] included other government officials and soldiers. At the same time, on the basis of countless documents they demonstrated, crucially, widespread "freedom of action" by these persons[123]—numerous cases in which "it emerges that another approach was entirely possible."[124] Sometimes, the documentation generated insight or encouraged those with a sober sense of the truth to speak out. We thus find Ansgar Skriver observing, in an article on theater in the Third Reich in a local Berlin paper, "Whoever reads this may no longer wish to hear the popular references to the 'National Socialist reign of violence' that are almost stereotypically used by our radio stations' news editors. . . . The violence did not descend on the German people but rather emerged from that people." "If Wulf's documentation were not there in black and white," Skriver continued, "it would be difficult to believe to what catastrophic extent German culture became National Socialist culture during those twelve years."[125]

At the heart of the historical contribution made by these books of Poliakov and Wulf was a focus on "the broad leeway and numerous variations that existed."[126] (This interpretive axis marked a basic distance from the approach taken in East Germany, where the documentation was attacked by Gerhard Strauß for obscuring "the lines of continuation of German fascism," its "colonialism" and "imperialism"; Wulf, Strauß indicated, could not hide his own bourgeois "constraints.") The first two volumes of the documentation were devoted to what Adler described as "the Nazi state . . . in its direct operations,"[127] although the "pioneers of the extermination" (the expression would be coined by Götz Aly and Susanne Heim in 1991) were here by no means neglected. In the third volume, they made, to again cite Adler, "the pulse of the National

Socialist era palpable": a "pulse" within which "foolhardiness as much as misguided idealism, confusion together with a fragile or destroyed sense of value,
overbearing intellect, arrogance, and often also sheer foolishness and stupidity
could all be heard."[128] At a time when the West German historical establishment avoided any mention of the Third Reich's "cultural underground" (Adler
again), Wulf and Poliakov considered the realms of religion, philosophy, education, scholarly activity, and natural-science research.[129] They drew no clear-
cut, systematic separating line between world-famous figures and third-ranking
nonentities in Germany's intellectual scene of the 1930s and 1940s, and their
documentation both brought together and carefully distinguished all orientations of forced and voluntary conformity: "woolgathering . . . oddballs" (again
Adler), fellow travelers, pure opportunists, and blind patriotic enthusiasts, together with virulent, believing biological racists, a panopticon of variously motivated personal and ideological viewpoints. The two authors thus presented an
"exemplary case . . . of a university's perversion" and, in that context, "situations that were nothing less than schizophrenic,"[130] consigning "the feeling-
laden outpourings of professors seeking a new mysticism" to readers' mockery.[131]
And although Wulf and Poliakov confirmed "that a large portion of German
natural scientists—whatever their inclinations or political convictions—kept
their laboratory doors firmly closed to racial mania," they also underscored
that the same profession had announced to "Nazi patriots" and their "Ger-
manism" "that only the Germanic spirit was capable of furthering science's
recognition of the truth."[132]

In a language marked by an undertone of pain, rage, and incomprehension, the two authors likewise attacked the "'representatives' of German legal
studies and culture" and their "struggle" over how to deal with the "menacing
problem of 'Mischlinge'"—of people with "mixed blood." Likewise, in page
after page they demonstrated the close connection between the "Wehrmacht
and Jew-baiting,"[133] a connection that would become firmly established in
West Germany's educated middle-class consciousness only following the fierce
debate sparked by the "Crimes of the Wehrmacht" exhibition starting in the
mid-1990s. But what remained decisive for Wulf was always "specific lines of
demarcation," the "border human beings sometimes cross, whether intentionally or through negligence."[134] For while in a highly differentiated manner, Poliakov and Wulf confirmed a complex consisting of "distancing, not wanting to
know, and complicity,"[135] they also cast scorn on "a general's shy mitigating
efforts" that sufficed to reinterpret his signed anti-Jewish orders as "mild" and
thus ease his conscience.[136] Here in the documentation's second volume as
well, it is clear that the authors considered it self-evident that "complicity with
or even shared guilt for the work of extermination" could be avoided only by

those who dared "stand up against it." Only those who consciously refused to go along preserved "dignity," hence "their nation's honor,"[137] a position also evident in the portrait emerging in Wulf's later documentation of "press and radio," as described by H. G. Sellenthin, of abject "failure, slavish acquiescence, absence of opinion, political disinterest, and German self-hate."[138]

In the introduction to *The Third Reich and Its Thinkers*, Poliakov and Wulf insist that although

> the promiscuous mix of thinkers and murderers saddens us, it also illuminates the complex problem of the Third Reich. [Cf. the directly following indication, in the foreword to the first, "Weltanschauung" chapter, that "the unbelievable tangle of texts and names marking this chapter furnishes the reader in advance with an idea of what our book describes."] . . . We considered it irreconcilable with our duty as historians to omit this or that excerpt simply because its author perhaps could show us that at the bottom of his heart he had been an opponent of National Socialism. . . . We may concede mitigating circumstances to the involuntary thinkers we chose here, but do they deserve the exoneration of silence?[139]

In responding to their question in the negative, the authors were laying out part of an effort to offer a "cross section of the German intellectual word under the National Socialist regime." In doing so, they explain, "Actually no commentary was needed. However, we were obliged to document not only Adolf Hitler and Heinrich Himmler, but also the authorial and rhetorical omissions of personalities who were well known and esteemed in the Third Reich, and are still so today. Many of them felt defamed through having such neighbors and expressed their displeasure about this to us."[140] For Wulf and Poliakov, this conveyed displeasure confirmed a clear distinction regarding motives, "complicity," excuses and ex post facto explanations: "Was it narrow-mindedness or schadenfreude, careerism, or nothing more than fear that was at play here? This is, in fact, simply of no importance! Individual-psychological factors can hardly have a place here. The sole thing really counting in this respect is made up of the uncanny forces, the flowing together of the most varied possible streams. In the end it had to inevitably culminate in the worst catastrophe in the history of Germany and indeed of Europe."[141] The main factors that Poliakov and Wulf identified in their own general assessment were "ice-cold rationalism" *and* a "will to murder," a "plainly sadistic rage directed at anything weak and innocent" leading directly to an "eradication of unworthy life."[142] But in light of the successful protests by ordinary Germans against the euthanasia program, the authors posed the following basic question to themselves and their readers:

"Why wasn't the public pressure strong enough in the case of the Jews as well?" "In this way," they continued, "we find ourselves facing a new complex of questions—facing, let us admit it, a horrible question." And the answer they suggested was itself to the point: "Defamation on such a scale, with that sort of vehemence and persistence, would have to bear fruit."[143]

"The German man," commented the authors with a touch of malice, "has certainly not lacked soldierly courage. . . . But the world is just as much aware of how closely his lack of civil courage between 1933 and 1945 was often tied to a fear of losing the authorities' favor, [and] to concern about public opinion— that of the dear neighbor or even the *Blockwart* [the Nazi block warden]." In this context, Poliakov and Wulf spoke bluntly of "weakness of character present to excess," a "lack of genuine inner conviction," and "a general joy in marching in rank and file without any responsibility and often against one's better knowledge." Such feelings, the authors added, continued to be encountered in Germany of the 1950s.[144]

In the last chapter of *The Third Reich and the Jews*, Wulf and Poliakov turned to the in fact "fortunately large number" of Germans who, facing the same, unavoidable choice between "villainy and heroism" as countless others, had differed from them in defying the Nazi system; the authors went so far in their introduction as to dedicate the volume to their memory.[145] Unfortunately, as they indicated in the foreword to that chapter, although whoever somehow "wished to help could do so," "by far the largest portion of the German people was concerned with other things,"[146] a basic reality also reflected by the situation in the German universities, as described in *The Third Reich and Its Thinkers*, a situation encapsulated in the observation that "among the teachers of true caliber, entirely rabid Hitlerites were certainly as rare as heroic temperaments cast in the mold of Professor [Kurt] Huber."[147]

Wulf's Motivation and
the Premise of Historical Objectivity

Joseph Wulf's intense engagement with his research object produced precision— no "commemorative pathos" emptied of concrete content. In remarks offered in an interview in the mid-1960s, Wulf indicated that he suffered from "archivitis," and that he was striving toward a synthesis of the historical sources with "what he experienced directly as a resistance fighter and Auschwitz prisoner."[148] He did not share Harry Pross's view of documents as "tools against evil"[149] but wished simply to inform and enlighten. As remarkable as it may still seem in retrospect, he was also one of the few historians writing in the 1950s to pose the most basic of all questions: in his words in an unpublished manuscript on excesses of the German idea of continuity, "How could it be that the annihilation of European Jewry could be planned and carried out in the twentieth century and in the center of the civilized world?"[150] Importantly, for Wulf the historical caesura grounding this question was not 1933 and the "seizure of power"—the long-lasting focus of discussion in Germany after the war—but 1942, hence the dictatorship's move into a policy of extermination. (For Wulf, "the year 1933" would remain an unsolved problem—the capacity of highly cultivated Germans to "suddenly function like idiots," a source of continued astonishment.[151])

Wulf always showed caution when it came to trying to "classify the entirety of the National Socialist conceptual world" (his way of putting it in a manuscript for a presentation to be given on Germany's Süddeutscher Rundfunk);[152] this caution was arguably a source of his ability to link what would emerge as the Holocaust with institutions, groups of perpetrators, and plans formed in the 1930s and 1940s, together with their historical locations, something that would again be undertaken only in the 1990s by Ludolf Herbst, Ulrich Herbert, Saul Friedländer, and Götz Aly. In Wulf's estate, we thus find a 130-page text, "Responsible High-Ranking Officers around Hitler: Studies in the History of the Reichswehr and Wehrmacht."[153] Here Wulf not only closely examined the relationship between the German army, on the one hand, the special killing units and SS extermination troops, on the other hand, together with the so-called Commissar Order, but in chapters on the mythology informing "Operation Tannenberg" and Nazi education in the Wehrmacht also explored, on a high level of historical scholarship, the question of the historical and institutional continuity of Nazi ideas and premises—another area that the historical establishment would only enter years later.[154] Wulf thus defined the Holocaust in terms of its intentionality—as a "war against the Jewish people,"[155] in this way anticipating the approach taken in 1975 by Lucy Dawidowicz in her best-selling book on *The War against the Jews*,[156] and pointed to the "ideology of murder" of the Reich Security Main Office: in their goals, Wulf indicated, the party and the SS were unified, but not in their methods and long-term planning.[157] He referred to the Volksdeutsche Mittelstelle (the SS's "Main Welfare Office for Ethnic Germans") and the general framework of the Nazi "Master Plan East" in this context, noting, "It is important to here keep in mind that plans for resettlement were not only Himmler's concern—there were countless such institutions."[158] (Again, Nazi resettlement policies would only be taken up systematically in the mid-1990s, first in a documentary volume edited by Czesław Madajczyk, then by Götz Aly.[159]) Also, he confronted the "excesses of the German idea of continuity"—a reference to Friedrich Meinecke's notion, discussed earlier, of a continuous authentic German tradition existing apart from and

above the Nazi catastrophe—by focusing with great precision both on traditions brought forward into Nazism from the Wilhelminian period, for instance,
a tradition of "hardness, violence, and contempt for human beings" and
Wagner's "musical images of the end of the world,"[160] and on the (sharply condemned) postwar careers of broad circles of former Nazi activists: their "disposition toward mystification," their postwar publications stamped with "documentary pathos," and their formation in the same period of various coteries. (Wulf
here refers to, among others, Generals Manstein and Reichenau; the founding
in 1950 of the Reich Fraternity in Bielefeld, which was frequented by Himmler's
daughter; and the Freikorps Deutschland, founded in August 1951 by Vienna's
former *Gauleiter*, Eduard Frauenfeld.[161]) Wulf found the appearance of a palliat-
ing obituary for Nazi legislator and SS theorist Wilhelm Stuckart in the *Frankfurter Allgemeine Zeitung* unbearable, together with, for example, the nomination
by the Christian Democrat and Free Democratic parties of Herbert Gerigk to
serve as the cultural-affairs director for the city of Bochum without taking into
account his virulent *Lexicon of Jews in Music* (1940) and the appointment of Alfred
Baum, former deputy director of Veit Harlan's notorious piece of antisemitic
film propaganda, *Jud Süß*, as director of Radio Free Berlin.

Taboo Breaking: Names, Places, Dates

From our present perspective, not only the contents and density of Wulf and
Poliakov's documentation is impressive, but perhaps even more so, the presen-
tational form of these texts and others written by Wulf alone—a "documentary
style" opening access, as H. G. Sellenthin indicated in a review of Wulf's 1963
book *Literatur und Dichtung im Dritten Reich*, to the Third Reich's "essential core."[162]
This "style" involves extended reflection on questions of objectivity, authorial
position, and survivors' accounts of the death camps, together with commentary
on the nature of the work itself. In general, the published texts, photos, facsim-
iles, and documentary excerpts represent an extraordinarily heterogeneous
inventory. As mentioned, they cover both the most prominent Nazi criminals
(Himmler, Stroop, etc.) and subalterns; readers are presented with key documents (for example, the Wannsee Conference minutes), on the one hand, and
peripheral, at times absurd discoveries revealing facets of Nazism, on the other
hand. While some already published material was incorporated, for instance,
the Gerstein Report together with the footnotes from the first volume of the
Vierteljahrshefte für Zeitgeschichte, the bulk of the sources presented were unpublished, with primary material (sometimes translated into German) here alternating with secondary research by other historians (for example, excerpts from
Reitlinger's book). All told, highly informative sources predominate, consistently

interspersed and supplemented by summaries and short essays (for example, in *The Third Reich and the Jews*: Léon Poliakov's essay "Six Million Are Statistically and Documentarily Confirmed"; Joseph Wulf's "Finland and Denmark Preserved Their Dignity"; and biographical essays about perpetrators (Jürgen Stroop) and victims (the Polish historian Emmanuel Ringelblum).[163]

The stylistic device of contrast is here very striking. In order to simultaneously describe ideology and reality, phraseology and daily life, in *The Third Reich and Its Servants* Poliakov and Wulf compiled various sources on one and the same page: where the main portion of individual pages was taken up by (usually) complete letters, laws and ordinances, summonses, messages, minutes, and file memoranda from the Nazi administration, they also included short excepts and sentence scraps from the ideological writing being promulgated at the time, set off by frames, a practice that generates strong tension through a form of mutual self-commentary. We thus find a citation of an army order of 2 October 1943 to the effect that "the action against the Jews [*Judenaktion*] in the night of 1 to 2 October" had been "carried out without incident."[164] On the page's bottom, one sentence from the Nazi Party's organizational book, "the Fuhrer is always right" (also 1943) is likewise printed. We find the same stylistic means applied in the volume on the Warsaw ghetto (which, to reiterate, Wulf wrote alone) in order to systematically present a double perspective of murderers and victims. Hence in the simple confrontation between the "Stroop Report" and the "Ringelblum Archive"—the presence of the latter tacitly informed by Wulf's own presence on 1 September 1946 at the unearthing of the first hidden metal milk jugs containing Emanuel Ringelblum's documentation of life in the Warsaw ghetto from the ruins of the house on Nowolipki Street 68[165]—a distance emerges that itself functions as eloquent commentary.[166] This commenting function is also at work in the headings chosen by Wulf and Poliakov for the presented source material.[167]

Already with a mere decade's distance, much of this selected documentation sounded so absurd—these "absurdities" dominating in the chapter on "Hitleriana"—that the authors could only suggest: "Laughing is healthy and can help make things clear."[168] Not rarely, they chose to use a paradoxical blend of irony and sarcasm. In the book on theater and film, in the course of a polemic aimed at the actor Werner Krauß—famous not only for his great roles in classic plays by Schiller and others but also for his contribution to *Jud Süß* and various other pro-Nazi activities, he was rehabilitated and much honored in Germany and Austria after the war—Wulf commented that "shame diminishes with increasing sin (free after Schiller)" to which he hastily added, however, "These lines are not meant to have either a polemical or ironic effect. The only thing of concern here is the cleanness and purity of modern historical documentation [*die Sauberkeit und Reinheit zeitgeschichtlicher Dokumentation*]." But again, accompanying that insistence on objectivity as a primary goal, we find authorial interjections such as the following, which is offered in relation to Nazi science and the Third Reich's "intellectual elite," in particular the "German physics" conceived by Professor Philipp Lenard: "We may be allowed to designate such an intellectual stance as a measure of madness so high as to be beyond comprehension, that stands there without precedent, and that could have not been reached without the enthused, assiduous emulation of the madman."[169]

What, then, was the understanding of objectivity that Wulf shared with Poliakov? In the short foreword to the chapter on Nazi German scholarship in *The Third Reich and Its Thinkers*,[170] the two authors argued that the Nazi view of history (what they termed the "reaction") had emerged from the cognitive doubt of figures such as Dilthey, Simmel, and Rickert, amounting to a sense that "there was no longer any objectivity," hence that "the door was wide open to any interpretation": "In this manner," they indicated, "subjectivity was granted citizenship within historiography." Their plain-spoken conclusion: "Science is defiled when placed in the service of the totalitarian state."[171] Objectivity was thus already necessary because its suppression between 1933 and 1945 itself helped explain the Third Reich's functioning. Wulf reflected further on the problem of objectivity in his book *Die bildenden Künste im Dritten Reich* (The Pictorial Arts in the Third Reich) from 1963, but now far more defensively: the historiography of contemporary events "self-evidently" occupied other dimensions than the historiography of earlier periods, since "means and instruments [are] . . . so to speak still immature, reflections more constrained, interpretation narrower."[172] For this reason, possibilities for shedding light on causal events were also more limited. Wulf's attenuation may seem surprising, but in the 1950s his rejection of claims to presenting the total picture, grand interpretations, and sweeping intellectual-historical classifications was so singular that it deserves to be emphasized: contemporary history simply represented a "stage for future historians." This was, of course, a relativization of his own work, but also a reflection—as articulated in the following citation from his unpublished essay on the excesses of the German idea of continuity—on "the limits of historiography," combined with a respect for pragmatism, empiricism, and concrete research: a perspective that especially in Germany would only strongly surface in work of the 1980s and 1990s:

> I would now like to once again speak, as it were, on my own account: I am referring to the double task that the historian of the Jewish catastrophe must fulfill. First and foremost, it is important to ascertain the facts—and already that is not at all easy. Those who were witnesses were murdered. . . .

The other, more difficult task is recognizing the limits of historiography. We cannot be neutral, detached researchers into the truth when we are writing about events determining the life and death of peoples. It is my duty to take the part of the victims, in the name of humanity and for a more humane future. We need to find ways and methods—and I mean exact scientific ways and methods—that can help us understand what the human beings in the concentration camps and death camps endured. We cannot remain indifferent when inquiring into the reasons for and sources of their murder.[173]

In their emphasis on the inherent lacunae of historical research on Germany's recent past, such passages clearly represent a modest retraction—but a necessary one in that Wulf was at the same time pressing forward into what then was perhaps the most delicate of postwar German terrain: that marked out by an overabundance of *concrete names*. The historian's duty was, he argued, to acknowledge their presence, as a key to the continued meaning of the events that had transpired:

On the one hand, the names belonged to individuals who still often live and continue to make their mark in a highly impressive way; on the other hand, it was often dilettantes, who could only develop into a mystifying force in the presence of a wicked totalitarian spirit. But who should or could be in a position to make the proper selection here? . . . In principle both are integral to contemporary history. How could the later historian otherwise gain a picture of the fear and obsessive ideas at work in the totalitarian state? Dilemmas of this sort are nothing short of distressing— especially of course when someone, like the author of these lines, is so often confronted with them.

It was impossible, Wulf summarized, to pass over all those comprising the Third Reich except Hitler's inner circle as "pure abstractions."[174]

When it comes to Wulf's basic approach, nothing carries more meaning than the role played by names in his sense of objectivity: in Germany, this was the age's great taboo, its breaking something that, in the framework of considerable concern by West Germany's postwar historians about their discipline's relationship to the Nazi past, always required reflection on their part. The discussion about naming names at the IfZ in response to Helmut Heiber's 1966 book *Walter Frank and the Reich Institute for the History of the New Germany*[175] here serves as a good example. In certain respects, Heiber (1924–2003) can in fact be considered a typological counterfigure to Wulf, above all in respect to a "stupendous knowledge of the sources" that rendered him indispensable at the IfZ for decades; his career thus merits a short description by way of contrast to Wulf's. Broszat named him a "master of critical biographical research and description"; since 1954, he had engaged in a "meticulous analysis" of the material of the Nuremberg trials, thus laying the foundations for the institute's archives.[176] The study of Walter Frank was his magnum opus and would become the standard reference work on the behavior of university teachers in the Third Reich, but he also published other biographical studies, for instance, of Hitler and Goebbels,[177] and his book on the Weimar Republic—published in a series that he edited together with Broszat—would achieve a wide West German readership. In the 1970s, Broszat (then the IfZ's deputy director) would commission him (together with Ino Arndt and Hildegard von Kotze) to reconstruct the "files of the party chancellery," a grandiose project doomed to failure. In the 1980s, Heiber left the IfZ, on bad terms; in his later, voluminous studies of the Third Reich, a "spoken" descriptive tone dominated that often slipped into regular resentment-laden tirades, for example, against scholarly methodology, a "solicitous" national masochism—and indeed against emancipation, the media, modernity in general, and not least of all Jews.[178]

Before its publication, the manuscript of Heiber's book on Frank had been passed along through IfZ review committees and received high praise by the institute's board; in Rothfels' words, it did justice to "the fate of one's own scholarly field [*der eigenen Wissenschaft*] in the Third Reich."[179] Heiber's book, Rothfels emphasized, had "no denunciatory tone," rested on "an enormous breadth of material," and simply suffered from deficits "in stylistic respects."[180] At the same time, Rothfels suggested that the book contain *no* index of names, in order to prevent "misuse," an idea that proved unpersuasive.[181] In the context of Heiber's monumental work, the basic question was discussed of what approach to citing the names of living persons was legally permissible and morally acceptable. For Hans Kaufmann, the use of letters as historical sources produces more "unpleasant indiscretion" than historical insight. As the minutes put it: "It is a question of tact, which is not always maintained by historians. . . . A feeling for discretion is often absent." The only person to raise objections was Karl Dietrich Bracher, for whom the "colorfulness of the events" could only be rendered by citing correspondence.[182]

The enthusiasm of both Rothfels and Hans Schieder for Heiber's book was duly reflected in an "emphatic and absolute" vote by both historians to have it published. Looking back, both the enthusiasm and the general aggressive defense of the book are hardly surprising: In the first place, the past behavior and careers of all the historians positively inclined toward it had gone unmentioned by Heiber. In the second place, all told, this often-cited book made no break

with the legitimatory function of postwar German historiography. In his edited
volume on precisely that function (emerging, in the late 1990s, from one of the
first German historians' conferences to confront the complicity of prominent
postwar historians with Nazism during the Third Reich), Peter Schöttler observes that

> despite, or as it seems to me precisely because of its unbelievable exhaus-
> tiveness . . . the research field that actually needed to be opened was imme-
> diately again closed. The impression Heiber left was that Nazi history
> consisted of endless propaganda battles plus personal quarrels. Nothing
> more. . . . Over no less than 1,200 pages Heiber rendered the entire collec-
> tion of Nazi historians ridiculous in such a way that no one could—indeed
> needed to—then take them seriously. Further research on the matter
> seemed superfluous. In this way the problem of Nazi history was buried
> beneath anecdotes and humorous dictums.[183]

In light of this basic functional reality of the book being so warmly received at
the IfZ, the contrast offered here to the reception of the books of Poliakov and
Wulf emerges as reflecting something more than a matter of scholarly/archival
diligence. Wulf, for his part, was certainly not concerned with "tact" or "discretion"; illustrative "colorfulness of the events" was also not what really mattered
to him. His main reason for naming names was a desire to appear as a witness—
or else as someone representing the witnesses. Not the role of the professional
historian—the fastidious and painstaking practitioner of historical *Wissenschaft*—
but that of someone staking a *claim to memory* was here the guiding principle.
And this is not the least of the reasons that Wulf's reflection on the connection
between historical objectivity and "names" was potentially so explosive. It
was, so to speak, the most sensitive point in his entire method—even earning
him an accusation of denunciation,[184] since, as he himself put it, "in 1963 or
1964" those bearing the names "could feel themselves shaken [*betroffen*]" or else
"somewhat funny if not even foolish" "when reading their own essays, letters,
or studies from the 1933–1945 period."[185] But Wulf was exposed to criticism by
the West German historians for another reason as well: he was inclined to grant
anonymous pamphleteers from the Nazi period somewhat more benefit of the
doubt than those who had prominence then or later—some of the former, he
granted, had composed their texts against their own convictions. Still, he did
not wish to follow prevalent custom and denounce some and spare others:
"Who could we remain silent about in good conscience, and why? Those
working in contemporary history cannot let themselves be influenced by feelings, emotions, or actions. But they should here not forget the dictum of an

Eastern European rabbi: 'I fear the possibility of becoming more clever than pious.'"[186]

Wulf received many "exonerating" missives in response to his publications. As he explained it, not rarely letter writers from "the judiciary," "the Wehrmacht," and the "Foreign Office" would mail him

> entire binders with solemn declarations, either in the original or in photocopy (naturally certified as a precaution). The things emerging from the documents are astonishing. Apparently the officials of the Thousand Years' Reich saw their most noble duty as consisting in helping preserve as many Jews as possible from death. . . . In line with conscientious scientific analysis, on the basis of such incontrovertible evidence it is necessary . . . to confirm that (a) the Third Reich's officials saved more Jews than perished; (b) a substantial percentage of these officials only remained in their distinguished positions with Hitler in order to have the possibility of saving the lives of more Jews.[187]

In actuality, Wulf underscored that his five volumes were not meant to document whether "someone was a Nazi (since many of those named were not even party members); rather they represent a documentation of the Third Reich. But that is a basic distinction." Readers should not forget, he added, that there were party members who were not Nazis and Nazis who were not in the party. "In case someone had friends named Cohn or Levi that is no reason to fail to mention his name in these books."[188] He bridled at "resistance fairy tales" as "an abuse in the higher humanitarian sense."[189] At the same time, he defended himself against the reproach of reviewers that he ended biographical details of the persons he was treating in 1945: "It is not the editor's task to indicate the present-day activities of those concerned. This is rather the responsibility of the press, various West German authorities, the universities, and perhaps especially both the Protestant and Catholic churches. A study of the reaction or silence of the persons mentioned would merit work and would likely deserve a book."[190]

The Status of Jewish Work on Nazism in 1950s Germany

When we read the introduction to *The Third Reich and the Jews*, one thing becomes perfectly clear: in the resistance shown to the intense engagement of Poliakov and Wulf with their theme, the taboo perceived as being broken, to one or another degree of conscious awareness, was not only a taboo of theme and style but also involved *Jewish authorship* in general; Wulf was very much aware that this was the case. In this regard, as a sympathetic Jewish commentator, H. G. Adler opined that Wulf and Poliakov may have shown "too much restraint."[191] And in fact, it is reasonable to speculate that the resentment the two authors faced was so great that they anticipated it and incorporated it into the volumes, hence the themes of "distance," "objectivity," and the difficulties of a historiography centered on the annihilation of the Jews—difficulties they viewed as stemming above all from the fact they were Jews, and thus purportedly stricken with resentment:

> Without suitable distance historiography is in this case especially difficult and awkward. But an additional aggravating factor is also at work here. A Jewish pen—however conscientious it wishes to be—when forced into the thankless role of the accuser, will necessarily run the risk of missing the right tone or foundering on two equally dangerous cliffs: first, the historian must refrain from any resentment (however understandable); and second, he must possess superhuman "scientific" objectivity that would be difficult for anyone in view of six million corpses, a third of the entire Jewish people.[192]

Harry Pross cited this passage in a review of a group of texts addressing "the Jewish-German catastrophe." He himself, Pross noted, had not succeeded in laying claim to "much-invoked objectivity, without which historiography is allegedly impossible." His "German pen" was incapable of such objectivity to the same extent "that it may elude a Jewish pen in this context."[193] For Wulf, "resentment" was a frequently voiced concern, the backdrop, for instance, of the following reflection, the basic distinction it addresses often repeated in one or another mode: "Before my colleague Léon Poliakov and I even began to work on the book . . . we discussed the nature of the project and its general conception. Should we publish a synthetic study based on collected and carefully examined and analyzed material consisting of innumerable documents or rather possibly present the reader with the original in something like a raw state?"[194] Wulf was completely convinced that a study of the Third Reich "would already signify a position or amount to that"—and this, as suggested, above all because Jews were presenting the study. Poliakov, he pointed out, came from Leningrad; he himself "was raised in Krakow (Galicia!)." Poliakov had been imprisoned; he himself had "landed in Auschwitz." And the two men had an additional "shared Jewish postwar characteristic: our families were exterminated. What would have been more natural than reproaching us with ressentiment, ancestral enmity, hate, and other humanly understandable qualities and attitudes?"[195] They were obliged, indicated Wulf, to preserve "absolute objectivity" and "simply add a title and foreword to the documents."[196] (Let us note that reviewers did not always deny Wulf such "objectivity"—Reginald Phelps thus speaking of the historian's "exemplary objectivity," manifest in a reliance on irrefutable documentation.)[197]

Wulf's reflections were not merely after the fact but represented convictions informing the planning of his volumes. The third chapter of *The Third Reich and the Jews*, consisting of around sixty pages of statements by survivors of the German extermination campaign, is here highly illuminating.[198] As "understandably a certain ressentiment" might "be suspected,"[199] the authors explain, only two forms of such statements were considered: in the first place, those of children, "since they are unprejudiced observers and still incapable of succumbing to national, racial, or even political considerations";[200] in the second place, those "of scholars and scientists [*Wissenschaftler*], whose feelings are tempered and held in bounds by observation and intellectual curiosity."[201] On the other hand, witnesses

> who have been through the fire of the extermination camps cannot be impartial. . . . These human beings will have to speak of the Third Reich and its facilities with passionate distaste, indeed with hate. . . . Historical truth, however, requires that in witness accounts such subjective feelings be put aside, and entirely eliminated as much as possible. For this reason reports by scholars have been placed at the beginning of this chapter; . . . these are compelling in their sober objectivity and exhaustiveness.

But the children, as Poliakov and Wulf formulate it, "do not name their executioners 'SS men' or 'Nazis,' rather registering them under the collective term 'Germans.' This should not cause annoyance—it was the way they saw things."[202]

Joseph Wulf was not the only author—and not the only Jewish author—to have reflected in the 1950s and 1960s on the relationship between "emotionality" and "sobriety," on the gap between the "emphasis conveyed by revulsion" and complete "freedom from prejudice."[203] Wolfgang Scheffler's writing, above all his *Judenverfolgung im Dritten Reich* (Persecution of Jews in the Third Reich),[204] made use of a similar rhetoric grounded in actuality, on the one hand, emotionality hidden in passing remarks, citations, and captions, on the other hand. (On the book's first page and in the conclusion, Scheffler regularly evokes "facts," "knowledge of the facts," "dissemination of the facts," depiction of the "actual events," "presentation of the truth," and the importance of "clean and proper information that conforms with the truth."[205]) The book both emphasizes the importance of documentation as "a direct introduction to the events"[206] and appropriates some documents from Wulf and Poliakov, as in fact did several other historians to a far greater extent.[207] For Scheffler as well, the rhetoric was basically a self-protective strategy we can now understand as allowing him to at least pose the "numerous painful questions" that otherwise would be written off as "resentful": to address broadly neglected critical matters such as the "political failure of the German people or the inadequate democratic solidity of the average citizen during those years."[208] And he addresses these matters in various ways, for example, in a simple caption under a photo of a transport in 1942 of Jews from Würzburg: "And no one knew?"[209] and in statements such as the following: alongside the SS, many administrative offices, police units, and so forth were "directly or indirectly involved"; the events between 1933 and 1941 "unfolded under full public gaze. . . . Every German has to recognize responsibility for them on his conscience."[210] Scheffler would frequently emphasize the importance of scrupulously documenting such questions and statements — and this over the next few decades. In 1988, we thus find him pointedly insisting that "photos, diary entries, letters, and business documents speak a more eloquent language than many abstract treatises. They tear the general fate of the Jews consigned to death out of their anonymity, make us aware that human beings with names were involved here, not unimaginable numbers of victims."[211]

In 1960, H. G. Adler was arguing in a similar manner: "When, fifteen years after the collapse of the National Socialist state, its concentration camps become a matter of discussion, the focus should not be on their well-known horrors. Rather, we should above all try to gain important insight on political, sociological, psychological, historical, and general human levels."[212] What counted, Adler now explained in his own concession to the prevalent West German discourse, was becoming acquainted with "human possibilities" in their "extreme and distorted manifestation." Such possibilities had been "unimaginable" before 1933 but slumbered in the "dark recesses of human nature"; in this light, his goal was, as he put it, "knowledge of the uncanny" (*Kenntnis des Unheimlichen*).[213] In what amounted to one facet of a double-bind situation, Adler not seldom took on a "representative" role in articulating the scholarly diction and tenets deemed acceptable at the time, for instance, in proposing, in 1958, a "totalitarian method of personality fragmentation" as a key to what had transpired.[214] The difficulty of his position surfaced in other ways, for example in voicing the criticism, on the occasion of the publication of the new edition of Kogon's *SS State*, that Kogon would have certainly been able to make more use of his "standard work" if he had integrated newer research literature.[215]

In 1966, the death-camp survivor Jean Améry would acknowledge and lay claim to public recognition of his "ressentiment" and "reactive anger." That claim and the "method" of his writing on Auschwitz were remarkably close, indeed in the end identical. As he described it, the identity imposed itself; it involved neither the pure account of a witness nor a form of scientific discourse confronting the reader "in distinguished objectivity," but rather highly reflective autobiographical writing—in other words, a public analysis of his own ressentiment: "Precisely where the 'I' was supposed to be entirely avoided it proved the only usable point of support. I had planned a reflective-essayistic work, and what emerged was a personal confession broken up by meditations. . . . Confessing and meditating I arrived at an examination—or if you will a description of the essence—of the victim's existence."[216]

Hence it would only be roughly a decade after the texts of Wulf and Poliakov, Scheffler and Adler that "the victim's existence," that is, to again speak with Améry, the status of the "overwhelmed" human being, would be presented openly, in direct relation to the "burden of [concretely described] experience." Only Améry could offer comments such as the following: "I do not feel at ease in this peaceful, lovely land, filled with capable and modern people. It is already clear why this is so: I belong to that happily slowly dying-out species of human being that through common agreement is called the 'victim of Nazism.' The people of which I am speaking and that I am here addressing have shown muted understanding for my reactive anger. . . . I am speaking as a victim and am examining my ressentiment."[217] For Wulf and Adler, taking such a position had been basically inconceivable. Where Améry could make a "description of the victim's subjective constitution" and an "analysis of ressentiment gained from introspection"[218] into a program, for Wulf in the 1960s, it was simply possible to propagate "absolute objectivity" and present documents having the force of proof, not to offer a historical account of the extermination process. We can assume that Wulf was well aware of the grounds for his highly defensive choice of "the only neutral and unprejudiced" approach, "a collection of documents and non-influenceable witness statements to a large extent stemming from the archives of the Third Reich itself";[219] otherwise, his chances of being heard would have amounted to nil.

The pressure exerted from the German side, aimed at dismissing the "question of collective guilt," could thus not fail to have an effect on the authors concerned. Already in the context of Kogon's book on the "history of evil" (meant here was the first, 1946 edition of his *SS State*), the Social Democratic *Süddeutsche Zeitung* found fault with "a series of serious psychological mistakes" by the Allies, one of the largest mistakes being "the unfortunate version of 'collective guilt,' combined with massive camp-atrocity propaganda [*KZ-Greuelpropaganda*]." (The article's broad conclusion: "Phariseeism there, obduracy here, on both sides this spirit must be expelled through a return to the moral foundations of

Western thought, if the chapter of the concentration camps, which even today continue to exist in many countries, is to finally have its end.")[220] Authors such as Kogon in the 1940s and Wulf and Adler a decade later were writing at a time when directly addressing the extermination of the Jews had to be justified, but not its being passed over in silence. Constantly present in the room, so to speak, was the sort of question an anonymous writer asked Kogon at the start of the 1950s: "Why are the Jews being pinned on us again?"[221] Years later, he was still receiving anonymous letters such as the following: "Those seeing from a distance see clearly; participants see through a fog. For this reason you would have done the right thing to burn your manuscript as you intended on a number of occasions while writing it. . . . Nothing but the truth can make us free. Indeed, but the truth is served poorly by slurs [*Verunglimpfungen*]. You should have stuck with your camp experiences and not generalized."[222] If those who had been victims wished to do precisely that—namely, generalize—and not merely offer personal reports, if they wished to present serious historical research and not personal reminiscences, then they were forced to invoke "objectivity" and "sobriety," lest they be marginalized or else declared literary "classics" and thus relegated to another sphere; sometimes direct warnings were issued not to read the work in question.[223] The postwar West German cultural establishment assessed the *SS State* as a "worthy counterpart to Dostoyevsky's *Memoirs from the House of the Dead*,"[224] or saw it as part of a series including Hemingway's *For Whom the Bell Tolls*, Mann's *Doctor Faustus*, Gottfried Benn's *Static Poems*, Plievier's' *Stalingrad*, and works of Arthur Koestler and Graham Greene.[225] Less refined journalists could continue to spin yarns, for instance, that the camps were "no German invention" but rather "a work of the devil";[226] that Kogon's book needed to be read as a "contemporary warning" "at once to Europe and the world: never to allow concentrationary states [*konzentrationäre Staaten*] to emerge in their realm."[227]

At one point, Poliakov and Wulf referred to their documentary procedure as "rendering unnecessary an explication of the painful complex of questions that has already entered history as the 'question of collective guilt.'"[228] They intentionally stayed away from that question, the authors explained. Although they spelled out what they *did* intend as pure understatement, indignation surfaced in the observation that "precisely in pedantic Germany," until then "not a single serious study has acknowledged the question."[229] The purpose of their own study was simply to contribute to both a "dissipation of unjustified unease" and "a better perception of relationships," while at the same time spurring "careful investigation."[230] That was far less, and far more defensively couched, than what Wulf and Poliakov were actually presenting. In that light, one retrospective statement of Wulf serves as a particularly eloquent comment on the social and academic history of West Germany in the 1950s: "We be-lieved that in a firmly defined framework we were doing as much as humanly possible."[231]

The Second Controversy between Wulf and the IfZ

Whereas in the 1950s key figures at the IfZ had responded to the documentary publications of Poliakov and Wulf in a manner ranging from critical to dismis-sive, the underlying conflict at work here escalated in the course of the 1960s. The form it took was an increasingly sharp confrontation between Wulf and both Broszat and Helmut Krausnick in a long series of private letters, in the context of the so-called Hagen Affair.[232] Dr. Wilhelm Hagen had been the president of the West German health ministry; in December 1942, as director of Warsaw's health authority, he had written Hitler on behalf of "Aryan" Poland, protesting that "proceeding the same way with a third of the Poles, seventy thousand old people and children under ten years old, as with the Jews means killing them." In his book on the Warsaw ghetto, Wulf had not cited this communication, but in one short (two-page) chapter he describes Hagen as an accomplice, referring to the Ringelblum archive to document his behavior in general.[233] Wulf here cites the Oath of Hippocrates, pointing to Hagen, head of the medical authorities within the ghetto administration, as an actor who showed total disregard for his professional ethos: he had been aware of the "nothing short of monstrously sparse distribution of food in the ghetto," had been informed better than anyone else of the catastrophic living circum-stances, and nevertheless threatened the ghetto's Jewish doctors with severe punishment and death should they be unable to fend off the danger of typhus. "These doctors," Wulf commented, "were then murdered together with their patients."[234]

In his capacity as an IfZ member, Broszat took marked distance from Wulf's documentation. Already in 1957, in a review of one of Wulf's publications, he had couched his reservations regarding Wulf's focus on the Nazi foreign office, judiciary, and army—hence regarding the natural expansion of Wulf's perspective to take in groups of those participating in the persecution of Jews and extermination policies—in a remarkable way, not as simply apologia but in terms of an elaborate methodology: "A [stamped] 'signed by' beneath a text in the area of the persecution of Jews does not yet prove anything and possibly indicates very little about the responsibility of this Herr X, indeed can be mis-leading if the entire network of competencies, individual and general political incentives and premises is not simultaneously unraveled."[235] Here the two main contending currents in historiographical debates about Holocaust origins, intentionalism and functionalism/structuralism, were played off against each other: "responsibility" on the one side, "a network of competencies," "general political incentives and premises," on the other.[236]

In a letter to Hagen, who had turned to the IfZ for help, at the same time sending documents placing him in the best possible light, Martin Broszat expressed his sympathies: "That you of all people should be the object of such distortion especially saddens us." Furthermore: "I may assure you that we are ourselves horrified at the blunder [*Mißgriff*] in Wulf's book. Our methodological objections to this sort of sweeping and context-free documentation have in this way been strengthened anew." And finally: "After [seeing] the numerous documents lying before us and the highly outstanding testimonial prepared for you on the Polish side, we have no doubts concerning the integrity of your conduct during the Nazi period as a public health officer in Warsaw, even after the documentation of Wulf."[237] Together with the letter, Broszat sent his book *Nationalsozialistische Polenpolitik, 1939–1945* (National Socialist Policies toward Poland), where, he explained, he mentioned Hagen "with this import." Broszat now decided to contact Wulf directly on Hagen's behalf, in a letter written on IfZ letterhead (and making repeated use of the personal pronoun "we"; according to Krausnick, Broszat was in any case acting on his own initiative[238]) dated 10 April 1963, stating: the material Wulf cited from the Ringelblum archive "in our view proves nothing in comparison. . . . in the interest of the cleanness [*Sauberkeit*] of contemporary historical and journalistic documentation, we consider this entire matter extraordinarily regrettable and for that reason would welcome it if you could take the step of providing Herr Prof. Hagen with amends." Already before 1933, Broszat emphasized, Hagen had been a strong opponent of the Nazi regime; in the war as well, he had "offered stubborn resistance to the health policies in Warsaw ordered by the SS and police" and had indeed been threatened with being sent to a concentration camp.[239]

Wulf's response on 16 April was both cutting and controlled: he had read Broszat's letter very carefully, but for him Dr. Ringelblum's statements were "just as authoritative as that of a health officer in the *Generalgouvernement*." He also addressed the differences between his Warsaw ghetto documentation and Broszat's book on Poland:

> In my book *The Third Reich and Its Executioners*, I document not . . . the rescue of Poles but the extermination of Jews. . . . I find it astonishing that you, Herr Broszat [*sehr verehrter Herr Broszat*], appeal to me "in the interest of the cleanness of contemporary historical and journalistic documentation." Please be assured that for years I wished to write nothing about the Third Reich, because I myself hardly accepted the idea that a former

ghetto inmate and prisoner at Auschwitz, the son of murdered parents, can be objective. Granted it required a great deal of strength to overcome all of that. In any event until now no one has reproached me as displaying ressentiment-filled thinking. On the other hand, I do not see why a Jew from the former *Generalgouvernement* should be any more subjective than any representative of the authorities in the *Generalgouvernement*. Please do not read this as ironic, as it is meant sincerely.[240]

Wulf added the following sentence: "It is after all not my fault if there was a time when a Globocnick, awarded the Iron Cross for his murderous operations, and Herr Prof. Hagen represented the same Germany formally and vis-à-vis the Jews."

Shortly afterward, Hagen threatened Wulf with a lawsuit. (That it took Hagen two years to raise his objections was due to Wulf's mistaken use of the initial "N." for Hagen's first name.[241]) In reaction to this, on 24 April Wulf once again wrote to the institute, this time not to Broszat but to the director, Helmut Krausnick, including a copy of Broszat's letter of 10 April and his reply, and asking whether Broszat's opinion was shared by the institute.[242] "For me," he explained, "whether a man who intervenes for so-called Aryan Poland in a letter to Hitler while calmly accepting the Golgotha road of Warsaw's Jews can be considered part of 'the other Germany' is of basic significance." Wulf also referred to "an endless amount of documentation" located in Jerusalem and Warsaw that went far beyond what he had made public. He considered it "impossible, in the interest of the cleanness of contemporary historical documentation to write positive things about a man while passing over his behavior as a health officer in the Warsaw ghetto."

Although Krausnick tried to deescalate matters, emphasizing that "despite all differences of personal concern [*Betroffenheit*], which I by no means underrate," in the end "[we] largely are in concord,"[243] he by no means indicated distance from Broszat's standpoint. It was in the "nature of the sort of 'compilation' [*Zusammenstellung*] also contained in your new book that inevitably a danger emerges of moral 'equation.'" Not only objectively but also humanly, Krausnick indicated to Wulf, Globocnik represented "a very different Germany" than Hagen. In his reply Krausnick in fact remained very close to Hagen's apologetics, while introducing a mix of theoretical-functionalist and general juridical arguments:

> From Hagen's formulation, which voices an objection to proceeding with Poles "as with the Jews, *which is to say killing them*," as a historian, under theoretically or comparatively imagined normal circumstances I would not draw the following conclusion . . . : So this man approved the murder

of the Jews, or even simply: "he accepts it calmly," as you express it. Juridical and, specifically, lawyers' logic is a thing in itself, as I know from my own (nonpolitical) experience. But as a historian I would consider that form of logic to be simply exaggerated. At the very least I would still have doubts and then, even according to the strict juridical principle: *in dubio pro reo*. Especially since it does not seem plausible to me that one and the same man is free of "racial prejudices"—for that is after all what is at issue here—regarding the Poles and is not meant to be so in respect to the Jews![244]

In Krausnick's view, the political-psychological situation under the Nazi regime also had to be taken into account: "Even at the highest official and administrative level, there was no desire to recognize that Jews were being 'killed'!"[245] And then: "Dear Herr Wulf," Krausnick politely admonished, engaging in a major search for inculpating material "only to show that one is 'right' at all costs, and with some effort to place a man who (according to our present knowledge) at the very least is even at a gratifying remove from the average German of his time back in the category of the '100 percent Nazis' [*Hundertprozentige*], a category to which he did not wish to belong then and does not wish to now, would seem to me, openly stated, misguided [*verfehlt*]."[246] In their strong distortion of Wulf's position, these somewhat convoluted lines are illuminating. In the first place, Wulf had precisely *not* described Hagen as a "100 percent Nazi"; rather, in all his documentary volumes he—as well as Poliakov—had taken pains to avoid such categorization whenever possible, one of the main arguments at work here being that the existence of very many 40, 50, 60, and 70 percent Nazis was sufficient for what took place. Furthermore, Krausnick's declaration that Hagen *wished* neither then or at present to belong to the Nazis is striking. For Wulf had neither expressed nor suggested the contrary. He had only ventured to make Hagen's real behavior in Warsaw and not any "actual" intentions or indeed retroactive explanation the basis or his assessment. And finally, Krausnick's suggestion that Wulf regularly sought inculpating material to show that he was "'right' at all costs"—that he was, as it were, more concerned with revenge on individuals than perceiving the broad context—contained a marked self-contradiction: criticizing Wulf's lawyer's logic, he himself pleaded the principle of "in doubt for the accused," hence likewise in a trial's framework.

Wulf was a prolific correspondent—usually letters left his house not singly but in batches. It is thus not surprising that Krausnick soon received a four-page reply. The indignation and distress at work in this text are evident; Wulf even forgot to date the letter.[247] He began with a critique of Krausnick's formula of "differences of personal concern," rebutted the reproach that he had ever placed Globocnik and Hagen on the same level; to the contrary, he pointed out to Krausnick, he had even described Hagen as an "accomplice" [*Helfershelfer*], emphasized his focus on Hagen's attitude toward the Jews for whom he was responsible, defended his documentary sources, rebutted the notion that he was concerned with "being right," and then turned to methodological questions he considered "essential." His thesis was, he explained, that documents had "in the end . . . not only to be analyzed or scrutinized, but also "expanded . . . through what has been experienced." With everyone reading "so many documents," he observed, "we often forget the human beings." He now noted his astonishment at Krausnick's skepticism that Hagen could have racist convictions, as he manifestly had no ideological reservations regarding non-Jewish Poles: "Now, I beg your pardon but you were simply never a Jew!"; for Jews what belonged to normalcy at the time was "Germans helping a Polish 'Aryan' while being entirely indifferent to the fate of the Jews." Wulf remained firm in his conviction that Hagen belonged in a book on the Warsaw ghetto, since, he argued, in the Third Reich it was not necessary to be a Nazi Party member or indeed to have had racial prejudices in order to quietly accept the fate of the Jews; "especially after 1939 this will have simply belonged to the realm of 'force majeur,' fatality, a chain of unfortunate circumstances." Wulf appears here to have been formulating an image of the perpetrator that in itself was, in a sense, "functionalist," or more precisely, an image of an accessory to crime who, as a functionary, could avoid becoming a perpetrator *in his own self image.* "Please simply consider the sanitary circumstances in Warsaw's ghetto!" he now rhetorically appealed to Krausnick. "One cannot have been formally responsible for all of that and nevertheless have wished to belong to the 'other Germany.'" In addition to such a fundamental position, Wulf made a few other things clear in his long letter: first, that he indeed resented the fact that after the war Hagen himself said nothing about the situation in the ghetto, although he now insisted that he had done everything he could to improve it; and second, that he, Wulf, considered the tone taken by Broszat in his first letter to be wounding: the tone of a "pope" in questions of contemporary German history. Although he considered Broszat's work "very important," that the German historian had written that Wulf's documentary evidence had "absolutely nothing" to say had, he explained, taken him aback. "These citations say a great deal to me," Wulf countered. We have no answer from Krausnick to this letter.

Hagen's Self-Image and His Legal Dispute with Wulf

Meanwhile the controversy had become public. *Der Spiegel* offered a detailed report, with accounts in various papers following.[248] The plaintiff, Wilhelm

Hagen, was after all a former director of the West German health authorities and an honorary professor at the University of Bonn. *Der Spiegel* defined the question at work here very precisely: whether with his typhus edict and other ghetto ordinances, the former director of Warsaw's health authority "had pursued responsible policies or was complicit in the fate of the Jews." And in fact, Hagen was as personally convinced that he had pursued "responsible policies" as Wulf was of the opposite, that Hagen was "personally complicit," an "accomplice." In a formal legal sense what was at stake here was Hagen's loss or recovery of repute. Through his lawyer, Hagen demanded that on account of "defamation" Wulf and the Arani Verlag see to the removal of his name by 1 May 1963 from all warehoused copies of *The Third Reich and Its Executioners*, together with a recall of all unsold copies and preparation of a rebuttal to be inserted by public libraries in all the volumes they had. The arguments Hagen used in making his case are here of special interest, in that they exemplify a self-image that the IfZ defended in the 1960s out of conviction, even when Wulf had long since furnished additional inculpating material. This involved maintaining, in effect, a "functionalistic" causal context into which individuals were totally absorbed. In 1964, Gerhard Schoenberner would thus accurately observe in his previously cited *Zeit* article that the case centered on the individual's role in dictatorships, with the difficulties in reconstructing that role twenty years later being revealed here.

Hagen himself appears to have had few difficulties in that respect. After Wulf categorically declined an out-of-court settlement, he described his activities at the time, as Schoenberner put it in a letter of 28 March 1964 to Wulf's publisher, Arno Scholz, "in a manner that was formally and substantively so extremely tendentious that an objectively false picture" emerged.[249] In his own five-page letter to Scholz—a letter expressly addressed to him as "personal"— dated 20 February, Hagen had referred to the scenario of a legal fight between an old socialist like himself and a socialist publishing house as "shameful."[250] Signed by Hagen "in socialist greeting," the letter clearly represents his effort to create tension between Wulf and his publisher: Wulf, Hagen explained, was "not open to an objective discussion." As a member of the Wandervogel and the youth movement, Hagen had, he declared, "constantly spoken up against nationalism and hatred of Jews." Following World War I, in which he participated as a medical orderly, he had "once and for all" decided for socialism and became "chairman of the socialist student group in Munich," withdrawing when the Bavarian Soviet Republic became Communist. His public-health career path was influenced, he explained, by a decision to demonstrate his socialist convictions no longer "with talk" but rather "with work," starting in 1923 in Höchst and Frankfurt am Main. In 1927, Hagen informed Scholz, he returned to the Social Democratic Party, where he struggled against the "trail-blazer for the Nazis" Ernst Krieck and became a city health councillor. "In 1933 I was naturally dismissed"; after plans to emigrate fell apart (in part due to his meanwhile having four children), a former school friend, now the *Gauamts-leiter* in Augsburg, brought him to Bavaria: "When in 1938 all doctors were transferred to the Nazi Party, I could not decline entry to it." After 1945 he was exonerated by the denazification board on account of "demonstrated resistance."

This was Hagen's own short CV. But he also offered an account of his time and role in Warsaw, many passages of which evoked something like a socialist underground struggle to weaken the Nazi enemy, other passages resembling a self-certification as someone with superb "professional capabilities." His initial explanatory comments to Scholz here were not entirely consistent with his references to "official duties"—*Dienstverpflichtungen*—in his separate reply to Wulf: "When in 1940 doctors were urgently needed for public health service [in the *Generalgouvernement*], I declared myself ready, because I believed that in the hardship of war I could offer better aid in my own professional realm." There he tried "to be a helper to Poles and Jews wherever I could." He himself, he emphasized, had no executive authority and was merely an "expert advisor of the civil administration of the *Generalgouvernement* in health questions," above all those tied to potential epidemics. Secretly and at risk to himself, he hired a "female colleague with the same views as my own"; he owed his good reputation after 1945 "above all to my behavior in Warsaw." In that light, he wrote, "Please understand that I perceive my inclusion on the list of liquidators and their accomplices from Globocnik to Frank to be a grievous injustice that I cannot accept. My behavior can be judged not according to single events but only in its totality."

He was forced, Hagen further explained, to follow certain "speech rules" in order to maintain any prospect of helping, and "helped many Poles and at first also the Jews and risked everything to do so. I was powerless against the extermination of the Jews by the SS." A skeptical Scholz confronted Hagen in a letter of response with Wulf's documents, above all with Hagen's nine-page, personally signed memo of 7 July 1941, which Wulf had obtained from the Jewish Historical Institute in Warsaw, titled "Die Fleckfieberepidemie im Warschauer Judenviertel—Vorschläge zu ihrer Bekämpfung" (The Typhus Epidemic in Warsaw's Jewish Quarter—Suggestions for Its Control), in which Hagen requested from Hans Frank that, among other of his disease-control measures, Jews who left the ghetto be punished with beatings and "Jews with possessions" (*besitzende Juden*) be also fined, while "vagabond Jews" (*vagabundierende Juden*) be shot[251]—a memo that Hagen did not consider worthy of mention in his first letter. Hagen replied with an additional explanation of his Warsaw period:[252] the memo was written at a time when "being shot for leaving the ghetto" was already customary; his communication was no "suggestion" but a "mitigation" (*Milderung*) of the procedure. He had, he assured Scholz, expressed his "indignation" at the murder operations and asked Hitler for immediate intervention to stop them. He only learned about euthanasia at the end of 1943 (a reference to additional incriminating documentation that Wulf had meanwhile acquired; see further details below) and never demanded its use against mentally ill Polish people: "In Warsaw I played cards with the devil. In doing so I risked everything and almost gambled myself away. Some tricks of mine succeeded in helping the Poles. I lost the game for the Jews. Who can reproach me for this?"

This text, which Hagen wanted to see forcibly inserted into Wulf's *The Third Reich and Its Executioners* as his counterstatement,[253] presented him as a resistor. Things did not reach such a nadir, but the settlement ending the conflict between the two men was without a doubt a defeat for Wulf, for it involved the removal of the aforementioned two-page chapter of the book (334 and 335) that had informed readers about the medical advisor and his role in the Warsaw ghetto. Until the present, there is a near-empty white leaf at this spot, the only text being a cryptic footnote explaining that on the basis of a decision of the Bonn regional court chapter 14 is absent "from this and further editions."

"In Our Case Methodological Objections Are Based on Reciprocity" (J. Wulf)

On 3 November 1967, before the end of the legal dispute, Wulf wrote Hagen: "A doctor and a later president of the health authority who suggests as a recommendation for battling epidemics 'that vagabond Jews be shot' must either have the gift of constantly only judging his own personality in a favorable light or else assume that people will not be in a position to shed light on his past." Wulf also depicted the material sacrifices the trial had meant for him—at that point it had lasted five years. His activities as a historian and director of the International Documentary Center for Research on National Socialism had also been harmed as well. "Although I in no way owe you an accounting," he continued,

> I would nevertheless like to inform you of this, so that it becomes clear how foolish it was to rail against very restrained depictions and thus even make use of the courts in the hope that other facts over activities of the time are no longer ascertainable. I consider it to be my duty to continue in this direction, for the sake of both enlightening and shaping public opinion.

> Please be assured that I will not allow the legal proceeding you initiated to deter me from continuing to denounce the Jewish persecution's fearful manifestations, especially in the Warsaw ghetto, so that in this way I can help prevent such horrifying persecutory measures being repeated anywhere in the world, their cause and facilitation often being the sort of perfected organization and specialization that are ascribed to you.[254]

Wulf had imagined that the process of illuminating the past to which he referred could be carried out in cooperation with the IfZ, but he had been mistaken. His correspondence with the institute's director, Helmut Krausnick, and Krausnick's most important colleague, Martin Broszat, developed into a parallel dispute to that with Hagen. In October 1967, after Hagen had filed his lawsuit, Wulf again wrote Krausnick, recommending literature on the basic theme at issue and asking him to clarify whether Broszat's letter to Hagen of 8 April was an "official" IfZ communication or a private opinion of the author, commenting as follows: "I do not need to explain to you, a historian of repute, that I consider it a blunder if after 1945 a German historian renders a doctor who in 1941 threatened Jewish doctors with being shot and was responsible for the Warsaw ghetto's sanitary circumstances into a resistance hero."[255] Wulf's hurt was deep seated. There were also solid grounds for anger, as the Broszat letter had been allowed into the proceeding as a positive assessment of Hagen by West Germany's most important institute for the study of contemporary history, although Broszat had not intended this. "Herr Dr. Broszat can have whatever personal opinion of my work that he wishes," noted Wulf, just as he, Wulf, had expressed his views regarding Broszat's book on Nazi policies toward Poland a few years earlier. But in this case, he continued, as part of a trial the matter had become public, and he would himself turn to the public if he did not receive a clear and unambiguous response. Wulf would have to again press the matter on 22 October[256] before receiving an answer from Krausnick, who assured him in somewhat tortuous words that the letter did not represent "any official statement of opinion by the Institut für Zeitgeschichte," although Hagen's letter of inquiry was sent officially to the institute and Broszat maintained his "scholarly convictions."[257]

Soon afterward, Wulf located Hagen's memo and sent copies to both Krausnick and Broszat; in April, Broszat would finally respond to the discovery by cautiously and reluctantly revising his judgment of Hagen.[258] But there would be no healing of the rift between Wulf and the IfZ: already in the previously mentioned letter to Krausnick of November 1963, the Polish Jewish historian had referred to "certain methodological objections to the nature of particular publications of the institute. . . . But in our case methodological objections are based on reciprocity." Wulf had certainly expected that after the new information reached the institute, the IfZ would issue some statement, perhaps even apologizing to him either officially or at least privately through Broszat. But he in fact received no response to his communications. This prompted him to now mail a fresh copy of the Hagen memo to the institute (7 January 1964); Krausnick then responded indignantly in twelve lines (9 January) to the effect that he would not suffer being corrected and had a surfeit of correspondence to take care of; furthermore, Wulf's earlier communication had been no inquiry and thus simply had been registered. Concerning the matter at hand, he stated, "For now, however, I must refrain from a conclusive judgment."[259] On 5 March, Wulf thus sent Krausnick additional material: a sworn statement indicating that in 1942–43 Hagen had spoken out for euthanizing mentally ill Poles in order to free the facilities of a mental institution for other uses.[260] In his response of 13 March, Krausnick's tone now became somewhat more engaging, and he conceded that if the matter indeed stood as such (*wenn es sich so verhalte*), then "in fact an important piece of evidence for judging all the facts of the case [*das Gesamtsachverhalt*] would have emerged."[261]

Such a response was, however, no longer sufficient for Wulf. In a letter to Broszat dated 20 March 1964, he thus asked whether despite the new documentation he stood by the contents of his communication to Hagen from April 1963 in which he had praised Hagen for his unambiguously "upright stance." Broszat answered on 6 April with a letter amounting to a diplomatic balancing act, with a carbon copy of it going to Hagen: the two letters he had written in April to, respectively, Hagen and Wulf, he indicated, had had another factual framework than the one now at hand:

> I would be a bad historian if I wished to dispute the fact that some things can appear differently on the basis of new documents. And it is in my (juridically nonauthoritative) opinion not to be excluded that with your recently material you are more correct than with your published documentation. It is the case that I am insufficiently familiar with the provenances and objective contexts of the new evidence you have offered. Furthermore, I do not know and have not assessed possible counter-arguments of Professor Hagen and for that reason alone would like to refrain from a judgment on the present state of affairs.[262]

But as an accompaniment to his ambivalent concessions ("I understand the motive for your letter"), Broszat could not resist again scolding Wulf. It is here important to underscore that Wulf had not circulated any imputations regarding Hagen but had simply wished to articulate the perspective of the "patients" in the Warsaw ghetto entrusted to him; he thus was not only objectively correct in his assessment but had proceeded fairly on the level of detail. Broszat, however, would not rescind the initial "impression of hastiness or oversimplification [*Vergröberung*] that I gained from your published documentation concerning Hagen." In what he referred to as a "forthright" (*unverblümt*) manner, he expressed his annoyance "that precisely an author like you, who has contributed to the development of an awareness of contemporary history in Germany through many widely circulating publications on important themes, should, on the other hand, through questionable methods of documentation and citation, place a man in the wrong who all the same had demonstrably resisted Nazi practices in the position he took, and not without personal courage." Now as before, Broszat emphasized, it was his opinion that "the 'debonair' [*flott*] method of your documentation concerning Hagen is strongly disproportionate to the gravity of the directly or indirectly expressed accusation it contains, and to that extent I cannot see it as a convincing characterization of the person and activities of Hagen."[263] In making use of this rhetoric, Broszat underestimated Wulf's intelligence. For the problem with the mix of praise and reproach was too transparent: Wulf had never "contributed to the development of an awareness of contemporary history in Germany" in any way other than through the "methods of documentation and citation" that Broszat was here condemning as "questionable." And the simultaneous explicitly retained valuation of Hagen's "person and activities" and concession that the discussion's framework had completely changed because of new evidence amounted to nothing more than blowing smoke for the sake of evading the problem, or "refraining from a judgment on the present state of affairs." Wulf answered on 7 April, in a sense defeated by the blatant self-contradictions: "For me, your position as a historian is absolutely incomprehensible and unacceptable, and worse than my 'questionable method of documentation and citation.'"[264]

On 8 April 1964, Wulf mailed Krausnick a letter with a short "résumé" offered from his perspective:[265] "Our controversy (unlike you I am not placing the word in quotation marks) in the Hagen matter began exactly two years ago. On 29 April 1963 you wrote me that we 'largely are in concord.' I would like to very formally indicate that we are not so, and that we have highly different opinions regarding problems that presently constitute the world's trauma." Beneath point 2, Wulf made the following observation:

> In your letter of 23 October 1963 you wrote me that "other colleagues at the institute as well have methodological reservations . . . regarding the mentioned documentation." I have absolute understanding of such

reservations and have read and heard such reproaches here in Germany
so many times. But for me the following fact is completely incomprehensible: I cannot understand why so many historians working on a high level
of scholarship in European countries that were occupied by Hitler or in
Israel, the United States, etc. have fewer professional reservations concerning my documentation. Naturally I draw no conclusions from this
fact; on the other hand, I consider it a phenomenon meriting reflection.

And finally, he repeated that now as before Broszat's decisive first letter lay
before the court, and apparently no measures would be taken at the institute to
correct this, in one or another way. Broszat's scruples in this respect despite the
newly presented documents, while showing "to be sure, the most extreme degree
of scientific concern [*äusserste wissenschaftliche Sorgfalt*] here in Germany," in this
case "did not exactly display courage." "I presume," Wulf concluded, "that
with this letter your have been precisely informed of what I think of you, your
colleagues, and your institute."

Wulf likewise did not spare Martin Broszat a confrontation with his,
Broszat's, opportunism. He took the revised edition of Broszat's Poland book
as a basis for a new letter of inquiry, dated 7 October 1965:[266] Wulf here referred
to a critical study by the Polish Jewish Holocaust historian Tatjana Berenstein,
published in the same year, which described the relationship between the SS
and civilian authorities in the *Generalgouvernement* as indeed a struggle, but one
over local influence and enrichment, and suggested that these finding might
prompt yet one more revision of Broszat's "in any event pioneering work." He
had, Wulf explained, looked through the just-published edition and found
the information on Hagen unaltered, despite a reference in the foreword to
"addenda" on the basis of "new knowledge or documents." In the case of Hagen,
Wulf indicated, there was both new knowledge and new documents, as Broszat
was aware: "You are . . . a good historian—and thus it would simply interest
me to understand why in this last edition you fail to mention the existence (in
my view that would represent a minimum) of new documents regarding the
case of Dr. Hagen."[267] On 15 October 1965, Broszat answered in a way he was
basically forced into by Wulf's inquiry, with further methodological reflections
illuminating the dynamic at work in his structuralist approach to Nazism:

> Mention of the conflict between Dr. Hagen and the leaders of the SS and
> police in Warsaw was, as can be seen from the context, only meant as a
> selected example of the opposition, emerging in various realms of compe-
> tence, between aggressive and ideological determined anti-Polish goals

226 "Prehistorical Excavations" and "Absolute Objectivity"

(represented above all by the SS), on the one hand, and a task-oriented [*sachbezogen*] idea of office, not essentially corrupted by Nazi ideology, on the part of individual representatives of the German civil administration.[268]

Hence Broszat here indicated that although the Hagen case did not fit into his study's specific framework (which was the so-called annexed eastern areas, not the *Generalgouvernement*), he had taken it up and retained it because he saw it as an example of policies based on a "task-oriented idea of office, not essentially corrupted by Nazi ideology" standing opposed and apart from an ideology-centered policy of aggression. "In other words, I have addressed the Warsaw public health officer Dr. Hagen as an exponent of this characterized conception of office, which necessarily had to run into conflict with the extreme demands of the SS."[269] He had not, Broszat emphasized, intended to offer a complete and final judgment on Hagen's official activities, but although "a member of the civil administration could resist extreme SS policies toward Poland by referring to objective necessities [*sachliche Notwendigkeiten*]," he "was at the same time powerless, or felt himself powerless, when it came to changing the much more strongly specified anti-Jewish policies and here even became entangled nolens volens in the apparatus of discrimination." Now as before, Broszat was thus convinced that Hagen was not a perpetrator but in fact a resister whose "entanglement" in the "apparatus of discrimination" was unavoidable, and he said so quite directly: "I stand by what I wrote earlier"; the "deferred state of assessment" resulting from the "documents you have produced concerning Dr. Hagen" could not overcome the "difference of opinion between us." He was, Broszat declared, "inclined toward a far more differentiated assessment of the activities of Dr. Hagen" than Wulf. He expressed thanks for the reference to Berenstein's book, which he had not known, but he doubted "very much this study's thesis . . . [got] at the essence of the matter."

In this respect Broszat was correct: what was at issue was "the essence of the matter." In his "far more differentiated assessment" of the facts, the person involved was an honorable official beyond even a suspicion of ideological prejudice and anti-Jewish ressentiment, a person who bravely and dutifully resisted the "extreme SS policies toward Poland," and in any event was drawn against his will and because of the specific characteristics of the "apparatus" into processes for which he was not responsible. For Broszat, this "entanglement" was perhaps of interest in view of the Nazi system as a whole, but not in respect to Hagen as a person; in his view Hagen's rejection of any responsibility for circumstances in the ghetto was not only subjectively understandable but objectively correct.

Wulf turned the entire argumentation on its head: as the highest-ranking responsible medical official and functionary, Hagen was very much to be held accountable for the ghetto's catastrophic conditions; he was a perpetrator who even in the conceivable absence of radical antisemitic convictions observed the fate of the Jews with complete indifference. Wulf interpreted this indifference personally, not structurally or functionally, and as social action, not as the inevitable acceptance of predetermined forces. He saw no logical contradiction between Hagen's documented efforts to work against the SS's policies toward non-Jewish Poles and the apparent fact that at the time Jews were not deigned worthy of such efforts. He did not try to impute the man responsible for health policies concerning the Warsaw ghetto with antisemitism; he simply asserted that this was unimportant when it came to concrete action. In any case, those who endured the social policies of people like Hagen were the Jews—and this without questions being raised at any level of responsible authority. From Wulf's reply to Broszat on 19 October, it is clear that Broszat's argumentation and self-assuredness left him perplexed. He addressed Broszat bluntly:

> I would like to know how you, as a historian concerned with contemporary problems, actually—and please pardon the following expression—function. I simply don't get it. For you the Hagen case is a 'selected example,' but for the uninitiated reader, because of your book and your arguments he emerges as a resister—as found with increasing frequency in West Germany from day to day.[270]

Here Wulf was without a doubt addressing what Broszat had termed the "essence of the matter." Wulf did mention his knowledge of Polish and his own role as a witness as allowing a different assessment of the documents, but in view of Broszat's basic attitude he had clearly begun to feel arguments were pointless. Nevertheless, he continued to pose questions: "Although it is hardly possible, let us leave aside the documents speaking against Hagen for a moment. Do you really believe that a man who intends to resist such an unjust regime, a man who knows the machinery and finally can and would have to use his good common sense—that such a person would write a letter to Hitler of the sort that Hagen wrote?" In this context, Wulf did not fail to understand that Broszat's explanation in his letter of 15 October that Hagen had "almost completely elided the *Judenpolitik* of the *Generalgouvernement*" was a discourse of avoidance. For in the question of Hagen's approach to euthanasia, the documents over which their dispute had unfolded also concerned non-Jewish Poles: a fact of which Wulf had to remind Broszat and that "at the least does not harmonize with, and may well completely contradict," the role of the civil administration

outlined by Broszat. In general, it is important to emphasize that despite whatever emotion emerges from remarks such as these, to a large degree Wulf
showed great concern with keeping the dispute on a rational and forthright
level. His basic stance, evident in many formulations in various published texts
and letters and maintained in his dispute with the IfZ despite growing consternation, was encapsulated in one remark in this last letter to Broszat: "I would not
be writing all of this to you if I were not convinced and did not believe that as a
historian you are engaged in an effort to write according to your best knowledge
and conscience."[271]

Although Wulf constantly based his research on documents, he was well
aware, as suggested, that he also spoke as a witness—as someone who had to
"sometimes laugh" when studying "documents about the *Generalgouvernement* at
our disposal and then confront them with what really took place. That will
sound trivial and somewhat simplified to you," he continued in his last letter to
Broszat, "but it is pure reality. For historians everything is clear when it comes
to the SS or Waffen SS in the *Generalgouvernement*. But I know a reality of pastors,
the Wehrmacht, and civil authorities in the *Generalgouvernement*—and this part of
the historical truth is, in my view, simply downplayed and trivialized in the
publications of *many* German historians. *In the best of cases* the German in the
Generalgouvernement who did not belong to the SS simply 'looked on' or 'looked
away.'"[272] We have no answer from Broszat to this letter from Wulf.

Historiography and Memory:
Wulf versus Broszat

In many respects the controversy over Hagen can be seen as anticipating important arguments exchanged between Broszat and Saul Friedländer twenty years
later, in the course of a debate over Broszat's call for a "historicization" of
Nazism. As would be the case then, what was here at issue were basic methodological and interpretive questions of Holocaust research: questions centered on
perspective, memory, and responsibility. And as in that debate, the conflict
here was informed by an assumption on the part of Broszat (and of the IfZ as
an institution) that their historical approach involved "scientific," "sober," and
"objective" interpretation; simultaneously, the Jewish "other" was assigned the
sublime role of "commemoration"; Wulf's interpretation here was not even
taken seriously, despite all the evidence emerging from the sources themselves.
In this regard, the controversy between Wulf and Broszat makes it especially
clear that, to put it mildly, Broszat's structural-historical reflections displayed
not an iota more fidelity to the sources being discussed than did Wulf's efforts
to establish the responsibility of individuals "literally" from the documents.
Against the backdrop of a conflict of this sort, Broszat's conviction and credo—

running through his work like a red thread—of an "intertwining of and discrepancy between subjective impulses and objective events"[273] takes on a highly particular meaning: "intertwining" indicates a simultaneity of or connection between what is separate or different, but in the context of the history of the genocide of the Jews, a "discrepancy" between intentional volition and "objective events" constitutes no explanation but rather is itself something that needs explaining. Broszat's picture of Hagen as a person indeed "intertwined" in an event but whose subjective impulses had nothing to do with that event was drastically inadequate as an objective explanation, simply failing to grasp the basic problem. His interpretation of the extermination process here had a blind spot; it was not free from unspoken exculpatory longing and generally indebted to a purely German perspective. *This* constituted the true conceptual provocation, to which Wulf was responding—not Wulf's decision to included Hagen in his book as an accomplice.

It is still clear in Broszat's debate with Friedländer that Broszat located a later version of that perspective in the vicinity of "objective" research, while designating an opposing perspective, represented by Friedländer and tied by Broszat, with a gesture of forbearance, to "memory" and "mourning," as "mythic" and hence best omitted from historiography of the Third Reich.[274] But the shaky foundations of Broszat's plea to remove the history of Auschwitz from "memory" and entrust it to what he defined as scientific history were exposed, at the latest, at the moment Friedländer underscored the space separating, precisely, the personal memories of the two historians. Was it mere coincidence, asked Friedländer, that the specific mnemonic backdrop of the generation of German historians born in the 1920s—for instance, their widespread membership in the Hitler Youth—was not being raised as a problem? Why, then, should German historians have any less pressing problems in describing the Nazi period with historical objectivity than the Jewish historians, like Wulf and Friedländer, whom they chronically wrote off as *betroffen*—inordinately effected by personal experience, hence incapable, in their assessment, of sober judgment?[275]

In 1988, Broszat addressed these questions indignantly, as "especially pushy" questions. He did not deign to acknowledge that the perspective he favored was itself a construct—and indeed one prone to encouraging German readers of the time to complacency regarding their attitudes and actions. In his reply to Broszat's reproaches, Friedländer got at the heart of the matter when he wrote that Broszat did not exactly expand his field of vision regarding events of the time, instead basically sticking with the focus of his own perception.

From the present perspective, above all since it became known that Martin Broszat was not simply a member of Hitler Youth, as Friedländer correctly assumed, but also became a member of the Nazi Party, the much-vaunted "pathos of sobriety" that he and his generation accorded themselves has lost some of its consistency. Broszat's self-image, which he encapsulated in the scarcely translatable formula *zwar betroffen, aber kaum belastet* (roughly: "indeed affected but hardly tainted") had to be purchased with silence in that respect, as otherwise the crucial normative tenor of his research on Nazism would certainly have been unsustainable. An assessment of Martin Broszat's special contribution to the historiography of the Nazi period must take into account such a constellation, especially because Broszat made a space between "research" and "memory" into a starting point for the problems he explored. In any event, it is clear that in his confrontation with what he viewed as a particular form of historical writing that needed to be rejected, and that not coincidentally was largely authored by Jewish historians, subjective memory did *not*, in fact, face objective research. Rather, operating in a framework of historical scholarship, two forms of memory here clashed.

The Fate of Joseph Wulf in Postwar Germany

As was the case in the 1950s, Joseph Wulf had little success in West Germany in the "progressive" 1960s and 1970s. From 1955 onward, he lived in Berlin; in Germany he would be sometimes designated a "Jewish historian in exile,"[276] sometimes a "Parisian author of Polish origin."[277] Both he and his wife liked the city on the Spree; Wulf was himself fascinated at being physically present in the former capital of the Third Reich. But the Wulfs had no desire at this point to become West German citizens. Quite to the contrary, Josef Wulf's personal relationship to Germany became increasingly tense over time; he was, he repeatedly stated, a "Jewish historian," "no German" but "stateless." In an interview given when he received the Ossietzky prize in Berlin, he referred to himself as a "foreigner."[278] Beginning in the late 1960s, he also began to refer to himself as a "*Churban* historian."[279] Dreams about his time in Auschwitz were becoming more frequent rather than less so, he privately indicated.[280] His goal was now to tie research to memory in a particular way: to transform the Wannsee villa into "a research center in the truest sense of the word and simultaneously make it into a memento for eternity";[281] if the project failed, he intended to leave Germany permanently. Since the 1950s, Wulf had increasingly suffered from West Germany's climate of restoration; in 1960 he mentioned a hundred gallstones in this context in another private letter.[282] In the late 1960s and early 1970s, his fighting spirit would be overtaken by a deep, objectively grounded melancholia, evident in the following excerpt from a letter to his son: "I have published eighteen books about the Third Reich here, and all this to no effect. You can document yourself to death for the Germans, the most democratic government can preside in Bonn—and the mass murderers walk around free, have their little houses and cultivate flowers."[283] The slap that Beate Klarsfeld delivered to West German Chancellor—and former Nazi propagandist—Kurt Kiesinger at a 1968 Christian Democratic Union convention in Cologne meant the same to him as Willy Brandt's famous genuflection before the Warsaw monument to the ghetto dead in 1970:[284] the Federal Republic did not understand that in Cologne it itself was being judged;[285] the republic was not identical with its official statements. "It is no democracy," Wulf commented, "when . . . [neo-Nazi journalist Helmut] Sündermann and I can both publish. That doesn't suffice for Germany."[286] And in April 1974, he asked the military advisor for the Social Democrats, Friedrich Beermann, why, in his letter to the president of the Bundestag on the occasion of the ratification of the Polish-German treaties, although he had spoken "movingly," he had also been oddly ambiguous, "anonymous," in the end phrasing things on "the model of Communist antisemitic Poland," speaking only of "human beings" having perished in the death camps in Poland: "Why . . . do you avoid the word 'Jews,' when they clearly and unmistakably perished as Jews in Belzec, Treblinka, and Auschwitz: . . . Please explain to me why you so completely avoided the word 'Jews' in your letter."[287]

The question arises of why Wulf moved to Germany in the 1950s. Although possessing a visa for the United States and considering Israel his homeland, he would never again leave Berlin. In a letter of 5 December 1967 to the liberal-conservative founder of the influential weekly Die Zeit, Marion Gräfin Dönhoff, Wulf himself acknowledged the apparent oddity: "Allow me, madam, to add a personal remark at the end of this letter: I am the only member of the Jewish fighters' organization in Poland (Krakow) who has ventured to live and function on German soil. My comrades—the few who survived—. . . live in Israel and reproach me severely for being here. They are probably right."[288] Nevertheless, Wulf's choice of domicile reflected a deep-seated rationality; his colleague Ulla Böhme thus recounted his determination to document what had taken place "in German for the Germans": "the Germans have to be beaten about the head" with that history "in German, in order that they read the material, concern themselves with it, and no longer can say 'we didn't know anything.'"[289] (In a March 1977 letter of Böhme to the journalist Joachim Wallasch, he put things more moderately: "His decision to live and write in Germany (or the reverse) rested on a conviction that it was necessary to present the Germans with the monstrous in their own language."[290]) Precisely because of the ferocious obstacles facing a Jewish historian in Germany, Wulf's central intention was filling "the gaps in a contemporary historiography that has scarcely used Polish, Hebrew, and Yiddish sources";[291] few of Wulf's German colleagues appear to have share Werner Wieberneit's insight to the effect that the sort of work he did "actually can be seen through only by institutes." (Wieberneit added that Wulf's accomplishment should finally be acknowledged in "undiminished" form and basically represented a "reproach to our scholarly institutes."[292]) Nevertheless, the emotional toll Wulf paid as a result of an uncompromising sense of vocation is clear. It is reflected in one passage in a letter he wrote Vienna-born Jewish author Anna Maria Jokl: "For an intensive Jew it is very difficult to *at once* live forcefully [*eindringlich*] with the Nazi years and effectively with Israeli reality. No people can bar that, no generation, and certainly no individual. . . . For the past twenty-five years I have only lived one-sidedly. Intensity of my sort cannot and must not be 50 percent. In any case I cannot function like that. Unimportant compromises are possible, but not those where essential things are at stake. This is difficult, very difficult. I will eventually come around."[293]

The Wannsee Villa Project

In the second half of the 1960s, Joseph Wulf was one of the first people to propose turning the site of the Wannsee Conference into a documentary center and institute for research on Nazism.[294] He considered this to be his actual life work. He did not live to see the idea realized (the second-floor library of the present House of the Wannsee Conference is named in his honor); to the contrary, the failure of his plans in the early 1970s shook him profoundly. Although the plans were focused on a matter of principle, it now seems that what was extraordinary about their failure was its details. Wulf emphasized the "quasi-extraterritoriality" of the Wannsee house;[295] only that, he felt, guaranteed that a microfilm archive organized according to international standards could be brought together with political awareness of the location's significance. At the beginning, his efforts to literally bring together research and memory had five points. Alongside establishing a museum concerned with the extermination of Europe's Jews in the Hitler period, setting up a representative "honorary committee composed of personalities from the Jewish and non-Jewish world," and publication of ten volumes of "minutes of exemplary trials of Nazi criminals," "demonstrating in a documentarily incontrovertible way the complex of concentration camps, ghettos, and *Einsatz*-units, the crimes against war prisoners, the last months of 1945, etc. on the basis of court records," above all two of the points were central: the "creation of an archive" for the "documentation of Nazism" and establishing an internationally oriented "Yearbook of Contemporary History" to be published by the Arani Verlag.

The dimensions of this project were immense; Wulf even envisioned a specially trained librarian capable of translating "from Yiddish, Hebrew, and Polish."[296] At the end of August 1966, together with Peter Heilmann and Friedrich Zipfel, Wulf founded the Association of the International Documentary Center for Research on Nazism and Its Aftereffects (IDC). Even at the end of the decade, he remained, according to his own account, "very optimistic": he could even persuade the eighty-two-year-old Karl Jaspers to be honorary chairman (he described his conversation with the philosopher as a "great experience"),[297] and prominent members included Fritz Bauer, Karl Dietrich Bracher, Heinz Galinski, Ralph Giordano, Helmut Gollwitzer, Hans Herzfeld, Max Horkheimer, Eugen Kogon, Hermann Langbein, Alexander Mitscherlich, Léon Poliakov, Wolfgang Scheffler, Gerhard Schoenberner, Wilhelm Weischedel, and Simon Wiesenthal. But as it happened, at this time the Wannsee villa was being used as an orphanage for the Berlin-Neukölln branch of the Social Democratic Party. The various other difficulties were themselves insurmountable. The authorities themselves were the main problem, against the backdrop of an absence of any broad social consensus for realizing the plans. Wulf's insistence on tying research to memory was either met with incomprehension or understood wrongly. Even well-meaning journalists asked questions such as the following: "If what is of concern here is research and only research, why can it only be undertaken in the Wannsee Villa?"[298] Letters from Jewish readers in periodicals such as *Die Zeit* themselves voiced skepticism regarding the plans; the architect Julius Posener thus argued along similar lines to the Evangelical theologian and politician (and participant in the plot to kill Hitler) Eugen Gerstenmaier before him: "It has to be torn down. It should have been torn down a long time ago. In its place a beautiful, light, innocent orphanage should be constructed."[299] Another reader's voice objected that "the ashes' embers should not be stirred up again"; there was even talk of a "restitution pressure-center" (a *Wiedergutmachungsdruckstelle*).[300] On 9 November 1967 (a day that was symbolically overdetermined as the anniversary of *Kristallnacht*), Wulf met with Nahum Goldmann, president of the World Jewish Congress, and with Berlin's mayor, Klaus Schütz (he had already met with Schütz's predecessor, Willy Brandt, a year earlier); Wulf here again emphasized the building's symbolic power "as a research center" and that he did not even "remotely envision a museum of National Socialism."[301] Eleven days earlier (29 October), in an open letter the author Rolf Hochhuth had called on the city of Berlin to support establishing the IDC. Hochhuth pointed to the fact "that even today there is no monument on German soil specifically recalling the so-called Final Solution."[302] As an answer from Klaus Schütz, however, he received a simple sentence that would achieve some fame: "I do not want any macabre cult-site."[303] A compromise failed; the Berlin senate then welcomed the plans but also indicated that it was "not of the opinion that the research center should be built in the house at Am Großen Wannsee 56–58."[304] For its part, the idea favored by the city officials of incorporating the project into the Free University of Berlin was unacceptable to the project's initiators. Wulf, who in those years had to be repeatedly placed under long-term police protection because of threats of violence,[305] gave up, disillusioned. In mid-September 1970 he resigned as chairman of the IDC, bluntly referring to the "senate's tactic of attrition" and inadequate support from Berlin's Jewish community as the reasons.[306] On 21 August 1971 he mailed off the circular inviting members to the association's last meeting; point 4 on the agenda was the proposal for its dissolution: "The years-long effort to establish the IDC have not been crowned with success."[307]

Following the bitter conflict between Wulf and the IfZ in the 1960s, in the 1970s there would be more disappointments, for a start concerning the small circle of people who proved more inclined to criticism of the project than support—among them IDC member Golo Mann, whom Wulf esteemed, and who had objected "that we so insisted on the house—the only important thing was after all the plan."[308] At the start of June 1973, Wulf would fall out with his friend Helmut Gollwitzer "as a Jew" on account of "dimensions of the unexpressed" in his address at the opening of the "week of brotherhood." Wulf reproached him "in all openness" for confounding all the misfortune on earth with the specific misfortune of the Jews: "We who have been stamped on also see Vietnam, Greece, South Africa, Bolivia, *but the nightmare of the Warsaw ghetto and Auschwitz will accompany us for generations.* . . . There as well entire dimensions seem missing to me [*Auch da vermisse ich Dimensionen*]."[309] And in the 1970s, the tensions between Wulf and the IfZ would again become visible, albeit in a de-escalated context; these were already evident in his comments at the closing meeting of the IDC committee ("I would like to also mention that on 23 February 1970 in Munich I had a detailed conversation with the director of the archive at the Institut für Zeitgeschichte, Herr Dr. Hoch, in which I succeeded in diminishing much of the existing ressentiment and made clear that the planned IDC would not compete but rather cooperate with the institute").[310]

Wulf closed the committee report with a frank remark: "It would certainly have been possible to formulate individual points of the report more sharply, for example, in respect to the attitude of the Berlin senate. In this report we have chosen not to express more strongly our bitter disappointment."[311] Sadly, disappointment would take over because recognition remained absent. His editor Dieter Struß at the Sigbert Mohn Verlag in Gütersloh financed him out of conviction and idealism but without an economic perspective and began ever more frequently to request help in letters to third parties. He wrote, for example, to the advisor on literature at the Berlin Senate for Science and Art that Wulf was actually facing a prospect of having "nothing, since all the connections and plans that he developed in order to further exist for us after the projects are finished have repeatedly fallen apart." Struß here referred to "advances of 75,000 marks"; the press had "gone to the utmost limits in the case of Herr Wulf," noting, "We can do no more for him and his plans." He felt it necessary to expressly emphasize to his correspondent that Wulf was "not writing his books on the Third Reich out of any feelings of revenge. They have far more likely allowed him to objectify his horrifying experiences as a scientifically working historian," adding, "I do not wish to watch while a man perishes whose value I believe I know."[312]

The honorary doctorate awarded Wulf by the Free University in 1970, which was a source of pride (in his letters he frequently mentioned that his own university had been Auschwitz)[313] was granted not by the university's historians but at the prompting of the theological faculty. The euphoria with which Wulf met this gesture is evident in a letter he wrote his friend Wolf von Baudissin on 19 January 1970 after receiving notification of the award: "This letter unintentionally has a double meaning for me—for one thing joy, because it signifies recognition of my up to now twenty-five-year work; for another thing 19 January 1945 was the first day I spent as a 'free man' after fleeing from the Auschwitz-evacuation transport on 18 January 1945. As a consequence this honor is also an obligation for me." But in fact, the honor occupied a basically symbolic and private realm; it was no real sign of recognition, although Wulf wished to believe this was so. A few years later (1973), he was insisting that the Jews had "become victims of [Christian-Jewish] reconciliation [*Aussöhnung*]";[314] he now became increasingly bitter, recalling the immediate postwar years almost positively, if also darkly, as "years in which the ashes and blood of millions of gassed and massacred persons still impressed the world!"[315] But Wulf's 1967 project of a "history of Zionism," directed at a leftist interpretation of the Zionist movement as intrinsically tied to colonialism and imperialism,[316] had already been initiated in such an intellectual and emotional framework. On 3 December of that year he had written his friend Rolf Hochhuth to ask the following question:

> Does a young German writer or dramatist have the right to write about the mistakes, baseness, or crimes of other people or politicians, and to make this manifest before a public that has not yet digested Auschwitz? I'll allow myself to say something to you, my dear Rolf—you know that I'm now fighting for the International Center of Documentation. What's at issue here is not the *Soldatenzeitung* writing about an "atonement center."

> But in the fight over the documentation center, all the disguised Nazis, potential fascists, and similar people will now, I say now—that is, 1967—come to the surface.

More than six years later, in August 1974, Wulf was continuing to aim what were nothing less than appeals at left-wing papers such as the *Berliner Extradienst*:

> Cease and desist from this antisemitic anti-Zionism in Berlin, city of the SS Reich Security Main Office and the notorious Wannsee Conference (Final Solution). . . . I have nothing against demonstrations fighting against fascism in Chile (concentration stadiums etc.), but demonstrate as well against the mass murderers of Habash's organization, whose sinister influence again and again torpedoes a peaceful solution in the Middle East. . . . Think through this problem in a rigorous way.[317]

At this time, Wulf's rejection of the "fascism" theory being presented in academic and public discussion was uncompromising: "No theory of state in our history—fascism included—can be treated analogously to the twelve years of the Third Reich. It represented the most psychopathological form of state centralization."[318]

Wulf's Suicide in October 1974

Privately and professionally, Wulf's last years were a single torture session. He wrote exposés, conceptual outlines, and thematic proposals—for instance, for a study of "cultural work in the Warsaw ghetto" (first submitted to the Berlin senator for science and art Werner Stein but taken up anew in 1970); for a "memoristics of the Third Reich" (submitted to the Friedrich Ebert Foundation in 1970, with an exposé sent to Baudissin in 1974)—and waited for rejections from publishers, foundations, and sponsors.[319] Already at the beginning of the 1960s, plans had been afoot to bring Wulf to Hamburg as a research associate in the founding phase of the Institute for the History of German Jews, which, it was hoped, would "grow into the role of a German Leo Baeck Institute."[320] Wulf had expressed his interest, but the idea could not be realized. A few years later, Hellmuth Becker at the Max Planck Society's Institute for Educational Research forwarded Hans Rothfels an appeal for help by Wulf to Dietrich Goldschmidt at that institute, in which Wulf wrote, on 5 July 1965, "Following the appearance of seventeen of my publications, I unfortunately have been forced to see that one simply cannot live from these." Becker wrote Rothfels that it was "after all problematic that such a person is unemployed."[321]

Rothfels' reaction was telling; in strikingly dry and brief words, he referred to the New York branch of the Leo Baeck Institute, noting: "This all the more as he received the Leo Baeck Prize in 1961 and in any case, as seems to emerge from the appended letter sent me by Herr Goldschmidt, tends strongly toward the United States [*stark nach U.S.A. hinübertendiert*]."[322]

Wulf responded to many of the rejections promptly with sharp words revealing wounded pride, for example to Wolf Jobst Siedler, who had declined "help as a patron," expressed annoyance at Wulf's "strategic" way of proceeding, and sneered at the fact that he had received appeals simultaneously "from all points of the compass" (by which he meant from Wulf himself, from Ernst Jünger, and from Helmut Gollwitzer). Wulf, who would have liked to have published with Ullstein on historical grounds, answered deeply wounded: "I ask you for nothing, as I am the son of a very rich and highly intellectual Yehoshua Wulf from Krakow."[323] Now as before he worked as if possessed,[324] rendering the reported imperative of the great eighty-year-old historian of Jewry Simon Dubnow to his co-religionists upon his deportation, "Record everything!" into his own maxim.[325] He even contemplated founding a university "department for the history of East European Jewry."[326] It was Germany's "duty to establish such an institute . . . here on German soil,"[327] for "as a cultural phenomenon" Eastern European Jewry no longer existed: "Between 1939 and 1945, Germany not only liquidated millions of East European Jews . . . but exterminated a culture."[328] Of Wulf's unrealized plans, the following are known: an overview of "a thousand years of East European Jewry,"[329] a "history of Hassidism," a description of the cultural work in the Warsaw ghetto (planned at seven hundred pages), and the publication of "Diaries of an Eastern Jew" (or: ". . . of an East European Jew"; ". . . of a Contemporary Historian") that he had begun in 1964–65.[330] Above all this project had great personal significance for Wulf: a "life work"[331] after the failure of the Wannsee project. He planned three years for its preparation and a length of five hundred pages; a publisher's acceptance letter would arrive on the day of his death, with the letter remaining unopened. Essentially, Wulf here planned to write the history of his own work as a private scholar in West Germany between 1954 and the 1970s. It was meant to constitute a historical-mnemonic effort to render his own "massive archive"[332] into the basis of a reflection on the history of the mentality of postwar West Germany. In a third-person description Wulf wrote (and supplied with his own quotation marks), he put it like this:

> Out of forty thick binders containing the correspondence with scholars, writers, poets, Nazis, rabbis, Christian theologians, famous politicians, and other personalities in German, Hebrew, Yiddish, Polish, and French

from all over Europe, the USA, and Israel," he wished to [examine] not
only the *history* of the Nazi regime but also *"problems* regarding the Nazi
period, historiography, and coping with the phenomenon of totalitarian
states . . . in literature, Judaism, antisemitism, Zionism, Israel, philosophy,
Jewish mysticism, the Yiddish language, etc."[333]

Wulf's main concern, he explained, was an ongoing process of manipulation,
silence, and falsification; his book was meant to be "a revision [*Korrektur*]—a
kind of review."[334]

At the beginning of 1974, he drafted a two-page "appeal to the German
intellectual public" for publication in *Die Zeit*, but this would not be published.[335]
Wulf had written this as an "open letter" to Helmut Gollwitzer under the immediate impression of a trip to Israel. He also apparently viewed the text as part of
his will, since at the start he indicated that "as a Jew, as a Jewish historian, and
after my experience in Germany between 1939 and 1974," he did not wish to be
buried in Germany.[336] His deeply seated bitterness was here directed explicitly
at "Christians," "Germans," and "the politically blind left": "For a conscious
Jew living and working in Europe, how you Christians forget what you have
done with Jews over two thousand years, how you Germans forget that you
have exterminated six million Jews, only becomes clear on Israeli soil. On Israeli
soil, all of Europe seems to be in a sort of Orwellian condition." Wulf was dis-
mayed by the pro-Palestinian demonstrations that he felt were being "hyped"
(*aufgebauscht*) by Germany's student-led protest movement, and this at Israel's
cost:

> Indeed, the left; any half-educated Jew, Jewish historians, have always
> known that antisemitism comes from the right. But now we have to note
> with astonishment and despair that via hostility toward Israel the left as
> well is becoming antisemitic. Within this leftism, which makes use of
> masks, an uncanny ignorance prevails concerning Israel, Zionism, the
> Jewish people, Jewish culture, and everything spiritual we have given the
> world. . . . I ask you why you German intellectuals and writers now speak
> so quietly about Jews, Zionism, and Israel.[337]

Wulf was now increasingly communicating with those around him as the
representative of a destroyed Jewish high culture. In an answer to a letter from
his son, he tried to explain his position as follows:

> Am I a Jew? I honestly don't know. I only know that (1) I am familiar—
> highly familiar—with Jewish history and culture, in all its shades. (2) For

that reason I know that we have been subject to murder for two thousand years. (3) I know that—with the exception of the United States—Israel is presently as isolated as the Jews were between 1939 and 1945. (4) I know that I am extraordinarily closely connected to the fate of the Jews. (5) I know that, for instance, thirty Einsteins, fifty Rubinsteins, etc., etc. were gassed. (6) I know that not only six million Jews were gassed but that a great, intellectual, poetic, etc. etc. East European culture was exterminated.[338]

Wulf then turned to the destruction of Judaism in the Soviet Union and Khrushchev's ban on a monument for the murdered Jews at Babi Yar. In any event, the increasingly bleak spiritual condition clearly apparent in such communications had its objective correlative in a financial situation that was nothing short of catastrophic. In a letter of 2 August 1970 to Baudissin, he described things clearly, if despairingly:

As you know, I have published eighteen books on the Third Reich. What you do not know is that I have not received any royalties from the books. Before and during my work on the books, I received advances from the publishers, simply to be able to write them—i.e., to do research, prepare photocopies, etc. Books of this sort are only published in very limited numbers and are a deficit business for both publishing houses and the author. . . . For over a year I have had no income. After twenty-five years of work I basically stand before a void. My theme—the Third Reich—is presently not in demand and not topical. I literally am facing the question of what I am to live on in the near future. I am here concerned not with a one-time fellowship but with having the status of an employee with a monthly income at an institution or organization for which I could prepare projects: documentation, reports, analyses, studies, etc. I am writing you because you know my work of twenty-five years and my publications. I believe you understand that I cannot now suddenly face "nil"—and I hope that you will understand when I ask you to write me should you see the possibility of that sort of security for me. I have, after all, accomplished something in the past twenty-five years; I wish to work and after all should—I believe you understand this—not now be in this situation.[339]

The death of Wulf's wife, Yenta, on 28 August 1973 was preceded by a period of extreme suffering. At several points Wulf collapsed psychically and physically; he was himself brought to a hospital but left it secretly and extremely ill on 10 July to be at the bedside of his dying wife.[340] He had to then be hospitalized on two further occasions—for several weeks in January and again in April 1974.

After Yenta's death, he lived "some months in shock, like a dead stone":[341] "Without my wife . . . I would never have been Joseph Wulf; without her I would have remained the spoiled child of a very rich Jew from Krakow," he remarked to Baudissin.[342] To Gollwitzer he indicated that "following my Auschwitz this was the most distressing experience of my time—itself difficult— after the war."[343]

On 10 October 1974 Wulf jumped to his death. The *Bild-Zeitung* reported the event; the *Nationalzeitung* crowed. (Wulf had, the paper indicated, "fabricated anti-German propaganda tomes, in the process sending "fantastical research results and numbers regarding Nazi crimes into the world."[344]) For years afterward, in Wulf's otherwise bare study a large white sign with an imperative in Hebrew hung over his work area: "Zachor!!!" (Remember!!!), with the figure "6000000" placed beneath (see Figure 9). In his contribution to a volume devoted to Wulf appearing fifteen years later, Wolfgang Scheffler recalled that "Wulf had the feeling that despite his nine documentary volumes, two biographies, a full-length historical study, and five smaller publications his work had been fruitless. The circumstances of his death recall the despairing leaps to death of his fellow sufferers from the windows of the Warsaw ghetto's burning houses."[345]

Empiricism and Typology

Wulf's research was untimely. And he died well into a period marked by a great distancing in general German awareness from the basic import of what had transpired between 1933 and 1945. Hence in February 1966, we find Hermann Langbein, first secretary of the Comité international des camps, writing Eugen Kogon that he wished to start preliminary work on his next book, to be called "Menschen in Auschwitz" and

> treating human problems behind and in front of the barbed wire under
> Auschwitz's extreme conditions, while also taking into account the results
> of the Auschwitz trial. But I . . . do not yet know how I will create the neces-
> sary conditions for such a project (that will require some time, for I do not
> want to skimp on this book). Do you know of an institution that could offer
> a research contract or something similar to a fool like me? I would very
> much like to consolidate my experiences (of Auschwitz and from the last
> decades) in a book; I believe this could be useful, but at the moment it
> seems that I could be the only person who believes in such usefulness.[346]

In contrast, in the intellectual scene efforts to update the Third Reich were being undertaken that, for example, caused Hannah Arendt to strictly decline any cooperation with the writer Hans Magnus Enzensberger. In his book on "politics and crime" of 1964, Enzensberger had declared that "Auschwitz" laid bare the roots of politics: "Yesterday's 'Final Solution'" could not be prevented, but "tomorrow's 'Final Solution' can be prevented." Its planning, Enzenberger argued, was proceeding publicly, rendering all those who witnessed 1964 into complicit parties. Enzensberger asked his publishers to see if Arendt would be willing to review the book; Arendt wrote back to the press as follows: "Saying that Auschwitz has exposed the roots of politics amounts to saying that the whole human race is guilty. And when everyone is guilty no one is guilty. Once again, the specific and the particular have here been drowned in the sauce. When a German writes that, it is questionable. It means: not our fathers, but all human beings created the calamity. Which simply is not true."[347]

When it comes to understanding the significance of Wulf's books, a modified version of a remark by H. G. Adler seems helpful here: they offered a great deal, but it was necessary to know how to read them.[348] But precisely that was avoided in Wulf's time. Holocaust research actually began with the work of Wulf and Poliakov. In the first place, in Gerhard Schoenberner's words, it was the first work "to have begun publishing Nazi documents, thus introducing research on this period on a broad scale."[349] In the second place, the documentation acknowledged the perspectives of both the victims and the perpetrators, travelers, and opportunists—what was here of interest was "the typology of these people," as Wulf put it.[350] The discovered and selected sources were meant to clarify "the narrow intertwining of political, racial-ideological, and economic goals" and point to the unity of the event in which the SS, the Wehrmacht, the judiciary, and the bureaucracy were participating. (The East German press thus understood Wulf's project as "progressive," which was basically a very accurate assessment, although also a transparent political instrumentalization, as made most luridly clear in the insinuation that the historian "lost his life in a way that has never been entirely clarified."[351])

Beyond this, the books were provocative and Wulf himself quarrelsome, attacking directly, offering for instance a public response to the wide range of letters that reached him because of what they revealed.[352] He liked to quote one particular Lichtenberg aphorism: It is not the lies but rather the very fine false assertions that hinder a clarifying of the truth. He felt his work superior to that of the institute-based West German specialists in contemporary history: "Why haven't German researchers long since produced the material—why did a Galician Jew have to come and do it?[353] As an autodidact, Wulf was, in Henryk Broder's words, "in his entire approach an annoyance and provocation for academic German historians," an observation confirmed by Gerhard Schoenberner: "He did not wait for the professional historians, only very few of whom were venturing to take on this theme; and he did not take up their later analyses.

He merely broke a taboo, drew attention to something being neglected, filled a gap, and forced a guild of historians to turn its scholarly attention to this long-neglected thematic field. The whole group never forgot that in him."[354]

Nevertheless, Wulf was no historian of Judaism per se.[355] The perspectives opened by his research and Poliakov's have, in the third place, remained convincing because they could take in a great deal while not losing touch with the central problem of the historical locus of the genocide of the Jews and *not* playing research off against memory. On the occasion of his receipt of the Heinrich Stahl prize in April 1964, Hans Lamm characterized Wulf as a "one-man research institute," but also as the "kaddish-author of his generation."[356] In his choice of sources, Wulf did not leave the slightest doubt that it was precisely not a handful of criminal subjects who drew Germany and the world into an abyss; and that Auschwitz, Treblinka, and Majdanek had been a civilizational break whose causes, unfolding, and consequences had to be explored and described on various—scientific, intellectual, and political—levels.

Notes

Introduction to the American Edition

1. Paul Ricœur, *Memory, History, Forgetting*, trans. Kathleen Blamley and David Pellauer, Chicago, 2004 (originally published as *La mémoire, l'histoire, l'oubli*, Paris, 2000).

2. Ricœur, *Memory, History, Forgetting*, 138.

3. Ibid., 16, 135.

4. Ibid., 135.

5. Ibid.

6. Ibid., 137.

7. For an overview of the development in East Germany, see, for example, Jürgen Danyel, "Vom schwierigen Umgang mit der Schuld: Die Deutschen in der DDR und der Nationalsozialismus," *Zeitschrift für Geschichtswissenschaft* 40 (1992): 915–28; Joachim Käppner, *Erstarrte Geschichte: Faschismus und Holocaust im Spiegel der Geschichtswissenschaft und Geschichtspropaganda der DDR*, Hamburg, 1999.

8. See esp. the chapter "The Language of Republicanism and West German Political Generations" in A. Dirk Moses, *German Intellectuals and the Nazi Past*, Cambridge, 2007, 38–54; Nicolas Berg, "Zeitgeschichte und generationelle Deutungsarbeit," in *Martin Broszat, der "Staat Hitlers" und die Historisierung des Nationalsozialismus*, ed. Norbert Frei, Göttingen, 2007, 161–80; Christoph Cornelißen, "Historikergenerationen in Westdeutschland nach 1945: Zum Verhältnis von persönlicher und wissenschaftlich objektivierter Erinnerung an den Nationalsozialismus," in *Erinnerungskulturen: Deutschland, Italien und Japan seit 1945*, ed. Christoph Cornelißen, Lutz Klinkhammer, and Wolfgang Schwendtker, Frankfurt a.M., 2003, 139–52.

9. On history writing and the Holocaust, see Norbert Frei and Wulf Kansteiner, eds., *Den Holocaust erzählen: Historiographie zwischen wissenschaftlicher Empirie und narrativer Kreativität*, Göttingen, 2013; Alon Confino, *Foundational Past: The Holocaust as Historical*

Understanding, Cambridge, 2012; on postwar German contemporary history, see Peter Pulzer, "Looking Back on the Third Reich: The Politics of German Historiography," in *Jüdische Geschichte als allgemeine Geschichte*, ed. Raphael Gross and Yfaat Weiss, Göttingen, 2006, 245–56; Martin H. Geyer, "Im Schatten der NS-Zeit. Zeitgeschichte als Paradigma einer (bundes-)republikanischen Geschichtswissenschaft," in *Zeitgeschichte als Problem: Nationale Traditionen und Perspektiven der Forschung in Europa*, ed. Alexander Nützenadel and Wolfgang Schieder, Göttingen, 2004, 25–53.

10. See esp. Klaus Kempter, *Joseph Wulf: Ein Historikerschicksal in Deutschland*, Göttingen, 2012; idem, "Joseph Wulf: Ein Churban-Historiker," *Jahrbuch des Simon-Dubnow-Instituts/Simon Dubnow Institute Yearbook* 10 (2011): 407–30. Also Gerd Kühling, "Schullandheim oder Forschungsstätte? Die Auseinandersetzung um ein Dokumentationszentrum im Haus der Wannsee-Konferenz (1966/67)," *Zeithistorische Forschungen/Studies in Contemporary History*, online ed., vol. 5, no. 2 (2008), http://www.zeithistorische-forschungen.de/16126041-Kuehling-2-2008. On early Holocaust research in general, see above all Laura Jockusch, *"Collect and Record!" Jewish Holocaust Documentation in Postwar Europe*, New York, 2012; Elisabeth Gallas, *"Das Leichenhaus der Bücher": Kulturrestitution und jüdisches Geschichtsdenken nach 1945*, Göttingen, 2013; Kathrin Stoll, "Erinnerungsreden Szymon Datners: Frühe Zeugnisse eines Holocaust-Überlebenden aus Białystok," *Jahrbuch des Simon-Dubnow-Instituts/Simon Dubnow Institute Yearbook* 11 (2012): 309–32; Roni Stauber, *Laying the Foundations for Holocaust Research: The Impact of Philipp Friedman*, Search and Research—Lectures and Papers, ed. Dan Michman, vol. 15, Göttingen, 2009; Natalia Aleksiun, "Rescuing a Memory and Constructing a History of Polish Jewry: Jews in Poland 1944–1950," *Jews in Russia and Eastern Europe* 1, no. 2 (2005); 5–27; Dan Michman, *Holocaust Historiography—A Jewish Perspective: Conceptualization, Terminology, Approaches, and Fundamental Issues*, London, 2003.

11. Saul Friedländer, *Kitsch und Tod: Der Widerschein des Nazismus*, expanded new ed., Frankfurt a.M., 1999, 141 (the cited material is found only in the new foreword to the second German edition of this book). Friedländer's extraordinarily important study *Nazi Germany and the Jews* has appeared in two volumes: *The Years of Persecution, 1933–1939*, New York, 1997; *The Years of Extermination, 1939–1945*, New York, 2007.

12. George Mosse, *The Crisis of German Ideology*, London, 1966, 4. Translator's note: As George Mosse suggests, in the Nazi context and its postwar aftermath, the German word *Volk*, commonly translated as "people," is especially loaded semantically, representing the core of the idea of the racial community and hence of the entire Nazi belief system. For this reason, throughout this book I will usually retain *Volk* in the original German rather than rendering it as "people" but will break with this approach when the context seems to call for it.

13. For one example for such argumentation, see the essay by the literary critic Hans Egon Holthusen (who was much honored in Germany well into the 1980s), "Freiwillig zur SS" ("An SS Volunteer"—a self-reference by Holthusen), *Merkur* 20 (1966). The article was then rebutted in a letter to *Merkur* by author and Holocaust survivor Jean Améry (*Merkur* 21 [1967]). On this controversy, see Nicolas Berg, "Jean Améry und Hans-Egon Holthusen: Eine 'Merkur'-Debatte in den 1960er Jahren,"

Mittelweg 36, no. 2 (2012): 28–48. On Holthusen, see also Joel Golb, "Dichtung und Politik im Nachkriegsdeutschland: Die Kontroverse um einen Brief von Celan an Jünger," in *"Ich staune, dass sie in dieser Luft atmen können": Jüdische Intellektuelle in Deutschland nach 1945*, ed. Monika Boll and Raphael Gross, Frankfurt a.M., 2013, 87–125, here 108. See also in general Konrad H. Jarausch, *After Hitler: Recivilizing Germans, 1945–1995*, Oxford, 2006.

14. See Neil Gregor, "Das Schweigen nach 1945 und die Spuren der 'Volksgemeinschaft': Zu den Grenzen eines Forschungskonzepts," in *"Volksgemeinschaft" als soziale Praxis: Neue Studien zur NS-Gemeinschaft vor Ort*, ed. Dietmar von Reeken and Malte Thießen, Paderborn, 2013, 341–53; Michael Wildt, "'Volksgemeinschaft'—Eine Zwischenbilanz," in *"Volksgemeinschaft" als soziale Praxis*, 355–69; idem, *Hitlers' Volksgemeinschaft and the Dynamics of Racial Exclusion: Violence against Jews in Provincial Germany, 1919–1939*, trans. Bernhard Heise, New York, 2012; Ian Kershaw, "'Volksgemeinschaft': Potenzial und Grenzen eines neuen Forschungskonzepts," *Vierteljahrshefte für Zeitgeschichte* 59, no. 1 (2011): 1–17; Frank Bajohr and Michael Wildt, eds., *Volksgemeinschaft: Neue Forschungen zur Gesellschaft des Nationalsozialismus*, Frankfurt a.M., 2009.

15. See Enzo Traverso, *Auschwitz denken: Die Intellektuellen und die Shoah*, Hamburg, 2000. For a Holocaust-focused perspective on the history of memory in Europe and beyond, see Dan Diner, *Gegenläufige Erinnerungen: Über Geltung und Wirkung des Holocaust*, Göttingen, 2007. For an overview of the present status of Holocaust research, see David Bankier and Dan Michman, eds., *Holocaust Historiography in Context: Emergence, Challenges, Polemics and Achievements*, Jerusalem, 2008; Marina Catturazza, "The Historiography of the Shoah: An Attempt at a Bibliographical Synthesis," *Totalitarismus und Demokratie: Zeitschrift für internationale Diktatur- und Freiheitsforschung* 3, no. 2 (2006): 285–321. On modern history focused on autobiographical texts, see Martin Sabrow, "Autobiographie und Systembruch im 20. Jahrhundert," in his *Autobiographische Aufarbeitung: Diktatur und Lebensgeschichte im 20. Jahrhundert*, Leipzig, 2012, 9–24; Ulrike Jureit, "Autobiographien— Rückfragen an ein gelebtes Leben," *Autobiographische Aufarbeitung*, 149–57; Carsten Heinze and Arthur Schlegelmilch, "Autobiographie und Zeitgeschichte: Einleitung," *Bios: Zeitschrift für Biographieforschung* 23, no. 2 (2010): 167–69; Volker Depkat, "Zum Stand und zu den Perspektiven der Autobiographieforschung in der Geschichtswissenschaft," *Bios: Zeitschrift für Biographieforschung* 23, no. 2 (2010): 170–87.

16. For an overview, see Nicolas Berg, "The Holocaust and the West German Historians: Historical Research and Memory," in *On Germans and Jews under the Nazi Regime: Essays by Three Generation of Historians, a Festschrift in Honor of Otto Dov Kulka*, ed. Moshe Zimmermann, Jerusalem, 2006, 85–103.

17. Monika Boll and Raphael Gross, introduction to *"Ich staune, dass Sie in dieser Luft atmen können,"* 9–20; Steven E. Aschheim, "The Tension of Historical *Wissenschaft*: The Émigré Historians and the Making of German Cultural History," in idem, *Beyond the Border: The German-Jewish Legacy Abroad*, Princeton, N.J., 2007, 45–81.

18. Siegfried A. Kaehler, *Briefe, 1900–1963*, ed. Walter Bußmann and Günther Grünthal, Deutsche Geschichtsquellen des 19. und 20. Jahrhunderts 58, Boppard, 1993, 300. Also "returning boomerang," ibid., 302; "our existence stands under the sign of the 'boomerang': eye for an eye," ibid., 311; similarly 319, 345.

19. Ibid., 325. For Kaehler, neither Jews nor emigrants had "cause for moral hubris [*moralische Überhebung*]. . . . The bombing terror [*Bombenterror*] very much allow[ed] a comparison with the genuine German atrocities" (ibid., 319).

20. Cited from Eduard Mühle, *Für Volk und deutschen Osten: Der Historiker Hermann Aubin und die deutsche Ostforschung*, Düsseldorf, 2005, 594; on Aubin see also Eduard Mühle, ed., *Briefe des Ostforschers Hermann Aubin aus den Jahren 1910–1968*, Quellen zur Geschichte und Landeskunde Ostmitteleuropas 7, Marburg, 2008.

21. Even in the mid-1960s, Hans Ebeling could ascertain what he termed a German "minority mentality," consisting of the following: "oversensitivity to criticism," "reactions of astonishment when gestures of goodwill are not immediately understood and accepted" (for example: "But we want reconciliation with the Jews; it's they who don't want it!"); "outbursts of self-hate." See Hans Ebeling, "Deutschland—wieder besucht (Podiumsdiskussion)," in *Haltungen und Fehlhaltungen in Deutschland: Ein Tagungsbericht*, ed. Hermann Glaser, Freiburg, 1966, 145–46.

22. Kaehler, *Briefe, 1900–1963*, 327.

23. Ibid., 362.

24. Gisbert Beyerhaus, "Neue Wege zur Erforschung des zweiten Weltkrieges," *Welt als Geschichte* 11 (1951): 58–63, here 58. For his part Kaehler spoke of the "dark riddle of German history"; see Siegfried A. Kaehler, "Vom dunklen Rätsel deutscher Geschichte," *Die Sammlung* 1, no. 3 (1945/46): 140–53.

25. Jan Eike Dunkhase, *Werner Conze: Ein deutscher Historiker im 20. Jahrhundert*, Göttingen, 2010, 235–56.

26. Dunkhase, *Werner Conze*, 260.

27. On the term *Geschichtspolitik*, see Edgar Wolfrum, *Geschichtspolitik in der Bundesrepublik Deutschland: Der Weg zur bundesdeutschen Erinnerung*, Darmstadt, 1999; for a brief introduction to the problem of "political-historical" argumentation by twentieth-century German historians, see idem, *Geschichte als Waffe: Vom Kaiserreich bis zur Wiedervereinigung*, Göttingen, 2001.

28. Werner Conze, "Die deutsche Opposition gegen Hitler," *Neue politische Literatur* 2 (1953): 210–15, here 210.

29. Dunkhase, *Werner Conze*, 231.

30. Hajo Holborn, "Irrwege in unserer Geschichte?," *Der Monat* 2 (1949): 531–35, here 535. For a similar rejection of such a stance, see Geoffrey Barraclough in *Der Monat* 2 (1949): 335–38.

31. Helene Wieruszowski, "Brief an Friedrich Meinecke vom 11. August 1946," in *Friedrich Meinecke: Akademischer Lehrer und emigrierte Schüler; Briefe und Aufzeichnungen, 1910–1977*, ed. Gerhard A. Ritter, Biographische Quellen zur Zeitgeschichte 23, Munich, 2006, 301–4, here 303.

32. See Waltraud W. Wende, "Kultur als Programm gegen Hitler: Diskursstrategien des Neuanfangs in der Periode zwischen 1945 und 1949," in *Totalitarismus und Literatur: Deutsche Literatur im 20. Jahrhundert—Literarische Öffentlichkeit im Spannungsfeld totalitärer Meinungsbildung*, ed. Hans Jörg Schmidt and Petra Tallafuss, Göttingen, 2005, 135–50, here 142.

33. On the term's untranslatability, see Amos Elon, *Journey through a Haunted Land: The New Germany*, New York, 1967, 179.

34. For one book showing the direction in which things were now moving, see Ulrich Herbert, ed., *National Socialist Extermination Policies: Contemporary German Perspectives and Controversies*, New York, 1999 (originally a 1995 lecture series given in the University of Freiburg's history department). The new research direction was anticipated by Wolfgang Scheffler (1929–2008), a student of Ernst Fraenkel and teacher of an entire generation of German researchers on the Holocaust, including Christian Gerlach, Dieter Pohl, Peter Klein, and Andrej Angrick.

35. Martin Broszat and Saul Friedländer, "A Controversy about the Historicization of National Socialism," in *Reworking the Past: Hitler, the Holocaust, and the Historians' Debate*, ed. James Baldwin, Boston, 1990, 102–32.

36. Dan Diner, *Beyond the Conceivable: Studies on Germany, Nazism, and the Holocaust*, Berkeley, 2000.

37. Herbert A. Strauss, "Der Holocaust: Reflexionen über die Möglichkeiten einer wissenschaftlichen und menschlichen Annäherung," in *Antisemitismus: Von der Judenfeindschaft zum Holocaust*, ed. Herbert A. Strauss and Norbert Kampe, Bonn, 1988, 215–33.

38. See Charles S. Maier, *The Unmasterable Past: History, Holocaust, and German National Identity*, with a new preface, Cambridge, Mass., 1997, passim. For contextualization and interpretation of the "historians' controversy," see the following relatively recent works: Klaus Große-Kracht, "Debatte: Der Historikerstreit, Version: 1.0," in *Docupedia-Zeitgeschichte*, 11 Jan. 2010, https://docupedia.de/zg/Historikerstreit?oldid=75521; idem, *Die zankende Zunft: Historische Kontroversen in Deutschland nach 1945*, Göttingen, 2005; Ulrich Herbert, "Der Historikerstreit. Politische, wissenschaftliche und biographische Aspekte," in *Zeitgeschichte als Streitgeschichte: Große Kontroversen seit 1945*, ed. Martin Sabrow, Ralph Jessen, and Klaus Große Kracht, Munich, 2003, 94–113; Doris L. Bergen, "Controversies about the Holocaust: Goldhagen, Arendt, and the Historians' Conflict," in *Historikerkontroversen*, ed. Hartmut Lehmann, Göttingen, 2000, 141–74.

39. Strauss, "Der Holocaust," 215.

40. Ibid., 216.

41. Ibid., 217.

42. Herbert A. Strauss, *In the Eye of the Storm: Growing Up Jewish in Germany, 1918–1943, A Memoir*, New York, 1999; on Strauss's life and work, see Nicolas Berg, *Der Holocaust und die westdeutschen Historiker: Erforschung und Erinnerung*, Göttingen, 2003; 2nd ed., 2003; 3rd ed., 2004, 629–33; Werner Bergmann, Christhard Hoffmann, and Denis E. Rohrbaugh, eds., *The Herbert A. Strauss Memorial Seminar at the Leo Baeck Institute New York, March 29, 2006*, Berlin, 2006. For the first published memoir by a historian who survived Nazi Germany, see Saul Friedländer, *When Memory Comes*, New York, 1979; this slim book received adequate attention only in later editions—not when the original French version appeared in 1978 or in the first editions of the English and German translations. For other autobiographical reflections by historians working in the same or related contexts, see Raul Hilberg, *The Politics of Memory: The Journey of a Holocaust Historian*, Chicago,

1996; Peter Gay, *My German Question*, New Haven, Conn., 1998; Fritz Stern, *Five Germanys I Have Known*, New York, 2006.

43. Otto Dov Kulka, *Landscapes of the Metropolis of Death: Reflections on Memory and Imagination*, trans. Ralph Mandel, New York, 2013; German ed.: *Landschaften des Todes: Auschwitz und die Grenzen der Erinnerung und Vorstellungskraft*, Munich, 2013.

44. See the chapter on "The Pogroms of November 1938," in Strauss, *In the Eye of the Storm*, 96–112.

45. Ibid., 127.

46. Ibid., 180.

47. Ibid., 213–14.

48. Christhard Hoffmann, "Deutsch-jüdische Geschichtswissenschaft in der Emigration," in *Die Emigration der Wissenschaften nach 1933: Disziplingeschichtliche Studien*, ed. Herbert A. Strauss, 257–79, here 269. The differing perspectives of witnesses and historians have stamped many international conferences—and have often enriched the connected debates. A starting point was the conference in Stuttgart in the mid-1980s titled "Entschlussbildung zum Völkermord" (Decisions toward the genocide), marking the first time Raul Hilberg was invited to give a lecture at a German university and the setting for the onset of the debate between Broszat and Friedländer.

49. Raul Hilberg, "Die Holocaustforschung heute: Probleme und Perspektiven," in *Die Macht der Bilder: Antisemitische Vorurteile und Mythen*, ed. Jüdischen Museum der Stadt Wien, Vienna, 1995, 403–9, here 408.

50. Pointedly and early, for instance, in Eberhard Jäckel and Jürgen Rohwer, *Der Mord an den Juden im Zweiten Weltkrieg*, Stuttgart, 1985, 48–49, 242–43; most recently: Saul Friedländer, "Ein Briefwechsel, fast 20 Jahre später," in Frei, *Martin Broszat, der "Staat Hitlers" und die Historisierung des Nationalsozialismus*, 188–94; idem, *Den Holocaust beschreiben: Auf dem Weg zu einer integrierten Geschichte*, Göttingen, 2010; idem, "Reply to Hayden White," in Frei and Kansteiner, *Den Holocaust erzählen*, 79–87.

51. Strauss, *In the Eye of the Storm*, 255. For a reflection on the heuristic distance between primary, and nontransmittable experiences inscribed like a "mass of lava" in those affected and secondary description by those who have not had the same experience or were born later, see Reinhart Koselleck, "Formen und Traditionen des negativen Gedächtnisses," in *Verbrechen erinnern: Die Auseinandersetzung mit Holocaust und Völkermord*, ed. Volkhard Knigge and Norbert Frei, Munich, 2002, 21–32, here 23ff.

52. Norbert Frei, "Mitläufergeschichten? Heute erscheint Nicolas Bergs Studie über die NS-Deutungen deutscher Zeithistoriker," in *Süddeutsche Zeitung*, 8 May 2003; Nathan Sznaider, "Der Holocaust gehört uns! Nicolas Berg erzählt, wie deutsche Historiker die Geschichtsschreibung vor den Juden retteten," in *Die literarische Welt*, 26 June 2003; Sebastian Conrad, "Geschichtsvergröbernde Erinnerung: Nicolas Berg wirft den westdeutschen Historikern vor, sie hätten bei der Erforschung des Holocaust die Opfer ausgeschlossen," in *Berliner Zeitung*, 7 July 2003; Volker Ullrich, "Forschung ohne Erinnerung: Nicolas Bergs Buch über den Holocaust und die deutschen Historiker sorgt für Streit," in *Die Zeit*, 10 July 2003; Arno Lustiger, "Den Grabstein ersetzen: Mein Weg zur Erforschung der Schoa," in *Frankfurter Allgemeine Zeitung*, 11 July 2003; Christian Geulen, "Zwischen Erinnerung und Erforschung: Positionen westdeutscher Historiker aus gut

fünf Jahrzehnten; Nicolas Berg schreibt eine Gedächtnisgeschichte des Holocaust" in *Frankfurter Rundschau*, 5 Sept. 2003; Wolfgang Benz, "Irritierendes Licht ins Dunkel: Abrechnung mit der Historikerzunft," in *Das Parlament*, 6 Oct. 2003 (special supplement for Frankfurt Book Fair), 2; Peter Schöttler, "Kritik ohne Kontext," in *Die Tageszeitung*, Feb. 2004.

53. Christoph Cornelißen, "'Apologie' ist sein Schlüsselbegriff: Zur Formierung des kollektiven Gedächtnisses; Nicolas Bergs Studie über die westdeutschen Historiker und den Holocaust," in *Badische Zeitung*, 15 July 2003; Friedhelm Zubke, "Streit um Schuld und Scham: Holocaust; Nicolas Berg zur Rolle der westdeutschen Historiker," in *Göttinger Tageblatt*, 18 Oct. 2003.

54. Dirk Rupnow, "Professionelle Geschichtsschreiber, der Massenmord und die vergessene Erinnerung," *Newsletter*, no. 26 (Fall 2003), ed. Fritz Bauer Institut (also online since May 2003); Philipp Stelzel, "Von Strukturalisten und anderen Apologeten: Nicolas Berg analysiert die westdeutsche Geschichtsschreibung über den Holocaust," www .literaturkritik.de/public/rezension.php?rez_id=6386 (ed. 10, 5, Oct. 2003); Wolfgang Braunschädel, untitled article, in *Archiv für die Geschichte des Widerstandes und der Arbeit* 17 (2003): 656–60; Hanno Loewy, "Die Geburt der Sachlichkeit aus dem Geist des tragischen Heroismus—Zu Nicolas Bergs fulminanter Historisierung der Historisier," *Tel Aviver Jahrbuch für deutsche Geschichte* 22 (2004): 328–40; Hans Mommsen, "Zeitgeschichtliche Kontroversen," *Neue Politische Literatur* 3 (2004): 15–24; Habbo Knoch, review of book in *H-Soz-u-Kult*, 4 Feb. 2004, http://hsozkult.geschichte.hu-berlin.de/rezensionen /2004-1-065; Stefanie Hardick, "Apologetische Reflexe: Nicolas Berg: *Der Holocaust und die westdeutschen Historiker*," *Die Berliner Literaturkritik*, 6 Jan. 2004, www.berlinerliteratur kritik.de/index.cfm?id=106mat=5072; Fabian Kettner, "Deutsche Geschichtsarbeit: Nicolas Berg macht die historische Forschung zur Shoah zum Gegenstand der historischen Forschung," *Context XXI*, nos. 6–7: 32–34; Irmtrud Wojak, n.t., in *Beiträge zur Geschichte des Nationalsozialismus*, vol. 20, Göttingen, 2004, 257–59; Constantin Goschler, review of book in *sehepunkte* 4 (10 Sept. 2004): 9, http://www.sehepunkte.historicum .net/2004/09/3361tml; Anthony Kauders, n.t., *Central European History* 38 (2005): 2, 344– 46; Eduard Mühle, n.t., *Zeitschrift für Ostmitteleuropa-Forschung* 54, no. 2 (2005): 276–77; Johnpeter Horst Grill, n.t., in *Holocaust and Genocide Studies* 19, no. 3 (2005): 523–25; Stefan Jordan, "Theorie in Geschichte und der Geschichtswissenschaft," *Geschichte in Wissenschaft und Unterricht* 56, no. 7/8 (2005): 426–38, here 428–29; Felix Dirsch, review of book, *Religion—Staat—Gesellschaft* 7, no. 1 (2006): 121–24.

55. Shelley Berlowitz, "Alles ganz sachlich? Nicolas Berg zeigt in seinem Buch, wie die westdeutsche Historikerzunft das Gedächtnis der jüdischen Opfer abwertete und ausblendete," *Die Wochenzeitung*, 25 Sept. 2003; Micha Brumlik, "Die Historisierung der Zeitgeschichte: Nicolas Bergs Studie über die deutsche Holocaust-Forschung," *Neue Zürcher Zeitung*, 19 Nov. 2003; Julian Schütt, "Die Zunfthistoriker," *Weltwoche* (Switzerland), 27 Oct. 2003.

56. Irene Armbruster, "Verzerrte Geschichte: Eine junge Generation von deutschen Historikern setzt sich kritisch mit der Generation ihrer Lehrer und Mentoren auseinander," in *Aufbau: The Transatlantic Jewish Paper*, 24 July 2003, 8–10; Anthony D. Kauders, n.t., *Central European History* 38, no. 2 (2005): 344–46; Imtrud Wojak, "Nicolas

Berg and the West German Historians: A Response to His 'Handbook' on the Historiography of the Holocaust," *German History* (2004): 101–18.

57. Natan Sznaider, "A Great Divide, Forever Divided," in *Haaretz* (English ed.), 24 Dec. 2003.

58. Ian Kershaw, "Beware the Moral High Ground," *Times Literary Supplement*, Oct. 2003, 10–11; Peter Pulzer, "Holocaust und hiesige Historiker," *Jahrbuch Extremismus und Demokratie* 16 (2004): 310–13.

59. Nicolas Le Mogne, n.t., *Bulletin d'Information de la Mission Historique Française en Allemagne* 40 (2004): 470–472.

60. H. W. von der Dunk, "Dadernatie over de shoah," *Historisch Nieuwsblad*, Nov. 2003, 54–55; a more detailed version of the latter review appeared in *European Review* 13, no. 2 (2005): 311–15.

61. Johan Östling, "Historien om Förintelsens historia," *Axess* (April 2004): 43–44.

62. Adam Krzeminski, "Kochajmy sie!," *Polityka*, 22 Oct. 2003, 60.

63. *Forum: "Der Holocaust und die westdeutschen Historiker,"* in *H-Soz-u-Kult*, 23 Feb. 2004, http://hsozkult.geschichte.hu-berlin.de/forum/id=412&type=diskussionen.

64. Tillmann Bendikowski, "Der Holocaust und die westdeutschen Historiker," Deutschlandfunk, 4 Aug. 2003; Rainer Volk, "Mitläufer und Aufklärer? Die deutschen Nachkriegshistoriker und der Holocaust," Bayerischer Rundfunk, 5 Aug. 2003; Patrick Horst, "Der Holocaust und die westdeutschen Historiker: Erforschung und Erinnerung," Südwestfunk, 2, 24 Jan. 2004.

65. Andreas Eckert, *Literaturen*, no. 7/8 (2003): 66–67; Heinrich Senfft, n.t., *Universitas*, Dec. 2003, 1306–7. See *Süddeutsche Zeitung*, 30 June 2003 (first place on the nonfiction book list for July 2003); *Die Zeit*, 17 July 2003 (first place on the nonfiction book list for July 2003); *Literaturen*, no. 7/8 (2003): 63; *H-Soz-u-Kult* (see note 63).

66. Volker Ulrich, "Forschung ohne Erinnerung," in *Die Zeit*, 10 July 2003; Kershaw, "Beware the Moral High Ground."

67. Gerd Wiegel, n.t., *Zeitschrift für Geschichtswissenschaft* 53, no. 1 (2005): 1, 90–92, here 90.

68. Mommsen, "Zeitgeschichtliche Kontroversen," here 15, 17.

69. Peter Longerich, "Der Fall Martin Broszat," *Die Zeit*, 14 Aug. 2003; Norbert Frei, "Hitler-Junge, Jahrgang 1926: Hat der Historiker Martin Broszat seine NSDAP-Mitgliedschaft verschwiegen—oder hat er nichts davon gewusst?," *Die Zeit*, 11 Sept. 2003; Sven F. Kellerhoff, "Verstehen heißt nicht verharmlosen: Was hinter dem Streit um den verstorbenen Zeithistoriker Martin Broszat und seine Mitgliedschaft in der NSDAP steckt," *Die Welt*, 12 Sept. 2003; Otto Köhler, "Was die Akten sagen, was sie nicht sagen: Günter Wallraff und Martin Broszat; Ein Versuch zu vergleichen, was nicht zu vergleichen ist," *Freitag*, 19 Sept. 2003; Rainer Blasius, "Keiner wäscht weißer: Ja, nein, weiß nicht: Der Disput um den Historiker Martin Broszat," *Frankfurter Allgemeine Zeitung*, 20 Sept. 2003; Christian Jostmann, "Kein Versehen: Ein Gutachten zeigt; Es gab keine unfreiwilligen NSDAP-Mitglieder," *Süddeutsche Zeitung*, 8 Oct. 2003; Viktor Winkler, "Ein gefährdetes Erbe: Zum 'Fall' Martin Broszat," *H-Soz-u-Kult*, 31 Oct. 2004, http://hsozkult.geschichte.hu-berlin.de/forum/2004-10-001.

70. Nicolas Berg, "Die Lebenslüge vom Pathos der Nüchternheit: Joseph Wulf, Martin Broszat und das Institut für Zeitgeschichte in den sechziger Jahren," *Südddeutsche Zeitung*, 17 July 2002.

71. Christian Jostmann and Frank Ebbinghaus, "Legt an, gebt Feuer! / Gebt an, legt Feuer! Rothfels I: Institut für Zeitgeschichte, München / Rothfels II: Centre Marc Bloch, Berlin," *Süddeutsche Zeitung*, 21 July 2003; Volker Ullrich, "Der Fall Rothfels: Der Streit um den berühmten Zeithistoriker und die Versäumnisse der Geschichtswissenschaft," *Die Zeit*, 24 July 2003; Matthias Berg, "Der Historiker Hans Rothfels (1891–1976)—'Ein Wanderer zwischen den Welten'? (Tagung am Centre Marc Bloch—Deutsch-Französisches Forschungszentrum für Sozialwissenschaften, 15 July 2003)," *H-Soz-u-Kult*, 12 Aug. 2003, http://hsozkult.geschichte.hu-berlin.de/tagungsberichte /id=274; Jochen Kirchhoff, "Hans Rothfels und die deutsche Zeitgeschichte (Tagung im Institut für Zeitgeschichte, München vom 16–17 July 2003)," *H-Soz-u-Kult*, 13 Aug. 2003, http://hsozkult.geschichte.hu-berlin.de/tagungsberichte/id=278.

72. Nicolas Berg, "Hidden Memory and Unspoken History: Hans Rothfels and the Post-War Refoundation of German Contemporary Historical Studies," *Leo Baeck Institute Yearbook* 49 (2004): 195–220. My extensive discussion of Rothfels in chapter 2 is a slightly revised version of this essay.

73. On Hans Rothfels, see Johannes Hürter and Hans Woller, eds., *Hans Rothfels und die deutsche Zeitgeschichte*, Munich, 2005; on Martin Broszat, see Frei, *Martin Broszat, der "Staat Hitlers" und die Historisierung des Nationalsozialismus.*

74. Hans Woller and Jürgen Zarusky, "Der 'Fall Theodor Eschenburg' und das Institut für Zeitgeschichte," *Vierteljahrshefte für Zeitgeschichte* 4 (2013): 551–65, here 562ff.

75. Mommsen, "Zeitgeschichtliche Kontroversen," 17.

76. Ibid.

77. For example Hans Mommsen, "Täter und Opfer—ein Streit um die Historiker," *Die Welt*, 13 Sept. 2003, 9; more extensively: idem, "Martin Broszat und die Erforschung der NS-Zeit," in Frei, *Martin Broszat, der "Staat Hitlers" und die Historisierung des Nationalsozialismus*, 19–31.

78. Hans Mommsen, *Beamtentum im Dritten Reich: Mit ausgewählten Quellen zur nationalsozialistischen Beamtenpolitik*, Stuttgart, 1962; idem, "Aus der Zeitgeschichte: Bilanzen und Forschungen," *Deutsche Rundschau* 87 (1962): 68–87; idem, "Aufgabenkreis und Verantwortlichkeit des Staatssekretärs der Reichskanzlei Dr. Wilhelm Kritzinger [1962]," in *Gutachten des Instituts für Zeitgeschichte*, vol. 2, Stuttgart, 1966, 369–98; see also Berg, *Der Holocaust und die westdeutschen Historiker*, 557–65.

79. See Alexandra Przyrembel, n.t., *Historische Anthropologie* 11 (2003): 3, 482–85, here 484–85.

80. See, for instance, Hermann Rudolph, "Die deutsche Katastrophe: Die Geschichtswissenschaft ist immer auch ein Kind ihrer Zeit; Wie Deutschlands Historiker nach dem Zweiten Weltkrieg mit dem Holocaust gerungen haben," *Der Tagesspiegel*, 8 Dec. 2003, 7.

81. Torben Fischer and Matthias N. Lorenz, eds., *Lexikon der "Vergangenheitsbewältigung" in Deutschland: Debatten- und Diskursgeschichte des Nationalsozialismus nach 1945*, Bielefeld,

2007; Thorsten Eitz and Georg Stötzel, eds., *Wörterbuch der "Vergangenheitsbewältigung": Die NS-Vergangenheit im öffentlichen Sprachgebrauch*, Hildesheim, 2007.

82. *Friedrich Meinecke: Akademischer Lehrer und emigrierte Schüler*, Mühle, *Briefe des Ostforschers Hermann Aubin*; Friedrich Meinecke, *Werke*, vol. 10: *Neue Briefe und Dokumente*, ed. Gisela Bock and Gerhard A. Ritter with Stefan Meineke and Volker Hunecke, Munich, 2012.

83. Jan Eckel, *Hans Rothfels: Eine intellektuelle Biographie im 20. Jahrhundert*, Göttingen, 2005; Mühle, *Für Volk und deutschen Osten*; David Thimme, *Percy Ernst Schramm und das Mittelalter: Wandlungen eines Geschichtsbildes*, Göttingen, 2006; Franz Hocheneder, *H. G. Adler (1910–1988): Privatgelehrter und freier Schriftsteller*, foreword by Wendelin Schmidt-Dengler, Vienna, 2009.

84. Christoph Nonn, *Theodor Schieder: Ein bürgerlicher Historiker im 20. Jahrhundert*, Düsseldorf, 2013.

85. See Stefan Reinecke, "Historisiert die NS-Historiker!" *Die Tageszeitung*, 18 Dec. 2006; Oliver Schmolke, "Die 'Historisierung' der Historiker," 30 July 2004, http://www.ifs.tu-darmstadt.de/npl/netz-rezensionen/berg.html.

86. Astrid M. Eckert, *The Struggle for the Files: The Western Allies and the Return of German Archives after the Second World War*, trans. Donna Geyer, Cambridge, 2007 (orig. German ed.: 2004); Ruth Nattermann, *Deutsch-jüdische Geschichtsschreibung nach der Shoah: Die Gründungs- und Frühgeschichte des Leo Baeck Institute*, Essen, 2004; Hartmut Lehman and Otto Gerhard Oexle, eds., *Nationalsozialismus in den Kulturwissenschaften*, vol. 1: *Fächer—Millieus—Karrieren*, Göttingen, 2004; vol. 2: *Leitbegriffe—Deutungsmuster—Paradigmenkämpfe: Erfahrungen und Transformationen im Exil*, Göttingen, 2004.

Chapter 1. Tragedy, Fate, and Breach

1. Hans-Günther Zmarzlik, "Einer vom Jahrgang 1922: Rückblick in eigener Sache," in idem, *Wieviel Zukunft hat unsere Vergangenheit*, Munich, 1970, 25, 31.

2. Julius Posener, *In Deutschland 1945 bis 1946: Kommentierte Ausgabe mit einem Nachwort von Alan Posener*, Berlin, 2001 (1st ed.: Jerusalem, 1947), 25. Posener observes sharply but judges gently; similarly Eugen Kogon, "Das deutsche Volk und die Konzentrationslager," in idem, *Der SS-Staat: Das System der deutschen Konzentrationslager*, Munich, 1946, 331ff.; cf. in contrast the relevant commentary on the German postwar mentality in William L. Shirer, *End of Berlin Diary*, New York, 1947; Stephen Spender, *European Witness*, London, 1946; Saul K.: Padover, *Experiment in Germany: The Story of an American Intelligence Officier*, New York, 1946.

3. Wolfgang Benz, "Die Deutschen und die Judenverfolgung: Mentalitätsgeschichtliche Aspekte," in *Die Deutschen und die Judenverfolgung im Dritten Reich*, ed. Ursula Büttner, Hamburg, 1992, 51–63. On this branch of research, see Ursula Büttner, "Die deutsche Gesellschaft und die Judenverfolgung—ein Forschungsproblem," in *Die Deutschen und die Judenverfolgung im Dritten Reich*, 7–29; Hans-Heinrich Wilhelm, "Wie geheim war die 'Endlösung'?," in *Miscellanea: Festschrift für Helmut Krausnick zum 75. Geburtstag*, ed. Wolfgang Benz, Stuttgart, 1980, 131–48; Ian Kershaw, "The Persecution of

Jews and German Popular Opinion in the Third Reich," *Leo Baeck Institute Yearbook* 26 (1981): 261–89; Hans Mommsen, "Was haben die Deutschen vom Völkermord an den Juden gewußt?," in *Der Judenpogrom 1938: Von der "Reichskristallnacht" zum Völkermord*, ed. Walter Pehle, Frankfurt a.M., 1988, 176–200; David Bankier, *The Germans and the Final Solution: Public Opinion under Nazism*, Oxford, 1992.

4. Thus Fritz Klein in an interview, in Stefanie Schüler-Springorum and Christl Wickert, "Unversöhnte Geschichte(n): Historiker in Ost und West," in *Geschichte als Möglichkeit: Über die Chance von Demokratie, Festschrift für Helga Grebing*, ed. Karsten Rudolph and Christel Wickert, Essen, 1995, 9–25, here 14.

5. Raul Hilberg in an interview with the *Hannoversche Allgemeine*, 5 Oct. 1995; in more detail: idem, *Unerbetene Erinnerung: Der Weg eines Holocaust-Forschers*, Frankfurt a.M., 1994; and an interview of Hilberg with Harald Welzer, "Der Holocaust war für mich Gegenwart," in *"Auf den Trümmern der Geschichte": Gespräche mit Raul Hilberg, Hans Mommsen und Zygmunt Baumann*, ed. Harald Welzer, Tübingen, 1999, 13–48. On the reception of Hilberg in Germany, see Nicolas Berg, "Lesarten des Judenmords," in *Wandlungsprozesse in Westdeutschland: Belastung, Integration, Liberalisierung, 1945-1980*, ed. Ulrich Herbert, Göttingen, 2002, 92, 98–102, 110–12, 132–34.

6. Gerd Tellenbach, *Die deutsche Not als Schuld und Schicksal*, Stuttgart, 1947, 49.

7. Ibid., 45.

8. Ibid., 46, 47.

9. Gerd Tellenbach, "Nachwort über heutige Perspektiven der deutschen Geschichte," in idem, *Die Entstehung des deutschen Reiches*, 3rd ed., Munich, 1949, 225–43, here 241. For the problem of differences between this afterword's phrasing in different editions of Tellenbach's book in relation to his general ideological perspective, see Berg, *Der Holocaust und die westdeutschen Historiker* (3rd ed.), 49n9.

10. Tellenbach, *Entstehung des deutschen Reiches*, 16–17.

11. Peter Rassow to Siegfried A. Kaehler, 31 May and 2 June 1945, in Winfried Schulze, *Deutsche Geschichtswissenschaft nach 1945*, Munich, 1989, 66–74, here 69.

12. Annelise Thimme, "Geprägt von der Geschichte," in *Erinnerungsstücke: Weg in die Vergangenheit; Rudolf Vierhaus zum 75. Geburtstag gewidmet; Mit Beiträgen von Karl Otmar Freiherr von Aretin, Karl Dietrich Bracher, Fritz Fellner, Iring Fetscher, Klaus Friedland, Irmgard Höß, Walther Hofer, Erich Kosthorst, Annelise Thimme, Eberhard Weis, Karl Ferdinand Werner und Wolfgang Zorn*, ed. Hartmut Lehmann and Otto G. Oexle, Vienna, 1997, 153–224, here 153–54.

13. Ulrich Herbert, "Der Holocaust und die deutsche Gesellschaft," in *Auschwitz: Sechs Essays zu Geschehen und Vergegenwärtigung*, ed. Klaus-Dietmar Henke, Berichte und Studien, no. 32, Dresden, 2001, 37–51, here 51.

14. Erich Kosthorst, "Mein Weg durch die Zeitgeschichte," in Lehmann and Oexle, *Erinnerungsstücke*, 137–52, here 143; on the same page *deutschen-möglich* is then extended to *menschen-möglich* (again translated roughly: "human-possible"). Kosthorst here presumed the biographical origins of the *Sonderweg* thesis—that of a "special path" to German history—"as a motive" long before its scholarly formulation "as a conclusion": "The testing of such a variant of the German special path . . . that, however, was not

only familiar to those born in 1920 through the tradition of German political thinking but somehow could not even appear wayward, remained the motive, not the conclusion, of my scholarly research" (142).

15. Fritz Klein, *Drinnen und draußen: Ein Historiker in der DDR; Erinnerungen*, Frankfurt a.M., 2000, 92.

16. Hans-Günther Zmarzlik, "Einer vom Jahrgang 1922: Rückblick in eigener Sache," in idem, *Wieviel Zukunft hat unsere Vergangenheit?*, Munich, 1970, 16–31, here 26.

17. Tellenbach, *Die deutsche Not*, 43; see also idem, *Aus erinnerter Zeitgeschichte*, Freiburg, 1981.

18. Zmarzlik, "Einer vom Jahrgang 1922," 26; very similarly: Waldemar Besson, "Wie ich mich geändert habe," *Vierteljahrshefte für Zeitgeschichte* 19 (1971): 398–403.

19. Nicolaus Sombart, *Rendezvous mit dem Weltgeist: Heidelberger Reminiszenzen, 1945–1951*, Frankfurt a.M., 2000, 217.

20. Ibid., 218.

21. Ludwig Dehio, *Deutschland und die Weltpolitik im 20. Jahrhundert*, Munich, 1955, 12; cf. 12, 13, 27, 30.

22. Ibid., 12, 25.

23. Ibid.

24. Friedrich Meinecke, *Die deutsche Katastrophe: Betrachtungen und Erinnerungen*, Wiesbaden, 1946, 96.

25. Sombart, *Rendezvous mit dem Weltgeist*, 145.

26. Dehio, *Deutschland und die Weltpolitik*, 39.

27. Niedersächsische Staats- und Universitätsbibliothek (Göttingen), estate of Kahrstedt, nos. 32 and 33, here *Hessische Post*, 19 April 1945; *Hannoversche Kurier*, 26 Oct. 1945.

28. Those whom Annelise Thimme ("Geprägt von Geschichte," 208–9) has described as the "rescuers and restorers of the image of German history" included Thimme herself, Hans Rothfels, Gerhard Ritter, and Karl Dietrich Erdmann.

29. This "paradoxical finding" is emphasized by Sebastian Conrad, *Auf der Suche nach der verlorenen Nation: Geschichtsschreibung in Westdeutschland und Japan, 1945–1960*, Göttingen, 1999. Conrad here points repeatedly (see, e.g., 12, 85, 105, 130–31, 410) to a discourse centered on an end of the national state accompanied by an actual intensified focus on a German national historiography.

30. See here the reference to the "end of the empire [*Reich*] of the Antichrist" in the diary entry of the prelate Josef Sauer, 23 April 1945, cited in Hugo Ott, "Schuldig—mitschuldig—unschuldig? Politische Säuberungen und Neubeginn 1945," in *Die Freiburger Universität in der Zeit des Nationalsozialismus*, ed. Eckhard John, Bernd Martin, Marc Mück, and Hugo Ott, Freiburg, 1991, 243–58, here 244–45.

31. Eva Reichmann, "Im Banne von Schuld und Gleichgültigkeit," in *Frankfurter Allgemeine Zeitung*, 23 March 1960; reprinted in idem, *Größe und Verhängnis deutsch-jüdischer Existenz, Zeugnisse einer tragischen Begegnung*, Heidelberg, 1974, 181.

32. Conrad, *Auf der Suche nach der verlorenen Nation*, 126–27; for a similar perspective, see Lutz Niethammer, "Methodische Überlegungen zur deutschen Nachkriegsgeschichte:

Doppelgeschichte, Nationalgeschichte oder asymmetrisch verflochtene Parallelge-schichte?," in *Deutsche Vergangenheiten — eine gemeinsame Herausforderung: Der schwierige Umgang mit der doppelten Nachkriegsgeschichte*, ed. Christoph Kleßmann, Hans Misselwitz, and Günter Wichert, Berlin, 1999, 307–29, here 319.

33. Max Picard, *Hitler in uns selbst*, Zurich, 1946, 31–37.

34. Ibid., 36.

35. Ibid.

36. Ibid., 247–48.

37. Ibid., 280–81.

38. Karl Jaspers, *Die Schuldfrage*, Heidelberg, 1946.

39. Dirk Blasius, "'Judenfrage' und Gesellschaftsgeschichte," *Neue Politische Literatur* 23 (1978): 17–33, here 17.

40. Picard, *Hitler in uns selbst*, 232, 205. On the partly impotent, partly opportunistic behavior of representative German philosophers between 1945 and 1948, see Gerwin Klinger, "Meisterdenker in staatsloser Zeit: Deutsche Philosophie zwischen 1945 und 1948," *Frankfurter Rundschau*, 29 June 1996. But Klinger fails to differentiate in view of the contemporary semantics so that the similarities between Carl Schmitt and Karl Jaspers emerge more strongly than the far greater differences. For a sense of the differences, see Dirk van Laak, *Gespräche in der Sicherheit des Schweigens: Carl Schmitt in der politischen Geistesge-schichte der frühen Bundesrepublik*, Berlin, 1993; and Ralf Kadereit, *Karl Jaspers und die Bundes-republik Deutschland: Politische Gedanken eines Philosophen*, Paderborn, 1999.

41. Siegfried A. Kaehler, "Die Problematik der Preußischen Geschichte im 19. Jahrhundert," *Die Sammlung* 9 (1954): 1–17, here 17.

42. Hermann Aubin, "Abendland, Reich, Deutschland und Europa," in *Schicksals-fragen der Gegenwart: Handbuch politisch-historischer Bildung*, ed. German Ministry of Defense, vol. 1, Tübingen, 1957, 29–63, here 58–59.

43. Hermann Aubin, "Die Deutschen in der Geschichte des Ostens," *Geschichte in Wissenschaft und Unterricht* 7 (1956): 512–45, here 516, 544. See also Conrad, *Auf der Suche nach der verlorenen Nation*, 388–89.

44. This the formulation of Justus Hashagen in reference to the "historians' duties" in the new Germany of 1920, cited from Annette Vowinckel, *Geschichtsbegriff und Historisches Denken bei Hannah Arendt*, Cologne, 2001, 15.

45. Johannes Kühn, *Über den Sinn des gegenwärtigen Krieges*, Heidelberg, 1940 — a book that prompted Victor Klemperer to refer to Kühn as a "traitor to scholarship"; see Victor Klemperer, *"Ich will Zeugnis ablegen bis zum Letzten": Tagebücher, 1933–1945*, 2 vols., Berlin, 1995, 1:667.

46. Johannes Kühn, *Die Wahrheit der Geschichte und die Gestalt der wahren Geschichte*, Oberursel, 1947, 55. For Detlev Junker, "Theorie der Geschichtswissenschaft am Histo-rischen Seminar der Universität Heidelberg," in *Geschichte in Heidelberg*, ed. Jürgen Miethke, Berlin, 1992, 159–74, here 171–72, this book by Kühn, although having an "unfortunate title," can nonetheless be read as "historiographically essential" because it poses "classical questions of historical theory." See also, uncritically, Eike Wolgast, "Die neuzeitliche Geschichte im 20. Jahrhundert," in Miethke, *Geschichte in Heidelberg*, esp.

147ff., criticized by Eberhard Demm, "Alfred Weber und die Nationalsozialisten," *Zeitschrift für Geschichtswissenschaft* 47 (1999): 211–36, here 232.

47. Cited from Joachim Radkau, *Die deutsche Emigration in den USA*, Düsseldorf, 1971, 227. The statement was made in 1941.

48. Kühn, *Die Wahrheit der Geschichte*, 69, 66–67.

49. Hans Freyer, *Weltgeschichte Europas*, 2 vols., Wiesbaden, 1948, 2:993.

50. Ibid., 1:xi, xii, xiii.

51. Ibid., 2:998; 1:87, 95.

52. Ibid., 2:998.

53. Ibid., 1:164.

54. Paul Egon Hübinger, "Um ein neues Geschichtsbild," *Geschichte in Wissenschaft und Unterricht* 1 (1950): 385–401, here 399.

55. Gisbert Beyerhaus, "Neue Wege zur Erforschung des Zweiten Weltkriegs," *Welt als Geschichte* 2 (1951): 58–63, here 58.

56. Golo Mann, *Deutsche Geschichte, 1919–1945*, Frankfurt a.M., 1961 (1st ed.: Frankfurt a.M., 1958), 105.

57. Kühn, *Die Wahrheit der Geschichte*, 65.

58. Ibid., 68.

59. See also Conrad, *Auf der Suche nach der verlorenen Nation*, 186, 215 (he uses modern terms for the same phenomenon, e.g., "selective perspective for problems" or "special focal points").

60. Annelise Thimme, "Geprägt von der Geschichte," in Lehmann and Oexle, *Erinnerungsstücke*, 191.

61. One of the few reviews of the time to problematize this idea was an (otherwise positively inclined) article by Johann Albrecht von Rantzau, "Die deutsche Katastrophe: Zum neuen Werk von Friedrich Meinecke," *Die Zeit*, 14 Nov. 1946. The reviewer related the word "catastrophe" to the year 1933.

62. Wilhelm Hoffmann, *Nach der Katastrophe*, Stuttgart, 2001 (1st ed.: 1946), 1.

63. Meinecke, *Die deutsche Katastrophe*, 38, 57, 70.

64. Johannes Haller, foreword to *Die Epochen der deutschen Geschichte*, new expanded ed., Stuttgart, 1940; on Haller, see Hans-Erich Volkmann, "Deutsche Historiker im Umgang mit Drittem Reich und Zweitem Weltkrieg 1939–1949," in *Ende des Dritten Reiches—Ende des Zweiten Weltkriegs: Eine perspektivische Rückschau*, ed. Hans-Erich Volkmann, Munich, 1995, 861–911; idem, "Von Johannes Haller zu Reinhard Wittram: Deutschbaltische Historiker und der Nationalsozialismus," *Zeitschrift für Geschichtswissenschaft* 45 (1997): 21–46; idem, "Als Polen noch der Erbfeind war: Zum 50. Todestag des politischen Historikers Johannes Haller," *Die Zeit*, 12 Dec. 1997; on the Nazi period in particular, see Heribert Müller, "Johannes Haller und der Nationalsozialismus," in *Gestaltungskraft des Politischen: Festschrift Eberhard Kolb*, ed. Wolfram Pyta and Ludwig Richter, Historische Forschungen 63, Berlin, 1998, 443–82; on Haller's autobiography, see also Nicolas Berg, "Zwischen individuellem und historiographischem Gedächtnis: Der Nationalsozialismus in Autobiographien deutscher Historiker nach 1945," *Bios* 13 (2000): 181–207, here 191ff. The dominant Goethian understanding of history at the time is

reflected in Klaus Ziegler, "Zu Goethes Deutung der Geschichte," *Deutsche Vierteljahrs-schrift für Literaturwissenschaft und Geistesgeschichte* 30 (1956): 232–67, who observes that for Goethe "historical chaos is largely presented as the manifestation of a chaos of nature at its foundation" (247).

65. This the formulation in Johannes Haller, "Zum Verständnis der Weltge-schichte," *Die Pforte* 1 (1947/48): 349–67, here 363; cf. 364. The historian Reinhard Wittram (discussed later) misinterpreted this credo of "natural religion" as the result of the dominance of a contemporary natural-scientific sense of the world. See Reinhard Wittram, "Erinnerung an Johannes Haller," *Welt als Geschichte* 10 (1950): 67–70, here 67–68.

66. F. A. Kramer, *Vor den Ruinen Deutschlands: Ein Aufruf zur geschichtlichen Selbstbe-sinnung*, Berlin, 1945, 86.

67. Fritz Helling, *Der Katastrophenweg der deutschen Geschichte*, Frankfurt a.M., 1947, 204.

68. Werner Conze, "Die deutsche Opposition gegen Hitler," *Neue Politische Literatur* 2 (1953): 210–15, here 210.

69. Theodor Schieder, "Die geschichtlichen Grundlagen und Epochen des deutschen Parteienwesens," in idem, *Staat und Gesellschaft im Wandel unserer Zeit*, Munich, 1958, 64.

70. For example, in Henry Picker, *Hitlers Tischgespräche im Führerhauptquartier, 1941–1942: Im Auftrage Verlags neu hrsg. von Percy Ernst Schramm, in Zusammenarbeit mit Andreas Hill-gruber und Martin Vogt*, Stuttgart, 1963, 23.

71. Siegfried A. Kaehler, "Die Problematik der Preußischen Geschichte im 19. Jahrhundert," *Die Sammlung* 9 (1954): 1–17, here 3–4.

72. Freyer, *Weltgeschichte Europas*, 2:994.

73. Dehio, *Deutschland und die Weltpolitik*, 19–20, 21, 26.

74. Eva Reichmann, "Flucht in den Haß" (foreword), in idem, *Größe und Verhängnis deutsch-jüdischer Existenz: Zeugnisse einer tragischen Begegnung*, Heidelberg, 1974, 166.

75. Hans Kohn, *Bürger vieler Welten: Ein Leben im Zeitalter der Weltrevolution*, introduced by Arnold J. Toynbee, Frauenfeld, 1965, 77.

76. Hans Kohn, *Wege und Irrwege: Vom Geist des deutschen Bürgertums*, Düsseldorf, 1962, esp. "Der Verlauf der neueren deutschen Geschichte," 7–26. On Kohn, see esp. Heinz Wolf, *Deutsch-jüdische Emigrantenhistoriker in den USA und der Nationalsozialismus*, Frankfurt a.M., 1988, 113–14; Bernd Faulenbach, "Der 'deutsche Weg' aus der Sicht des Exils: Zum Urteil emigrierter Historiker," *Exilforschung: Ein internationales Jahrbuch* 3 (1985): 11–30.

77. Kohn, *Bürger vieler Welten*, 242. An anthology edited by Kohn and already pre-senting the same thesis was harshly criticized by Werner Conze, "Deutsche Geschichte in neuer Sicht?," *Neue Politische Literatur* 3 (1954): cols. 719–21 ("Whoever is afraid to neutralize the devil," Conze declares, "does not confront history in its inexorability").

78. Friedrich Meinecke, "Straßburg—Freiburg—Berlin, 1901–1919 (1945)," in idem, *Autobiographische Schriften*, ed. and introduced by Eberhard Kessel, Stuttgart, 1969, 310, 313.

79. Meinecke, *Die deutsche Katastrophe*, 5, 7, 9. See also 96, where Meinecke speaks of the "present fearful catastrophe that sprang from Hitlerism and put an end to it."

80. Friedrich Meinecke to Gerhard Masur, 7 Feb. 1947, Institut für Zeitgeschichte, Munich (henceforth IfZ), estate of Masur, no. 58.

81. Fritz Stern, ed., *Geschichte und Geschichtsschreibung: Möglichkeiten—Aufgaben—Methoden. Texte von Voltaire bis zur Gegenwart*, Munich, 1966, 274.

82. Edgar Wolfrum, *Geschichte als Waffe: Vom Kaiserreich bis zur Wiedervereinigung*, Göttingen, 2001, 62ff. Wolfrum emphasizes the "pilot's function" of the Meinecke text for the postwar German sense of history. Conrad, *Auf der Suche nach der verlorenen Nation*, 61, stresses the "oscillation" between a European and a specifically German localization of Nazism.

83. See Lehmann and Oexle, *Erinnerungsstücke*, 133; Jost Nolte, "Respektvolles Lob eines altmodischen Denkers," *Die Welt*, 27 Jan. 1996.

84. Friedrich Meinecke to Heinrich Ritter v. Srbik, 8 May 1946, in Friedrich Meinecke, *Ausgewählter Briefwechsel*, ed. and introduced by Ludwig Dehio and Peter Classen (=Friedrich Meinecke, *Werke*, vol. 6), Stuttgart, 1962, 249.

85. Meinecke, *Autobiographische Schriften*, 321–445; on the autobiographical genre: Schulze, *Deutsche Geschichtswissenschaft nach 1945*, esp. 50ff.

86. Meinecke, "Straßburg—Freiburg—Berlin," 253.

87. Friedrich Meinecke to Siegfried A. Kaehler, 16 April 1950, in Meinecke, *Ausgewählter Briefwechsel*, 555.

88. Meinecke, *Die deutsche Katastrophe*, 7–8.

89. Friedrich Meinecke to Siegfried A. Kaehler, 29 Jan. 1945, in Meinecke, *Ausgewählter Briefwechsel*, 514.

90. Meinecke to Gerhard Masur, 26 April 1947, IfZ, estate of Masur; see also the 1948 essay on Ranke and Burckhardt, and the remarks in Schulze, *Deutsche Geschichtswissenschaft nach 1945*, 56–57, together with Schulze's accurate observation of the difference in this respect between Meinecke and Gerhard Ritter, who showed no desire to follow up on Burckhardt's "demystification of the political."

91. Meinecke, *Die deutsche Katastrophe*, 7–8.

92. Friedrich Meinecke to Eduard Spranger, 18 Dec. 1947, in Meinecke, *Ausgewählter Briefwechsel*, 609.

93. Friedrich Meinecke to Ludwig Dehio, 21 July 1947, ibid., 280ff.

94. Friedrich Meinecke, "Deutung eines Ranke-Wortes," in idem, *Zur Theorie und Philosophie der Geschichte*, ed. and introduced by Eberhard Kessel, vol. 4 of his *Werke*, Stuttgart, 1959, 117–39 (first published 1942).

95. Friedrich Meinecke, "Irrwege in unserer Geschichte?," *Der Monat* 2 (1949): 3–6.

96. Meinecke, *Die deutsche Katastrophe*, 26.

97. Ibid., 121ff., 123.

98. Ibid., 124.

99. Benedetto Croce, "Friedrich Meineckes Geschichtsphilosophie," *Der Monat* 3 (1951): 313–15.

100. Meinecke, "Irrwege in unserer Geschichte?," 6.

101. Friedrich Meinecke to Gerhard Masur, 7 Feb. 1947, IfZ, estate of Masur, no. 58.

102. Walther Hofer, "Weltgeschichte als Tragödie: Gedanken zum Tode Friedrich Meineckes," *Schweizer Monatshefte* 34 (1954/55): 94–97, here 95. See also idem, "Dämonie und Geschichte: Weg und Wandlung Friedrich Meineckes," *Der Tagesspiegel*, 6 Feb. 1957, 4. Hofer's Meinecke biography, *Geschichtsschreibung und Weltanschauung: Betrachtungen zum Werk Friedrich Meineckes*, was published in Munich in 1950.

103. Meinecke, "Irrwege in unserer Geschichte?," 5.

104. Ibid., 6.

105. Meinecke, "Straßburg—Freiburg—Berlin," 228. The most convincing and at the same time balanced critique of Meinecke's "aestheticizing" of historical thought was offered early on by Ernst Schulin, "Das Problem der Individualität: Eine kritische Betrachtung des Historismus-Werkes von Friedrich Meinecke," *Historische Zeitschrift* 197 (1963): 102–33; and then by Jörn Rüsen, "Die Krise des Historismus in unzeitgemäßer Erneuerung—Friedrich Meineckes 'Entstehung des Historismus,'" in his *Konfigurationen des Historismus: Studien zur deutschen Wissenschaftskultur*, Frankfurt a.M., 1993, 331–56. See also the critical overview by Jonathan B. Knudsen, "Friedrich Meinecke (1862–1954)," in *Paths of Continuity: Central European Historiography from the 1930s to the 1950s*, ed. Hartmut Lehmann and James van Horn Melton, Washington, D.C., 1994, 49–71; here as well the specific mixture of anti-Enlightenment and classical-liberal elements in Meinecke's role as postwar German moderator is emphasized (see 51).

106. Meinecke, "Irrwege in unserer Geschichte?," 5.

107. "Keine Irrwege—?," *Der Monat* 2 (1949/50): 330–35, here 331, 334.

108. Karl Dietrich Erdmann, "Anmerkungen zu Friedrich Meineckes 'Irrwege in unserer Geschichte' und 'Die deutsche Katastrophe,'" *Geschichte in Wissenschaft und Unterricht* 2 (1951): 85–91, here 85, 87.

109. Hans Schlange-Schöningen, *Am Tage danach*, Hamburg, 1946, 205.

110. See Gerhard Ritter to Friedrich Meinecke, 1 Jan. 1940, in Gerhard Ritter, *Ein politischer Historiker in seinen Briefen*, ed. Klaus Schwabe and Rolf Reichardt, with the assistance of Reinhard Hauf, Schriften des Bundesarchivs 33, Boppard/Rh., 1984, 346–47. The letter was a response to Meinecke's "Geschichte und Gegenwart" (in idem, *Vom geschichtlichen Sinn und vom Sinn der Geschichte*, Leipzig, 1939, 7–22), where the historian already formulated his "vertical historiography."

111. Hans Rothfels to Siegfried A. Kaehler, 8 May 1948 and 17 Nov. 1947, in Kaehler–Rothfels correspondence, Niedersächsische Staats- und Universitätsbibliothek (Göttingen), estate of Kaehler, nos. 268 and 271. For another, brief discussion of the reception history of Meinecke's text, see Schulze, *Deutsche Geschichtswissenschaft nach 1945*, 56–58.

112. Eduard Spranger to Friedrich Meinecke, 25 Sept. 1946, in Meinecke, *Ausgewählter Briefwechsel*, 597–99. See also Spranger's effusive praise for Meinecke's oeuvre nearly three years later: Eduard Spranger to Friedrich Meinecke, 15 June 1949, ibid., 619; here Spranger extols Meinecke for his oeuvre's role "in the rebuilding of German self-assurance and morale, whose old strength is embodied in you, dear friend. As you know, our entire *Volk* is rising toward that."

113. Siegfried A. Kaehler, "'Die deutsche Katastrophe': Zu dem neuesten Buch von Friedrich Meinecke," *Göttinger Universitäts-Zeitung* 1, no. 20 (15 Nov. 1946): 3–5.

114. Siegfried A. Kaehler to Friedrich Meinecke, 30 Oct. 1946, in Meinecke, *Ausgewählter Briefwechsel*, 505 (elision is in that volume).

115. Kaehler, "'Die deutsche Katastrophe,'" 3.

116. Siegfried A. Kaehler to Friedrich Meinecke, 30 Oct. 1946, in Meinecke, *Ausgewählter Briefwechsel*, 506; Friedrich Meinecke to Siegfried A. Kaehler, 8 Dec. 1946, ibid., 509.

117. Kaehler to Meinecke, 30 Oct. 1946, ibid., 502.

118. Numerous similar assessments in Geheimes Staatsarchiv Preußischer Kulturbesitz (Berlin-Dahlem) [henceforth: Prussian State Archives], Rep. 92 Meinecke, nos. 140, 154, and 187. Examples of the few exceptions: Hanz Holldack, "Eine Selbstkritik des Bürgertums," *Hochland*, no. 39 (1946): 169–76; Hermann L. Mayer, "Revision des deutschen Zeitgeschichtsbildes," *Süd-West-Echo* (Rastatt), 18 Jan. 1947; Heinz Weniger, "Ursache oder Schuld in der Geschichte?," *Rheinische Zeitung*, 9 Nov. 1946. Weniger criticized Meinecke's invocation of "coincidence" and "the tragic" as a "questionable sign in a historical thinker."

119. Albert Brackmann to Friedrich Meinecke, 7 Nov. 1946, Prussian State Archives, Rep. 92, no. 4.

120. Gerhard Brück to Friedrich Meinecke, 4 April 1947, Prussian State Archives, Rep. 92, no. 5.

121. Erich Boehringer to Friedrich Meinecke, 22 Aug. 1946, Prussian State Archives, Rep. 92, no. 4.

122. Karl Dietrich Erdmann, "Friedrich Meinecke: Die deutsche Katastrophe," *Kölner Universitätszeitung*, no. 7 (n.d.).

123. Franz Schnabel, "Das Urteil der Geschichte," *Hessische Nachrichten*, 26 Nov. 1946; Friedrich Baethgen to Friedrich Meinecke, 29 May 1946, Prussian State Archives, Rep. 92, no. 2; IfZ to Meinecke, Prussian State Archives, Rep. 92, no. 278; German Historian's Association to Meinecke, Prussian State Archives, Rep. 92, no. 278.

124. Gerhard Schröder and Ernst Lemmer to Friedrich Meinecke, Prussian State Archives, Rep. 92, no. 278.

125. Heinz Gaessner to Friedrich Meinecke, 1 May 1947, Prussian State Archives, Rep. 92, no. 12.

126. Michael Müller-Claudius, *Deutsche und jüdische Tragik*, Frankfurt a.M., 1955, 184, 9.

127. *Süddeutsche Zeitung*, 1 Oct. 1946, 3.

128. Gerd Bucerius to Friedrich Meinecke, 28 Nov. 1946, Prussian State Archives, Rep. 92, no. 5.

129. *Hamburger Abendblatt*, 30 Oct. 1952.

130. Bruno Wachsmuth, "Zwischen Schuld und Verhängnis," *Der Tagesspiegel*, 4 Sept. 1946; anon., "Die klärende Katastrophe," *Schwäbische Zeitung*, 30 Aug. 1946.

131. Partial reprinting of the "coincidence" chapter in *Der Mannheimer Morgen*, 30 Jan. 1947; further examples: Hermann Fiebing, "Zufälle?," *Südkurier*, 7 Aug. 1946, 1; Maximilian v. Hagen, "Eine erste Geschichte unserer Katastrophe," *Neue Zeit*, 26

Oct. 1946. The sharpest criticisms were also directed at this point: Gustav Zerres, "Die deutsche Katastrophe," *Rheinischer Merkur*, 29 Oct. 1946, referred to the chapter as "somewhat plaintive all-purpose theory"; another newspaper termed it "naive" ("Die Herrschaft des Nationalsozialismus," *Trierische Volkszeitung*, 12 Nov. 1946); Leonhard v. Muralt, "Die deutsche Katastrophe. Zum Buch von Friedrich Meinecke," *Bücher-Rundschau* (n.d.), 338–40, likewise criticize the "coincidence" factor in Meinecke's account for masking the responsibility of the Germans (Prussian State Archives, Rep. 92, no. 254).

132. Anon., "Die deutsche Katastrophe," *Nürnberger Nachrichten*, 26 Feb. 1947.

133. Leibniz Verlag (prev. R. Oldenbourg publishers) to Friedrich Meinecke, 30 Sept. 1946, Prussian State Archives, Rep. 92, no. 254.

134. Hans Kudszus, "Die Tragik der Geschichte," *Der Tagesspiegel* (n.d.), Prussian State Archives, Rep. 92, no. 278.

135. Felix E. Hirsch, "Tribute to a Great European," *New York Herald Tribune*, 29 Oct. 1952; Sidney B. Fay (who translated the book into English) to Friedrich Meinecke, 5 May 1947, Prussian State Archives, Rep. 92, no. 10; Aage Friis, "Meinecke über die deutsche Katastrophe," *Svenska Dagbladet* (Stockholm), 14 March 1947.

136. Walther Hofer, "Ein geschichtlicher Denker zur deutschen Katastrophe," *Der kleine Bund: Literarische Beilage des "Bund"* 27, no. 38 (1946): 149–51. Meinecke's book was translated into Japanese in 1951 under the telling title "The German Tragedy"; its Japanese reception was "animated" (see Conrad, *Auf der Suche nach der verlorenen Nation*, 161).

137. Hofer, "Ein geschichtlicher Denker," 150–51.

138. Eugen Kogon, *Der SS-Staat: Das System de Deutschen Konzentrationslager*, Munich, 1946; translated as *The Theory and Practice of Hell: The German Concentration Camps and the System behind Them*, New York, 1950.

139. Erich Boehringer to Friedrich Meinecke, 22 Aug. 1946, Prussian State Archives, Rep 92, no. 4.

140. Kogon, *Der SS-Staat*, Munich, 1946, vii. All the following citations are from the first German edition (foreword and introduction), v–xv.

141. The table of contents itself covers eight pages; many headings and subchapters are formulated in a deliberately scientific tone, for example, "The Total Number and Average Endurance of Camp Prisoners," "Mixing of Prisoner Categories and Mutual Ratio," and the account of "The Relativity of Statistical Information."

142. Kogon, *Der SS-Staat*, vii; next citation vi.

143. Ibid., vii.

144. Ibid., 328.

145. Ibid., v; next two citations, viii, x.

146. Ibid., vi, ix.

147. Ibid., vii.

148. Eugen Kogon, "Beginn der Geschichtsrevision," *Frankfurter Hefte* 1 (1946): 776–79, here 776, 777.

149. Ibid., 779.

150. Gisbert Beyerhaus, "Notwendigkeit und Freiheit in der deutschen Katastrophe: Gedanken zu Friedrich Meineckes jüngstem Buch," *Historische Zeitschrift* 169 (1949): 73–87, here 73.

151. Ibid., 75ff.

152. Gisbert Beyerhaus to Friedrich Meinecke, 31 May 1949, Prussian State Archives, Rep. 92, no. 3.

153. Gisbert Beyerhaus to Friedrich Meinecke, 17 Oct. 1949, Prussian State Archives, Rep. 92, no. 3.

154. Siegfried A. Kaehler, "Der 20. Juli 1944 im geschichtlichen Rückblick," *Die Sammlung* 9 (1954): 436–45, here 440, 442.

155. Paul Kluke, "Der deutsche Widerstand. Eine kritische Literaturübersicht," *Historische Zeitschrift* 169 (1949): 136–61, here 137.

156. Greifenverlag to Friedrich Meinecke, 15 Aug. 1946, Prussian State Archives, Rep. 92, no. 13.

157. Friedrich Meinecke to Siegfried A. Kaehler, 16 April 1947, in Meinecke, *Ausgewählter Briefwechsel*, 514.

158. Ibid.

159. Friedrich Meinecke to G. P. Gooch, 15 April 1947, in Meinecke, *Ausgewählter Briefwechsel*, 277.

Chapter 2. "A Large Dark Stain on the German Shield of Honor"

1. On Ritter in general: Christoph Cornelißen, *Gerhard Ritter: Geschichtswissenschaft und Politik im 20. Jahrhundert*, Düsseldorf, 2001; the most important older literature: Werner Berthold, "Zur Entstehung, Wirkung und Bewertung des Buches '. . . großhungern und gehorchen' aus der Sicht des Jahres 1997," in *Historiographischer Rückspiegel: Georg G. Iggers zum 70. Geburtstag*, ed. Gerald Diesener, Leipzig, 1997, 13–24; Hans-Günter Zmarzlik, "Lebendige Vergangenheit: Eine Würdigung Gerhard Ritters," *Historische Zeitschrift* 207 (1968): 55–74; Andreas Dorpalen, "Gerhard Ritter," in *Deutsche Historiker*, ed. Hans-Ulrich Wehler, 9 vols., Göttingen, 1971–82, 1:86–99; Max Müller, "Gerhard Ritter: Ein politischer Historiker," *Historisches Jahrbuch* 106 (1986): 119–34. The first larger introduction to Ritter's life and work was by one of his students: Klaus Schwabe, "Gerhard Ritter— Werk und Person," in *Gerhard Ritter, Ein politischer Historiker*, ed. Klaus Schwabe and Rolf Reichardt, Boppard/Rhein, 1984, 1–170; idem, "Change and Continuity in German Historiography from 1933 into the early 1950s: Gerhard Ritter (1888–1967)," in *Paths of Continuity: Central European Historiography from the 1930s to the 1950s*, ed. Hartmut Lehmann and James van Horn Melton, Washington, D.C., 1994. Important in respect to the year 1945: Agnes Blänsdorf, "Gerhard Ritter 1942–1950: Seine Überlegungen zum kirchlichen und politischen Neubeginn in Deutschland," *Geschichte in Wissenschaft und Unterricht* 42 (1991): 67–91. For a critical look at Ritter's role in reconstructing his own historical mission in Germany, see Peter Schumann, "Gerhard Ritter und die deutsche Geschichtswissenschaft nach dem Zweiten Weltkrieg," in *Mentalitäten und Lebensverhältnisse: Beispiele*

aus der Sozialgeschichte der Neuzeit; Rudolf Vierhaus zum 60. Geburtstag, hrsg. von Mitarbeitern und Schülern, Göttingen, 1982, 399–415.

2. Gerhard Ritter, *Geschichte als Bildungsmacht: Ein Beitrag zur historisch-politischen Neubesinnung,* Stuttgart, 1946 (2nd ed.: 1949), 16, 17.

3. Schwabe, "Gerhard Ritter—Werk und Person," 103, contradicts this interpretation of Ritter. But the citations he takes from Ritter's work are mostly subordinate differentiations after which he returns to the thesis that the special German development in the political realm has no evident connection with the rise of Nazism.

4. This from Ritter's most concise formulation of his views regarding National Socialism: Gerhard Ritter, "The Historical Foundations of the Rise of National Socialism," in *The Third Reich,* ed. International Council for Philosophy and Humanistic Studies, London, 1955, 381–417.

5. Dieter Hein, "Geschichtswissenschaft in den Westzonen und der Bundesrepublik 1945–1950," in *Einführung in die Fragen an die Geschichtswissenschaft in Deutschland nach Hitler, 1945–1950,* ed. Christoph Cobet, Frankfurt a.M., 1986, 30–40.

6. The "constants in Ritter's picture of the world and history" are also emphasized by Michael Matthiesen, *Gerhard Ritter: Studien zu Leben und Werk bis 1933,* 2 vols., Egelsbach, 1993, 2:1287.

7. Siegfried A. Kaehler, "Der Wunsch als Vater der Historie: Wandlungen unseres Geschichtsbildes," *Deutsche Zeitung und Wirtschaftszeitung,* no. 22, 19 March 1950.

8. Siegfried A. Kaehler to Friedrich Meinecke, 26 Oct. 1949, in Meinecke, *Ausgewählter Briefwechsel,* 550–51.

9. Siegfried A. Kaehler to Friedrich Meinecke, 28 Oct. 1950, ibid., 562–63.

10. Heinrich Heffter, "Forschungsprobleme der Geschichte des Nationalsozialismus," *Geschichte in Wissenschaft und Unterricht* 3 (1952): 197–215, here 208. Heffter refers as an alternative to the "Romanic concept of an elite" (ibid.).

11. Max Picard, *Hitler in uns selbst,* Zurich, 1946, here 232, 205.

12. Ritter, *Geschichte als Bildungsmacht,* 24.

13. The controversy was termed a "first turn" by Hans-Ulrich Wehler, "Geschichtswissenschaft heute," in *Stichworte zur geistigen Situation der Zeit,* ed. Jürgen Habermas, vol. 2: *Politik und Kultur,* Frankfurt a.M., 1979, 709–53, here 727. See in this context the following two anthologies: Ernst W. Lynar, ed., *Deutsche Kriegsziele, 1914–1918: Eine Diskussion,* Frankfurt a.M., 1964; Wolfgang Schieder, ed., *Erster Weltkrieg: Ursachen, Entstehung und Kriegsziele,* Cologne, 1969. On the debate itself, see above all George W. F. Hallgarten, "Deutsche Selbstschau nach 50 Jahren: Fritz Fischer, seine Gegner und Vorläufer" (1967), in idem, *Das Schicksal des Imperialismus im 20. Jahrhundert,* Frankfurt a.M., 1969, 57–135; and from the viewpoint of the Fischer school: Imanuel Geiss, "Die Fischer-Kontroverse. Ein kritischer Beitrag zum Verhältnis zwischen Historiographie und Politik in der Bundesrepublik," in idem, *Studien über Geschichte und Geschichtswissenschaft,* Frankfurt a.M., 1972, 108–98; Volker Berghahn, "Die Fischer-Kontroverse—15 Jahre danach," *Geschichte und Gesellschaft* 6 (1980): 403–19.

14. Gerd Krumeich, "Das Erbe der Wilhelminer: Vierzig Jahre Fischer-Kontroverse; Um die deutschen Ziele im Ersten Weltkrieg stritten die Historiker, weil

man vom Zweiten geschwiegen hatte," in *Frankfurter Allgemeine Zeitung*, 4 Nov. 1999. Konrad H. Jarausch, "Normalisierung oder Re-Nationalisierung? Zur Umdeutung der deutschen Geschichte," *Geschichte und Gesellschaft* 21 (1995): 571–84, here 574, discusses the question of whether the Fischer controversy "broke apart" the narrow ties between German historiography and a nationalist orientation or simply carried them forward in the "critical" cloak of the *Sonderweg* thesis.

15. Krumeich, "Das Erbe der Wilhelminer."

16. Ritter, *Geschichte als Bildungsmacht*, 40. On Ritter's "political pedagogics" after 1945 see also Schwabe, "Gerhard Ritter — Werk und Person," 97–121; Cornelißen, *Gerhard Ritter*, 371–622.

17. Gerhard Ritter to Pieter Geyl, 16 Jan. 1962, in Bundesarchiv (Koblenz) (henceforth German Federal Archives), estate of Ritter 1166, no. 351.

18. As coined by Norbert Frei to designate West Germany's early postwar efforts to "come to terms" with the Nazi past, the expression is perhaps best translated as "a policy for the past." See Norbert Frei, *Adenauer's Germany and the Nazi Past: The Politics of Amnesty and Integration*, trans. Joel Golb, New York, 1997 (original ed.: *Vergangenheitspolitik: Die Anfänge der Bundesrepublik und die NS-Vergangenheit*, Munich, 1996).

19. Bernd Weisbrod, ed., *Akademische Vergangenheitspolitik: Beiträge zur Wissenschaftskultur der Nachkriegszeit*, Göttingen, 2002, passim; the citation in Gerhard Kaiser and Matthias Krell, "Ausblenden, Versachlichen, Überschreiben: Diskursives Vergangenheitsmanagement in der Sprach- und Literaturwissenschaft nach 1945," ibid., 190–214, here 194.

20. Gerhard Ritter to Fritz T. Epstein, 20 June 1961, in German Federal Archives, estate of Ritter 1166, no. 350.

21. For material on the different interrogations in the so-called Lörracher case and Ritter's travel ban, see his personal files in the Freiburg University archives, B24/1046–1049.

22. See Cornelißen, *Gerhard Ritter*, 232–46, here 245.

23. "Die Universität Freiburg im Hitlerreich! Persönliche Eindrücke und Erfahrungen: Niederschrift auf Tonband aufgenommener Ausführungen von Prof. Gerhard Ritter anläßlich eines Besuches von Dr. Helmut Heiber am 22. Mai 1962," in German Federal Archives, estate of Ritter 1166, no. 414. See Helmut Heiber, *Walter Frank und sein Reichsinstitut für Geschichte des neuen Deutschland*, Stuttgart, 1966 (on this book, see chapter 5, note 175).

24. "Die Universität Freiburg im Hitlerreich!," 1.

25. Ibid., 28. It is the case that following three postponements of the planned "great book-burning" *Aktion* on the Exerzierplatz because of rain (10, 17, 31 May 1933) it took place in symbolic form on 17 June at 9:15 p.m. before Freiburg's Münsterportal, with a torchlight procession from the Karlsplatz to the victory monument and Kaiserstraße (now Kaiser-Joseph-Straße). See "An die Bevölkerung Freiburgs!," *Der Alemanne*, 17 June 1933. Although planned in detail, the "great book-burning" itself never took place. For more information on the plans, see Berg, *Der Holocaust und die westdeutschen Historiker* (3rd ed.), 113–14n22.

26. Ritter, "Die Universität Freiburg im Hitlerreich!," 2.

27. Ibid., 3.

28. Ibid., 11.

29. Ibid., 16, 4–5.

30. Ibid., 17, 27.

31. Ibid., 6, 7.

32. On Ritter's concrete role in the University of Freiburg's *Reinigungsausschuß* (purging committee), see Cornelißen, *Gerhard Ritter*, 371–400; Silke Seemann, *Die politischen Säuberungen des Lehrkörpers der Freiburger Universität nach dem Zweiten Weltkrieg (1945–1957)*, Freiburg 2002, 238–40.

33. Cornelißen, *Gerhard Ritter*, 384.

34. Gerhard Ritter to Pieter Geyl, 16 Jan. 1961, in German Federal Archives, estate of Ritter 1166, no. 350; shortened in Gerhard Ritter, *Ein politischer Historiker in seinen Briefen*, ed. Klaus Schwabe and Rolf Reichardt, with the assistance of Reinhard Hauf, Schriften des Bundesarchivs 33, Boppard/Rhein, 1984, 563–64.

35. Gerhard Ritter to Pieter Geyl, 16 Jan. 1961; the last two sentences are not in the Schwabe/Reichardt selected correspondence.

36. Ibid.

37. English ed.: Fritz Fischer, *Germany's Aims in the First World War*, London, 1977.

38. On Ritter's behavior during the Third Reich, see, in addition to the above-cited literature, Henryk Olszewski, "Gerhard Ritter und der Nationalsozialismus," in idem, *Zwischen Begeisterung und Widerstand: Deutsche Hochschullehrer und der Nationalsozialismus*, Poznan, 1989, 111–29. The more recent assessment is largely generous; see, for instance, Michael Matthiesen, *Verlorene Identität: Der Historiker Arnold Berney und seine Freiburger Kollegen, 1923–1938*, Göttingen, 1998 (a study of the role of both Ritter and Hermann Heimpel in the expulsion of Arnold Berney from Freiburg University). Likewise, the picture offered by several students of Ritter is of a German nationalist historian who sharply opposed Marxism in the Nazi period but could nonetheless maintain critical independence and remained decent toward Jewish colleagues and students; see Käthe Vordtriede, *"Es gibt Zeiten, in denen man welkt": Mein Leben in Deutschland vor und nach 1933*, ed. and with an introduction by Detlef Garz, Lengwil, 1999, 156; Annelise Thimme, "Geprägt von der Geschichte," 153–224, esp. 171–73 and 180–81. For the 1933–45 period Thimme refers to Ritter's "critique, which he expressed openly or tacitly in his lectures. As hedged as his remarks occasionally were, we students always noticed them and offered enthusiastic applause, which he sometimes rebuffed rather testily."

39. Jan Eckel, "Intellektuelle Transformationen im Spiegel der Widerstandsdeutungen," in Herbert, *Wandlungsprozesse in Westdeutschland*, 140–76, here 140.

40. Cited from Franz Worschech, *Der Weg der deutschen Geschichtswissenschaft in die institutionelle Spaltung (1945–1965)*, Kohlberg, 1990, 55.

41. Leo Stern, *Gegenwartsaufgaben der deutschen Geschichtsforschung*, Berlin, 1952, 47–48.

42. Gerhard Ritter to Werner Jäger, 5 March 1946, in Ritter, *Ein politischer Historiker in seinen Briefen*, 412.

43. Gerhard Ritter to Wilhelm Röpke, 13 Nov. 1945, ibid., 404–5., here 404.

44. Gerhard Ritter, *Carl Goerdeler und die deutsche Widerstandsbewegung*, Stuttgart, 1956

(1st ed.: 1954); idem, "Carl Goerdeler und das Ende des deutschen Widerstands," *Der Monat* 7 (1955): 387–401.

45. Cited from Cornelißen, *Gerhard Ritter*, 548.

46. Gerhard Ritter to Deutsche Verlags-Anstalt, 20 Aug. 1954, cited from Cornelißen, *Gerhard Ritter*, 554.

47. Ritter, "Carl Goerdeler und das Ende des deutschen Widerstands," passim; idem, *Carl Goerdeler und die deutsche Widerstandsbewegung*, 387–88, 391.

48. Jan Eckel, "Intellektuelle Transformationen im Spiegel der Widerstandsdeutungen," in Herbert, *Wandlungsprozesse in Westdeutschland*, 141.

49. Ritter, "Carl Goerdeler und das Ende des deutschen Widerstands," 390.

50. Eckel, "Intellektuelle Transformationen," 143, 144.

51. Gerhard Ritter to G. Goerdeler, 15 March 1955, cited from Cornelißen, *Gerhard Ritter*, 559.

52. Eckel, "Intellektuelle Transformationen," 175.

53. Siegfried A. Kaehler to Hans Rothfels, 12 Nov. 1946, in Rothfels–Kaehler correspondence, Niedersächsische Staats- und Universitätsbibliothek (Göttingen).

54. Cornelißen, *Gerhard Ritter*, 557–58.

55. Gerhard Ritter to Hermann Oncken, 5 Oct. 1939, in Ritter, *Ein politischer Historiker in seinen Briefen*, 344.

56. This already was the contemporary assessment of Joachim A. von Rantzau, "Politische Geschichtsschreibung und Patriotismus," *Frankfurter Allgemeine Zeitung*, 16 March 1951.

57. Heinrich Bornkamm, "Gerhard Ritter: Grabrede," *Archiv für Reformationsgeschichte* 58 (1967): 145–48, here 146.

58. Schulze, *Deutsche Geschichtswissenschaft nach 1945*, 159–82; Schumann, "Gerhard Ritter," passim; Cornelißen, *Gerhard Ritter*, 437–43. In respect to the effects of the division of Germany on postwar German historiography, see Worschech, *Der Weg der deutschen Geschichtswissenschaft*, esp. 36ff. and 57ff. It is the case that we here find nothing about the many problems and controversies emerging in the association's founding and its first convention. Rather, we read that the founding proceeded "without major difficulties" (39).

59. Fritz Hartung to Gerhard Ritter, 20 June 1949, in Archiv des Verbandes der Historiker Deutschlands, Max Planck Institute, folder no. 1.

60. See, for instance, a letter to a section leader in the East German interior ministry, Korfes, 24 April 1952, as cited in Worschech, *Der Weg der deutschen Geschichtswissenschaft*, 43. Worschech himself lays emphasis on the "tradition of an objectivistic understanding of scholarship," with many simultaneous examples of political instrumentalization.

61. See "Protokoll über die Sitzung des vorläufigen Ausschusses des Verbandes der Historiker Deutschlands" (minutes of the Historical Association's provisional board), 5 and 6 Feb. 1949, in Archiv des Verbandes der Historiker Deutschlands, Max Planck Institute, folder no. 1.

62. Gerhard Ritter to W. Philipp, 18 March 1949, ibid.

63. Gerhard Ritter to Rudolf Stadelmann, 26 Dec. 1948, ibid.

64. Gerhard Ritter, "Gegenwärtige Lage und Zukunftsaufgaben deutscher Geschichtswissenschaft," in *Über das Studium der Geschichte*, ed. Wolfgang Hardtwig, Munich, 1990, 288–311, here 288 (first published in *Historische Zeitschrift* 170 [1950]: 1–22).

65. Ibid., 292.

66. Ibid., 296.

67. Ibid., 289, 294; see also Gerhard Ritter to Percy E. Schramm, 1 July 1947, in Ritter, *Ein politischer Historiker in seinen Briefen*, 431–32. Ritter here emphasized "the sober question of political responsibility" and rejected the "philosophical-historical constructions" through which all great "value conflicts" were traditionally declared to be fate.

68. Ritter, "Gegenwärtige Lage," 289.

69. Ibid., 294.

70. Ibid., 293; the dichotomy between the two viewpoints regarding Bismarck is discussed in Cornelißen, *Gerhard Ritter*, 507–21, who describes the debate as being between "unequal partners" (509).

71. Ritter, "Gegenwärtige Lage," 299.

72. Ibid., 306.

73. Ibid., 308.

74. Ibid., 298–99.

75. This is also the view of Worschech, *Der Weg der deutschen Geschichtswissenschaft*, 59, who also cites the historian Franz Herre's reference to the "blare of old tones." See Franz Herre, "Selbstbesinnung der deutschen Geschichtswissenschaft," *Neues Abendland* 4 (1949): 306; additional critical voices: Ernst Deuerlein, in *Tagespost*, 4 Oct. 1949; Walter Markov, "Krise der deutschen Geschichtsschreibung," *Sinn und Form* 2 (1950): 109–55.

76. Herre, "Selbstbesinnung," 306 and 308.

77. Gerhard Ritter to Hermann Heimpel, 23 Sept. 1949, in Archiv des Verbandes der Historiker Deutschlands, Max Planck Institute, folder no. 1.

78. Hans Nabholz to Gerhard Ritter, 4 Oct. 1949, cited from Worschech, *Der Weg der deutschen Geschichtswissenschaft*, 61.

79. Gerhard Ritter, *Europa und die deutsche Frage: Betrachtungen über die geschichtliche Eigenart des deutschen Staatsdenkens*, Munich, 1948, 7.

80. Ritter, *Goerdeler und die deutsche Widerstandsbewegung*, 92.

81. Ritter, *Europa und die deutsche Frage*, 116ff.; Conrad, *Auf der Suche nach der verlorenen Nation*, 173–74, speaks ironically of Ritter's "logic of import."

82. Ritter, *Europa und die deutsche Frage*, 118.

83. Ritter, *Goerdeler und die deutsche Widerstandsbewegung*, 91.

84. Ibid., 93, 94.

85. Karl Dietrich Erdmann, "Anmerkungen zu Friedrich Meineckes 'Irrwege in unserer Geschichte' und 'Die deutsche Katastrophe,'" *Geschichte in Wissenschaft und Unterricht* 2 (1951): 85–91, here 90–91, had himself insisted that National Socialism was "historically preshaped as a type" both "analogically" and "genealogically." For Werner Conze, "Die deutsche Geschichtswissenschaft seit 1945: Bedingungen und Ereignisse,"

Historische Zeitschrift 225 (1977): 1–28, here 13, Ritter's book tied "honest new orientation and apologia together in unbroken self-awareness."

86. See Gerhard Ritter to Hans Rothfels, 14 March 1949, in Archiv des Verbandes der Historiker Deutschlands, Max Planck Institute, folder no. 1.

87. Ludwig Dehio to Gerhard Ritter, 13 Nov. 1948, ibid.

88. Ludwig Dehio, "Deutschland und die Epoche der Weltkriege," *Historische Zeitschrift* 173 (1952): 77–94, here 78, 91.

89. See Christoph Cornelißen, "Staatskunst und Kriegshandwerk: Gerhard Ritter und Ludwig Dehio," in idem, *Gerhard Ritter*, 568–88, here 587. In the opponents' personal copies, the language was clearer than in the public objections and counter-statements: Dehio was annoyed by Ritter's "stubborn apologetics," and Ritter named Dehio's objections "tin" (586).

90. Ritter, *Geschichte als Bildungsmacht*, 15.

91. Stern, *Gegenwartsaufgaben der deutschen Geschichtsforschung*, 42 and 45ff. See also Gerhard Lozek and Horst Syrbe, *Geschichtsschreibung contra Geschichte: Über die antinationale Geschichtskonzeption führender westdeutscher Historiker*, East Berlin, 1964. The authors here referred to West German "NATO historians."

92. Gerhard Ritter, "Der deutsche Professor im 'Dritten Reich,'" *Die Gegenwart* 1, no. 1 (1945): 23–26; see Hannah Arendt to Karl Jaspers, 9 July 1946, in Hannah Arendt–Karl Jaspers, *Briefwechsel, 1926–1969*, ed. Lotte Köhler and Hans Saner, Munich, 1985, 87. The English version of Ritter's essay: "The German Professor in the Third Reich," *Review of Politics* 8 (April 1946): 242–54.

93. Johann Albrecht von Rantzau, "Politische Geschichtsschreibung und Patriotismus," *Frankfurter Allgemeine Zeitung*, 16 March 1951. Already beforehand: idem, "Individualitätsprinzip, Staatsverherrlichung und deutsche Geschichtsschreibung," *Die Sammlung* 5 (1950): 284–99; idem, "Das deutsche Geschichtsdenken der Gegenwart und die Nachwirkungen von Ranke," *Geschichte in Wissenschaft und Unterricht* 1 (1950): 514–24.

94. Kroll would later become editor of the Catholic journal *Neues Abendland*; see Axel Schildt, *Zwischen Abendland und Amerika: Studien zur westdeutsche Ideenlandschaft der 50er Jahre*, Munich, 1999, here 45–46. Schildt describes a mélange of concepts of *das Abendland*, the "Occident," of which the "autochthonous conservative-Protestant" version (33) was only a side branch of a dominant intellectual Catholicism. Its most important institution, the journal *Neues Abendland*, became the organ for the sharpest critique of Ritter, above all in articles by the young historians Ernst Deuerlein and Franz Herre (both born in 1926). On the general context, see Schulze, *Deutsche Geschichtswissenschaft*, 173; Dagmar Pöpping, *Abendland: Christliche Akademiker und die Utopie der Antimoderne, 1900–1945*, Berlin, 2002.

Three older studies exist on the founding of the IfZ: Robert Koehl, "Zeitgeschichte and the New German Conservativism," *Journal of Central European Affairs* 20 (1960): 131–57; John Gimbel, "The Origins of the 'Institut für Zeitgeschichte': Scholarship, Politics and the American Occupation, 1945–1949," *American Historical Review* 70 (1965): 714–31; and Helmuth Auerbach, "Die Gründung des Instituts für Zeitgeschichte," *Vierteljahrshefte für Zeitgeschichte* 18 (1970): 529–54. A summary of Auerbach in Wolfgang Benz,

"Wissenschaft oder Alibi? Die Etablierung der Zeitgeschichte," in *Wissenschaft im geteilten Deutschland: Restauration oder Neubeginn nach 1945?*, ed. Walter H. Pehle and Peter Sillem, Frankfurt a.M., 1992, 11–25, esp. 18ff. See also the memoirs of Karl Buchheim, *Eine sächsische Lebensgeschichte: Erinnerungen 1889–1972*, ed. Udo Wengst and Isabel F. Pantenburg, Biographische Quellen zur Zeitgeschichte 16, Munich, 1996, who is extremely critical of Gerhard Ritter. The approach taken by the IfZ to the genocide of the Jews is discussed in detail in chapter 4 of this book.

95. Gerhard Ritter, "Vaterlandsliebe und Nationalismus," *Frankfurter Allgemeine Zeitung*, 2 Feb. 1951.

96. Gerhard Ritter to Friedrich Meinecke, 10 Sept. 1946, in Ritter, *Ein politischer Historiker in seinen Briefen*, 419 ("To a high degree I feel responsible for the future fate of German history").

97. Gerhard Ritter to Golo Mann, 9 April 1959, ibid., 535. On Ritter's attitude toward emigrants and foreigners, see also Karina Urbach, "Zeitgeist als Ortsgeist: Die Emigration als Schlüsselerlebnis deutscher Historiker?," in *Der Zeitgeist und die Historie*, ed. Hermann Joseph Hiery, Dittelbach, 2001, 161–79, here 161ff.; Cornelißen, "Ein deutscher Historiker und die 'ausländische Geschichtswissenschaft,'" in idem, *Gerhard Ritter*, 457–83. On Robert Vansittart see Jörg Später, *Vansittart: Britische Debatten über Deutsche und Nazis, 1902–1945*, Göttingen, 2003.

98. Gerhard Ritter to editors of the *Neue Zeitung*, 31 Dec. 1948, in Ritter, *Ein politischer Historiker in seinen Briefen*, 449.

99. Friedrich Meinecke to Adolf Leschnitzer, 15 Nov. 1951, in idem, *Werke*, 10:475–76.

100. See Heinrich A. Winkler, "Ein Erneuerer der Geschichtswissenschaft: Hans Rosenberg 1904–1988," *Historische Zeitschrift* 248 (1989): 532–52, here 545. Even during the *Historikerstreit*, Rosenberg was a critic of "alarming regression to German nationalist thinking" (553).

101. Ibid., 545.

102. See Hans Rosenberg, foreword to idem, *Politische Denkströmungen im deutschen Vormärz*, Göttingen, 1972, 7–17.

103. Winkler, "Ein Erneuerer der Geschichtswissenschaft," 549, emphasizes the influence of Rosenberg's thesis on Hans-Ulrich Wehler's *Kaiserreich* interpretation.

104. See Peter Th. Walther, "Emigrierte deutsche Historiker in den USA," *Berichte zur Wissenschaftsgeschichte* 7 (1984): 41–52, here 46.

105. See Winkler, "Ein Erneuerer der Geschichtswissenschaft," 542.

106. Cf. Wehler, "Geschichtswissenschaft heute"; Hans-Ulrich Wehler, *Sozialgeschichte heute: Festschrift für Hans Rosenberg zum 70. Geburtstag*, Göttingen, 1970, 16.

107. In the context of the historiography of Auschwitz, the influence Rosenberg exerted on Raul Hilberg was likewise extremely important; in contrast to his contribution to the genesis of the *Sonderweg* thesis, it has been largely neglected. See Raul Hilberg, "Die Holocaustforschung heute: Probleme und Perspektiven," in *Die Macht der Bilder: Antisemitische Vorurteile und Mythen*, ed. Jüdisches Museum der Stadt Wien, Vienna, 1995, 403–9, here 403. Hilberg has pointed more than once to the strong formative role

that a seminar held by Rosenberg in 1947, and above all Rosenberg's idea of the "inde-structability of bureaucracy," played in his own interest in administrative structures (Hilberg's master's thesis, which he wrote under Franz Neumann, had the title "The Role of the German Civil Service in the Destruction of Jews" [typescript 1950, in Butler Library, Columbia University, New York]). On Rosenberg's influence see also Raul Hilberg and Alfons Söllner, "Das Schweigen zum Sprechen bringen: Ein Gespräch über Franz Neumann und die Entwicklung der Holocaust-Forschung," in *Zivilisationsbruch: Denken nach Auschwitz*, ed. Dan Diner, Frankfurt a.M., 1988, 175–200, here 176, 190. For a more critical perspective: Raul Hilberg, *Unerbetene Erinnerung: Der Weg eines Holocaustforschers*, Frankfurt a.M., 1994, 50ff.

108.   Corneließen, *Gerhard Ritter*, 461–62.

109.   Ibid., 483.

110.   See also Gerhard Ritter, "Nationalbewußtsein und Geschichtswissenschaft," in *Nationalbewußtsein: Sechs Aufsätze*, ed. Robert Rodenhausen, Mühlhausen, 1920, 12–20.

111.   Corneließen, *Gerhard Ritter*, 458–59, 460, 468.

112.   Urbach, "Zeitgeist als Ortsgeist," 175; see also Heinz Wolf, *Deutsch-jüdische Emigrantenhistoriker in den USA und der Nationalsozialismus*, Frankfurt a.M., 1988.

113.   Urbach, "Zeitgeist als Ortsgeist," 177.

114.   Gerhard Ritter, "Geschichtsunterricht oder Gemeinschaftskunde?," *Geschichte in Wissenschaft und Unterricht* 13 (1962): 281–94, here 290.

115.   Ibid., 294. See also Gerhard Ritter, *Wissenschaftliche Historie, Zeitgeschichte und "Politische Wissenschaft,"* Heidelberg, 1959.

116.   Ritter, *Wissenschaftliche Historie*, 23.

117.   Ritter, "Geschichtsunterricht oder 'Gemeinschaftskunde'?," 290. See the energetic refutation by Karlludwig Rintelen, "Gemeinschaftskunde und Geschichtsunterricht: Eine Entgegnung auf Gerhard Ritters Aufsatz 'Geschichtsunterricht oder Gemeinschaftskunde?,'" *Geschichte in Wissenschaft und Unterricht* 13 (1962): 705–12.

118.   Steven P. Remy, *The Heidelberg Myth: The Nazification and Denazification of a German University*, Cambridge, MA, 2002, 2.

119.   Gerhard Ritter, "Wissenschaftliche Historie einst und jetzt: Betrachtungen und Erinnerungen," *Historische Zeitschrift* 202 (1966): 574–602, here 585.

120.   Hajo Holborn, "Irrwege in unserer Geschichte?," *Der Monat* 2 (1949/50): 532.

121.   Ritter, "Geschichtsunterricht oder 'Gemeinschaftskunde'?," 290–91.

122.   Gerhard Ritter to Hans Rothfels, 27 April 1932, in Ritter, *Ein politischer Historiker in seinen Briefen*, 246, 247.

123.   Ritter, "Gegenwärtige Lage und Zukunftsaufgaben deutscher Geschichtswissenschaft," 311. On Ritter's *Historik* in general, see Schwabe, "Gerhard Ritter—Werk und Person," 154–70; Cornelißen, *Gerhard Ritter*, 129–44.

124.   Gerhard Ritter to Heinrich Bornkamm, 13 Oct. 1932, in Ritter, *Ein politischer Historiker in seinen Briefen*, 253.

125.   Ibid.

126.   Gerhard Ritter to Hermann Witte, 11 Feb. 1933, ibid., 261–62, here 262.

127. Ibid.

128. Gerhard Ritter to Karl Alexander v. Müller, 1 Dec. 1935, ibid., 285ff., here 288.

129. Gerhard Ritter to Hermann Witte, 11 Feb. 1933, ibid., 262.

130. Gerhard Ritter to Paul Mollenhauer, 28 Jan. 1946, ibid., 408.

131. Gerhard Ritter, "Deutsche Geschichtswissenschaft im 20. Jahrhundert," *Geschichte in Wissenschaft und Unterricht* 1 (1950): 81–96, 129–37, here 136.

132. Ritter, *Carl Goerdeler und die deutsche Widerstandsbewegung*, 93.

133. Elliot Cohen, "Deutsche und Juden: Eine Rede in Berlin," *Der Monat* 3 (1950/51): 375–79.

134. *Der Monat* 3 (1950/51): 211–12.

135. Cohen, "Deutsche und Juden," 376.

136. Max Picard, *Die Welt des Schweigens*, Erlenbach, 1948, 11, 67, 117.

137. Gerd Tellenbach, *Die deutsche Not als Schuld und Schicksal*, Stuttgart, 1947, 7.

138. Picard, *Die Welt des Schweigens*, 61, 92.

139. Ibid., 89; Karl Heinz Roth, "Hans Rothfels: Geschichtspolitische Doktrinen im Wandel der Zeiten; Weimar—NS-Diktatur—Bundesrepublik," *Zeitschrift für Geschichtswissenschaft* 49 (2001): 1061–73, here 1070, 1071, and 1073, likewise explores *Beschweigen*, "hushing up," as an active act.

140. Hermann Lübbe, "Der Nationalsozialismus im deutschen Nachkriegsbewusstsein," *Historische Zeitschrift* (1983): 579–99.

141. Mitchell G. Ash, "Verordnete Umbrüche—Konstruierte Kontinuitäten: Zur Entnazifizierung von Wissenschaftlern und Wissenschaften nach 1945," *Zeitschrift für Geschichtswissenschaft* 43 (1995): 903–23; Bernd Weisbrod, "Dem wandelbaren Geist: Akademisches Ideal und wissenschaftliche Transformation in der Nachkriegszeit," in idem, ed., *Akademische Vergangenheitspolitik: Beiträge zur Wissenschaftskultur der Nachkriegszeit*, Göttingen, 2002, 11–35, here 30–31; Otto G. Oexle, "'Zusammenarbeit mit Baal': Über die Mentalität deutscher Geisteswissenschaftler 1933—und nach 1945," *Historische Anthropologie: Kultur, Gesellschaft, Alltag* 8 (2000): 1–27; idem, "Zweierlei Kultur: Zur Erinnerungskultur deutscher Geisteswissenschaftler nach 1945," *Rechtshistorisches Journal* 16 (1997): 358–90. See also Konrad H. Jarausch and Martin Sabrow, eds., *Verletztes Gedächtnis: Erinnerungskultur und Zeitgeschichte im Konflikt*, Frankfurt a.M., 2002.

142. On Rothfels as a "special case," see interview with Reinhard Rürup in Rüdiger Hohls and Konrad Jarausch, eds., *Versäumte Fragen: Deutsche Historiker im Schatten des Nationalsozialismus*, Stuttgart, 2000, 278–79.

143. Conrad, *Auf der Suche nach der verlorenen Nation*, 344; for a contrary view, see Claus-Dieter Krohn, "Unter Schwerhörigen? Zur selektiven Rezeption des Exils in den wissenschaftlichen und kulturpolitischen Debatten der frühen Nachkriegszeit," in Weisbrod, *Akademische Vergangenheitspolitik*, 118.

144. See the interviews with Wolfram Fischer and Hartmut Lehmann, in Hohls and Jarausch, *Versäumte Fragen*, 101, 322. Hans Rothfels recalls his own mentor Hintze as a "knight in armor"; see idem, "Erinnerungen an Otto Hintze," MS [3 pp.], in Bundesarchiv Koblenz, estate 213, no. 36 (dated "Tübingen, July 1965").

145. Wolfgang Mommsen, in Hohls and Jarausch, *Versäumte Fragen*, 196 and 203.

146. Peter Thomas Walther, "Von Meinecke zu Beard? Die nach 1933 emigrierten deutschen Neuzeithistoriker," PhD diss., State University of New York, 1989; idem, "Emigrierte deutsche Historiker in den USA," *Berichte zur Wissenschaftsgeschichte* 7 (1984): 41–52; idem, "Emigrierte deutsche Historiker in den Vereinigten Staaten, 1945–1950: Blick oder Sprung über den Großen Teich?," in *Einführung in Fragen an die Geschichtswissenschaft in Deutschland nach Hitler, 1945–1950,* ed. Christoph Cobet, Frankfurt a.M., 1986, 41–50.

147. Hans Mommsen, "Geschichtsschreibung und Humanität: Zum Gedenken an Hans Rothfels," in *Aspekte deutscher Außenpolitik im 20. Jahrhundert,* ed. Wolfgang Benz and Hermann Graml, Stuttgart, 1976, 9–27; idem, "Hans Rothfels," in *Deutsche Historiker,* ed. Hans-Ulrich Wehler, 9 vols., Göttingen, 1971–82, 9:127–47; Werner Conze, "Hans Rothfels," *Historische Zeitschrift* 237 (1983): 311–60.

148. Theodor Schieder, "Hans Rothfels zum 70. Geburtstag am 12. April 1961," *Vierteljahrshefte für Zeitgeschichte* 9 (1961): 117–23.

149. Lothar Machtan, "Hans Rothfels und die Anfänge der historischen Sozialpolitikforschung in Deutschland," *Internationale Wissenschaftliche Korrespondenz zur Geschichte der Arbeiterbewegung* 28 (1992): 161–210; Wolfgang Neugebauer, "Hans Rothfels Weg zur vergleichenden Geschichte Ostmitteleuropas, besonders im Übergang von früher Neuzeit zur Moderne," *Berliner Jahrbuch für Osteuropäische Geschichte* 3 (1996): 333–78.

150. See, for example, Karen Schönwälder, *Historiker und Politik: Geschichtswissenschaft im Nationalsozialismus,* Frankfurt a.M., 1992, 53ff.; Willi Oberkrome, *Volksgeschichte: Methodische Innovation und völkische Ideologisierung in der deutschen Geschichtswissenschaft, 1918–1945,* Göttingen, 1993, 95ff. and 133ff. (See also notes 71, 72, and 73 on page 251.)

151. Peter Schöttler, "Einleitende Bemerkungen," in idem, ed., *Geschichtswissenschaft als Legitimationswissenschaft, 1918–1945,* Frankfurt a.M., 1997, 7–30, here 23.

152. Ingo Haar, *Historiker im Nationalsozialismus: Deutsche Geschichtswissenschaft und der "Volkstumskampf" im Osten,* Göttingen, 2000 (2nd rev. ed.: 2002), esp. 70ff.; see also idem, "'Revisionistische' Historiker und Jugendbewegung: Das Königsberger Beispiel," in Schöttler, *Geschichtswissenschaft als Legitimationswissenschaft,* 52–103.

153. Thomas Etzemüller, *Sozialgeschichte als politische Geschichte: Werner Conze und die Neuorientierung der westdeutschen Geschichtswissenschaft nach 1945,* Munich, 2001, 11, 25–26, 32 ("father figure"), 45 ("patriarch"), 47 ("authority"), 134 ("mentor"), 213 ("chieftain").

154. For citation, see Etzemüller, *Sozialgeschichte als politische Geschichte,* 46.

155. Volker Ullrich, "Der Fall Rothfels: Der Streit um den berühmten Zeithistoriker und die Versäumnisse der Geschichtswissenschaft," *Die Zeit,* 24 July 2003, 38. The article comments on a pair of simultaneous conferences on Rothfels at the Centre Marc Bloch in Berlin ("Hans Rothfels 1891–1976—ein 'Wanderer zwischen den Welten'?") and the Institute for Contemporary History in Munich ("Hans Rothfels und die deutsche Zeitgeschichte") in the summer of 2003; see also the preceding debate in the Internet discussion group H-Soz-u-Kult, with contributions by Peter Thomas Walther, "Eine kleine Intervention und ein bescheidener Vorschlag in Sachen Rothfels"; Karl Heinz Roth, "Hans Rothfels: Neo-konservative Geschichtspolitik diesseits und jenseits des Atlantiks"; Thomas Etzemüller, "Suchen wir Schuld oder wollen wir Gesellschaft analysieren? Eine Anmerkung zur aktuellen Debatte um Hans Rothfels"; Karen Schönwälder,

"Repräsentant der Übergänge"; Jan Eckel, "Historiographie als Personalgeschichte. Bemerkungen zu einer neuen Diskussion über deutsche Historiker"; Mathias Beer, "Wo bleibt die Zeitgeschichte? Fragen zur Geschichte einer Disziplin," http://hsozkult .geschichte.hu-berlin.de/forum/id=281&type=diskussionen. See now most recently, Karsten Borgmann, ed., "Hans Rothfels und die Zeitgeschichte," *Historisches Forum* 1 (2004), publications of Clio-online, no. 2, http://edoc.hu-berlin.de/e_histfor/1/PDF /HistFor_1–2004.pdf. This volume includes an extensive bibliography compiled by Nina Balz: "Zitierte und ergänzte Literatur zum 'Rothfels-Streit,'" 95–106.

156. See the debate between Heinrich August Winkler and Ingo Haar with the following contributions: Heinrich August Winkler, "Hans Rothfels—ein Lobredner Hitlers? Quellenkritische Bemerkungen zu Ingo Haars Buch 'Historiker im Nationalsozialismus,'" *Vierteljahrshefte für Zeitgeschichte* 49 (2001): 643–52; Ingo Haar, "Quellenkritik oder Kritik der Quellen? Replik auf Heinrich August Winkler," *Vierteljahrshefte für Zeitgeschichte* 50 (2002): 497–505; Heinrich August Winkler, "Geschichtswissenschaft oder Geschichtsklitterung? Ingo Haar und Hans Rothfels: Eine Erwiderung," *Vierteljahrshefte für Zeitgeschichte* 50 (2002): 635–51.

157. Karl Heinz Roth, "Geschichtspolitische Doktrinen im Wandel der Zeiten. Weimar—NS-Diktatur—Bundesrepublik," *Zeitschrift für Geschichtswissenschaft* 49 (2001): 1061–73; idem, " 'Richtung halten': Hans Rothfels und die neo-konservative Geschichtsschreibung diesseits und jenseits des Atlantik," *Sozial. Geschichte. Zeitschrift für historische Analyse des 20. und 21. Jahrhunderts*, n.s, 18 (2003): 41–71.

158. Winfried Schulze, "Hans Rothfels und die deutsche Geschichtswissenschaft nach 1945," in *Von der Aufgabe der Freiheit: Politische Verantwortung und bürgerliche Gesellschaft im 19. und 20. Jahrhundert: Festschrift für Hans Mommsen*, ed. by Christian Jansen, Lutz Niethammer, and Bernd Weisbrod, Berlin 1995, 83–98; cf. Winfried Schulze, *Deutsche Geschichtswissenschaft nach 1945*, Munich, 1989.

159. Schulze, "Hans Rothfels," 86; see also the interview with Winfried Schulze, in Hohls and Jarausch, *Versäumte Fragen*, 417–18; for a detailed biography see Jan Eckel, *Hans Rothfels: Eine intellektuelle Biographie im 20. Jahrhundert*, Göttingen, 2005; idem, "Intellektuelle Transformationen im Spiegel der Widerstandsdeutungen," in *Wandlungsprozesse in Westdeutschland: Belastung, Integration, Liberalisierung, 1945–1980*, ed. Ulrich Herbert, Göttingen, 2002, 140–76.

160. Walther, "Von Meinecke zu Beard?," 49.

161. Ibid.

162. Konrad Kwiet, "Judenverfolgung und Judenvernichtung im Dritten Reich: Ein historiographischer Überblick," *Militärgeschichtliche Mitteilungen* 27 (1980): 149–92; cited from the article's revised version published in Dan Diner, ed., *Ist der Nationalsozialismus Geschichte? Zu Historisierung und Historikerstreit*, Frankfurt a.M., 1987, 295.

163. As an initial approach, see Nicolas Berg, "Perspektivität, Erinnerung und Emotion: Anmerkungen zum 'Gefühlsgedächtnis' in Holocaustdiskursen," in *Kontexte und Kulturen des Erinnerns: Maurice Halbwachs und das Paradigma des kollektiven Gedächtnisses; Mit einem Geleitwort von Jan Assmann*, ed. Gerald Echterhoff and Martin Saar, Constance, 2002, 225–51.

164. Mommsen, "Geschichtsschreibung und Humanität," 11.

165. Theodor Schieder, "Betroffenheit einer Generation: Zum Tode des Historikers Hans Rothfels," *Rheinischer Merkur*, 2 July 1976.

166. Werner Conze, "Geschichte in Ideen und Personen: Zum Tode von Hans Rothfels," *Frankfurter Allgemeine Zeitung*, 25 June 1976. In a similar vein, in his famous lecture at the Mannheim conference of historians in 1976, Conze noted that Rothfels brought "his own bitter personal experiences to bear in research on contemporary history." In Rothfels' methodologically pioneering introduction to the first volume of the *Vierteljahrshefte für Zeitgeschichte*, Conze stressed, he had "objectified" his experiences in a classic manner; see idem, "Die deutsche Geschichtswissenschaft seit 1945," *Historische Zeitschrift* 225 (1977): 1–28, here 15.

167. Hans Mommsen, "Hans Rothfels," 129.

168. Hans Rothfels, *Theodor Lohmann und die Kampfjahre der staatlichen Sozialpolitik (1871–1905): Nach ungedruckten Quellen bearbeitet*, Berlin, 1927.

169. Haar, "'Revisionistische' Historiker und Jugendbewegung"; idem, *Historiker im Nationalsozialismus*, passim.

170. Hans Rothfels to Reinhard Wittram, 25 October 1946, quoted in Roth, "'Richtung halten,'" 41–42; see also Hans Rothfels, "Die Geschichte in den dreißiger Jahren," in *Deutsches Geistesleben und Nationalsozialismus: Eine Vortragsreihe der Universität Tübingen*, ed. Andreas Flitner, Tübingen, 1965, 90–107, here 106. He too, Rothfels confirmed, had "for a time been entangled"; nevertheless his lecture's basic thrust is to protect his colleagues (106).

171. Representative of the party's central office to the deputy of the Führer, 2 July 1934, in Bundesarchiv Koblenz, estate of Rothfels 213, no. 20.

172. Open letter to Hans Rothfels, 2 July 1934, ibid.

173. Ibid.

174. *Kurator* of the Albertus University Königsberg to the Minister for Science, Art and National Education, 8 April 1933, in German Federal Archives, estate of Rothfels 213, no. 20.

175. Hans Rothfels, "Abschiedsworte beim Zusammensein mit dem Seminar in Juditten," 25 July 1934, in German Federal Archives, estate of Rothfels 213, 20 (unnumbered, 6).

176. Interview with Hans Rothfels by Viktor von Oertzen and Hubert Locher for the Südwestfunk (n.d.), in German Federal Archives, estate of Rothfels 213, no. 20.

177. Erich Kosthorst, "Mein Weg durch die Zeitgeschichte," in Hartmut Lehmann and Otto G. Oexle, eds., *Erinnerungsstücke: Wege in die Vergangenheit; Rudolf Vierhaus zum 75. Geburtstag gewidmet*, ed. Hartmut Lehmann and Otto G. Oexle, Vienna, 1997, 139–40.

178. Siegfried A. Kaehler to Friedrich Meinecke, 20 April 1950, in Meinecke, *Ausgewählter Briefwechsel*, 557.

179. Friedrich Meinecke, "Zum Geleit," in Werner Conze, ed., *Deutschland und Europa: Historische Studien zur Völker- und Staatenordnung des Abendlandes, Festschrift für Hans Rothfels*, Düsseldorf, 1951, 9–11, here 10.

180. Ibid.

181. Ibid., 11.

182. Friedrich Meinecke to Hans Rothfels, 3 June 1946, in Meinecke, *Ausgewählter Briefwechsel*, 250.

183. Marita Krauss, *Heimkehr in ein fremdes Land: Geschichte der Remigration nach 1945*, Munich, 2001; Krohn, "Unter Schwerhörigen?," 97ff.

184. Gottfried Benn to Friedrich Wilhelm Oelze, 19 March 1945, in Gottfried Benn, *Briefe an Oelze (1882–1945)*, Wiesbaden, 1977, 388; see Nicolas Berg, "Intellektuelle Distanzen: Versuch über Gottfried Benn, Peter de Mendelssohn und die Frage nach dem Gegenteil von Gedächtnis," *Freiburger Literaturpsychologische Gespräche* (2004): 111–24.

185. Friedrich Lütge, "Parteigenosse—Nichtparteigenosse," *Zeitschrift für Politik*, n.s., 10 (1963): 170–91. The following citations are from this source.

186. Helmut Schelsky to Carl Schmitt, 28 September 1950, quoted in Dirk van Laak, "'Nach dem Sturm schlägt man auf die Barometer ein . . .' Rechtsintellektuelle Reaktionen auf das Ende des 'Dritten Reiches,'" *Werkstatt Geschichte* 6 (1997): 25–44, here 37.

187. Quoted in Hans Maier, "Ein Schwieriger zwischen den Fronten. Erinnerungen an Eric Voegelin," *Frankfurter Allgemeine Zeitung*, 8 April 2000.

188. Arnold Bergsträsser, ed., *Deutsche Beiträge zur geistigen Überlieferung*, vol. 1, Chicago, 1947; untitled review of the volume by Ludwig Dehio in *Historische Zeitschrift* 169 (1949): 339–40.

189. Hans Rothfels, "Stein und die Neugründung der Selbstverwaltung," in Bergsträsser, *Deutsche Beiträge zur geistigen Überlieferung*, 154–67 (reproduced in *Zeitschrift für Religions- und Geistesgeschichte* 1 [1948]: 210–21).

190. Heinrich Ritter von Srbik to Hans Rothfels, 10 February 1949, in Heinrich Ritter von Srbik, *Die wissenschaftliche Korrespondenz des Historikers, 1912–1945*, ed. Jürgen Kämmerer, Boppard/Rhein, 1988, 563–65.

191. Hellmut Becker to Hermann Mau, 24 February 1951, in archives of the IfZ: IfZ/Gründungsunterlagen ID 101, vol. 1; Otto Vossler to Hermann Mau, 19 October 1951, ibid.

192. Hans Rothfels, *Die deutsche Opposition gegen Hitler*, Krefeld, 1949, 20.

193. Hans Rothfels, "Das politische Vermächtnis des deutschen Widerstands," *Vierteljahrshefte für Zeitgeschichte* 2 (1954): 329–43, here 333; this article appeared under the same title as an offprint published by the Bundeszentrale für Heimatdienst (Central Federal Office for Homeland Services) (untitled series, no. 14, Bonn, 1955).

194. Ibid., 334, 337, 341, 343; see also Hans Rothfels, "Zum 20. Jahrestag der Erhebung des 20. Juli 1944," *Aus Politik und Zeitgeschichte*, no. 29 (15 July 1964): 3–6, here 6.

195. Hans Rothfels, untitled review of Allen Welsh Dulles, *Germany's Underground* (New York, 1947), *Historische Zeitschrift* 169 (1949): 133–35, here 135.

196. Paul Kluke, "Der deutsche Widerstand: Eine kritische Literaturübersicht," *Historische Zeitschrift* 169 (1949): 136–61; on the broader framework of this body of texts see Eckel, "Intellektuelle Transformationen."

197. Gerhard Ritter, untitled review of Rothfels, *German Opposition*, *Historische Zeitschrift* 169 (1949): 402–5.

198. Hans Rothfels to Friedrich Meinecke, 24 September 1948, Prussian State Archives, estate of Meinecke, Rep. 92, no. 221.

199. Ulrich Raulff, "Erträumte Autobiographie," *Frankfurter Allgemeine Zeitung*, 11 July 1994.

200. Hans Rothfels to Siegfried A. Kaehler, 17 November 1947, in Kaehler–Rothfels correspondence, Niedersächsische Staats- und Universitätsbibliothek (Göttingen), no. 268.

201. Rothfels, *Die deutsche Opposition gegen Hitler*, 24.

202. Ibid., 22.

203. Ibid., 23–24.

204. Ibid., 24.

205. Ibid., 19–26.

206. Cited from Schulze, *Deutsche Geschichtswissenschaft*, 136; idem, "Hans Rothfels und die Deutsche Geschichtswissenschaft nach 1945," 84.

207. Hans Rothfels to Freiherrn von Guttenberg, 1 June 1947, in German Federal Archives, estate of Rothfels 213, no. 20; see also Hans Rothfels to Siegfried A. Kaehler, 12 October 1946, in Kaehler–Rothfels correspondence, Niedersächsische Staats- und Universitätsbibliothek (Göttingen), (Cod. Ms., no. 1, 144, d.).

208. Mommsen, "Geschichtsschreibung und Humanität," 21.

209. Hans Rothfels to Paul Kluckhohn, November 1949 (transcript), in Kaehler–Rothfels correspondence, Niedersächsische Staats- und Universitätsbibliothek (Göttingen), no. 286.

210. Ritter, untitled review of Rothfels, *German Opposition*; Karl Dietrich Erdmann, untitled review, in *Geschichte in Wissenschaft und Unterricht* 1 (1950): 313.

211. Ritter, untitled review of Rothfels, *German Opposition*, 402.

212. Siegfried A. Kaehler, "Der 20. Juli im geschichtlichen Rückblick," *Die Sammlung* 9 (1954): 440, 442; see also Werner Conze, "Die deutsche Opposition gegen Hitler," *Neue Politische Literatur* 2 (1953): cols. 719–21; Schieder, "Hans Rothfels zum 70. Geburtstag," 123.

213. Friedrich Meinecke to Hans Rothfels, 22 August 1948, in Meinecke, *Ausgewählter Briefwechsel*, 293–94.

214. Ibid.

215. Martin Krapf to Hans Rothfels, 16 July 1965, in German Federal Archives, estate of Rothfels 213, no. 36; Theo Kordt to Hans Rothfels, 23 May 1951, ibid., no. 158.

216. Hans Rothfels to Siegfried A. Kaehler, n.d. (1948?), in Kaehler–Rothfels correspondence, Niedersächsische Staats- und Universitätsbibliothek (Göttingen), (Cod. Ms., no. 1, 144, d).

217. Hans Rothfels to Siegfried A. Kaehler, 7 April 1947, in Kaehler, *Briefe, 1900–1963*, 336.

218. Hans Rothfels to Siegfried A. Kaehler, 8 May 1948, in Kaehler–Rothfels correspondence, Niedersächsische Staats- und Universitätsbibliothek (Göttingen), no. 271, 2.

219. Siegfried A. Kaehler to Hans Rothfels, 12 November 1946, ibid.

220. Hans Rothfels to Siegfried A. Kaehler, 7 Feb. 1947, ibid.

221. Ibid.

222. Peter de Mendelssohn, "Gegenstrahlungen: Ein Tagebuch zu Ernst Jüngers Tagebuch," *Der Monat* 2 (1949): 149–74, here 157.

223. Wilma und Georg Iggers, *Two Lives in Uncertain Times: Facing the Challenges of the Twentieth Century as Scholars and Citizens*, New York, 2006 (quoted from the German ed.: *Zwei Seiten der Geschichte: Lebensbericht aus unruhigen Zeiten*, Göttingen, 2002, 92).

224. Ibid.

225. Georg Iggers, "Eine Kindheit in Deutschland: Erinnerungen 1926–1938," *Sozialwissenschaftliche Informationen* 18 (1989): 170–76, here 172; see also George and Wilma Iggers, *Zwei Seiten der Geschichte*, 51–65; Franz Fillafer, "Gespräch mit Georg G. Iggers," *Sozial. Geschichte. Zeitschrift für historische Analyse des 20. und 21. Jahrhunderts*, n.s., 19 (2004): 84–99.

226. See the comments by Hans Mommsen in Hohls and Jarausch, *Versäumte Fragen*, 172.

227. Georg G. Iggers, *The German Conception of History: The National Tradition of Historical Thought from Herder to the Present*, Middletown, CT, 1968 (German trans.: *Deutsche Geschichtswissenschaft: Eine Kritik der traditionellen Geschichtsauffassung von Herder bis zur Gegenwart*, Vienna, 1997 [revised and expanded version of first German edition of 1971]).

228. Iggers, *Zwei Seiten der Geschichte*, 93.

229. Iggers, *Deutsche Geschichtswissenschaft*, 309–10, 339, 364 (on Rothfels' conservative nationalist views); 318, 322, 326 (on his assessments of the role of the historical sciences in National Socialism); 345ff. (on the reductionist approach taken in his book *Die deutsche Opposition*); 350 (on his apologia for Bismarck); 357–58 (on "defensive" research in contemporary history at the IfZ).

230. See, for example, Georg Iggers, "Die deutschen Historiker in der Emigration," in *Geschichtswissenschaft in Deutschland: Traditionelle Positionen und gegenwärtige Aufgaben*, ed. Bernd Faulenbach, Munich, 1974, 97–111, here 103; on the broader picture, see Ernst Schulin, "Deutsche und Amerikanische Geschichtswissenschaft: Wechselseitige Impulse im 19. und 20. Jahrhundert," in idem, *Arbeit an der Geschichte: Etappen auf dem Weg zur Moderne*, Frankfurt a.M., 1997, 164–91, here 190.

231. Wolf, *Deutsch-jüdische Emigrantenhistoriker in den USA und der Nationalsozialismus*, 179.

232. See Bernd Faulenbach, *Ideologie des deutschen Weges: Die deutsche Geschichte in der Historiographie zwischen Kaiserreich und Nationalsozialismus*, Munich, 1980; on the fundamental impact of the Great War on subsequent German historiography, see the persuasive description of the young Gerhard Ritter by Christoph Cornelißen, "Der Erste Weltkrieg: Fronterfahrung und historisch-politisches Denken," in idem, *Gerhard Ritter*, 65–105. Referring to Siegfried A. Kaehler's expression, in a letter he wrote to G. Ritter on 1 Nov. 1950, "spiritual comradeship on the march" (1950), Cornelißen notes (8) that generation-specific experiences structure the experiential process itself and are not some sort of confection of retrospective historiography. On the broader context, see also Fritz Stern, "Die Historiker und der Erste Weltkrieg: Privates Erleben und öffentliche Erklärung," *Transit* 5 (1994): 116–34.

Chapter 3. Hermann Heimpel, Reinhard Wittram, and Fritz Ernst

1. Carl Linfert, program director of Westdeutscher Rundfunk, had conceived the program because of what he saw as a lamentable "historical loss of memory" in respect to Prussia. See Carl Linfert to Peter Rassow, 7 Nov. 1957, in German Federal Archives, estate of Rassow, N 1228, no. 188.

2. Ibid.

3. See Siegfried A. Kaehler to Peter Rassow, 14 Aug. 1958, ibid.

4. Peter Rassow to Carl Linfert, 11 Nov. 1957, ibid.

5. Hermann Heimpel, "Geschichte und Geschichtswissenschaft," *Vierteljahrshefte für Zeitgeschichte* 5 (1957): 1–17, here 8.

6. Reinhard Wittram, *Das Interesse an der Geschichte: Zwölf Vorlesungen über Fragen des zeitgenössischen Geschichtsverständnisses*, Göttingen, 1958 (3rd ed.: 1968), 17.

7. Gerwin Klinger, "Meisterdenker in staatsloser Zeit: Deutsche Philosophie zwischen 1945 und 1948," *Frankfurter Rundschau*, 29 June 1996. On the new existentialism of the period, see Jost Hermand, *Kultur im Wiederaufbau: Die Bundesrepublik Deutschland, 1945–1965*, Munich, 1965, 73–77.

8. Werner Näf, "Heinrich Ritter v. Srbik (1878–1951)," *Historische Zeitschrift* 173 (1952): 95–101, here 95, 101.

9. Georg Brun, *Leben und Werk des Rechtshistorikers Heinrich Mitteis unter besonderer Berücksichtigung seines Verhältnisses zum Nationalsozialismus*, Frankfurt a.M., 1991, 152, 176. The texts referred to are Heinrich Mitteis, "Rechtsgeschichte und Gegenwart," *Neue Justiz: Zeitschrift für Recht und Rechtswissenschaft* 1 (1947): 27–29 (a summary of idem, *Vom Lebenswert der Rechtsgeschichte*, Weimar, 1947); idem, *Die Rechtsgeschichte und das Problem der historischen Kontinuität*, Abhandlung der Deutschen Akademie der Wissenschaft, no. 1, Berlin, 1947; idem, *Über das Naturrecht*, Deutsche Akademie der Wissenschaften zu Berlin: Vorträge und Schriften, Berlin, 1948.

10. Heinrich Mitteis to Christa Dempf-Dulckeit, 30 Oct. 1945, cited from Brun, *Leben und Werk des Rechtshistorikers Heinrich Mitteis*, 177.

11. Mitteis, "Über das Naturrecht," 29; cited from ibid., 150; Heinrich Mitteis to Christa Dempf-Dulckeit, 20 April 1947, cited from ibid., 151.

12. Heinrich Mitteis, "Staatliche Konzentrationsbewegungen im großgermanischen Raum," in *Abhandlungen zur Rechts- und Wirtschaftsgeschichte*, Weimar, 1941, 53–86; cited from Brun, *Leben und Werk des Rechtshistorikers Heinrich Mitteis*, 152–53. Brun, ibid., also refers to another article by Mitteis in *Tägliche Rundschau*, no. 157, 13 Nov. 1945.

13. Heinrich Mitteis to Christa Dempf-Dulckeit, 7 April 1946, cited from Brun, *Leben und Werk des Rechtshistorikers Heinrich Mitteis*, 153.

14. Diethard Aschoff, introduction to Fritz Ernst, *Im Schatten des Diktators: Rückblick eines Heidelberger Historikers auf die NS-Zeit*, ed. Diethard Aschoff, Heidelberg, 1996, 5–37, here 23. Aschoff praises Ernst exaggeratedly for his behavior in 1933–45, presenting him as an example of a historian's clear opposition through double entendres, allusions in the scholarly literature, and so on. He can thus be accorded, Aschoff argues, "a straight

line before and after 1945," borrowing the formulation from Ernst himself. See Fritz Ernst, *Die Deutschen und ihre jüngste Geschichte: Beobachtungen und Bemerkungen zum deutschen Schicksal der letzten fünfzig Jahre (1911–1961)*, 2nd ed., Stuttgart, 1964 (first published 1963), 131, where the phrasing is general but actually refers to Ernst.

15. Ernst, *Die Deutschen und ihre jüngste Geschichte*, 135.

16. Fritz Ernst, "Zeitgeschehen und Geschichtsschreibung," *Welt als Geschichte* 17 (1957): 137–89.

17. Cited from Aschoff, introduction to Ernst, *Im Schatten des Diktators*, 7.

18. All three formulations in Ernst, *Die Deutschen und ihre jüngste Geschichte*, 125.

19. Wolfgang J. Mommsen, "Die Deutschen und ihre jüngste Geschichte," *Neue Politische Literatur* 11 (1966): 94–95.

20. Ernst, *Die Deutschen und ihre jüngste Geschichte*, 159.

21. Ibid., 8.

22. Ibid., 9.

23. Ibid., 10.

24. Ibid., 19, 20 (similarly 122), 102.

25. Ibid., 109, 114, esp. 118, again 120, 123 (the parenthetical example), and 158 (where Ernst sings the praises of none other than General von Reichenau).

26. Ibid., 119, 130.

27. Ibid., 114, 125.

28. Ibid., 109; also 106–7, 110, 111.

29. Ibid., 118.

30. Ibid., 120.

31. Ibid., 19.

32. Ibid.

33. Ibid., 16–17.

34. Ibid., 17.

35. Ibid., 11.

36. Ibid., 109.

37. Ibid., 122, 124.

38. Ibid., 125, 126.

39. Ibid., 132.

40. Ibid., 137.

41. Fritz Ernst, "Rückblick auf jene zwölf Jahre des Dritten Reichs" (18 pp., probably written between 1956 and 1959), now in idem, *Im Schatten des Diktators*, 39–72.

42. Aschoff, introduction to Ernst, *Im Schatten des Diktators*, 36; example taken from Ernst, *Die Deutschen und ihre jüngste Geschichte*, 8.

43. Ernst, *Im Schatten des Diktators*, 115–17, passim. The theologian Helmut Thielicke ("Kleine Biographie," in Elga Kern, ed., *Wegweiser in der Zeitenwende: Selbstzeugnisse bedeutender Menschen, Selbstzeugnisse von Bertrand Russell, Helmut Thielicke, Hein Herbers u.a.*, Munich, 1955, 22–40), who was the same age as Ernst, presented this complex of conformity, belated repentance, and appeals for understanding to the following generation even more succinctly: "To be sure I myself became familiar with the conflict of a young man chasing

after a fervently desired lifetime career and now, in a dictatorship, continuously facing the problem of either being completely consistent and dispensing with any genuflection before those holding power and then also giving up his career and the strived for life-purpose; or else indeed chasing after the career goal, more or less crumbling away from consistency, and observing how without becoming a scoundrel, more or less maneuvers his way through. Now, afterward, it seems entirely clear which solution would have been the upright and only acceptable one." His intent, Thielicke indicated, was "to make clear the entire weight of the decision and to appeal for understanding for many actions that someone who has not lived under an ideological *tyrannis* cannot understand as self-evident" (29).

44. Fritz Ernst, "Zeitgeschehen und Geschichtsschreibung," *Welt als Geschichte* 17 (1957): 137–89.

45. Ernst, "Rückblick," 69.

46. Ibid., 68.

47. Aschoff, introduction to Ernst, *Im Schatten des Diktators*, 17.

48. See *K. H. Bauer and Karl Jaspers, Briefwechsel, 1945–1968*, ed. Renato de Rosa, Berlin, 1983.

49. Aschoff, introduction to Ernst, *Im Schatten des Diktators*, 26.

50. Ernst, "Rückblick," 40–41.

51. Ibid., 42–43.

52. Ibid., 68–69.

53. Ernst, *Die Deutschen und ihre jüngste Geschichte*, 110.

54. Ernst, *Im Schatten des Diktators*, 72, 71.

55. Wittram, *Das Interesse an der Geschichte*, 95.

56. See, for example, Hans-Ulrich Wehler, "Geschichtswissenschaft heute," in *Stichworte zur geistigen Situation der Zeit*, ed. Jürgen Habermas, vol. 2: *Politik und Kultur*, Frankfurt a.M., 1979, 709–53, here 718; similarly the comment of Wolfgang J. Mommsen, in Hohls and Jarausch, *Versäumte Fragen*, 211.

57. Siegfried A. Kaehler to Peter Rassow, 13 May 1945, in Kaehler, *Briefe, 1900–1963*, 295–98, here 297.

58. Obenaus, "Geschichtsstudium und Universität nach der Katastrophe von 1945: Das Beispiel Göttingen," in *Geschichte als Möglichkeit. Über die Chancen der Demokratie. Festschrift für Helga Grebing*, ed. Karsten Rudolph and Cristel Wickert, Essen, 1959, 307–37.

59. Gerhard Sauter, "Endzeit- oder Endvorstellungen und geschichtliches Denken," in *Jahrhundertwenden*, ed. Manfred Jakubowski-Tiessen, Hartmut Lehmann, and Johannes Schilling, Göttingen, 1999, 377–402.

60. This assessment in Joachim Radkau, "Geschichtswissenschaft heute—Ende der Selbstmystifikation?," *Neue Politische Literatur* 17 (1972): Part I: "Die Historie aus der Grenzperspektive," 1–14; part II: "Selbstdarstellungen der Historie," 141–167, here 144. See in general the critical essay by Hans-Erich Volkmann, "Von Johannes Haller zu Reinhard Wittram: Deutschbaltische Historiker und der Nationalsozialismus," *Zeitschrift für Geschichtswissenschaft* 45 (1997): 21–46, here esp. 30ff. For a defense of Wittram's post-war period, see Klaus Neitmann, "Reinhard Wittram und der Wiederbeginn der

baltischen Studien in Göttingen nach 1945," *Nordost-Archiv: Zeitschrift für Regionalgeschichte*, n.s., 7 (1998): 1, 11–32. Neitmann has a very high opinion of the "intensity of Wittram's self-critique" (25); he views the "deep, indeed penetrating seriousness with which Wittram pursued the problem" as undeniable (26). This argument is developed against both Volkmann and Eduard Mühle, "'Ostforschung': Beobachtungen zum Aufstieg und Niedergang eines geschichtswissenschaftlichen Paradigmas," *Zeitschrift für Ostmitteleuropa-Forschung* 46 (1997): 317–50, who while speaking of critical gestures on Wittram's part nevertheless emphasizes that they remained "carefully superficial" (320). Without critical analysis but evocative of the time: Manfred Hagen, "Göttingen als 'Fenster zum Osten' nach 1945," in *Geschichtswissenschaft in Göttingen: Eine Vorlesungsreihe*, ed. Hartmut Boockmann and Hermann Wellenreuther Göttinger Universitätsschriften, Ser. A, Schriften, vol. 2, Göttingen, 1987, 321–43.

61. Obenaus, "Geschichtsstudium und Universität nach der Katastrophe von 1945," 316. Obenaus places special emphasis on the competition between Wittram and Heimpel.

62. Reinhard Wittram, "Das öffentliche Böse und das achte Gebot," *Die Sammlung* 8 (1953): 16–26 (reprinted in idem, *Zukunft in der Geschichte: Zu Grenzfragen der Geschichtswissenschaft und Theologie*, Göttingen, 1966, 60–75).

63. Wittram, "Das öffentliche Böse," 17.

64. Ibid., 20.

65. Ibid., 19.

66. Ibid., 25.

67. Ibid., 20.

68. Ibid.

69. Werner Terpitz, "Die Nation ist das Vergängliche: Schon 1954 protestierten Studenten gegen den falschen Konsens der Bundesrepublik," *Frankfurter Allgemeine Zeitung*, 31 July 1999.

70. Reinhard Wittram, "Das Faktum und der Mensch: Bemerkungen zu einigen Grundfragen des Geschichtsinteresses," *Historische Zeitschrift* 185 (1958): 55–87, here 59, 60.

71. Ibid., 62.

72. Ibid., 63.

73. Ibid., 62.

74. Nicolai Hartman, *Das Problem des geistigen Seins*, Berlin, 1949, 31.

75. *Geschichtsauffassungen*; *Lehre vom Menschen*." Cf. Wittram, "Das Faktum und der Mensch," 69, 71, 85.

76. See Hagen, "Göttingen als 'Fenster zum Osten' nach 1945," 336.

77. Wittram, "Das Faktum und der Mensch," 71–72 (with references to Karl Barth and others).

78. Ibid., 73.

79. Ibid.

80. Hagen, "Göttingen als 'Fenster zum Osten' nach 1945," 336.

81. Wittram, "Das Faktum und der Mensch," 78ff.

82. Ibid., 84.

83. Ibid., 75.

84. Ibid.

85. Ibid., 77.

86. Ibid., 75.

87. Ibid., 77.

88. Ibid., 85.

89. Günther Stökl, "Zum Selbstverständnis des Faches Osteuropäische Geschichte," *Jahrbücher für Geschichte Osteuropas*, n.s., 32 (1984): 481–87, here 485.

90. Cohen, "Deutsche und Juden," 376.

91. Cited from Hugo Ott, "Schuldig—mitschuldig—unschuldig? Politische Säuberungen und Neubeginn 1945," in *Die Freiburger Universität in der Zeit des Nationalsozialismus*, ed. Eckhard John, Bernd Martin, Marc Mück, and Hugo Ott, Freiburg, 1991, 243–58, here 243.

92. Michael Kohlstruck, *Zwischen Erinnerung und Geschichte: Der Nationalsozialismus und die jungen Deutschen*, Berlin, 1997, 14.

93. Ibid., 22–23. In our period Kohlstruck is the first author to have recognized Heimpel's role in this respect. But already in Heimpel's time: Hans Wenke, "'Bewältigte Vergangenheit' und 'Aufgearbeitete Geschichte': Zwei Schlagworte, kritisch beleuchtet," *Geschichte in Wissenschaft und Unterricht* 11 (1960): 60–65.

94. Heimpel, "Geschichte und Geschichtswissenschaft," 16.

95. See, on the basis of new sources, Michael Matthiesen, *Verlorene Identität: Der Historiker Arnold Berney und seine Freiburger Kollegen, 1923–1938*, Göttingen, 1998, esp. 51–55.

96. Winfried Schulze, *Deutsche Geschichtswissenschaft nach 1945*, Munich, 1989, 42; Matthiesen, *Verlorene Identität*, 9; Helmut Heiber, *Universität unterm Hakenkreuz, Teil I: Der Professor im Dritten Reich: Bilder aus der akademischen Provinz*, Munich, 1991, 370; Hartmut Boockmann, *Der Historiker Hermann Heimpel*, Göttingen, 1990, esp. 53, 59. The lecture in Frankfurt on Heimpel was given by Pierre Racine; see idem, "Hermann Heimpel à Strasbourg," in *Deutsche Historiker im Nationalsozialismus*, ed. Winfried Schulze and Otto Gerhard Oexle, Frankfurt a.M., 1999, 142–56.

97. Walter Hinck, *Im Wechsel der Zeiten: Leben und Literatur*, Bonn, 1998, 151–52.

98. Heinrich Schmidt, "Erinnerungen an drei Göttinger Historiker: Hermann Heimpel, Karl Gottfried Hugelmann, Siegfried A. Kaehler," in *Nationalsozialismus und Region: Festschrift für Herbert Obenaus zum 65. Geburtstag*, ed. Marlies Buchholz, Claus Füllberg-Stolberg, and Hans-Dieter Schmid, 2nd ed., Bielefeld, 1997, 15–39, here 16, 18, 35.

99. Siegfried A. to Hans Rothfels (undated: April 1948?), in Kaehler–Rothfels correspondence, Niedersächsische Staats- und Universitätsbibliothek (Göttingen), estate of Kaehler, no. 270, 4.

100. Schmidt, "Erinnerungen an drei Göttinger Historiker," 34–35. The same perspective is found already in Karl Ferdinand Werner, *Das NS-Geschichtsbild und die deutsche Geschichtswissenschaft*, Stuttgart, 1967, 90; similarly in Karen Schönwälder, *Historiker und Politik: Geschichtswissenschaft und Nationalsozialismus*, Frankfurt a.M., New York, 1992, 280; Arnold Esch, "Denken und doch Schauen, Schauen und doch Denken: Zum Tode von

Hermann Heimpel," in *Deutsche Akademie für Sprache und Dichtung, Jahrbuch 1988*, Darmstadt, 1989, 154–55; idem, "Über Hermann Heimpel," in Schulze and Oexle, *Deutsche Historiker*, 159–60.

101. Reinhard Rürup, in Hohls and Jarausch, *Versäumte Fragen*; see also Obenaus, "Geschichtsstudium und Universität nach der Katastrophe von 1945," 316; Ernst Schulin, *Hermann Heimpel und die deutsche Nationalgeschichtsschreibung*, Schriften der Philosophisch-historischen Klasse der Heidelberger Akademie der Wissenschaften 9, Heidelberg, 1997.

102. Hermann Heimpel to Leipzig publisher K. W. Hiersemann, 3 April 1946, cited from Heimpel, *Aspekte: Alte und neue Texte*, ed. Sabine Krüger, Göttingen, 1995, 263.

103. Hermann Heimpel to Gerhard Ritter, 12 May 1949, in Archiv des Verbandes der Historiker Deutschlands, Max Planck Institute, folder no. 1.

104. Hermann Heimpel, "Die Erforschung des deutschen Mittelalters im deutschen Elsaß," *Straßburger Monatshefte* (1941): 738–43; regarding this period of his career, see Ursula Wolf, *Litteris et patriae: Das Janusgesicht der Historie*, Stuttgart, 1996, 248–64.

105. Wolf, *Litteris et patriae*, 260.

106. Cited from ibid., 262.

107. Ibid., 261.

108. Hermann Heimpel to Gerhard Ritter, 16 Jan. 1946, cited from Matthiesen, *Verlorene Identität*, 111.

109. Hermann Heimpel to Gerhard Ritter, 4 Dec. 1949, in Archiv des Verbandes der Historiker Deutschlands, Max Planck Institute, no. 1.

110. See, on the basis of the same sources, Schumann, "Gerhard Ritter und die deutsche Geschichtswissenschaft nach dem Zweiten Weltkrieg," passim.

111. Josef Fleckenstein, "Gedenkrede auf Hermann Heimpel," in *In Memoriam Hermann Heimpel: Gedenkfeier am 23. Juni 1989 in der Aula der Georg-Augusta-Universität; Mit einer Gedenkrede von Josef Fleckenstein und Gedenkworten von Norbert Kamp u.a.*, Göttinger Universitätsreden 87, Göttingen, 1989, 47–60, here 27–45, esp. 28–29.

112. Hermann Heimpel, "Erinnerungen an Siegmund Hellmann," in idem, *Aspekte*, 151.

113. Ibid., 147.

114. Hermann Heimpel, "Rede, gehalten am 19. 10. 1981," in *Hermann Heimpel zum 80. Geburtstag*, ed. Max-Planck-Institut für Geschichte, Göttingen, 1981, 42.

115. Hermann Heimpel, "Dank für den am 25. Juli 1966 dargebrachten Fackelzug," in idem, *Aspekte*, 190.

116. Thomas Etzemüller, "Kontinuität und Adaption eines Denkstils: Werner Conzes intellektueller Übertritt in die Nachkriegszeit," in Weisbrod, *Akademische Vergangenheitspolitik*, 123–46, here 124.

117. In *In Memoriam Hermann Heimpel*, 47–60, here 59–60.

118. Martin Sabrow, "Der Historiker als Zeitzeuge: Autobiographische Umbruchsreflexionen deutscher Fachgelehrter nach 1945 und 1989," in Jarausch and Sabrow, *Verletztes Gedächtnis*, 125–52, here 145–52.

119. Ibid., 152.

120. Hinck, *Im Wechsel der Zeiten*, 147. Hinck is referring here to the Germanist Wolfgang Kayser.

121. Thimme, "Geprägt von der Geschichte," 191–92, in reference to Friedrich Gogarten and Otto Weber.

122. Christian Graf von Krockow, *Zu Gast in drei Welten: Erinnerungen*, Stuttgart, 2000, 157.

123. Hermann Mau, "Der Nationalsozialismus als aktuelle Forschungsaufgabe," in IfZ, MS 49-1338/54.

124. Both Schulze, *Deutsche Geschichtswissenschaft nach 1945*, 238, and Ulrich von Hehl, "Kampf um die Deutung. Der Nationalsozialismus zwischen 'Vergangenheitsbewältigung,' Historisierungspostulat und 'neuer Unbefangenheit,'" *Historisches Jahrbuch* 117 (1997): 2, 406–36, here 413, cite the term's later use by Mau as its first usage, although Hehl also indicates (414) that the origins of this "verbal monstrosity" have "not been sufficiently clarified."

125. Hermann Mau, "Die Akten der großen Nürnberger Kriegsverbrecherprozesse als Geschichtsquelle," typescript, dated 22 Dec. 1950, in IfZ, MS 49-2367/59, 2.

126. Cited from Kohlstruck, *Zwischen Erinnerung und Geschichte: Der Nationalsozialismus und die jungen Deutschen*, Berlin, 1997, 13–14. For emphasis on the Protestant milieu in which the term was coined, see Claudia Fröhlich and Michael Kohlstruck, "Vergangenheitspolitik in kritischer Absicht," in Fröhlich and Kohlstruck, eds., *Engagierte Demokraten: Vergangenheitspolitik in kritischer Absicht*, Münster, 1999, 7–30, here 16.

127. Heimpel, "Neujahr 1956," radio address transmitted by the Norddeutsche Rundfunk and the Westdeutsche Rundfunk on 1 Jan. 1956, in the radio series (directed by J. Eggebrecht) *Gedanken zur Zeit*; in Hermann Heimpel, *Kapitulation vor der Geschichte? Gedanken zur Zeit*, Göttingen, 1956, 86–91, here 87.

128. Ibid.

129. Ibid.

130. Ibid.

131. Ibid.

132. Ibid.

133. Sabrow, "Der Historiker als Zeitzeuge," 145.

134. Heimpel, "Neujahr 1956," 91.

135. Ibid.

136. Hermann Heimpel, "Über den Tod für das Vaterland," *Die Sammlung* 11 (1956): 1–11; reprinted in *Kapitulation vor der Geschichte?*, 32–45. See above all the essay's beginning.

137. Heimpel, *Kapitulation vor der Geschichte*, 32.

138. Ibid., 32–33.

139. Patrick Bahners, "Die Zeit, in der nicht tot zu sein ein Vorwurf ist" (a long article on Heimpel marking his hundredth birthday), *Frankfurter Allgemeine Zeitung*, 22 Sept. 2001.

140. Heimpel, "Über den Tod für das Vaterland," 41, 42; also 30, 35–36.

141. See Kohlstruck, *Zwischen Erinnerung und Geschichte*, 15–16.

142. Hermann Heimpel, *Der Mensch in seiner Gegenwart: Sieben historische Essays*, Göttingen, 1954; 2nd, expanded ed., 1957.

143. Heimpel, "Neujahr 1956," 90.

144. Hermann Heimpel, *Die halbe Violine*, Stuttgart, 1949; there is no study of Heimpel's autobiography, just reviews following its publication and a few remarks in letters.

145. Fridolin Solleder, untitled review, *Historische Zeitschrift* 171 (1951): 605–7.

146. See Siegfried A. Kaehler to Friedrich Meinecke, 30 March 1950, in Meinecke, *Ausgewählter Briefwechsel*, 554. Several efforts by Kaehler to present his own experiences in this manner failed; his estate preserved the remaining fragments.

147. See Herman Nohl, "Vergangenheit und Zukunft," *Die Sammlung* 6 (1951): 62–63.

148. Heinrich Schmidt, "Bemerkungen zu den Selbstbiographien dreier Historiker," *Die Sammlung* 8 (1953): 511–16.

149. Schmidt, "Erinnerungen an drei Göttinger Historiker," 37.

150. Boockmann, *Der Historiker Hermann Heimpel*, 8; Fleckenstein, "Gedenkrede auf Hermann Heimpel," 30–31.

151. Heimpel, *Der Mensch in seiner Gegenwart*, 198.

152. Ibid., 31, 41, 12.

153. Heimpel, *Die halbe Violine*, 257.

154. Ibid., 152.

155. Ibid., 163.

156. Ibid., 149–50.

157. Ibid., 280.

158. Heimpel, "Traum im November," *Insel-Almanach auf das Jahr 1961*; also in *Geschichte in Wissenschaft und Unterricht* 32 (1981): 521–25. The following citations in the main text are all from this short article.

159. Hermann Heimpel, "Gedanken zu einer Selbstbesinnung der Deutschen," *Die Sammlung* 9 (1954): 417–28, here 417.

160. Harald Weinrich, *Lethe: Kunst und Kritik des Vergessens*, Munich, 1979, 38.

161. Translated from the following source: Augustinus, *Bekenntnisse* (Latin and German), introduced and annotated by Joseph Bernhart, Frankfurt a.M., 1987, 487.

162. Wolfgang Berkefeld, "Hermann Heimpel—Freude an der Geschichte," *Westermanns Monatshefte* 103 (1962): 48–54, here 54.

163. "The moralist Burckhardt declines to name evil good because of good consequences; the historian Burckhardt acknowledges [*anerkennt*] power as an element of the historical economy. Not judgments and condemnations but *knowledge* [*Erkenntnis*] *and its ascesis* is Burckhardt's final word." Hermann Heimpel, *Zwei Historiker: Friedrich Christoph Dahlmann. Jacob Burckhardt*, Göttingen, 1962, 35.

164. Ernst Schulin, *Hermann Heimpel und die deutsche Nationalgeschichtsschreibung: Vorgetragen am 14. Februar 1997*, Schriften der Philosophisch-historischen Klasse der Heidelberger Akademie der Wissenschaften 9, Heidelberg, 1997; the citation of Heimpel on 50–51.

165. Ibid., 50.

166. Ibid., 15.

167. Ibid., 51.

168. Heimpel, *Aspekte*, 243.

169. Ibid., 168.

170. Heimpel, *Der Mensch in seiner Gegenwart*, 211.

171. Heimpel, *Über Geschichte und Geschichtswissenschaft in unserer Zeit*, Vortragsreihe der Niedersächsischen Landesregierung 13, Göttingen, 1959, 5.

172. Ibid., 6.

173. Ibid.

174. Ibid., 13.

175. Ibid., 13–14.

176. Ibid., 14. Schulin (*Hermann Heimpel und die deutsche Nationalgeschichtsschreibung*, 13) had himself criticized Heimpel's "hasty" rhetoric of reconciliation in the early 1950s "in view of the state of knowledge of contemporary history."

177. Heimpel, *Über Geschichte und Geschichtswissenschaft in unserer Zeit*, 15.

178. Ibid., 15–16; for the general context, see the important study by Mathias Beer, "Im Spannungsfeld zwischen Politik und Zeitgeschichte: Das Großforschungsprojekt 'Dokumentation der Vertreibung der Deutschen aus Ost-Mitteleuropa' im Spannungsfeld von Politik und Zeitgeschichte," *Vierteljahrshefte für Zeitgeschichte* 46 (1998): 345–89.

179. Alexander Dallin, *Deutsche Herrschaft in Rußland, 1941–1945: Eine Studie über Besatzungspolitik*, Königstein, 1981 [first German translation: 1958; English-language original: *German Rule in Russia*, 1956].

180. Heimpel, *Über Geschichte und Geschichtswissenschaft*, 16.

181. See, for example, Heimpel, *Über Geschichte und Geschichtswissenschaft*, 25: "The German historian. . . ."

182. Ibid., 19.

183. Ibid.

184. Ibid.

185. Ibid., 23–24.

186. Ibid., 24.

187. Ibid., 24–25.

188. Ibid., 25.

189. Jean Améry, "Ressentiments," in idem, *Jenseits von Schuld und Sühne: Bewältigungsversuche eines Überwältigten*, new ed., Stuttgart 1977 (1st ed.: 1966, ed. Gerhard Szczesny), 108–9.

190. On the conflicts over Thielicke, see also Wolfgang Faßnacht, *Universitäten am Wendepunkt? Die Hochschulpolitik in der französischen Besatzungszone (1945–1949)*, Freiburg im Breisgau, 2000.

191. Thielicke, "Kleine Biographie," 22–40, here 38.

192. Conversation between Ernst Schulin and the author, 14 June 1999. Years later, following a "reflexive learning process" by Schieder that Hans-Ulrich Wehler praised very highly, the tone was very different. In a letter to Rothfels, Schieder expressed thanks for a talk—it became famous—on German historiography of the 1930s,

adding the following comment: "In any case, you have succeeded in thoroughly exploring things that have often been suppressed, although I also believe that precisely in my generation far more have constantly confronted them inwardly." See Theodor Schieder to Hans Rothfels, 16 Feb. 1965, in German Federal Archives, estate of Rothfels 213, no. 36. In contrast, even in the 1970s, without naming names, Werner Conze ("Die deutsche Geschichtswissenschaft seit 1945: Bedingungen und Ereignisse," *Historische Zeitschrift* 225 [1977]: 1–28, here 14) stereotypically spoke of the "revision of the German idea of history" being carried out "under the mental pressure of the victors' scolding and one's own scruples."

193. Rudolf Diels to Carl Schmitt, 27 Nov. 1949, cited from Dirk van Laak, "'Nach dem Sturm schlägt man auf die Barometer ein . . .': Rechtsintellektuelle Reaktionen auf das Ende des Dritten Reiches," *Werkstatt Geschichte* 6 (1997): 17, 25–44, here 44.

194. Götz Aly, "Rückwärtsgewandte Propheten: Willige Historiker; Bemerkungen in eigener Sache," in idem, *Macht—Geist—Wahn: Kontinuitäten deutschen Denkens*, Berlin, 1997, 153–83; idem, "'Daß uns Blut zu Gold werde': Theodor Schieder, Propagandist des Dritten Reichs," *Menora: Jahrbuch für deutsch-jüdische Geschichte* (1998): 13–27. See also Peter Schoettler, ed., *Geschichtsschreibung als Legitimationswissenschaft, 1918–1945*, Frankfurt a.M., 1997; Schulze and Oexle, *Deutsche Historiker im Nationalsozialismus*.

195. Van Laak, "'Nach dem Sturm schlägt man auf die Barometer ein . . . ,'" 36; Dirk van Laak, *Gespräche in der Sicherheit des Schweigens: Carl Schmitt in der politischen Geistesgeschichte der frühen Bundesrepublik*, Berlin, 1993.

Chapter 4. "How Difficult It Is *Not* to Write Powerfully about Auschwitz!"

1. Horst Möller, "Das Institut für Zeitgeschichte und die Entwicklung der Zeitgeschichtsschreibung in Deutschland," in *50 Jahre Institut für Zeitgeschichte: Eine Bilanz*, ed. Horst Möller and Udo Wengst, Munich, 1999, 1–68.

2. Ibid., 50, 2.

3. Ibid., 34.

4. Ibid., 31; see IfZ board meeting minutes (board of trustees and advisory board), 9 March 1951, 12–13, in IfZ ED 105 (1). The most important discussion of the IfZ's early phase remains Schulze, *Deutsche Geschichtswissenschaft nach 1945*, 229–42; see also Auerbach, "Die Gründung des Instituts für Zeitgeschichte"; and the festschrift-anthologies between 1975 and 2000, including *25 Jahre Institut für Zeitgeschichte: Statt einer Festschrift*, Stuttgart 1975; Möller and Wengst, eds., *50 Jahre Institut für Zeitgeschichte*.

5. Conrad, *Auf der Suche nach der verlorenen Nation*, 239ff. Conrad's view of the institute's early approach to recent German history is extremely critical; see esp. the chapter "Zeitgeschichte als Methode," which, however, does not so much evaluate the IfZ institutionally as discuss concepts of contemporary historiography in postwar Germany in general. Early studies on the IfZ are mentioned in note 94 on page 268.

6. See IfZ board of trustees meeting minutes (henceforth: IfZ board meeting minutes), 9 Jan. 1952, 2, in IfZ ED 105 (1).

7. See Christoph Weisz and Ingrid Baass, "Die Bibliothek des Instituts für Zeitgeschichte," in Möller and Wengst, *50 Jahre Institut für Zeitgeschichte*, 88.

8. Möller, "Das Institut für Zeitgeschichte," 50, 51.

9. Benz, "Wissenschaft oder Alibi? Die Etablierung der Zeitgeschichte," 25.

10. Paul Kluke, "Aufgaben und Methoden zeitgeschichtlicher Forschung," *Europa-Archiv* 10 (1955): 7429–38, here 7436.

11. A.D., "Nationalsozialismus—wissenschaftlich betrachtet," *Stuttgarter Zeitung*, 8 Aug. 1950. The following above all based on the holdings of the IfZ archive: IfZ/Allg., (1946–1950), in: IfZ ED 105 (1).

12. A.D., "Nationalsozialismus—wissenschaftlich betrachtet."

13. Hans-Dietrich Loock, "War's so? Erinnerungen an die Entstehung der Zeitgeschichte," in *25 Jahre Institut für Zeitgeschichte*, 38–54, here 49.

14. Lutz Niethammer, "Methodische Überlegungen zur deutschen Nachkriegsgeschichte: Doppelgeschichte, Nationalgeschichte oder asymmetrisch verflochtene Parallelgeschichte?," in *Deutsche Vergangenheiten—eine gemeinsame Herausforderung: Der schwierige Umgang mit der doppelten Nachkriegsgeschichte*, ed. Christoph Kleßmann, Hans Misselwitz, and Günter Wichert, Berlin, 1999, 307–29, here 325.

15. Ibid., 315.

16. See Otmar Freiherr von Aretin, "Deutschlands Geschichtswissenschaft seit dem 2. Weltkrieg," *Deutsche Rundschau* 83 (1957): 358–62, here 362.

17. German Federal Archives, N. Goetz, no. 49. On Goetz and his role in the early IfZ trench battles, see above all Wolf Volker Weigand, *Walter Wilhelm Goetz, 1867–1958: Eine biographische Studie über den Historiker, Politiker und Publizisten*, Boppard am Rhein, 1992, esp. 352ff.

18. Hans Günter Hockerts, "Zugänge zur Zeitgeschichte: Primärerfahrung, Erinnerungskultur, Geschichtswissenschaft," in Jarausch and Sabrow, *Verletztes Gedächtnis*, 39–72, here 62.

19. On Eschenburg, see his memoirs: Theodor Eschenburg, *Also hören Sie mal zu: Geschichte und Geschichten, 1904 bis 1933*, Berlin, 1995; idem, *"Letzten Endes meine ich doch: Erinnerungen, 1933–1999*, Berlin, 1999. Also Hans-Peter Schwarz, "Nachruf auf Theodor Eschenburg," *Vierteljahreshefte für Zeitgeschichte* 47 (1999): 593–600; Hans Karl Rupp and Thomas Noetzel, "Theodor Eschenburg: Stilkritik aus Sorge um die Institution," in Rupp and Noetzel, eds., *Macht, Freiheit, Demokratie: Anfänge der westdeutschen Politikwissenschaft; Biographische Annäherungen*, Marburg, 1991, 107–20. On the *Vierteljahreshefte für Zeitgeschichte*, see the jubilee volume 51 (2003). In 2012 a debate began about Eschenburg's membership in the "Motor-SS" in particular, his Nazi years in general, and his silent personal politics of memory about this after 1945. The controversy started with Rainer Eisfeld, "Theodor Eschenburg: Übrigens vergaß er noch zu erwähnen . . . Eine Studie zum Kontinuitätsproblem in der Politikwissenschaft," *Zeitschrift für Geschichtswissenschaft* 59, no. 1 (2011): 27–44; Hannah Bethke, "Theodor Eschenburg in der NS-Zeit (Gutachten 3 Sept. 2012)," https://www.dvpw.de/fileadmin/docs/Kongress2012/Paperroom/Eschenburg-Gutachten.pdf; see also Udo Wengst, "Der 'Fall Theodor Eschenburg': Zum Problem der historischen Urteilsbildung," *Vierteljahreshefte für Zeitgeschichte* 61, no. 3

(2013): no. 3, 411–44; and the answer to Wengst from Hans Woller and Jürgen Zarusky, "Der 'Fall Theodor Eschenburg' und das Institut für Zeitgeschichte: Offene Fragen und neue Perspektiven," *Vierteljahreshefte für Zeitgeschichte* 61, no. 4 (2013): 551–65.

20. Konrad Heiden, *Geschichte des Nationalsozialismus—Die Karriere einer Idee*, Berlin, 1932.

21. Theodor Eschenburg, "Aufgaben der Zeitgeschichte," *Geschichte in Wissenschaft und Unterricht* 6 (1955): 356–61, here 358. In general, and in contrast to his objectivity fetish, Eschenburg was of the pragmatic opinion that contemporary history was above all "an instrument for aiding political evaluation," representing a "great reservoir of experience for politicians"; see 359–60.

22. See, for example, Günter Moltmann, "Zeitgeschichtlicher Unterricht: Bildungswert und methodische Probleme," *Geschichte in Wissenschaft und Unterricht* 7 (1955): 158–77, who likewise inquires into the "positive features" of recent German history and warns against "damning judgments."

23. Eschenburg, "Aufgaben der Zeitgeschichte," 359, 360.

24. Conrad, *Auf der Suche nach der verlorenen Nation*, 238, 241, 245.

25. Eschenburg, "Aufgaben der Zeitgeschichte," 360.

26. Ibid., 359, 358, 360.

27. Ibid., 361.

28. Hermann Graml, "Die fünfziger Jahre," in Möller and Wengst, *50 Jahre Institut für Zeitgeschichte*, 77–83, here 80.

29. Hans Buchheim to H. G. Adler, 16 May 1958, in Deutsches Literaturarchiv (Marbach am Neckar) (henceforth German Literary Archives), estate of Adler A II 89.

30. Loock, "War's so?," 49.

31. Helmut Heiber, *Joseph Goebbels*, Berlin, 1962, 15.

32. Loock, "War's so?," 40–41 (*Wissenschaftsgläubigkeit*). Loock even suggests a connection between the beginnings of contemporary history in Germany's postwar period and the "dehistoricization of social consciousness" (42).

33. Ibid., 42–43.

34. Wenke, "'Bewältigte Vergangenheit' und 'Aufgearbeitete Geschichte,'" 70.

35. Loock, "War's so?," 45, 40.

36. See, for example, Auerbach, "Die Gründung des Instituts für Zeitgeschichte," passim.

37. Loock, "War's so?," 44–45.

38. Ibid., 44.

39. See Graml, "Die fünfziger Jahre," 78.

40. Ibid., 44 and 46.

41. Thus the famous formulation of Martin Broszat, in Martin Broszat and Saul Friedländer, "Um die Historisierung des Nationalsozialismus: Ein Briefwechsel," *Vierteljahrshefte für Zeitgeschichte* 36 (1988): 339–72, here 361 (for the English translation, see note 35 on page 247).

42. Loock, "War's so?," 45.

43. Ibid., 46.

44. Ibid., 48: "We were sometimes uneasy."

45. IfZ board meeting minutes, 4th session, 30 May 1949, 10, in IfZ archives (henceforth IfZ archives), Kuratorium (Sitzungsprotokolle) 1 (1949–1961).

46. Ibid., 4.

47. Theodor Heuss to the Deutsche Institut zur Erforschung des Nationalsozialismus, 24 June 1949, in IfZ archives, ED 105 (1). Imanuel Geiss, "Die westdeutsche Geschichts-wissenschaft seit 1945," *Jahrbuch des Instituts für Deutsche Geschichte* 3 (1974): 422–55, here 434, equated the IfZ with the "institutionalized interest of politics in contemporary history." As a general claim this seems overstated, especially in respect to Heuss.

48. IfZ board meeting minutes, 7, in IfZ archives, Kuratorium: Sitzungsprotokolle 1 (1949–1961).

49. IfZ board meeting minutes (board of trustees and advisory board), 17 May 1952, 2, in IfZ archives, ED 105 (1).

50. Benz, "Wissenschaft oder Alibi?," 21.

51. Citation of Schwend before the Bavarian State Chancellery in IfZ board meeting minutes, 3rd session, 27 Feb. 1949, 6, in IfZ archives, Kuratorium: Sitzungsprotokolle 1 (1949–1961).

52. Ibid., 5.

53. IfZ board meeting minutes, 27 Feb. 1949, 8.

54. Preliminary discussion,16–17 Oct. 1947, 4, in IfZ archives, Kuratorium: Sitzungsprotokoll 1 (1947–1961).

55. IfZ board meeting minutes, 3, in IfZ archives, Kuratorium: Sitzungsprotokolle 1 (1949–1961).

56. Ibid., 7.

57. Ibid., 6. The list is cited in Hans Buchheim's account from 1990, "Die fünfziger Jahre," in Müller and Wengst, *50 Jahre Institut für Zeitgeschichte*, 69–77, here 70.

58. Buchheim, "Die fünfziger Jahre," 70–71.

59. IfZ board meeting minutes (board of trustees and advisory board), 9 March 1951, 5, in IfZ archives, Kuratorium: Sitzungsprotokolle 1 (1949–1961).

60. Ibid., 6–8, here 7–8.

61. Ibid., 27 July 1953, 2, in IfZ archives, ED 105 (1).

62. IfZ board meeting minutes (board of trustees and advisory board), 1–2 July 1955, 8, ibid.

63. IfZ board meeting minutes, 25 June 1954, 6–7, ibid.

64. This formulation in response to publication of the book's third edition in 1960: Waldemar Besson, "Neuere Literatur zur Geschichte des Nationalsozialismus," *Viertel-jahrshefte für Zeitgeschichte* 9 (1961): 314–30, here 327; on the negative reception of Reit-linger's books, see also Berg, "Lesarten des Judenmords," in Herbert, *Wandlungsprozesse in Westdeutschland*, 91–139, here 103.

65. IfZ board meeting minutes (board of trustees and advisory board), 1–2 July 1955, 9, in IfZ archives, ED 105 (1).

66. Ibid., 8.

67. Ibid., 22 April 1958, 13.

68. Ibid., 20 Oct. 1956, 12.

69. Ibid., 22 Jan. 1960, 4. See also Helmut Krausnick, "Zur Zahl der jüdischen Opfer des Nationalsozialismus," in *Aus Politik und Zeitgeschichte* (appendix to *Das Parlament*), no. B 32/54, 11 Aug. 1954, 426–27.

70. See the accounts of the institute by Hellmuth Auerbach, Hermann Weiß, and Udo Wengst, in Möller and Wengst, *50 Jahre Institut für Zeitgeschichte*, 507–38.

71. IfZ board meeting minutes (board of trustees and advisory board), 20 Oct. 1956, 3–4, 11, in IfZ archives, ED 105 (1).

72. Kurt Sontheimer, *Antidemokratisches Denken in der Weimarer Republik: Die politischen Ideen des deutschen Nationalismus zwischen 1918 und 1933*, Munich, 1962. The book was begun by Sontheimer in the mid-1950s, when he was in his mid-twenties; it was finished in 1959 but only appeared three years later. In the foreword, we read nothing of the controversies surrounding publication. To the contrary, Sontheimer expresses thanks for the "pleasant working and conversational climate in the Institute for Contemporary History." He did receive an IfZ stipend and published two essays as preliminary presentations of his main theme: Kurt Sontheimer, "Antidemokratisches Denken in der Weimarer Republik," *Vierteljahrshefte für Zeitgeschichte* 5 (1957): 42–62; idem, "Der Tatkreis," *Vierteljahrshefte für Zeitgeschichte* 7 (1959): 229–60. On Sontheimer's own generational view of German postwar intellectual history from the perspective of the late 1990s, see Kurt Sontheimer, *So war Deutschland nie: Anmerkungen zur politischen Kultur der Bundesrepublik*, Munich, 1999; the necessary critique was offered briefly and clearly by Ulrich Herbert, "So war Deutschland wirklich nie: Anmerkungen zu Kurt Sontheimers Buch über die politische Kultur der Bundesrepublik," *Süddeutsche Zeitung*, 17 May 1999. Unrewarding: Hans Heigert, "Von innen ausgehöhlt: Kurt Sontheimers 'Antidemokratisches Denken in der Weimarer Republik,'" *Süddeutsche Zeitung*, 24–25 June 1995; see also Wilhelm Bleek, "Kurt Sontheimer: Politikwissenschaft als öffentlicher Beruf," in *Macht, Freiheit, Demokratie*, ed. Hans Karl Rupp and Thomas Noetzel, vol. 2: *Die zweite Generation der westdeutschen Politikwissenschaft*, Marburg, 1994, 27–43.

73. IfZ board meeting minutes (board of trustees and advisory board) in IfZ archives, ED 105 (1). In an appendix to the minutes, we read that Sontheimer was expected above all to follow up on "the connection of ideas located at the highest level with their dull simplification." A year and a half later, someone at the institute would finally speak up in defense of Sontheimer's project—Otto Heinrich von der Gablentz, who issued a reminder about the "illumination of the ideological backgrounds of National Socialism."

74. Ibid., 21 Oct. 1960, 7. Today what seems worth mentioning is not so much the absence of "Weimar's left-wing opponents" as rather the absence of any discussion of the antisemitic radicalism of the time. See Jean-Paul Bier, "The Holocaust, West Germany, and Strategies of Oblivion, 1947–1979," in *Germans and Jews since the Holocaust: The Changing Situation in West Germany*, ed. Anson Rabinbach and Jack Zipes, New York, 1986, 185–207, here 194.

75. IfZ board meeting minutes (board of trustees and advisory board), 4 Nov. 1961, 7, in IfZ archives, ED 105 (1).

76. Ibid., 6.

77. In this respect Rothfels' student Heinrich A. Winkler has an especially high opinion of the role of both Rothfels and some of his students (above all of Waldemar Besson, who died prematurely). See Winkler's statement in Hohl and Jarausch, *Versäumte Fragen*, 369–82. Interesting in this context is the separation of Rothfels' students into a "Rothfelsian left" and "Rothfelsian right" (374).

78. IfZ board meeting minutes, 1 Aug. 1963, 9, in IfZ archives, ED 105 (2) Hausarchiv/Stiftungsrat (Sitzungsprotokolle) A (1962–1978).

79. Hans Herzfeld, review of Rothfels' "Zeitgeschichtliche Betrachtungen," *Historische Zeitschrift* 202 (1966): 657.

80. Conze, "Die deutsche Geschichtswissenschaft seit 1945," 15. See Hans Rothfels, "Zeitgeschichte als Aufgabe," *Vierteljahrshefte für Zeitgeschichte* 1 (1953): 1–8; see also idem, "Sinn und Aufgabe der Zeitgeschichte," in idem, *Zeitgeschichtliche Betrachtungen: Vorträge und Aufsätze*, Göttingen, 1959, 9–16. This conceptualization has made its way into, for instance, the widely distributed "Fischer lexicon" on history. See Waldemar Besson, ed., *Das Fischer Lexikon Geschichte*, Frankfurt a.M., 1961, esp. the article by Besson, a student of Rothfels, on "Zeitgeschichte," 264–69, also 332–51.

81. Eva Reichmann, "Zeitgeschichte als politische und moralische Aufgabe," in *Schriften der Bundeszentrale für politische Bildung*, Bonn, 1964, 3–12, here 6–7.

82. Ibid., 6–7. Cf. Rothfels, "Zeitgeschichte als Aufgabe," 2.

83. Rothfels, "Zeitgeschichte als Aufgabe," 8.

84. Hans Rothfels, "Sinn und Aufgabe der Zeitgeschichte," in idem, *Zeitgeschichtliche Betrachtungen*, 16; idem, "Vorwort," ibid., 5.

85. Hans Freyer, *Theorie des gegenwärtigen Zeitalters*, Stuttgart, 1955, 11.

86. Reichmann, "Zeitgeschichte als politische und moralische Aufgabe," 7.

87. Ernst, "Rückblick auf jene zwölf Jahre des Dritten Reichs," in idem, *Im Schatten des Diktators*, 68–69.

88. Karl Dietrich Erdmann, "Die Geschichte der Weimarer Republik als Problem der Forschung," *Vierteljahrshefte für Zeitgeschichte* 3 (1955): 1–19, here 1.

89. Ulrich Herbert, "Drei deutsche Vergangenheiten: Über den Umgang mit der deutschen Zeitgeschichte," in *Doppelte Zeitgeschichte: Deutsch-deutsche Beziehungen, 1945–1990*, ed. Arnd Bauerkämper, Martin Sabrow, and Bernd Stöver, Bonn, 1998, 376–90, here 380.

90. Erdmann, "Die Geschichte der Weimarer Republik als Problem der Forschung," 19, 2–3.

91. Ibid., 1.

92. See IfZ board meeting minutes (board of trustees and advisory board), 8–9 May 1959, 5–6, in IfZ archives, ED 105 (1).

93. Ibid., 6.

94. Ibid.

95. IfZ board meeting minutes ("Remarks of Ministerial Advisor Kordt and Ministerial Director Hagelberg"), 11 March 1964, 12, in IfZ archives, ED 105 (2) Hausarchiv/Stiftungsrat (Sitzungsprotokolle) A (1962–1978).

96. Hans Rothfels, 8 March 1964, transcribed in ibid., 10–11.

97. David Hoggan, *Der erzwungene Krieg: Ursachen und Urheber des 2. Weltkrieges*, Tübingen, 1961; the book would be reprinted many times. On the general context, see Hans-Jürgen Schröder, "Pseudowissenschaftlicher Mißbrauch der Zeitgeschichte," in Matthias Peter and Hans-Jürgen Schröder, *Einführung in das Studium der Zeitgeschichte*, Paderborn, 1994, 116–26.

98. See Möller and Wengst, *50 Jahre Institut für Zeitgeschichte*, 112; Gotthard Jasper, "Über die Ursachen des Zweiten Weltkrieges Zu den Büchern von A. J. P. Taylor und David L. Hoggan," *Vierteljahrshefte für Zeitgeschichte* 10 (1962): 311–40. This was Hoggan's "official" refutation by the IfZ: his work was "nothing other than a straight-out falsification" (329), possessing no scholarly status (338).

99. Hoggan, *Der erzwungene Krieg*, 4th ed., 1963, 793. As late as 1987, in the aftermath of the *Historikerstreit*, Rolf Kosiek (*Historikerstreit und Geschichtsrevision*, Tübingen, 1987) was one of several authors who tried to rehabilitate Hoggan's ideas.

100. See Hermann Glaser, *Deutsche Kultur, 1945–2000*, Munich, 1997, 303.

101. Rothfels pointed to the Nazi backdrop of an organization that awarded Hoggan a prize in a letter to the editor, *American Historical Review* 69 (1963/64): 1222. Among the important reviews of the Hoggan book: Jasper, "Über die Ursachen des Zweiten Weltkrieges"; idem, "Fibel für alte und neue Nazis," *Die Zeit*, 5 Oct. 1962; Graml, *Geschichte in Wissenschaft und Unterricht* 14 (1963): 8 (also as IfZ reprint); article series in *Rhein-Neckar-Zeitung*; Frank Thiess, "Wie entstand der Zweite Weltkrieg?," *Rhein-Neckar-Zeitung*, 21–22 July 1962; Werner Conze, "Wie entstand der Zweite Weltkrieg?," *Rhein-Neckar-Zeitung*, 28–29 July 1962; Wolfgang Schieder and Volker Wieland, "Wie entstand der Zweite Weltkrieg?," *Rhein-Neckar-Zeitung*, 4–5 Aug. 1962.

102. Armin Mohler to Hans Rothfels, 22 June 1964, in German Federal Archives, estate of Rothfels 213, no. 36.

103. Ibid.

104. Hans Rothfels to Armin Mohler, 18 June 1964, ibid.

105. Armin Mohler to Hans Rothfels, 22 June 1964, ibid.

106. Hans Rothfels to Armin Mohler, 25 June 1964, ibid.

107. Armin Mohler to Hans Rothfels, 30 June 1964, ibid.

108. Hermann Heimpel, "Marburger Historikertag," *Historische Zeitschrift* 173 (1952): 215–18, here 215.

109. See *Geschichte in Wissenschaft und Unterricht* 2 (1951): 626; cited in Worschech, *Der Weg der deutschen Geschichtswissenschaft*, 71.

110. See Amos Elon, *In einem heimgesuchten Land: Reise eines israelischen Journalisten in beide deutsche Staaten*, Munich, 1966 (*Journey through a Haunted Land: The New Germany*, New York, 1967), 6off.; for the public reaction to the Eichmann trial, see Matthias Weiß, "Journalisten: Worte als Taten," in *Karrieren im Zwielicht: Hitlers Eliten nach 1945*, ed. Norbert Frei, Frankfurt a.M., 2001, 280; Peter Krause, *Der Eichmann-Prozeß in der deutschen Presse*, Wissenschaftliche Reihe des Fritz-Bauer-Instituts 8, Frankfurt a.M., 2002.

111. IfZ board meeting minutes (board of trustees and advisory board), 19 June 1965, 12, in IfZ archives, ED 105 (2).

112. Ibid., 3 Dec. 1957, 7, ibid. (1).

113. See request by Hübinger, in ibid., 6.

114. Expert opinion of IfZ, printed by IfZ, in *Gutachten des Instituts für Zeitgeschichte*, vol. 1, Munich 1958; *Gutachten des Instituts für Zeitgeschichte*, vol. 2, Stuttgart, 1966.

115. Paul Kluke, "Vorwort," in *Gutachten des Instituts für Zeitgeschichte*, 1:10.

116. Martin Broszat, *Die Judenpolitik Rumäniens*, in ibid., 102–83.

117. For instance of Reitlinger: *Gutachten des Instituts für Zeitgeschichte*, 2:56, 60, 63, 64, 67, 68, 75, 74, 78, 90, 91, 92, etc.

118. See Loock, in *Gutachten des Instituts für Zeitgeschichte*, 2:448–68, 399–447.

119. Kluke, "Vorwort."

120. In *Neue Politische Literatur* 3 (1958): col. 922.

121. Examples of the international resonance: "Höss, de goede moordenaar?," *De Linie* (Brussels), 9 Jan. 1959, 3; Stig Janasson, "Kommendanten i Auschwitz," *Stockholm-Tidningen* 20 Feb. 1959; "The Nazi Mentality," *Times Literary Supplement*, 17 July 1959.

122. IfZ board meeting minutes (board of trustees and advisory board), 3 Dec. 1957, 6, in IfZ archives, ED 105 (1).

123. Ibid., 22–23 April 1958, 6–7.

124. See Broszat's introduction to Rudolf Höß, *Kommandant in Auschwitz: Autobiographische Aufzeichnungen*, introduction and commentary by Martin Broszat, Stuttgart, 1958, 14.

125. For one Polish historian, the memoirs represent "the first scholarly effort in Germany to offer a firsthand demonstration of the truth about Auschwitz." See Franciszek Ryszka, "Martin Broszat, die Wiederaufnahme der kulturellen Beziehungen und die Aussöhnung mit Polen," in *Mit dem Pathos der Nüchternheit: Martin Broszat, das Institut für Zeitgeschichte und die Erforschung des Nationalsozialismus*, ed. Klaus-Dietmar Henke and Claudio Natoli, Frankfurt a.M., 1991, 59–69, here 68.

126. Gerhard Fritsch, "Autobiographie eines Ja-Sagers und Massenmörders," *Die Presse* (Vienna), 11 Jan. 1959.

127. For the following, see IfZ archives, ED 105 Hausarchiv/Höß, Rudolf.

128. Walter Hähnle, "Judenvernichtung," *Zeitwende* (Hamburg), June 1960, 413.

129. Gottfried Vetter, "Der Maschinist des Teufels," *Telegraf* (Berlin), 1 Feb. 1959.

130. Hellmut Becker, "Der Henker von Auschwitz lebt unter uns," *Volkshochschule im Westen*, nos. 9 and 10 (1958): 232–33.

131. Anon., "Was einmal war: Deutsche Wirklichkeiten," *Gegenwart* (Frankfurt a.M.), Dec. 1958.

132. Günter Hönicke in a radio essay for the Norddeutscher Rundfunk, in NDR (Das politische Buch), 28 Oct. 1958, in IfZ archives, ED 105 Hausarchiv, Höß.

133. Anon., "Der Henker von Auschwitz macht Bilanz," *Süddeutsche Zeitung*, 1 Oct. 1958.

134. H. L., "Die totalitäre Krankheit," *Außenpolitik* (Stuttgart), May 1959.

135. Werner Jochmann, "Roboter der Pflichterfüllung," *Sonntagsblatt* (Hamburg), 11 Feb. 1959.

136. Helmut Lindemann, "Das Grauen von Auschwitz," *Stuttgarter Zeitung*, 5 Dec. 1958, 3.

137. The picture of Höß as a perpetrator was above all formed by the account of Helga Grebing, *Der Nationalsozialismus: Ursprung und Wesen*, Munich, 1959; Karl Dietrich Erdmann, "Die Zeit der Weltkriege," in Bruno Gebhardt, *Handbuch der deutschen Geschichte*, ed. Herbert Grundmann, 8th, new ed., vol. 4, Stuttgart, 1959, likewise gives Höß a prominent place, although, for instance, Eichmann is still falsely described and referred to as "Wilhelm Eichmann" at a few points (244–328, 289, 291).

138. Paul Noack, "Die Gaskammer als Handwerkszeug," *Münchner Merkur*, 27 Feb. 1959.

139. Erdmann, "Die Zeit der Weltkriege," 290.

140. See the statements by Becker and Rothfels, IfZ board meeting minutes (board of trustees and foundation board), 19 June 1965, in IfZ archives, ED 105 (2), 11f.

141. IfZ board meeting minutes (board of trustees and advisory board), 8–9 May 1959, 7, ibid., (1).

142. Scholarly board, minutes 16 July 1966, ibid., (2), 1. The comment was made by Helmut Krausnick.

143. Hans Buchheim to H. G. Adler, 21 Aug. 1959, in German Literary Archives, estate of Adler, A II 89.

144. H. G. Adler to Hans Buchheim, 5 Sept. 1959, ibid.

145. H. G. Adler, *Der verwaltete Mensch: Studien zur Deportation der Juden aus Deutschland*, Tübingen, 1974, xvii.

146. H. G. Adler to Hans Buchheim, 19 May 1958, in German Literary Archives, estate of Adler, A II 89.

147. H. G. Adler to Martin Broszat, 31 Oct. 1963, ibid.

148. H. G. Adler to Helmut Krausnick, 5 March 1959, ibid.

149. H. G. Adler to Hans Buchheim, 3 Jan. 1962; Hans Buchheim to H. G. Adler, 13 March 1962, ibid.

150. Hans Buchheim to H. G. Adler, 7 May 1963, ibid.

151. IfZ board meeting minutes (board of trustees and foundation board), 24 July 1964, in IfZ archives, ED 105 (2), 8f.

152. Helmut Krausnick to H. G. Adler, 6 Nov. 1964, in German Literary Archives, estate of Adler, A II 89.

153. H. G. Adler to Helmut Krausnick, 9 Nov. 1964, ibid.

154. Hans Buchheim to H. G. Adler, 16 May 1958, ibid.

155. H. G. Adler to Hans Buchheim, 18 June 1958, ibid.

156. H. G. Adler to Hans Buchheim, 6 Dec. 1958, ibid.; see H. G. Adler to Hans Buchheim, 27 Jan. 1959, ibid.

157. Hans Buchheim to H. G. Adler, 2. Feb. 1959, ibid.

158. H. G. Adler to Hans Buchheim, 6 Feb. 1959, ibid.

159. Hans Buchheim to H. G. Adler, 23 Feb. 1959 and 11 May 1959, ibid.

160. H. G. Adler to Heinz Förster (administrative head of the IfZ), 9 Dec. 1964, ibid.

161. H. G. Adler to Hans Buchheim, 5 March 1959, ibid.

162. Ibid.

163. H. G. Adler to Hans Buchheim, 27 Feb. 1961, ibid.
164. H. G. Adler to Hans Buchheim, 27 Jan. 1961, ibid.
165. H. G. Adler to Heinz Förster, 10 March 1961, ibid.
166. H. G. Adler to Anton Hoch, 18 Dec. 1961, ibid. Similarly in H. G. Adler to Anton Hoch, 19 Feb. 1962, ibid.
167. H. G. Adler to Hans Buchheim, 2 March 1964, ibid.
168. H. G. Adler to Hans Buchheim, 27 Feb. 1961, ibid.
169. H. G. Adler to Hans Buchheim, 27 Jan. 1961, ibid.
170. H. G. Adler to Hans Buchheim, 8 July 1960, ibid.; on Langbein see Katharina Stengel, *Hermann Langbein: Ein Auschwitz-Überlebender in den erinnerungspolitischen Konflikten der Nachkriegszeit*, Frankfurt a. M., 2013.
171. Ibid.
172. Hans Buchheim to H. G. Adler, 27 July 1960, ibid.
173. H. G. Adler to Hans Buchheim, 2. Sept. 1960, ibid.
174. H. G. Adler to Hans Buchheim, 15 Oct. 1960 and 27 Oct. 1960, ibid.
175. Adler, *Der verwaltete Mensch*, xix–xx.
176. Ibid., 1–2.
177. Hans Buchheim to H. G. Adler, 6 Oct. 1965, in German Literary Archives, estate of Adler A II 89.
178. Adler, *Der verwaltete Mensch*, xx.
179. Ibid., 2.
180. Ibid., 3, 2.
181. Ibid., 2–3.
182. Ibid., 3.
183. Ibid., xx.
184. Hans Buchheim, Martin Broszat, Hans-Adolf Jacobsen, and Helmut Kraus-nick, *Anatomie des SS-Staates*, 2 vols., Olten, 1965.
185. On the entire complex, see above all *Der Frankfurter Auschwitz-Prozess (1963–1965): Kommentierte Quellenedition*, ed. Raphael Gross and Werner Renz, 2 vols., Frankfurt a. M., 2013 (here Devin O. Pendas, "Der 1. Frankfurter Auschwitz-Prozess 1963–1965: Eine historische Einführung," 1:55–85); Hermann Langbein, *Der Auschwitz-Prozeß: Eine Dokumentation*, 2 vols., Vienna, 1965 (new ed.: Frankfurt a.M., 1995); Bernd Naumann, *Auschwitz: Bericht über die Strafsache gegen Mulka und andere vor dem Schwurgericht Frankfurt*, Frankfurt a.M., 1965 (an edition revised and abridged by the author appeared as a Fischer Verlag paperback; first ed., 1968; new edition, with a foreword by Werner Renz, Hamburg, 2013); Peter Reichel, "Strafsache gegen Mulka u.a. Der Auschwitz-Prozeß," in idem, *Vergangenheitsbewältigung in Deutschland: Die Auseinandersetzung mit der NS-Diktatur von 1945 bis heute*, Munich, 2001, 158–81 (a short overview); Wolfgang Benz, "'Bürger als Mörder und die Unfähigkeit zur Einsicht': Der Frankfurter Auschwitz-Prozess," in *Große Prozesse: Recht und Gerechtigkeit in der Geschichte*, ed. Uwe Schultz, Munich, 1996, 382–91. Two more-recent publications have offered a kind of balance sheet: Ulrich Schneider, ed., *Auschwitz—Ein Prozeß: Geschichte, Fragen, Wirkungen*, Cologne, 1994; Gerhard Werle and Thomas Wandres, *Auschwitz vor Gericht: Völkermord und bundesdeutsche*

Strafjustiz: Mit einer Dokumentation des Auschwitz-Urteils, Munich, 1995. On the question of German historiography of the legal proceedings, see Norbert Frei, "Der Frankfurter Auschwitz-Prozeß und die Zeitgeschichtsschreibung," in *Auschwitz: Geschichte, Rezeption und Wirkung*, ed. Fritz Bauer Institute, Frankfurt a.M., 1996, 123–38.

186. Christian Meier, "Nachruf auf Martin Broszat," *Vierteljahrshefte für Zeitgeschichte* 38 (1990): 23–42, here 26; Ulrich Herbert, ed., *Nationalsozialistische Vernichtungspolitik, 1939–1945: Neue Forschungen und Kontroversen*, Frankfurt a.M., 1998, 14.

187. Robert Gellately, "Situating the 'SS-State' in a Social-Historical Context," *Journal of Modern History* 64 (1992): 338–65, here 364.

188. Jens Banach, *Heydrichs Elite: Das Führerkorps der Sicherheitspolizei und des SD, 1936–1945*, Paderborn, 1998, 13.

189. Irmtrud Wojak, "Die Verschmelzung von Geschichte und Kriminologie: Historische Gutachten im ersten Frankfurter Auschwitz-Prozeß," in *Geschichte vor Gericht: Historiker, Richter und die Suche nach Gerechtigkeit*, ed. Norbert Frei, Dirk van Laak, and Michael Stolleis, Munich, 2000, 29–45.

190. On the details of the judicial terms, interests, and questions and their forensic usage, see Reinhard Henkys, "Geschichte und Gericht in nationalsozialistischen Gewaltverbrechen," in idem, *Die nationalsozialistischen Gewaltverbrechen: Geschichte und Gericht*, Stuttgart, 1964, 25–266; Jürgen Baumann, "Die strafrechtliche Problematik der nationalsozialistischen Gewaltverbrechen," Henkys, *Die nationalsozialistischen Gewaltverbrechen*, 267–321. On the criminology of collective crimes, see Herbert Jäger, *Verbrechen unter totalitärer Herrschaft: Studien zur nationalsozialistischen Gewaltkriminalität*, Frankfurt a.M., 1982. On the public discourse, see Mirjam Wenzel, *Gericht und Gedächtnis: Der deutschsprachige Holocaust-Diskurs der sechziger Jahre*, Göttingen, 2009.

191. Those warning of this danger included Norbert Frei, "Die Rückkehr des Rechts: Justiz und Zeitgeschichte nach dem Holocaust—eine Zwischenbilanz," in Bauerkämper, Sabrow, and Stöver, *Doppelte Zeitgeschichte*, 431.

192. Hans Buchheim, "Die SS in der Verfassung des Dritten Reiches," *Vierteljahrshefte für Zeitgeschichte* 3 (1955): 127–55, here 127.

193. Ibid.

194. Kogon, *Der SS-Staat*, 325–26.

195. Hans Buchheim, foreword to Buchheim, Broszat, Jacobsen, and Krausnick, *Anatomie des SS-Staates*, 1:9–11.

196. Ibid., 9.

197. For this and following citation, ibid.

198. Ibid., 11; in his foreword to Buchheim, Broszat, Jacobsen, and Krausnick, *Anatomie des SS-Staates*, vol. 2, Broszat refers to Kogon's book as "certainly a masterful text," while at the same time expressing distance from it (11).

199. Gerald Reitlinger, *The SS: Alibi of a Nation, 1922–1945*, London, 1955; idem, *Die S.S.: Tragödie einer deutschen Epoche*, trans. Hans B. Wagenseil, Munich, 1957; see Berg, "Lesarten des Judenmords," 103ff.

200. Hans Buchheim, "Zur Geschichte des Dritten Reiches, Führer und Organisation," *Neue Politik* 2 (1957): 181–98, here 193ff.

201. Buchheim, foreword to Buchheim, Broszat, Jacobsen, and Krausnick, *Anatomie des SS-Staates*, 10.

202. Reitlinger, *Die S.S.: Tragödie einer deutschen Epoche*, 438 ("Die Bedeutung der überzeugten, hartgesottenen SS-Leute wird heute vielfach übertrieben").

203. Ibid., 439.

204. Lord Russell of Liverpool, *The Scourge of the Swastika: A History of Nazi War Crimes during World War II*, London, 1954; idem, *Geißel der Menschheit: Kurze Geschichte der Nazi-Verbrechen*, Frankfurt a.M., 1955.

205. Buchheim, "Zur Geschichte des Dritten Reiches, Führer und Organisation," 195f.

206. IfZ board meeting minutes (board of trustees and advisory board), 5 Nov. 1951, 24, in IfZ archives, ED 105 (1), 18. Gerhard Ritter thus wrote off a study by Hedwig Conrad-Martius, *Die Entwicklung des Sozialdarwinismus in Deutschland und seine Bedeutung für die Entstehung des nationalsozialistischen Menschenbildes* (The Development of Social Darwinism in Germany and Its Significance for the Emergence of the National Socialist View of Human Beings), judged positively by Theodor Litt, by indicating that he did not know "how this work can be useful to the institute."

207. Hans-Peter Schwarz, "Warum eine Festschrift? Einführende Überlegungen des Beiratsvorsitzenden," in Möller and Wengst, *50 Jahre Institut für Zeitgeschichte*, xv–xxv.

208. For this reason the reference to the IfZ and Joseph Wulf by Bernhard Sutor, "Restauration oder Neubeginn? Politische Bildung 1945–1960," in *Aus Politik und Zeitgeschichte* (appendix to *Das Parlament*), B7–8/99, 12 Feb. 1999, 3–12, in his account of the public consciousness of the Holocaust in the 1950s, without any mention of the differences between the institute and the Jewish outsider, can only be termed a skewed interpretation (see esp. 6–7).

209. Schwarz, "Warum eine Festschrift?," xx.

210. Ibid.

211. Loock, "War's so?," 52.

212. Ibid., 49–50.

213. Ibid., 50.

214. Ibid., 49.

215. Ibid., 50.

Chapter 5. "Prehistorical Excavations" and "Absolute Objectivity"

1. Hartmut Berghoff, "Zwischen Verdrängung und Aufarbeitung Die bundesdeutsche Gesellschaft und ihre nationalsozialistische Vergangenheit in den fünfziger Jahren," *Geschichte in Wissenschaft und Unterricht* 49 (1998): 96–114, here 108.

2. For this and the following figures, see Peter Reichel, "'Über Auschwitz wächst kein Gras': Zur Auseinandersetzung mit dem Holocaust in der westdeutschen Gesellschaft," *Tribüne* 38 (1999): 160–72, here 164. See also Wolfgang Benz, "Mythos Anne Frank," in idem, *Bilder vom Juden: Studien zum alltäglichen Antisemitismus*, Munich, 2001,

86–95. Both articles emphasize the problem of instrumentalization, while criticizing the "media event and construction of a victim icon."

3. *Der Tagesspiegel*, 19 March 1957, cited from Norbert Muhlen, "Anne Franks Heimkehr," *Der Monat* 9 (1957): 81.

4. Ibid., 79.

5. Ibid., 82.

6. Ibid., 80.

7. Ibid., 80–81.

8. Gerhard Schoenberner, "Vom Tagebuch zum Film: Das Schicksal der Anne Frank," *Frankfurter Hefte* 14 (1959): 913.

9. Ibid.

10. Ibid., 915.

11. See Rina Frauendörfer, "Anne Frank in Deutschland," *Der Monat* 9, no. 107 (1957): 91–92.

12. Muhlen, "Anne Franks Heimkehr," 80 (*"Reißerfabrikanten"*).

13. Albrecht Goes, foreword to *Das Tagebuch der Anne Frank*, Heidelberg, 1950 (Dutch original: *Het Achterhuis*, 1946; German paperback ed.: Frankfurt a.M., 1955), 7.

14. Eva Reichmann, "Drei Stufen: Zur Aufführung des 'Tagebuchs der Anne Frank,'" in idem, *Größe und Verhängnis deutsch-jüdischer Existenz: Zeugnisse einer tragischen Begegnung*, Heidelberg, 1974 (1st ed. 1958), 170–72.

15. This formulation in Harry Pross, "Die jüdisch-deutsche Katastrophe," *Neue Politische Literatur* 1 (1956): cols. 243–58, here 245. On the reception history of the diary in Germany and the United States, see Hanno Loewy, "Das gerettete Kind: Die 'Universalisierung' der Anne Frank," in *Deutsche Nachkriegsliteratur und der Holocaust*, ed. Stephan Braese, Holger Gehle, Doron Kiesel, and Hanno Loewy, Wissenschaftliche Reihe des Fritz Bauer Instituts 6, Frankfurt a.M., 1998, 19–41; idem, "Märtyrerromanzen: Die 'befreite' Anne Frank," in *Geschichte im Film: Mediale Inszenierungen des Holocaust und kulturelles Gedächtnis*, ed. Waltraud Wende, Stuttgart, 2002, 94–122. James E. Young, "Das Anne-Frank-Haus," in *Mahnmale des Holocaust: Motive, Rituale und Stätten des Gedenkens*, ed. James E. Young, Munich, 1994, 107–13, examines the political function of the Anne Frank memorial in Amsterdam's Prinsengracht. The hasty appropriation of the victim's perspective, leading to an evasion of the Holocaust's history through an overemphasis on its prehistory, is also emphasized by Ulrich Herbert, "Der Holocaust in der Geschichtsschreibung der Bundesrepublik Deutschland," in Ulrich Herbert and Olaf Groehler, *Zweierlei Bewältigung: Vier Beiträge über den Umgang mit der NS-Vergangenheit in den beiden deutschen Staaten*, Hamburg, 1992, 67–86, here 68ff.

16. On these three examples, see Ulrich Herbert, "Zwischen Beschaulichkeit und Massenmord: Die Kriegswende 1943 aus der Perspektive des Alltags," *Neue Politische Literatur* 40 (1995): 185–89; Hannes Heer, ed., *Im Herzen der Finsternis: Victor Klemperer als Chronist der NS-Zeit*, Berlin, 1992; Hamburger Institut für Sozialforschung, ed., *Eine Ausstellung und ihre Folgen: Zur Rezeption der Ausstellung "Vernichtungskrieg. Verbrechen der Wehrmacht, 1941–1944*, Hamburg, 1999.

17. Walter Anger, ed., *Das Dritte Reich in Dokumenten*, Frankfurt a.M., 1956.

18. Ibid., 7 (foreword). For criticism of Anger's collection from the period, see Max Braubach, "Zeitgeschichte," *Historisches Jahrbuch* 79 (1960): 233–312, here 235.

19. Walther Hofer, ed., *Der Nationalsozialismus: Dokumente, 1933–1945*, Frankfurt a.M., 1957, 7. This collection would be published in Danish, French, and Spanish (all 1963), Italian (1964), and Portuguese; in Germany alone over a million copies have been sold in many editions, some of them newly prepared.

20. Objections to this dictum were already raised by Eberhard Jäckel, "Dokumente zur Geschichte des Dritten Reiches," *Neue Politische Literatur* 3 (1958): col. 29.

21. Hans Mommsen, "Holocaust und die deutsche Geschichtswissenschaft," in *The Historiography of the Holocaust Period*, ed. Yisrael Gutman and Gideon Greif, Jerusalem, 1988, 79–97, here 84.

22. Buchheim, "Zur Geschichte des Dritten Reiches, Führer und Organisation," 185. We should here note that Mommsen's article, "Holocaust und die deutsche Geschichtswissenschaft," refers to Hans Frank's *Im Angesicht des Galgens* (Neuhaus bei Schliersee, 1955; self-published by Brigitte Frank), the famous "Gerstein Report" published in the first volume of the *Vierteljahrshefte für Zeitgeschichte*, and the facsimile reproduction of the Stroop Report on the destruction of the Warsaw Ghetto; these sources have little to do with one another from a systematic scholarly perspective.

23. Julius Lippert, *Lächle . . . und verbirg die Tränen: Erlebnisse und Bemerkungen eines deutschen "Kriegsverbrechers,"* Leoni, 1955; Buchheim, "Zur Geschichte des Dritten Reiches," 185.

24. Harald Welzer, "Albert Speers Erinnerungen an die Zukunft: Über das Geschichtsbewußtsein einer Führungsfigur des 'Dritten Reiches,'" in *Erzählung, Identität und historisches Bewußtsein: Die psychologische Konstruktion von Zeit und Geschichte*, ed. Jürgen Straub, Frankfurt a.M., 1998, 389–403, here 394, 399, 401.

25. Buchheim, "Zur Geschichte des 'Dritten Reiches,'" 181, 178, 182.

26. Ibid., 184.

27. Welzer, "Verweilen beim Grauen," 123.

28. Gerhard Ritter, "Zur Einführung," in Henry Picker, *Hitlers Tischgespräche im Führerhauptquartier, 1941–1942: Im Auftrage Verlags neu hrsg. von Percy Ernst Schramm, in Zusammenarbeit mit Andreas Hillgruber und Martin Vogt*, Stuttgart, 1963, 11–29, here 11.

29. See Horst Möller, "Das Institut für Zeitgeschichte und die Entwicklung der Zeitgeschichtsschreibung in Deutschland," in Möller and Wengst, *50 Jahre Institut für Zeitgeschichte*, 1–68, here 35ff. A few years later (1958), the IfZ would restore its damaged reputation by publishing its scholarly edition of the Höß memoirs.

30. See *Quick*, nos. 23–28, 10 June–15 July 1951. On the image of Nazism and war conveyed by German glossy magazines in the 1950s, see the material in Michael Schorstheimer, *Die leuchtenden Augen der Frontsoldaten: Nationalsozialismus und Krieg in den Illustriertenromanen der fünfziger Jahre*, Berlin, 1995; and the critical but fair review by Winfried von Bredow, "Kurzzeitgedächtnis mit Lücken," *Neue Politische Literatur* 41 (1996): 529–30.

31. IfZ board meeting minutes (board of trustees and advisory board), 9 March 1951, 4 and 5–6, in IfZ archives, ED 105: Kuratorium und Beirat, Sitzungsprotokolle (1).

32. Ibid., 6; Hermann Mau, "Arbeitsbericht für den Zeitraum vom 10. März bis 5.

November 1951" (23 pp.), 14, in IfZ archives, Tätigkeitsberichte 1951–1961, ED 105 (1); Mau here emphasizes that although Ritter was commissioned, he had in reality played no role in the project.

33. IfZ board meeting minutes (board of trustees and advisory board), 5 Nov. 1951, 2ff., in IfZ archives, ED 105: Kuratorium und Beirat, Sitzungsprotokolle (1).

34. Ibid., 2–3 and 9.

35. Ibid., 6.

36. Ibid., 5.

37. Ibid., 6.

38. Ibid., 7.

39. Ibid.

40. IfZ board meeting minutes, 9 Jan. 1952, 1, ibid.

41. Ritter, "Zur Einführung," in Picker, *Hitlers Tischgespräche*, 545 (note).

42. Ibid., 11.

43. Ibid., 13.

44. Ibid., 13, 16, 17, 18.

45. Hermann Mau, "Der Nationalsozialismus als aktuelle Forschungsaufgabe" (typescript, dated in handwriting to 12 March 1952), IfZ archives, ED 105 and ID 1, 1338/54.

46. Ritter, "Zur Einführung," in Picker, *Hitlers Tischgespräche*, 11, 13, 16.

47. Picker himself began with an assurance that his documentary collection was meant "neither to justify nor to condemn" (ibid., 33). Underscoring the unique nature of the material, he remained under the spell of Hitler's "downright hypnotic" ability to blank out "the best ideas for resistance and defense of his advisors" (35). Here as well we find reflections on the "blending of good and evil motives, the noble with the shabby," the effort to salvage the honor of Hjalmar Schacht, admiration for Eva Braun. A commentary, Picker explained, was to be dispensed with "for the sake of the direct effect of the documents" and "to capture and transmit an unfalsified impression of Hitler's thinking in a literary manner" (38). Picker saw the didactic value of his publication as lying in the timeless "essence of the dictator," in a warning against absolute rule — "despite all recognition of the superior [*überragend*] possibilities of revolutionary men of action" — and in a dictatorship that in its planning for peace "initially has a seductive effect" (38).

48. Ibid., 18, 27, 28.

49. Hannah Arendt, "Bei Hitler zu Tisch," *Der Monat* 4, no. 37 (1951/1952): 85–90.

50. Ibid., 85, 90.

51. Ibid., 90.

52. Ibid., 86.

53. Ibid.

54. Ibid., 88, 90.

55. Henry Picker, *Hitlers Tischgespräche im Führerhauptquartier, 1941–42: Im Auftrag des Verlags neu hrsg. von Percy E. Schramm, in Zusammenarbeit mit Andreas Hillgruber und Martin Vogt*, Stuttgart, 1963, 48.

56. Ibid., 12.

57. For a biographical overview, see David Thimme, *Percy Ernst Schramm und das Mittelalter: Wandlungen eines Geschichtsbildes*, Göttingen, 2006; on his role in the Nazi period, see Manfred Messerschmidt, "Karl Dietrich Erdmann, Walter Bußmann und Percy Ernst Schramm: Historiker an der Front und in den Oberkommandos der Wehrmacht und des Heeres," in *Nationalsozialismus in den Kulturwissenschaften*, ed. Hartmut Lehmann and Otto Gerhard Oexle, vol. 1, *Fächer—Milieus—Karrieren*, Göttingen, 2004, 417-44.

58. Percy Ernst Schramm, *Kriegstagebuch des Oberkommandos der Wehrmacht (Wehrmachtführungsstab)*, Frankfurt a.M., 1961; idem, *Hitler als militärischer Führer: Erkenntnisse und Erfahrungen aus dem Kriegstagebuch des Oberkommandos der Wehrmacht*, Frankfurt a.M., 1962; idem, *Die Niederlage 1945: Aus dem Kriegstagebuch des Oberkommandos der Wehrmacht*, Munich, 1962.

59. Percy Ernst Schramm, preface to Picker, *Hitlers Tischgespräche*, 25. Here as well, Schramm certifies his interpretation with a reference to the "experiential treasure" he enjoyed as a witness. See also idem, "Über die schwierige Fixierung zeitgenössischer Vorgänge: Wo liegen die Schwierigkeiten?," in *Festschrift für Leonhard v. Muralt zum 70. Geburtstag*, Zurich, 1970, 24-33.

60. Schramm, preface, 94, 118.

61. Ibid., 34ff.

62. Ibid., 39.

63. Ibid., 46-52.

64. Ibid., 89.

65. Ibid., 111.

66. Martin Broszat, "Aufgaben und Probleme zeitgeschichtlichen Unterrichts," cited from idem, *Nach Hitler: Der schwierige Umgang mit unserer Geschichte*, ed. Hermann Graml and Klaus-Dietmar Henke, Munich, 1986, 18.

67. Hans Rothfels, "Vorbemerkungen des Herausgebers," *Vierteljahrshefte für Zeitgeschichte* 1 (1953): 177-85; the Gerstein Report itself: "Dokumentation. Augenzeugenbericht zu den Massenvergasungen," ibid., 185-94.

68. Cited from Saul Friedländer, *Kurt Gerstein oder die Zwiespältigkeit des Guten*, Gütersloh, 1968, 196 (French original: *Kurt Gerstein ou L'ambiguité du bien*, Paris, 1967; English ed.: *Kurt Gerstein: The Ambiguity of Good*, translated from the French and German by Charles Fullman, New York, 1969), 194.

69. "Belcec und Treblinka: Ein SS-Offizier und ein Jude berichten über die Todeslager in Polen," *Frankfurter Hefte* 8 (1953): 548-57.

70. Friedländer, *Kurt Gerstein oder die Zwiespältigkeit des Guten*, 196.

71. See Walter Boeckh, "Du sollst ein Mahnmal bauen," *Frankfurter Allgemeine Zeitung*, 23 June 1999.

72. See, for example, Rothfels, "Vorbemerkungen," 181.

73. Ibid., 182.

74. "Dokumentation: Augenzeugenbericht zu den Massenvergasungen," 188.

75. Rothfels, "Vorbemerkungen," 185.

76. Armin Mohler, n.t., *Das Historisch-Politische Buch* 8 (1960): 244.

77. Joseph Wulf and Léon Poliakov, *Das Dritte Reich und die Juden*, Berlin, 1955; idem, *Das Dritte Reich und seine Diener*, Berlin, 1956; idem, *Das Dritte Reich und seine Denker*, Berlin, 1959; Joseph Wulf, *Das Dritte Reich und seine Vollstrecker: Die Liquidation von 500.000 Juden im Ghetto Warschau*, Berlin, 1961. See also idem, *Die Nürnberger Gesetze*, Berlin, 1960; idem, *Heinrich Himmler*, Berlin, 1960. None of these volumes has appeared in English.

78. Wulf and Poliakov, *Das Dritte Reich und seine Denker*, 433.

79. A friend of both Alexandre Kojève and Emanuel Lévinas, Poliakov was the author of a nine-volume history of antisemitism that remains a standard work.

80. Wulf in an interview with the newspaper *Der Aufbau* (New York), 22 Dec. 1967, cited from *Sachor: Nicht Vergessen; Erinnerungen an Joseph Wulf*, ed. Aktion Sühnezeichen, Friedensdienste, Berlin, 1989, 7.

81. The following discussion is based on research in the Zentralarchiv zur Erforschung der Geschichte der Juden in Deutschland (Central Archives for Research on the Jews in Germany, Heidelberg; henceforth HCA), which holds Wulf's estate. I thank the late Naomi Wulf for facilitating access to Wulf's manuscripts and papers. Important work on Wulf's person and writing before the biography of Klaus Kempter from 2012: Henryk M. Broder, "Wer war Joseph Wulf?," *Frankfurter Rundschau*, 24 Oct. 1981; Gerhard Schoenberner, "Joseph Wulf—Die Dokumentation des Verbrechens," in *Engagierte Demokraten: Vergangenheitspolitik in kritischer Absicht*, ed. Claudia Fröhlich and Michael Kohlstruck, Münster, 1999, 132–42; Barbara Breysach, "Joseph Wulfs Zeugenwissen in der deutschen und frühen polnischen Nachkriegsöffentlichkeit," *Amsterdamer Beiträge zur neueren Germanistik* 50 (2001): 405–14. The cited volume *Sachor: Nicht Vergessen* consists of personal recollections from friends and colleagues. For Wulf's biography I have also drawn on his own information in CVs, letters, and interviews, together with letters of his collaborator Ulla Böhme; contemporary press reports were likewise important. I have also made use of interviews conducted by Henryk Broder at the beginning of the 1980s with many of Wulf's contemporaries; these are also held in the HCA. Attention should also be drawn to an impressive film by Broder—*Porträt eines Gerechten. Wer war Joseph Wulf?* (*Portrait of a Just Man: Who Was Joseph Wulf?*); his article is only an abbreviated summary of the film. I would also like to thank both Henryk Broder for his suggestions and, especially, the director of the archives, Peter Honigmann, for his comprehensive and friendly assistance.

82. Joachim March, "Joseph Wulf: Historiker der jüdischen Tragödie." From the series *Diener des Gewissens*, radio-broadcast ms. (15 pp.) of Sender Freies Berlin (23–24 March 1977), 2, in HCA, B 2/7 (91/15), no. 37.

83. See *Der Spiegel*, 3 Jan. 1956; see also the autobiography of Bräutigam, *So hat es sich zugetragen*, Würzburg, 1968.

84. Joseph Wulf, "Geständnisse eines Autors," *Deutsche Rundschau*, 84 (1958): 9; reprinted in *Sachor: Nicht vergessen*, 29–36, here 30.

85. Ibid., 31.

86. Ibid. The following reviews exemplify that sort of response, including to the later books: Paul Arnsberg, "Vom Mißbrauch der Sprache" (review of Joseph Wulf, *Aus dem Lexikon der Mörder: "Sonderbehandlung" und verwandte Worte in nationalsozialistischen*

Dokumenten, Gütersloh, 1963), *Frankfurter Allgemeine Zeitung*, 9 Oct. 1963 (Arnsberg speaks of "the capability of a professional"); Heinz Joachim, "Die Musik in Hitlers Herrschaft" (review of Joseph Wulf, *Musik im Dritten Reich*, Gütersloh, 1963), *Die Welt*, 10 Oct. 1963 (inaccuracies, but a necessary book); similarly H. H. Stuckenschmidt, "Gegängelte Musik," *Frankfurter Allgemeine Zeitung*, 19 Oct. 1963; Albert Buesche, "Es war kein Spuk, sondern Wirklichkeit" (review of Joseph Wulf, *Die bildenden Künste im Dritten Reich*, Gütersloh, 1963), *Der Tagesspiegel*, 10 March 1963 (the author, "disgusted by what is described, but at the same time fascinated by the uncovering of the events," recommends the book as a "vaccination").

87. Wulf, "Geständnisse eines Autors." One example of a total hatchet job: Bodo Scheurig, "Hitlers rückgratloser Diener" (review of Joseph Wulf, *Martin Bormann: Hitlers Schatten*, Gütersloh, 1962), *Kurier*, 4 Dec. 1962 ("a complete failure," "nonsense," "contradictions," "a hasty verdict").

88. Poliakov and Wulf are mentioned in a sentence or footnote in, for example, Mommsen, "Holocaust und die deutsche Geschichtswissenschaft"; Otto Dov Kulka, "Die deutsche Geschichtsschreibung über den Nationalsozialismus und die 'Endlösung': Tendenzen und Entwicklungsphasen," *Historische Zeitschrift* 240 (1985): 599–640, here 611; Konrad Kwiet, "Judenverfolgung und Judenvernichtung im Dritten Reich: Ein historiographischer Überblick," in *Ist der Nationalsozialismus Geschichte? Zu Historisierung und Historikerstreit*, ed. Dan Diner, Frankfurt a.M., 1987, 237–64, here 298. Their work is not mentioned in two otherwise excellent introductions to Holocaust historiography: Ian Kershaw, *Der NS-Staat: Geschichtsinterpretationen und Kontroversen im Überblick*, Reinbek, 1988 (English original: London, 1985; expanded new ed.: Reinbek, 1999), 148–206 ("Hitler and the Holocaust") and 329–55 ("'Normality' and Genocide: The Problem of 'Historicization'"); Ulrich Herbert, "Vernichtungspolitik: Neue Antworten und Fragen zur Geschichte des 'Holocaust,'" in Herbert, *Nationalsozialistische Vernichtungspolitik*, 9–66. Wulf is, however, mentioned in Ulrich Herbert, "Deutsche und jüdische Geschichtsschreibung über den Holocaust," in *Jüdische Geschichtsschreibung heute: Themen, Positionen, Kontroversen*, ed. Michael Brenner and David N. Myers, Munich, 2002, 247–58, here 252–53.

89. Thilo Vogelsang, n.t. (review of Léon Poliakov and Joseph Wulf, *Das Dritte Reich und seine Diener: Dokumente*, Berlin 1956), *Das Historisch-Politische Buch* 5 (1957): 242–43.

90. Joseph Wulf, *Martin Bormann: Hitlers Schatten*, Gütersloh, 1962; Max Braubach, "Veröffentlichungen zur Zeitgeschichte: Eine Nachlese," *Historisches Jahrbuch* 85 (1965): 119–57, here 134.

91. See Manfred Hagen, "Göttingen als 'Fenster nach Osten' nach 1945," in *Geschichtswissenschaft in Göttingen: Eine Vorlesungsreihe*, ed. Hartmut Boockmann and Hermann Wellenreuther, Göttinger Universitätsschriften, ser. A, Schriften, 2, 321–43, here 332.

92. Hans-Günther Seraphim, n.t. (review of Léon Poliakov and Joseph Wulf, *Das Dritte Reich und die Juden: Dokumente und Aufsätze*, Berlin, 1955), *Das Historisch-Politische Buch* 4 (1956): 215.

93. See Martin Broszat, "Probleme zeitgeschichtlicher Dokumentation," *Neue Politische Literatur* 2 (1957): cols. 298–304, here col. 298; the following citations: cols. 298 and 300.

94. Ibid., col. 301; following citations: col. 302.

95. H. G. Adler, Review of Poliakov and Wulf, *Das Dritte Reich und seine Diener*, radio-broadcast ms., 8 and 1, in German Literary Archives, estate of Adler, A II 33.

96. Ibid.

97. Poliakov and Wulf, *Das Dritte Reich und seine Diener*, xiv.

98. Joseph Wulf, *Presse und Funk im Dritten Reich*, Gütersloh, 1964, 9.

99. Broszat, "Probleme zeitgeschichtlicher Dokumentation," 300.

100. See John Felstiner, "'Alle Dichter sind Jidn': Paul Celans Sprache als Ort des Erinnerns," *Dachauer Hefte* 11 (1995): 133–44, here 135. Felstiner points to the influence of Reitlinger's book on Celan's poem "Tenebrae" (1957).

101. Raul Hilberg, "Die Holocaustforschung heute: Probleme und Perspektiven," in *Die Macht der Bilder: Antisemitische Vorurteile und Mythen*, ed. Jüdisches Museum der Stadt Wien, Vienna, 1995, 403–9, here 403.

102. Poliakov and Wulf, *Das Dritte Reich und die Juden*, 3.

103. Ibid., 4.

104. Ibid., 3.

105. Ibid., 9.

106. Ibid., 3.

107. Ibid., 81–248.

108. Poliakov and Wulf, *Das Dritte Reich und seine Diener*, xiii.

109. Ibid., vii.

110. Poliakov and Wulf, *Das Dritte Reich und die Juden*, 2.

111. Ibid.

112. Wulf, *Presse und Funk im Dritten Reich*, 10.

113. Ibid., 148, 10, 9.

114. Ibid., 86.

115. Poliakov and Wulf, *Das Dritte Reich und seine Diener*, vii, xii.

116. Ibid., vii.

117. Ibid.

118. Ibid.

119. Ibid., 7.

120. See, for example, Joseph Wulf, "Partisan der Menschlichkeit: Der Fall Raoul Wallenberg," radio-broadcast ms. for Germany's Südwestrundfunk, 1 Sept. 1966 (34 pp.), 2, in HCA, B 2/7 (91/15), no. 7.

121. Adler, review of Poliakov and Wulf, *Das Dritte Reich und seine Diener*, 1.

122. Poliakov and Wulf, *Das Dritte Reich und seine Diener*, 341.

123. Ibid., ix.

124. Ibid., 175.

125. Ansgar Skriver, "Theater im Dritten Reich," *Spandauer Volksblatt*, 5 Aug. 1964.

126. Poliakov and Wulf, *Das Dritte Reich und seine Diener*, 341. See Gerhard Strauß, "Dokumentation über nazistische Kunst" (review of Wulf, *Die bildenden Künste im Dritten Reich*), *Neues Deutschland*, 4 Sept. 1965.

127. Adler, review of Poliakov and Wulf, *Das Dritte Reich und seine Diener*, 1.

128. Ibid., 3 and 8.

129. Ibid.

130. Poliakov and Wulf, *Das Dritte Reich und seine Denker*, 73.

131. Ibid., 167.

132. Ibid., 291.

133. Poliakov and Wulf, *Das Dritte Reich und seine Diener*, ix.

134. Joseph Wulf, *Theater und Film im Dritten Reich*, Gütersloh, 1964, 9.

135. Poliakov and Wulf, *Das Dritte Reich und seine Diener*, x.

136. Poliakov and Wulf, *Das Dritte Reich und seine Denker*, xi.

137. Poliakov and Wulf, *Das Dritte Reich und seine Diener*, xi, 341.

138. H. G. Sellenthin, "Auf dem Pressefriedhof des III. Reiches" (review of Wulf, *Presse und Funk im Dritten Reich*), *Telegraf-Illustrierte*, 13 June 1965, 18.

139. Poliakov and Wulf, *Das Dritte Reich und seine Denker*, vii.

140. Ibid., vii.

141. Ibid., 3.

142. Poliakov and Wulf, *Das Dritte Reich und seine Diener*, xiii.

143. Ibid., xiv.

144. Ibid.

145. Poliakov and Wulf, *Das Dritte Reich und die Juden*, 4.

146. Ibid., 405.

147. Poliakov and Wulf, *Das Dritte Reich und seine Denker*, 73.

148. Joachim Hemmerle, "Dokumentarist des Dritten Reiches: Eine Begegnung mit dem Historiker Joseph Wulf," *Frankfurter Rundschau*, 29 Oct. 1965.

149. Pross, "Die jüdisch-deutsche Katastrophe," col. 253.

150. Joseph Wulf, "Auswüchse des deutschen Kontinuitätsgedankens in der Bundesrepublik" (ms., 30 pp.), ca. 1954–55, in HCA, B 2/7 (91/15), no. 12, 1.

151. See Joseph Wulf to Graf von Baudissin, 7 July 1964, ibid., no. 36.

152. Joseph Wulf, "Generalplan Ost: Ein Kapitel nationalsozialistischer Politik," radio-broadcast ms. for Süddeutscher Rundfunk, 16 Feb. 1967 (41 pp.), ibid., no. 11.

153. Joseph Wulf, "Die verantwortlichen hohen Offiziere um Hitler: Studie zur Geschichte der Reichswehr und Wehrmacht" (ms., 129 pp), ibid., no. 40.

154. Only the study of Christian Streit, *Keine Kameraden: Die Wehrmacht und die sowjetischen Kriegsgefangenen*, Stuttgart, 1978 (new ed.: 1996), can here be considered an early standard work.

155. Wulf, "Auswüchse des deutschen Kontinuitätsgedankens," 2.

156. See also Ludolf Herbst, "Der Krieg vor dem Krieg: Die Forcierung der nationalsozialistischen Judenpolitik," in idem, *Das nationalsozialistische Deutschland 1933–1945*, Frankfurt a.M., 1996, 200–217; on Lucy Dawidowicz, see Gallas, *Das Leichenhaus der Bücher*, 232–36, 249–52, 270–74.

157. Wulf, "Generalplan Ost," 20. On the thematic complex of racism and the rational calculus of practical constraints," see Ulrich Herbert, *Best: Biographische Studien über Radikalismus, Weltanschauung und Vernunft, 1903–1989*, Bonn, 1996, 42ff., 88ff. and esp. 203ff., 245ff.

158. Wulf, "Generalplan Ost," 10.

159. Czesław Madajczyk, ed., *Vom Generalplan Ost zum Generalsiedlungsplan*, Munich, 1994; Götz Aly, *"Endlösung": Völkerverschiebung und der Mord an den europäischen Juden*, Frankfurt a.M., 1995.

160. Wulf, "Auswüchse des deutschen Kontinuitätsgedankens," 4, 5. On the same intellectual-affective complex Wulf was addressing, see Ulrich Herbert, "'Generation der Sachlichkeit': Die völkische Studentenbewegung der frühen 20er Jahre in Deutschland," in *Zivilisation und Barbarei: Die widersprüchlichen Potentiale der Moderne*, ed. Frank Bajohr et al., Hamburg, 1991, 115–44; Karin Orth, *Das System der nationalsozialistischen Konzentrationslager*, Hamburg, 1999; and Saul Friedländer, *Das Dritte Reich und die Juden*, 87–128 (discussing the *Erlösungsantisemitismus*, "salvational" or "redemptive" antisemitism that emerged with Wagner).

161. Wulf, "Auswüchse des deutschen Kontinuitätsgedankens," 4 and passim. On the general context as appoached in recent research, see Frei, *Karrieren im Zwielicht*; Wilfried Loth and Bernd-A. Rusinek, eds., *Verwandlungspolitik: NS-Eliten in der westdeutschen Nachkriegsgesellschaft*, Frankfurt a.M., 1998; Ulrich Herbert, "Als die Nazis wieder gesellschaftsfähig wurden," *Die Zeit*, 10 Jan. 1996.

162. H. G. Sellenthin, "Die dichtende Rassenseele," *Telegraf-Illustrierte*, 2 Feb. 1964, 18.

163. Poliakov and Wulf, *Das Dritte Reich und die Juden*, 234–38, 407–15.

164. Poliakov and Wulf, *Das Dritte Reich und seine Diener*, 392.

165. See Ruta Sakowska, *Die zweite Etappe ist der Tod: NS-Ausrottungspolitik gegen die polnischen Juden, gesehen mit den Augen der Opfer; Ein historischer Essay und ausgewählte Dokumente aus dem Ringelblum-Archiv, 1941–1943*, Publikationen der Gedenkstätte Haus der Wannsee-Konferenz 3, Berlin, 1993, 101 (photo).

166. See Joseph Wulf, *Das Dritte Reich und seine Vollstrecker: Die Liquidation von 500 000 Juden im Ghetto Warschau*, Berlin, 1961, 47. See also Josef [*sic*] Wulf, "Dr. Emanuel Ringelblum und sein Untergrundarchiv im Warschauer Ghetto," *Deutsche Rundschau* 87 (1961): 241–49, here 241.

167. H. G. Adler, review of Poliakov and Wulf, *Das Dritte Reich und die Juden*, radio-broadcast ms., in German Literary Archives, estate of Adler, A II 33, 2.

168. Poliakov and Wulf, *Das Dritte Reich und die Juden*, 4.

169. Poliakov and Wulf, *Das Dritte Reich und seine Diener*, 311ff.

170. Poliakov and Wulf, *Das Dritte Reich und seine Denker*, 355.

171. Ibid., 393.

172. Wulf, *Die bildenden Künste im Dritten Reich*, 10.

173. Wulf, "Auswüchse des deutschen Kontinuitätsgedankens," 9ff.

174. Wulf, *Presse und Funk im Dritten Reich*, 11.

175. Helmut Heiber, *Walter Frank und sein Reichsinstitut für Geschichte des Neuen Deutschlands*, Stuttgart 1966.

176. Horst Möller, "Die Entstehung der Zeitgeschichtsschreibung," 16–17.

177. Martin Broszat, "Helmut Heiber zum 65. Geburtstag," *Vierteljahrshefte für Zeitgeschichte* 37 (1989): 353–56.

178. See the harsh assessments in Walter Bußmann, *Historische Zeitschrift* 257 (1993): 829–31; Bernd Martin, "Die Entlassung der jüdischen Lehrkräfte an der Freiburger Universität und die Bemühungen um ihre Wiedereingliederung nach 1945," *Freiburger Universitätsblätter* 34, no. 129 (1995): 7–46, here 9.

179. IfZ board meeting minutes (board of trustees and advisory board), 19 June 1965, 9, in IfZ archives, ED 105 (2).

180. Ibid., 9, 6.

181. Ibid., 9.

182. Ibid., 6ff.

183. Peter Schoettler, ed., *Geschichtsschreibung als Legitimationswissenschaft, 1918–1945*, Frankfurt a.M., 1997, 13–14.

184. Thus Alphons Silbermann, "Was heißt Dokument? Joseph Wulfs Sammlung," in *Die Welt*, 27 May 1965.

185. Wulf, *Presse und Funk im Dritten Reich*, 11.

186. Ibid.

187. Wulf, "Geständnisse eines Autors," 29–30.

188. Ibid.

189. Ibid., 12.

190. Ibid.

191. Adler, review of Poliakov and Wulf, *Das Dritte Reich und die Juden*, radio-broadcast ms., in German Literary Archives, estate of Adler, A II 33, p. 2.

192. Poliakov and Wulf, *Das Dritte Reich und die Juden*, 4.

193. Pross, "Die jüdisch-deutsche Katastrophe," cols. 243–44.

194. Wulf, "Geständnisse eines Autors," 29–30.

195. Ibid.

196. Ibid., 30.

197. RP, review of Wulf, *Das Dritte Reich und seine Vollstrecker, Deutsche Rundschau* 87 (1961): 1168–69.

198. Poliakov and Wulf, *Das Dritte Reich und die Juden*, here section on witness accounts, 249–306.

199. Ibid., 4.

200. Ibid.; see section on accounts by children, 278–88.

201. Ibid.; see section on accounts by scholars and scientists, 253–77.

202. Ibid., 251.

203. H. G. Adler, "Selbstverwaltung und Widerstand in den Konzentrationslagern der SS," *Vierteljahrshefte für Zeitgeschichte* 8, no. 3 (1960): 221–36, here 221.

204. Wolfgang Scheffler, *Judenverfolgung im Dritten Reich, 1933–1945*, Berlin, 1960 (expanded ed.: Berlin, 1964).

205. Ibid., 5, 115–16.

206. See the documentary collection: ibid., appendix, 65–114.

207. For example, in Anger, ed., *Das Dritte Reich in Dokumenten*, in the section on "the struggle [*Kampf*] against the Jews" (52–63), a third of the fifteen source excerpts are from Poliakov and Wulf, *Das Dritte Reich und die Juden*; and in Walther Hofer, ed., *Der*

Nationalsozialismus, the chapter on "Persecution and Extermination of the Jews" (267–312) consistently relies on the work of those authors. A third, again, of the twenty-two reprinted sources are taken from the first two volumes of Poliakov and Wulf.

208. Scheffler, *Judenverfolgung*, 115, 116.

209. Ibid., between 80 and 81.

210. Ibid., 59.

211. Helge Grabitz and Wolfgang Scheffler, *Letzte Spuren: Ghetto Warschau, SS-Arbeitslager Trawniki, Aktion Erntefest: Fotos und Dokumente über Opfer des Endlösungswahns im Spiegel der historischen Ereignisse*, Berlin, 1988, 7 (here in the context of documentation of the fate of the Jewish employees of the Schultz company).

212. Adler, "Selbstverwaltung und Widerstand," 221.

213. Ibid.

214. Adler, "Methoden der Persönlichkeitszertrümmerung," *Neue Politische Literatur* 4 (1959), cols. 257–72.

215. Ibid., 271–72.

216. Jean Améry, *Jenseits von Schuld und Sühne: Bewältigungsversuche eines Überwältigten*, new ed., Stuttgart, 1977 (1st ed.: 1966, ed. Gerhard Szczesny), 16. On Améry's autobiographical texts, see Petra S Fiero, *Schreiben gegen das Schweigen: Grenzerfahrungen in Jean Amérys autobiographischem Werk*, Hildesheim, 1997; Irene Heidelberger-Leonard, "Jean Amérys 'Meisterliche Wanderjahre,'" *Jahrbuch zur Geschichte und Wirkung des Holocaust* (1997): 289–302.

217. Améry, *Jenseits von Schuld und Sühne*, 103.

218. Ibid., 104.

219. Poliakov and Wulf, *Das Dritte Reich und die Juden*, 4.

220. Ernst Müller-Meiningen, "Nie und nirgends wieder," in *Süddeutsche Zeitung*, 11 Feb. 1947.

221. Anon. to Eugen Kogon, 10 Jan. 1952, in private estate of Michael Kogon.

222. Anon. to Eugen Kogon, 2 May 1953, in private estate of Michael Kogon. These were the less malicious letters. See, for instance, Erich Schüler to Eugen Kogon, 15 Dec. 1948, ibid.: "Who is now forcing you, as the slave of a Christian myth based on your Jewish religion, to lead a concentration-camp life in a spiritual sense? I . . . advise you urgently to no longer present yourself as a spokesman for the German *Volk*. You are a spokesman for Zionism and Stern Gang gangsterism and for nothing else. Palestine is responsible for your expectorations."

223. See, for example, *Das neue Buch* (Bonn), no. 4 (1958), on the 4th ed. of Kogon's *SS-Staat*: "To be sure only the religiously and morally solid, well-trained citizen will be able to safely read this book." Likewise, *Jugendnachrichten* (Munich), August 1953, on the 3rd ed.: "Few books have ever been located so close to the boundary of what is morally possible."

224. O. H. E. Becker, "Die nackte Wahrheit," *Der Tagesspiegel*, 10 July 1948.

225. This in the Hessischer Rundfunk discussion series *Das Abendstudio*, directed by Alfred Andersch, which looked at "great books of recent years" with Axel Eggebrecht and Klaus-Peter Schultz. On Andersch in Germany's postwar years, see the superb

critical essay by W. G. Sebald, "Der Schriftsteller Alfred Andersch," in idem, *Luftkrieg und Literatur*, Munich, 1999, 121–60.

226. On the 3rd ed. of Kogon's *SS-Staat*, in *Die Freiheit* (Vienna), 26 Jan. 1952.

227. Ibid.

228. Poliakov and Wulf, *Das Dritte Reich und die Juden*, 2.

229. Ibid.

230. Ibid.

231. Ibid.

232. The correspondence is kept in the Wulf estate, HCA, B 2/7 (91/11) and B 2/1 (92/21). The exchange was discussed for the first time in Berg, "Die Lebenslüge vom Pathos der Nüchternheit," *Süddeutsche Zeitung*, 17 July 2002. That the controversy was worth presenting publicly was something Wulf and Krausnick agreed on. Namely, when Wulf officially inquired at the IfZ whether he could examine the correspondence for documentation in his "Diaries of a Contemporary Historian," Helmut Krausnick answered as follows: "I thank you . . . for communicating the intended publication of your 'diaries.' It seems to me we need have no hesitation to shed public light on the fact that different people apply themselves with the same uprightness to clarifying complicated modern historical matters but arrive (as in the Hagen case) at judgments marked by controversy." Helmut Krausnick to Joseph Wulf, 29 March 1965, ibid.

233. Wulf, *Das Dritte Reich und seine Vollstrecker*, 334–35. On the person of Hagen, see Götz Aly and Susanne Heim, *Vordenker der Vernichtung: Auschwitz und die deutschen Pläne für eine neue europäische Ordnung*, Hamburg, 1991, 216–17. Hagen's memoirs (Wilhelm Hagen, *Auftrag und Wirklichkeit: Sozialarzt im 20. Jahrhundert*, Munich-Gräfelfing, 1978) shed no light on his role in the Warsaw ghetto.

234. Wulf, *Das Dritte Reich und seine Vollstrecker*, 335.

235. Broszat, "Probleme zeitgeschichtlicher Dokumentation," cols. 300–301.

236. To briefly summarize the opposing positions at work here in their "hard" form: "intentionalist" historians of the Holocaust maintain that its catalyst was anti-semitic ideology, as already laid out by Hitler in *Mein Kampf* in 1925–26; functionalists point to the absence of any concrete master plan to exterminate the Jews prior to 1941, instead underscoring the role played by competition and cumulative radicalization inside the Nazi Party apparatus.

237. Martin Broszat to Wilhelm Hagen, 8 April 1963, in HCA, B 2/7 (91/15), no. 3.

238. Helmut Krausnick to Joseph Wulf, 29. April 1963, ibid.

239. Martin Broszat to Joseph Wulf, 10 April 1963, ibid.

240. Joseph Wulf to Martin Broszat, 16 April 1963, ibid.

241. Wulf, *Das Dritte Reich und seine Vollstrecker*, 334.

242. Joseph Wulf to Helmut Krausnick, 24 April 1963, in HCA, B 2/7 (91/15), no. 3.

243. Helmut Krausnick to Joseph Wulf, 29 April 1963, ibid.

244. Ibid.; emphasis is Krausnick's.

245. Ibid.

246. Ibid.

247. Joseph Wulf to Helmut Krausnick (probably beginning May 1963), ibid.

248. "Gesundheit im Ghetto," *Der Spiegel*, 8 May 1963, 38–42. The article probably was written at Wulf's initiative. H[?]. Ly[?], "Ein Rechtsstreit," *Allgemeine Zeitung des Judentums*, 29 Nov. 1963; P[?], "Autor will Namen nicht streichen," *Generalanzeiger* (Bonn), 5 Dec. 1963; Gerhard Schoenberner, "Helfer oder Helfershelfer? Anmerkungen zu einem Prozeß um das Warschauer Getto," *Die Zeit*, 3 Jan. 1964; "Vagabunden an die Wand: Amtsarzt Dr. Hagen und das Warschauer Getto," publication unclear (see HCA, B 2/7 [91/15], no. 39), 17 May 1964.

249. Gerhard Schoenberner to Arno Scholz, 28 March 1964, in HCA, B 2/7 (91/15), no. 39.

250. Wilhelm Hagen to Arno Scholz, 20 Feb. 1964, ibid., no. 4. (for following citations as well).

251. See Ernst Klee, *Das Personenlexikon zum Dritten Reich*, Frankfurt a.M., 2007, 218–19. Wulf also received information about the development of the situation in the ghetto from Hanns von Krannhals, among others. See Hanns von Krannhals to Joseph Wulf, 9 April 1964 (5 pp.), in HCA, B 2/7 (91/15), no. 7.

252. Arno Scholz to Wilhelm Hagen, 2 March 1964; Wilhelm Hagen to Arno Scholz, 5 March 1964. Both in HCA, B 2/7 (91/15), no. 4.

253. Wilhelm Hagen to Arno Scholz, 18 March 1964; also Wilhelm Hagen, "Zu Josef Wulf: Das Dritte Reich und seine Vollstrecker," ibid.

254. Joseph Wulf to Wilhelm Hagen, 3 Nov. 1967, ibid., no. 7.

255. Joseph Wulf to Helmut Krausnick, 9 Oct. 1963, ibid. Wulf sent the letter via registered mail.

256. Joseph Wulf to Helmut Krausnick, 22 Oct. 1963, ibid.

257. Helmut Krausnick to Joseph Wulf, 23 Oct. 1963, ibid.

258. Joseph Wulf to Helmut Krausnick, 19 Nov. 1963; Joseph Wulf to Martin Broszat, 20 March 1964; Martin Broszat to Joseph Wulf, 6 April 1964, all ibid.

259. Helmut Krausnick to Joseph Wulf, 9 Jan. 1964, ibid.

260. Joseph Wulf to Helmut Krausnick, 5 March 1964, ibid.

261. Helmut Krausnick to Joseph Wulf, 13 March 1964, ibid.

262. Martin Brosazt to Joseph Wulf, 6 April 1964, ibid.

263. Ibid.

264. Joseph Wulf to Martin Broszat, 7 April 1964, ibid.

265. Joseph Wulf to Helmut Krausnick, 8 April 1965, ibid.

266. Joseph Wulf to Martin Broszat, 7 Oct. 1965, ibid.

267. Ibid. On Wulf's positive assessment of other IfZ books, see Jürgen Zarusky, "Die Schriftenreihe der Vierteljahrshefte für Zeitgeschichte," *Vierteljahrshefte für Zeitgeschichte* 51 (2003): 89–106, here 96.

268. Martin Brosazt to Joseph Wulf, 15 Oct. 1965, HCA, B 2/7 (91/15), no. 7.

269. Ibid.

270. Joseph Wulf to Martin Broszat, 19 Oct. 1965, ibid.

271. Ibid.

272. Ibid.; emphasis is Wulf's.

273. Broszat, "Aufgaben und Probleme zeitgeschichtlichen Unterrichts," 16.

274. For the entirety of the Broszat–Friedländer corespondence referred to later, see Broszat and Friedländer, "Um die Historisierung des Nationalsozialismus. Martin Brosazt to Saul Friedländer, 28 Sept. 1987, ibid., 342–43. On Broszat's term "mythic memory," see the essay by Dieter Heger, "Was heißt 'mythische Erinnerung' in Erzählungen von Überlebenden der Shoah?," in *Archiv der Erinnerung: Interviews mit Überlebenden der Shoah*, ed. Cathy Gelbin, Eva Lezzi, Geoffrey H. Hartmann, and Julius H. Schoeps, vol. 1, *Videographierte Lebenserzählungen und ihre Interpretation*, Potsdam, 1998, 157–91.

275. Saul Friedländer to Martin Broszat, 6 Oct. 1987, in Broszat and Friedländer, "Um die Historisierung des Nationalsozialismus," 346–47.

276. H. G. Sellenthin, "Das große Drama der Unmenschlichkeit," in *Telegraf-Illustrierte*, no. 241/16, 15 Oct. 1961, 25.

277. H. G. Sellenthin, *Telegraf*, 27 April 1958.

278. Joseph Wulf, "Diskrepanz in der Demokratie" (interview mit Ulla Böhme), *Spandauer Volksblatt*, 11 Dec. 1964. See Wulf's three-page letter to the German chancellor proposing that 8 May be made a "national memorial day": Joseph Wulf to Helmut Schmidt, 2 July 1974, in HCA, B 2/7 (91/15), no. 41.

279. See, for example, "Die Prozesse gegen die nationalsozialistischen Gewaltverbrecher als Basis für den Churban-Historiker," speech given at Brandeis University, referred to in Joseph Wulf to Anna Maria Jokl, 24 Dec. 1967, HCA, B 2/7 (91/15), no. 25.

280. Wulf, "Diskrepanz in der Demokratie."

281. Wulf to Anna Maria Jokl, 24 Dec. 1967, HCA, B 2/7 (91/15), no. 25.

282. Joseph Wulf to Wolf Graf Baudissin, 17 March 1960, ibid., no. 36.

283. Joseph Wulf to David Wulf, 2 Aug. 1974, ibid., no. 42.

284. On the significance of Willy Brandt's genuflection in Warsaw, see Joseph Wulf to Julius Kardinal Döpfner, 27 April 1973, and Joseph Wulf to Helmut Schmidt, 2 July 1974, ibid. no. 41. Germany's popular literary critic, the late Polish-German Jewish Holocaust survivor Marcel Reich-Ranicki, *Mein Leben*, Stuttgart, 2000, 550, has indicated that at that time he could not know he would be thankful to Brandt for the gesture "until the end of my life." On the general context, see Adam Krzemiński, "Der Kniefall," in *Deutsche Erinnerungsorte*, ed. Etienne François and Hagen Schulze, vol. 1, Munich, 2001, 638–53.

On the slapping episode and the public scandal it represented, see Joseph Wulf to David Wulf, 2 Aug. 1974, in HCA, B 2/7 (91/15), no. 42: "Namely beautiful Beate understood that the former Nazi simply needed a punch in the mouth." Beate Klarsfeld's sentencing to a year in jail on 10 July 1974 was commented on by Hermann Korte, *Eine Gesellschaft im Aufbruch: Die Bundesrepublik Deutschland in den sechziger Jahren*, Frankfurt a.M., 1985, 41, in relation to the "sometimes minimal punishments" meted out in the Frankfurt Auschwitz trial as follows: "The complete absence of at least political-moral reactions by prominent politicians with Nazi pasts needing to be judged in one way or another . . . strengthened the idea in at least a portion of the younger generation that at least part of the older generation had learned nothing and had not become true democrats, whatever lip service they showed."

285. See Wulf's comments on the verdict against Beate Klarsfeld, *Die Welt*, 17 and 27 July 1974.

286. Joseph Wulf, "Diskrepanz in der Demokratie" (interview with Ulla Böhme), *Spandauer Volksblatt*, 11 Dec. 1964. Sündermann's Holocaust-denying pamphlet, directed at Hans Buchheim: Helmut Sündermann, *Das Dritte Reich: Eine Richtigstellung in Umrissen*, Freising, 1959.

287. Joseph Wulf to Friedrich Beermann, 5 April 1973, in HCA, B 2/7 (91/15), no. 36.

288. Joseph Wulf to Marion Gräfin Dönhoff, 5 Dec. 1967, ibid., no. 27.

289. Böhme's formulation is cited in Broder, "Wer war Joseph Wulf?" See HCA, B 2/7 (91/15), no. 37.

290. Ibid.

291. "Joachim Hemmerle, Dokumentarist des Dritten Reiches: Eine Begegnung mit dem Historiker Joseph Wulf," *Frankfurter Rundschau*, 29 Oct. 1965. See also Wulf, interview with Edouard Kalic (1965), in HCA, B 2/7 (91/15), no. 3: "My formal place of residence remains Paris. I am only working in Germany at present because I here have the best archives for my theme and also—I would like to emphasize this—receive great support for my work in Germany. It was my strong desire to publish on the Third Reich precisely in Germany *itself* and in the German language. Additionally I maintain the standpoint that with my theme I can fill great gaps in Germany."

292. Werner Wieberneit, "Von Büchern und Schriftstellern," radio-broadcast ms. (12 pp.), RIAS (American Sector Radio) Berlin, 14 April 1964, 9, HCA, B 2/7 (91/15), no. 13.

293. Joseph Wulf to Anna Maria Jokl, 5 Oct. 1969, ibid., no. 25.

294. On Wulf's role in this context, see Kühling, "Schullandheim oder Forschungsstätte?"; Peter Heilmann, "Ein gescheitertes Projekt: Das Internationale Dokumentationszentrum," in *Sachor: Nicht vergessen*, 37–42; Johannes Tuchel, *Am Großen Wannsee 56–58: Von der Villa Minoux zum Haus der Wannsee-Konferenz*, Berlin, 1992, 150ff.

295. Joseph Wulf, reader's letter published in *Die Zeit*, 1 Dec. 1967.

296. Wulf, "Bericht von meinem Besucht in den USA vom 5.–20. Dezember 1967," Berlin, 22 Dec. 1967, 3, in HCA, B 2/7 (91/15), no. 27.

297. Internationales Dokumentationszentrum zur Erforschung des Nationalsozialismus und seiner Folgeerscheinungen e.V., "Information Nr. 1" (3 Nov. 1966), ibid.; also Joseph Wulf to Anna Maria Jokl, 28 Nov. 1967, in HCA, B 2/7 (91/15), no. 25.

298. Horst Rieck, "Tauziehen um die Wannsee-Villa: Wo die Endlösung beschlossen wurde," *Die Zeit*, 17 Nov. 1967.

299. Julius Posener, reader's letter, *Die Zeit*, 1 Dec. 1967. Posener's memoirs do not offer any clarification of this episode from his perspective. Instead, he mentions his successful objections to the planned demolition of a house built by the architect Hermann Muthesius. He also expresses annoyance that Berlin had not managed to transform the villa of the German Jewish painter Max Liebermann (located near the "Wannsee villa") into a museum (this project has meanwhile been realized). See Julius Posener, *Fast so alt wie das Jahrhundert*, Basel, 1993 (expanded new ed.; first published 1990), 300–301.

Bundestag president Eugen Gerstenmaier had proposed tearing down the "Wannsee villa" during a trip to Israel; see Tuchel, *Am Großen Wannsee*, 152.

300. Jacqueline Rouge, reader's letter, *Die Zeit*, 1 Dec. 1967.

301. See Rudolf Steinbeck, "Um das 'Haus der Endlösung': Ein Gespräch mit Joseph Wulf," *Der Tagesspiegel*, 9 Nov. 1967.

302. Rolf Hochhuth, "Herr Regierender Bürgermeister! Ein offener Brief," *Welt am Sonntag*, 29 Oct. 1967.

303. Klaus Schütz, "Meine Antwort an Rolf Hochhuth," in *Welt am Sonntag*, 5 Nov. 1967.

304. Klaus Schütz to Direktorium des Internationalen Dokumentationszentrums zur Erforschung des Nationalsozialismus und seiner Folgeerscheinungen e.V., 20 Dec. 1967, in HCA, B 2/7 (91/15), no. 27.

305. See *Volksblatt*, 2 Dec. 1967.

306. See *Der Tagesspiegel*, 13 Sep. 1970 (AP news item).

307. Internationales Dokumentationszentrum zur Erforschung des Nationalsozialismus und seiner Folgeerscheinungen e.V., circular to members, 21 Aug. 1971, in HCA, B 2/7 (91/15), no. 27. A the same time, in Duisburg an interdisciplinary research center was approved devoted to "the religion and history of Judaism"; fifteen years later, the Salomon Ludwig Steinheim Institute for German Jewish history would emerge from this center. In a personal essay, Julius H. Schoeps, initiator and director of the project over a number of years, observes that official support was probably offered not least of all "because we tried to see German Jewish history not exclusively from the perspective of Auschwitz." Such an approach naturally has much in its favor; but in my view the contrast between the successful Duisburg project and the failure of Wulf's plan in Berlin is nevertheless telling. See Julius H. Schoeps, "Never Forget Thy People Israel! Autobiographical Remarks," in *Speaking Out: Jewish Voices from United Germany*, ed. Susan Stern, Chicago, 1995, 67–81, here 75.

308. Internationales Dokumentationszentrum zur Erforschung des Nationalsozialismus und seiner Folgeerscheinungen e.V., board report, 21 Oct. 1967–22 Sept. 1971 (5 pp.), in HCA, B 2/7 (91/15), no. 27.

309. Joseph Wulf to Helmut Gollwitzer, 1 June 1973, ibid., no. 40 (Wulf's emphasis).

310. Internationales Dokumentationszentrum zur Erforschung des Nationalsozialismus und seiner Folgeerscheinungen e.V., board report, 21 Oct. 1967–22 Sept. 1971.

311. Ibid.

312. Dieter Struß to Senat für Wissenschaft und Kunst, Referent für Literatur, 2 March 1964, in HCA, B 2/7 (91/15), no. 24.

313. Joseph Wulf to Marion Gräfin Dönhoff, 5 Dec. 1967, ibid., no. 27; in a letter to the *Berliner Extradienst*, 8 Aug. 1974, ibid., no. 42., Wulf referred to that death camp as the "greatest university in the world."

314. Joseph Wulf to Cardinal Julius Döpfner, 27 April 1973, in B 2/7 (91/15), no. 41.

315. Wulf, *Theater und Film im Dritten Reich*, 10.

316. Joseph Wulf, "Geschichte des Zionismus" (synopsis), ms. (104 pp.), 1972, in HCA, B 2/7 (91/15), no. 18.

317. Wulf, letter to *Berliner Extradienst*, 8 Aug. 1974.

318. Wulf, *Presse und Funk im Dritten Reich*, 9.

319. See, for example, Joseph Wulf, project outline, "Kulturarbeit im Ghetto Warschau" (3 pp.); also Joseph Wulf to Werner Stein (Berlin senator for science and art), 3 July 1964, in HCA, B 2/7 (91/15), no. 24; after putting aside this project, Wulf took it up again in 1970, while also initiating plans for a project on "Memoristik des Dritten Reiches," for which he asked for support from the Friedrich Ebert foundation. See Joseph Wulf to Wolf Graf von Baudissin, 2 Sep. 1970, ibid., no. 36. For another exposé, see Joseph Wulf to Wolf Graf von Baudissin, 9 Aug. 1974, ibid.

320. Peter Freimark, "Vom Hamburger Umgang mit der Geschichte einer Minderheit: Vorgeschichte und Gründung des Instituts für die Geschichte der deutschen Juden," in *Juden in Deutschland: Emanzipation, Integration, Verfolgung und Vernichtung; 25 Jahre Institut für die Geschichte der deutschen Juden (Hamburg)*, ed. Peter Freimark, Alice Jankowski, and Ina Lorenz, Hamburg, 1991, 466–77 (first ed.: 1989), 472. Envisioned in the 1950s, the institute was officially opened in 1966.

321. Beatrix Brandi-Dohrn to Hans Rothfels, 12 July 1965, in German Federal Archives, estate of Rothfels 213, no. 36.

322. Hans Rothfels to Hellmut Becker, 19 July 1965, ibid.

323. Joseph Wulf to Wolf Jobst Siedler, 1 Aug. 1974, in HCA, B 2/7 (91/15), no. 42.

324. This and the following information based on the Broder interviews with Scholz, Struß, Gaus, Prusch, Schoenberner, Lüth, and Gollwitzer, ibid., 43.

325. Joseph Wulf to David Wulf, 2 Aug. 1974, ibid., no. 42.

326. Joseph Wulf to Helmut Gollwitzer, 16 May 1973, ibid., no. 40.

327. Ibid.

328. Ibid.

329. Joseph Wulf, "1000 Jahre Geschichte des osteuropäischen Judentums" (ms. exposé, 5 pp.), ibid.

330. Joseph Wulf, "Tagebuch eines osteuropäischen Juden (Titel-Vorschlag) ab 1945 bis ich das Buch zu Ende schreibe" (3 pp.), July 1974, ibid., no. 36.

331. Joseph Wulf to Madame Raymond and Dr. Willy Guggenheim, 25 July 1974, ibid., no. 41.

332. Wulf, "Tagebuch eines osteuropäischen Juden."

333. Ibid.

334. Ibid.

335. Joseph Wulf to Helmut Gollwitzer, 23 Jan. 1974, ibid., no. 40.

336. Ibid.

337. Ibid.

338. Joseph Wulf to David Wulf, 2 Aug. 1974, ibid., no. 42.

339. Joseph Wulf to Wolf Graf von Baudissin, 2 Aug. 1970, ibid., no. 36.

340. Wulf left a deeply disturbing account of these weeks in a diary: Joseph Wulf, "Jenta 7. VI. 1973–28. VIII. 1973" (ms., 37 pp.), dated 5 Nov. 1973, ibid., no. 12.

341. Joseph Wulf to Jacob Taubes, 13 June 1974, ibid., no. 41; similarly: Joseph Wulf to Wolf Graf von Baudissin, 9 Aug. 1974, ibid., no. 36.

342. Joseph Wulf to Wolf Graf von Baudissin, 9 Aug. 1974, ibid., no. 36.

343. Joseph Wulf to Helmut Gollwitzer, 18 June 1974, ibid., no. 40.

344. "Wulf macht ein Ende," *Die Nationalzeitung*, 18 Oct. 1974. Tuchel, *Am Großen Wannsee*, 154, speculates that Wulf's suicide resulted from despair at the failure of his plans for an International Center of Documentation.

345. Wolfgang Scheffler, "Über den Publizisten Joseph Wulf," in *Sachor: Nicht vergessen*, 47–52, here 52.

346. Hermann Langbein to Eugen Kogon, 18 Feb. 1966, in estate of Eugen Kogon.

347. Hannah Arendt–Hans Magnus Enzensberger, "Politik und Verbrechen: Ein Briefwechsel," *Merkur* 19 (1965): 380–85, here 381.

348. H. G. Adler, review of Wulf, *Das Dritte Reich und seine Vollstrecker*, radio-broadcast ms., 4, in German Literary Archives, A: H. G. Adler, A II 33.

349. Gerhard Schoenberner, "Ein Blatt für Joseph Wulf," in *Sachor: Nicht vergessen*, 15–20, here 18.

350. Cited from *Der Spiegel*, 28 Oct. 1964, 133–36, here 133.

351. See anon., "Dokumente: Das Dritte Reich uns seine Diener; Naziverbrechen, die nie verjähren dürfen," *Neues Deutschland*, 14 Feb 1979.

352. See, for example, Joseph Wulf, "An die Briefschreiber!," *Volksblatt*, 3 May 1964, in HCA, B 2/7 (91/15), no. 31.

353. Cited from *Der Spiegel*, 28 Oct. 1964, 133–36, here 133.

354. Schoenberner, "Ein Blatt für Joseph Wulf," 18.

355. Thus, somewhat inaccurately, Annemarie Doherr, "Ein Historiker des Juden-tums," *Frankfurter Rundschau*, 20 Aug. 1974.

356. Hans Lamm, "Der Kaddisch-Schreiber einer Generation," *Allgemeine Wochen-zeitung*, 21 April 1967.

Index

Adenauer, Konrad, 192
Adler, H. G.: as Auschwitz survivor, 165; biography of, 16; on Holocaust historiography, 211; IfZ and, 9, 165–70, 175; on Joseph Wulf's work, 241; *Vergangenheitbewältigung* and, 146–47; Wulf and Poliakov documentary volumes and, 193, 197–98, 209
Aly, Götz, 10, 94, 197, 201
Améry, Jean, 139, 211–12, 244–45n13
Anger, Walter, 181
Angrick, Andrej, 247n34
Annäherung, 11
Anrich, Ernst, 120
Arani Verlag, 192, 219, 232
Arendt, Hannah, 66, 166, 185–88, 194, 240–41
Aretin, Karl Otmar von, 145
Arndt, Ino, 206
Aschoff, Diethard, 111, 278–79n14
Ash, Mitchell G., 75
Association of the International Documentary Center for Research on Nazism and Its Aftereffects (IDC), 233, 234, 235–36
Aubin, Hermann, 6, 15, 16, 25
Auerbach, Hellmuth, 161–62
Augustine, 129, 132–33

Auschwitz: "Auschwitz report" and, 170–74; Auschwitz trials and, 163, 170, 172, 312n284; versus Buchenwald, 18; centralization versus marginalization of, 171–72; as event on the surface, 26; in German history, 134; German Jewish history not from sole perspective of, 314n307; historiographical avoidance of, 28, 168; IfZ focus on, 141–42; Joseph Wulf and, 235; knowledge of the Holocaust and, 17–18, 20; *menschen* in, 240; as obstacle to emergence of contemporary history, 144; politics and, 240–41; Reinhard Wittram's grappling with, 114–15; Rudolf Höß on, 162–65; as rupture in civilization, 10–11; sea change in West Germany's discourse about, 161, 163; as theme in early Holocaust study, 23

Baethgen, Friedrich, 39
Banach, Jens, 170
Barraclough, Geoffrey, 69
Barth, Karl, 117
Bauch, Kurt, 54, 119
Baudissin, Wolf von, 235, 236, 240
Bauer, Fritz, 233

Heimpel, Hermann (*continued*)
of, 8; public displays of remorse and, 140; rhetoric of reconciliation and, 286n176; role of in Nazi period, 113; scholars' assessment of, 120–21, 123, 129; silence about Holocaust and, 118; students of, 7; *Vergangenheitbewältigung* and, 99, 122–28, 132, 134, 135–36; on *Zeitgeschichte*, 160
Heinrich Stahl prize, 242
Helling, Fritz, 30
Hellmann, Siegmund, 8, 120, 122–23, 132
Herbert, Ulrich, 10, 170, 201, 299n15
Herbst, Ludolf, 201
Herder University, 113
Herre, Franz, 268–69n94
Herzfeld, Hans, 153–54, 157–58, 169, 233
Heuss, Theodor, 109, 140, 149, 150, 290n47
Hilberg, Raul, 9–10, 12, 18, 194, 248n48, 269–70n107
Hillgruber, Andres, 162
Himmler, Heinrich, 185, 201
Hinck, Walter, 124
Hintze, Otto, 45, 80
Hirsch, Felix E., 40
historiography and historians: acknowledgment of Holocaust as historical theme and, 116; aestheticization of historical thought and, 259n105; ancient Greece and Rome and, 26–27; anthropological turn in, 137–38; anti-catastrophic interpretive model and, 34–36; apologetics in early discussions of Holocaust and, 22–23, 28, 86; from apologia to guilty sadness in, 106–9; aristocratic versus democratic perspective in, 68; authenticity of documents and, 189–90; autobiography and, 10, 11–13, 59, 60, 86; avoidance of Final Solution in, 190, 194; as body of approximations, 5; Catholic versus Protestant historians and, 66–67, 268–69n94; change versus authenticity among historians and, 75; choice of language and, ix; Christian conception of history and, 113–16; communicative silence in, 90; contemporary

history and those experiencing it and, 143–46, 147–48, 153, 157; continuity and discontinuity as template for, 50; defensiveness of German historians and, 13–14; deferred, 183; dehistoricization of social consciousness and, 289n32; denazification standards and, 144; in a dictatorship, 114; documentary methodology in Germany versus elsewhere and, 224–25; documentary principle and, 180–83; East German versus West German, 65; emigrant historians and, 145–46; European and American responses to author's work in, 13–15; exculpatory, 88–89; factual whole versus personal self in, 118; failure to perceive Jewish catastrophe and, 90; Fischer controversy and, 263–64n14; Fischer lexicon and, 292n80; generational differences in approach to Holocaust and, 154, 161; generational differences in responses to author's work and, 13–14, 15; generation-specific experiences and, 277n232; Gerhard Ritter and, 65–70, 72; German catastrophe and, 28–35, 36–42, 44–46, 64–65; of German consciousness, 70–72; German Historians' Conference of 1998 and, 10, 94; German nationalism and, 269n100; German resistance in, 86–87, 88, 90; guilt as a historical question and, 103–5, 135–36; guilt versus shame and, 126; Hans Rothfels' influence and, 76–77, 78, 86–87, 88–89, 97, 156; Hermann Heimpel and, 119–22, 123–24; historian as sage and, 26; historians' blind spots and, 15; historians' controversy of 1980s and, 10, 11; historians' correspondence and, 15; historian's proximity to events and, 6; historians' self-preservation during Third Reich and, 279–80n43; historians serving the present and, 138–39; historical consciousness and self-consciousness and, 138; historicism and, 135–36;

Hitler, Adolf, and Hitlerism (*continued*)
German catastrophe and, 257n79;
German monopoly capitalism and,
65; Hagen affair and, 214; high-
ranking officers around, 201; Hitlerism of individual Germans and, 32;
Hitler's willing executioners and,
195–96; Holocaust as exception to
good policies of, 171; IfZ and, 150; as
improper focus of German history,
70; as individual man bringing misfortune, 48; master plan of Holocaust
and, 15; medical and psychological
explanations for, 186–87; *Mein Kampf*
by, 19–20, 310n236; as monster, 89;
officers' revolt against, 46; plot to kill
Hitler and, 125, 233; "positive contents of Hitlerism" and, 39, 44; propaganda of, 62; reasons for rise of, 40;
resistance from within and, 208; as
revolt of the masses, 64; Russian
Revolution and, 10; satanic principle
and, 34, 45; source of fascism of, 63;
"table talk" of, 175, 183–87, 300–
301n32, 301n47; as tempter and seducer, 21; timing of Germans' rejection of, 109; Versailles Treaty and
rise of, 7; young listeners to, 131–32.
See also Nazis and Nazism
Hoch, Anton, 167, 234
Hocheneder, Franz, 16
Hochhuth, Rolf, 233, 235–36
Hockerts, Hans Günter, 145
Hofer, Walther, 8, 35, 40–42, 181, 300n19
Hoffmann, Christhard, 12
Hoffmann, Wilhelm, 29
Hoggan, David, 158–59, 293n101,
293nn98–99
Hohls, Rüdiger, 75
Holborn, Hajo, 7, 71, 82
Hölderlin, Friedrich, 36
Holocaust: acknowledgment of as histori-
cal theme, 116; acknowledgment of
at 1955 *Volkstrauertag*, 127; acknowl-
edgment of responsibility for, 110;
atonement and, 104–5; Berlin monu-
ment and, 189; burden of proof and,

18; camp system in, 42–44; character
of perpetrators of, 163–64; collective
versus individual guilt and, 5–7, 21–
22, 25, 43–44, 112, 244–45n13; concentration camps as propaganda
and, 90; cultural underpinnings of,
197–98; in definition of *Zeitgeschichte*,
156; denial of, 313n286; discontinuity
and, 50–51; early documentation of,
189–94; establishment of as theme in
German universities, 174–75, 177;
evasion of through emphasis on prehistory of, 299n15; as exception to
good policies of Third Reich, 171;
extent of killing and, 18; extermination process in, 164; as extraordinary
within the ordinary, 177; framework
in which SS operated and, 172–74;
Gerald Reitlinger's *The Final Solution*
and, 152; as German and Jewish
tragedy, 39; Germans' complicity in
and distancing from, 198–200; Germans' defensiveness in, 51; Germans
in concentration camps and, 90; guiltless versus guilty silence about, 73;
Hans Rothfels' reductionist account
of, 86–87; IfZ's approach to, 141–43,
149, 151–53, 161, 176; as industry, 194;
intentionality of, 201; international
diplomacy and, 196; knowledge of,
17–21, 55, 56, 108–13, 151, 177, 211,
231; lack of postwar general study of,
176; living recollection and scholarly
method and, 119–20; long-term intellectual traditions setting stage for, 68;
master plan for, 14–15, 19–20, 241,
310n236; memory versus history of,
109; mentally ill victims of, 188, 223;
naming names and, 205–6, 207–8,
211; news clippings about, 23; number of victims of, 153, 240; orders and
obedience in, 172; origins of, 214–15,
310n236; public disinterest in, 171;
public displays of remorse and, 140;
reasons given for persecution of Jews
and, 19; report on mass gassings and,
187–89; silence about, 73, 74, 118,

George L. Mosse Series in Modern European Cultural and Intellectual History

Series Editors

Steven E. Aschheim, Stanley G. Payne, Mary Louise Roberts, and David J. Sorkin